Dear Peggy

Peggy Vaughan
answers questions about
extramarital affairs

Dialog Press
San Diego, CA

ISBN 978-0-936390-29-1
Manufactured in the United States of America

For more information about Peggy's work
Visit her Website: www.dearpeggy.com

Table of Contents

So jealous I can't breath
They were found naked

Need Advice in Confronting Wife
Getting the Truth about an Affair
Why is he angry and mean?
I haven't confronted her...
Dilemma
Finally told the truth

Marriage on the Rocks
Devastated by wife's affair
Shock and Devastation
My Husband and my Friend
Husband's affairs
Mid-life crisis and extramarital affairs
Roller-coaster Ride
Will I Overcome The Pain?
The Hurt
When an affair ends
How long does it take to get over?
Lied to for 7 years
My husband had an affair
Getting over the anger
He won't discuss his affair
Lingering pain of wife's affair
Extra, Extra, Extra
Embarrassed
Will an affair help me forget?
The pain is overwhelming
Online and Off-line Affair

Should I tell the kids?
Staying for the Sake of the Children?
Extramarital affair resulted in child
Child by Lover
She's pregnant

Obsessed With the Other Woman

4-year affair
Hate the Other Woman
Anger after the affairs
Still confused
The Other Woman
Harassment by other woman

Should I give up?
I'm trapped
Numb to Affairs, Still in Love
Settling for Stability
Affair with an employee
Best friend/more?
Confused
Why won't they stop?
Should I stay or should I go?
Why can't I leave?
What's wrong...?
A Soap Opera
Surrender
My husband's affair
Anxiety about moving on...
Second husband had affair
Wandering husband
Back and forth
Better to move on?
I fell in love
Can't deal with this
Angry and Hurt
HELP???
Lost and confused...
Help—Age Difference
Do I stay or start over?

My husband had an affair
Telling all the details?
Can I get through this?
Should I get pregnant despite the affair?
What's happening here?
Lies about having an affair
Am I just as guilty?

A Personal Note from the Author

I have dedicated the past three decades to working with people who are struggling to deal with the impact of extramarital affairs in their lives. I have heard from thousands of men and women (on all sides of this issue), giving me a window on the world of affairs, providing valuable insights about this all-too-common experience.

My understanding is strengthened by the fact that I also know about this subject from firsthand experience. Since 1955, I have been married to my childhood sweetheart. I, like many people, never expected my marriage would be vulnerable to affairs—but I learned the hard way that no marriage is immune.

The sense of blame, shame and devastation that is so common to this experience is intensified by the secrecy that surrounds it. We need much more "responsible honesty" about this life-altering experience. Since 1980, when my husband and I began speaking publicly about our experience, we have tried to educate the public about the prevalence of affairs and the need for a societal effort to deal with it.

This book provides new perspective on this issue through hearing the voices of the men and women who have "been there." It contains letters from those who have had affairs, from the hurt spouses, and from the third parties. The common thread of all the letters is the pain and devastation experienced by everyone who finds themselves involved in any of the various roles.

In my responses, I do not give individual advice; rather, I address the *issues* presented in the letters, using rational thinking to address this very emotional situation. (Note that all of my responses are directed to you, the Reader—*not* to the specific individual who wrote the letter.)

These letters are *not* taken from the thousands of personal letters I have received through the years. All the letters in this book were submitted specifically to be answered in a public forum. They were submitted during a time when I served as the expert on extramarital affairs for AOL's Online Psych. I have received letters through my own website at www.dearpeggy.com and have compiled those into three Collections sold through the site.

I hope this book will provide information, understanding and perspective for all those who are currently struggling with this issue—as well as for those who can use this information to avoid facing this situation in their own lives. In fact, everyone needs this kind of perspective because everyone is likely to be touched by affairs in some way—either personally or in responding to a friend or family member who needs help in sorting through their own experience with affairs.

I hope you will use this book to become better informed about affairs and to engage in responsible discussions with all those who are important in your life.

Peggy Vaughan
April 2010

Quotes about Peggy's Work

- It's such a relief to hear some "realistic" advice. It's just the kind of information I needed so desperately.
- Your work has been a life saver for me at this difficult time!
- You have really helped me start to put things in perspective. It's so helpful to find out that I am not really alone during this devastating period of my life.
- I am in awe of your courage and honesty. This is the most difficult subject in the world. God bless you.
- You have helped me calm down a great deal; I'm pretty sure my dad is having an affair and felt I had nowhere to turn for help.
- What can I say! Astonishing! Admirable! And Super! I have learned lots of good points other "experts" never touched.
- Thank you for helping me to deal with the pain and the anger.
- It's extremely helpful to hear your point of view of having "been there" I hope that you can continue to be helpful to others.
- Great information and perspectives!
- I applaud your work and feel fortunate to live in a time among people willing to tackle our important social problems, that in the long run affect the fabric of our society.
- Your information has given me hope for the first time. Thanks!
- I've found your approach to be such a relief. Thank you for your level-headed approach.
- Your information has been a constant source of comfort and knowledge. More helpful than support group meetings, or counseling sessions.
- You are an incredible resource!
- Thank you for dealing with this subject in a way that represents the way society really is, rather than just condemn everyone who is involved in an affair.
- I draw comfort from your work; I know I am not alone.
- You have a very nice treatment of a important subject—free from hyperbole and filled with understanding and compassion.
- What a pleasant surprise, to find someone so open and honest.
- I wish I and everyone could read your comments when we first get married, it would sure save a lot of grief.

1: Affairs 101

How do you "define" an affair?

Dear Peggy,
Some time ago my wife became involved with another man who is also married. Their relationship lasted for several months. During this time they went out on dates, met in secret, kissed, fondled each other, etc. About the only thing they did not do is have intercourse. I have, and always will, consider this an "affair." My wife disagrees. Is there a "definition" of an affair?

Dear Reader,
I receive *many* letters asking me to "define" an affair. The classic definition of an affair is when a married person has sex (intercourse) with someone other than their spouse. However, that narrow definition no longer fits the experience of many people today. In fact, a person is likely to feel that an extramarital affair has taken place whenever they are in a committed relationship (whether or not they are married) when their partner:
— secretly engages in a relationship with another person that involves any kind of sexual activity.
— secretly becomes involved in a sexually-charged relationship with another person, without actual sexual activity.
— secretly develops a deeply meaningful emotional connection, whether sexual or platonic.
— secretly engages in any variation or combination of the above.
The primary factor in defining an extramarital affair is that secrecy and deception are involved. Deception is an integral part of an affair, regardless of the particular form it takes. In fact, people often recover from the fact that their partner had sex with someone else before they recover from the fact that they have been deceived.
In the final analysis, it's up to each couple (and indeed, each *person*) to determine for themselves whether their particular situation fits the "definition." Actually, a focus on defining an affair often distracts from getting down to the issue of *dealing* with the situation—because in practical terms, it's an issue that needs to be addressed in a serious way, no matter *how* it is defined.

* * * * * * * * * * * * *

Are affairs normal?

Dear Peggy,
Are affairs normal for men—and do they ever stop?

Dear Reader,

I'd like to differentiate between "having" affairs and *wanting* to have affairs. Being attracted to others is totally normal—for both men *and* women. And even "wanting" to act on that attraction is normal. But even if a desire for affairs is normal, that doesn't dictate whether someone *acts* on that desire. Obviously, we don't *do* everything we *want* to do. And the key factor in whether or not someone actually *has* an affair depends on their willingness to be dishonest and deceptive.

For instance, if someone wants to have an affair and decides to keep it secret, they're *more* likely to go ahead and do it. However, if they're honest about their desire and openly acknowledge it, they're *less* likely to pursue an affair. Unless there is a willingness to lie about an affair, most people will *choose* to be monogamous—because most people simply can't handle a sexually open marriage.

So when we focus specifically on *having* affairs, the argument that men are not "naturally" monogamous is really irrelevant. There's no way to know for sure whether we are naturally monogamous or naturally not monogamous—because different societies/cultures take on certain norms. And no one has lived outside a culture in order to see what would be normal. In the meantime, every person has a choice as to what to do. If they're dishonest about their desires, they're likely to make one choice (have an affair), but if they're honest, they're likely to make a different choice (*not* to have an affair). It's all a matter of choice, not what's "normal."

* * * * * * * * * * * * *

Why do women cheat?

Dear Peggy,

Why do women cheat? Is it different from men?

Dear Reader,

Of course, there's not ONE single reason why women have affairs. But there are some *general* differences in the factors that contribute to a woman having an affair vs. a man having an affair.

In fact, I had a close personal friend (Dr. Lynn Atwater, now deceased) who did one of the earliest studies on why women have affairs. She wrote a book back in 1982 titled "The Extramarital Connection: Sex, Intimacy, and Identity" in which she said that *in general*, while for men having affairs, sex is likely to be a significant factor—for women it's much more a combination of factors, including (as the subtitle of the book indicates) sex, intimacy and identity.

While the sexual chemistry component is likely to be present, it's augmented by the inclination toward combining the sex with intimacy, a feeling of closeness. And further, the impact on women's sense of themselves (their "identity" beyond their role as wife/mother, etc.) is usually an important part of the whole equation.

2

So the major difference between women and men having affairs may simply be that for women the reasons are somewhat more complex than those for men. Many men will say they feel generally satisfied with their marriages but want the *additional* satisfaction they get from an affair. Whereas, most women engaging in affairs indicate (whether it's real or a justification in their own minds) that one of the main reasons for the affair is their dissatisfaction with their marriages.

None of these general explanations, however, can be applied to any specific person (whether man or woman) without more knowledge about the particular person and the particular situation.

* * * * * * * * * * * * *

Marital Fidelity

Dear Peggy,

I am fortunate to know a married couple who has been happily married for more than forty years and they have never engaged in extramarital affairs. Whatever happened to moral integrity? If people commit to be married to a particular person, why can't they commit to be faithful to them? It is sad that so many people live by the philosophy of "if it feels good do it?"

Don't women or men think about the pain and suffering they cause their spouse before they decide to have an affair? I've had a married man suggest an extramarital affair and even though somewhat attracted to him, I said no.

Doesn't the third person think of how the married person must feel? I believe in honest communication and monogamous relationships—not reasons to justify infidelity. Do you have answers to these questions?

Dear Reader,

These questions represent the way most people think things *should* be. Every survey ever done shows that approximately 85 percent of all people polled think affairs are wrong—but this doesn't keep large numbers of people from having affairs. Unfortunately, we don't "practice what we preach." And, contrary to common thinking, it's not a question of bad people having affairs and good people avoiding them. All kinds of people from all walks of life are vulnerable to having affairs.

As for whether they "think about the pain and suffering they cause their spouse?"—No, they usually don't think about consequences; they try to focus on the positive feelings they get from the affair. Inherent in having an affair is blocking out a focus on the potential consequences. In order to rationalize their behavior, there's an unrealistic belief that "what they don't know won't hurt them," or "they'll never find out."

Usually, the same is true of the third party. Anyone involved in an affair, regardless of which role they play, focuses on the positive things they are experiencing while ignoring, denying, or rationalizing about any negatives. And as for how people can *decide* to have an affair, most people don't sit down and decide; they usually report that it "just happened." Having an affair is not a rational, thoughtful decision.

Finally, the comment about "believing in honest communication and monogamy" goes to the heart of one of the basic problems with affairs. While as a society we profess monogamy, we don't practice it—precisely because we are willing to be dishonest and deceptive. Unfortunately, what happens most often is that people *profess* monogamy but *practice* secret, deceptive extramarital affairs. And saying it *should* be different probably won't change this. But more open, responsible discussion of the realistic impact of affairs just may be able to make a difference.

* * * * * * * * * * * *

One-night stands...

Dear Peggy,

I have trouble applying the word "affair" to my husband's infidelity because, based on what I know so far, he did not have a relationship with the women, meaning he had "one-night stands." My understanding of extramarital affairs was that your partner had an ongoing relationship with someone else, usually a long-lasting relationship and also usually while you were still in the same area code.

My husband travels for long periods of time in his line of work. The first time this happened, he was gone for a year and when he came back, I found a letter in his luggage from another woman... That's how I found out he had cheated on me. He swore it was just a one-night stand and he had stopped seeing her after that. It was very difficult to regain the trust (don't know if I ever did...) but fast forward 7 years later and he had to go again...5 months into that absence, I went to join him... and soon enough I found out he, again, had been with someone else. Oddly enough, he has never given me any reason to doubt him when we are both living at home...This seems to happen only when we are separated.

Somehow, the fact that this happened with such a wide margin of time in between, makes me feel a bit "relieved"...sort of "it can't be that bad..." but deep inside I just can't convince myself it's only been bad luck or circumstance. It's still kind of hard to relate to stories about men who lie about coming home late from work, or having women on the side while you wait at home...because that's never happened to me. The cheating has been going on while I've been thousands of miles away and totally unaware of what he was doing... But I do relate to the pain and the sense of betrayal you feel when you discover that the person you trusted most in this world is a total stranger... someone you do not know... someone who you never thought would hurt you this way or ANY way, for that matter...

My question is...how do you really know? How do you trust them again? How do you know when it's just circumstances and not a deliberate and well thought out plan to lie and cheat and do something morally wrong? I hope you can give me some insight into this issue.

Dear Reader,

The above letter provides an opportunity to reflect on *patterns* that often develop in affairs. Often there's a pattern of gradually increasing the risk and the activities. At first, affairs may only be "while we're apart and can't be together anyway;" but if there are no *apparent* consequences, the degree of activity is likely to escalate. (Again, a reminder that this is not inevitable; just typical. There's no plan or deliberateness to this pattern; it's just a gradually evolving way things tend to happen.) In any life experience that someone finds enjoyable (which could be sports or any other activity), there's a tendency toward taking more and more risks—not just continuing to do things the same way over an extended period of time.

So to come back to the issue of affairs, if the first experience is *successful* (in that there were no regrets or bad feelings or immediate consequences), there is a likelihood that it will be repeated the next time there's an opportunity. Eventually, even without that same opportunity, there may be a rationalization that it's somehow OK to expand to another level. Of course, anyone may stop at any point, but that may not happen without some kind of significant event that leads to a clear decision to stop.

Finally, a word about what behavior constitutes an affair: whether it's a one-night stand, cyber-sex, long-term affair, prostitute, emotional affair, or any other type of *SECRET* relationship involving sexual overtones—it's an affair! As I've mentioned before, and as is alluded to in the above letter, it's the *deception* that often hurts longer than anything else. And that feeling of deception usually exists, regardless of the particular *type* of affair.

* * * * * * * * * * * * *

Faithful??

Dear Peggy,

Recently my wife of 24 years admitted to engaging in oral sex with her boss, but insists that she is still faithful to me...in that they have not had intercourse... My question to you is, why would she make this distinction in her behavior?

Dear Reader,

People do all kinds of mental gymnastics (rationalizations) in order to feel OK about themselves. Naturally, it makes no sense to draw this kind of distinction, but it's a very common kind of thinking used by people to somehow justify or explain away their behavior. Most of us have done this kind of magical thinking at one time or another when we're trying to kid ourselves about what we're really doing. For instance, I remember when I was a teenager having sex with my then boyfriend (now husband of more than 40 years) that we did just about everything we could think of *besides* intercourse—so I could continue to think of myself as not doing anything *wrong* and still being a "virgin." This

5

was back in the early 50s and was a common way of dealing with sex during that era, especially among good/religious Southern girls like me.

In fact, this kind of splitting hairs to make our actions fit certain parameters is something we all do in various ways. While our actions may not be sexual, there's a tendency to rationalize whatever behaviors we want to somehow deny or explain away. An effort to equate oral sex with still being "faithful" is a classic example of such rationalization. A person making such a statement may be doing it in an effort to convince *herself* that she's still faithful—not just to convince her husband. It's doubtful, however, that anyone could seriously see this as anything more than a desperate effort to avoid dealing with the reality of what has happened. Sometimes when people don't know how to deal with something, they simply try to deny it—even to themselves.

* * * * * * * * * * * * *

Questions, questions, questions...

Dear Peggy,

I am very much in love with my wife but cannot help but wanting after other women. I am first of all confused as to how I can be capable of so many emotions, and second of all wondering if I should do this? Can a marriage withstand an extramarital affair? Can an affair ever be helpful in a marriage? Are online emotional affairs the same as cheating if you are just as attached as if you had been meeting in real life in your mind? Am I typical of other people my age? I am 36 years old.

Dear Reader,

Lots of questions here—no easy answers—but I'll make some comments about each one:

1. Can a marriage withstand an extramarital affair?

   Yes, it's possible. However, simply "withstanding" an extramarital affair can leave the marriage deadened and meaningless. It's important to thoroughly deal with the affair in order to fully recover.

2. Can an affair ever be helpful in a marriage?

   This is a common rationalization in trying to somehow justify an affair. While an affair may be "helpful" for the individual involved in the affair (in that it's an ego-boost and fun), it's certainly not helpful to the spouse or to the marriage. Usually, it's devastating. (And even if an affair is never discovered, keeping the secret creates an emotional distance within the marriage that is difficult to overcome.) It is possible, however, for the tremendous work involved in overcoming an affair to be used to improve the marriage by virtue of creating a new bond after the earlier bond has been broken. But this would never justify an affair because it's not the most likely outcome.

3. Are online emotional affairs the same...?

6

To the spouse who discovers an online emotional affair, the devastated feelings are very similar to discovering an actual physical affair. It's the secrecy and deception that is the most difficult to overcome.

4. Am I typical of other people my age (36 years old)?

Being attracted to other people is typical of people of any age. Attractions, in and of themselves, are not the problem. It's what you do with the attractions. And the secret fantasy gives them a kind of power that makes it more likely that someone will act on them. So ongoing honesty between a couple diminishes the power of the normal attractions to others and gives a couple the best chance of avoiding having this become a threat to the relationship.

* * * * * * * * * * * * *

How long do affairs last?

Dear Peggy,
How long does the average extramarital affair last?

Dear Reader,

This may be the shortest question I've ever received, but it's very important because it brings attention to a situation that people who are just beginning an affair seldom consider.

Due to the secretive nature of affairs, it's very difficult to get precise numbers. But the best estimate of people who have studied this for years (and one which fits with my own experience of working with people over the past 20 years) indicates:

1. When an affair is quickly discovered by a spouse, it may bring an abrupt halt.
2. If the initial encounter produces some negative feelings or reactions, it may not proceed.
3. If it goes beyond the initial few encounters (and is not interrupted by outside forces), most affairs "run their course" in from 6 months to 2 years.

Naturally, as with anything, there are exceptions. There are documented cases of affairs that go on for many, many years. But the fact that we've heard of them is a reflection of the fact that they are the exception rather than the rule.

The "6 months to 2 years" is, of course, impacted by many factors: frequency of the meetings, intensity of the relationship, etc. But the overriding factor that almost always plays a major role is the inevitable time when the first flush of the euphoria involved with a new relationship begins to fade.

Whether a person is first dating the person they eventually marry or having an affair outside their marriage, there's a kind of *fantasy* period where two people are discovering each other and are blinded by the newness of the experience. (The added *secrecy* of an affair may prolong that period beyond the time that it lasts while openly dating.)

Unfortunately, people tend to attribute special qualities to a person with whom they're having an affair, when it's far more likely that the specialness has more to do with the newness of the relationship than with the particular person.

7

This is why we see people go from one affair to another—or from one marriage to another—always trying to recapture that special feeling that comes only with starting a new relationship.

So focusing on this question of "how long an affair usually lasts" may help put this experience in perspective. Ironically, most people don't ask this question until after an affair is well underway—when they gradually come to grips with the fact that it won't last and begin to wonder when it will end. So while no one can predict in a given situation, most affairs do tend to follow this general pattern.

* * * * * * * * * * * * *

Affairs are in a way a good thing

Dear Peggy,

I think that affairs are in a way a good thing. On the negative side, they can break up relationships and hurt the people involved. But it is also a test of love. If someone cheats on you once and never does it again you know that this man/woman is the one for you. She/he is very much in love with you and you can continue your life. But if someone cheats on you once, then does it again repeatedly, you know that it is time to leave the relationship before anyone else gets hurt. I would never stoop so low as to say that it is ok to cheat on someone, I am merely saying that if someone does commit this falsehood to you, stop and think before calling it off. The person may have been only caught up in the moment, but still love you. You could be making a bigger mistake by leaving the one you really love.

Dear Reader,

While this is a thoughtful reflection on the relationship between love and having affairs, there are several statements that cry out for more comment.

First, the idea that "affairs are in a way a good thing" is unlikely to *ever* be embraced by a person whose partner has an affair. While it's true that the process of doing the hard work necessary to cope with the fallout from an affair *may* eventually lead to some benefit, this is very different from saying the affair itself was a good thing. (For instance, my husband and I developed a stronger relationship following his affairs than we had before, but his affairs might just as easily have led to divorce. It was the *work* we did after confronting the affairs—rather than the affairs themselves—that made the difference.) As with any crisis, it's not the crisis that makes people better/stronger/whatever. It's how they respond to the crisis.

Second, the idea that affairs are a "test of love" feeds into the false way of thinking that if someone loves you, they won't have an affair. While married women who have affairs often convince themselves that they no longer love their husbands, many men having affairs are clear that they still love their wives; they just want *both* the affair and the marriage.

Third, the idea that "If someone cheats on you once and never does it again, you know that this man/woman is the one for you" reflects the false idea that there is *one* special person for you. There is no such thing as just one person who could be "the one" for you.

Last, the idea that "...if someone cheats...repeatedly, you know that it is time to leave the relationship..." is in keeping with much of the rigid way of thinking about when you can or can't rebuild the relationship. It's not nearly as simple as this would make it appear. Sometimes it's best to leave after the first time it happens; other times it might not be best to leave even after several instances. Nothing about dealing with affairs is as cut-and-dried as we'd like to think it is. Whether to stay or leave depends on many, many factors—mostly related to the possibilities for the future of the relationship rather than why/how many times/with whom the affairs took place. This is a far more complex issue than most people realize—which is why there is such a need to broaden the general understandings about affairs.

* * * * * * * * * * * * *

Affair in a 21-year Marriage

Dear Peggy,

I have an extraordinary situation. My husband is a very successful business man. He has made his work his life and is very committed to it. We lived in another area for awhile, but I came home while he stayed and finished his job there. I was raising our children and missing him terribly, but my husband had an affair while we were apart. I found the evidence (a very intimate letter from someone I knew) in his briefcase. I was crushed, humiliated and in so much pain, but I kept it to myself. I knew about the affair for several days before I told him I knew. He, of course, told me that nothing happened and flatly denied that it took place.

He went back to a new job in still another location and we still are not communicating about the affair. I have no idea how long it has been going on, or whether he is still seeing her. I am having a very difficult time understanding this. The pain is so great that I have lost a great deal of weight in the last month since I've known. I've seen a therapist that has helped a lot, but how do I ever get over the pain of the betrayal. This is so out of character for him that I am at a loss as to what to do. How can I get the marriage on the right track, and how to trust him again. And I'm concerned about the children. The older ones have a sense of something wrong, but my youngest does not. Do they need to be told the truth; and if so, who tells them?

Dear Reader,

The situation described in this letter understandably feels "extraordinary," (and it *is* extraordinary to the person dealing with it), but having heard the personal affair experiences of thousands of people, this situation follows a very typical pattern. There's far more involved than can adequately be addressed in a short response, but I'll try to cover a few key points that might help anyone in this situation:

1. Being "successful" (especially when involving travel and living apart) makes it easier for someone to compartmentalize their life and keep their family relationship and outside relationships separate in their own mind—as if one has nothing to do with the other.
2. Being "crushed, humiliated and in pain" are almost always the reactions to learning of a partner's affair (even if there was a suspicion beforehand, but even moreso if there was no suspicion). The most common word used is *devastation*.
3. "Flatly denying" the affair and "not communicating about the affair" are also quite common. There's an unwritten rule among people having affairs: "Never tell. If questioned, deny it. If caught, say as little as possible."
4. "Having a difficult time understanding this" is also predictable (and understandable) because it doesn't "make sense." (People having affairs tend to rationalize their behavior in order to feel OK about themselves.)
5. Losing a lot of weight is also typical. In fact, the struggle to physically deal with the pain and loss is the first order of business for most people.
6. Seeing a therapist can help, but getting over the pain of the betrayal and learning to trust again takes a lot of time and work. It can't be rushed. Some key factors are: willingness to answer questions, hanging in through the inevitable emotional impact, and severing contact with the third party. (These are not absolute, but usually indicate a willingness to resolve this issue instead of trying to bury it alive, where it just keeps coming back.)
7. Concern about the children is, of course, quite common as well. In general, when kids know there's something wrong and don't know what it is, they tend to imagine that it has something to do with them. In our own case, our children were 11 and 13 when we told them about my husband's affairs. We did it together, reassuring them that we would work it out. Our kids are now grown, and the strongest lesson they gained from knowing, was learning to appreciate the importance of honesty. Of course, each parent must make their own decision about whether/when/how to tell, based on the ages of the children and their own knowledge of what's best for them.

* * * * * * * * * * * * *

Renew Old Flame Online

Dear Peggy,

I recently discovered that my husband of 20 years has renewed a relationship with his air force lover online. He tells me that he still loves me, that she only has a small part of him, but that he also believes God brought them back together, and he can't cut off the relationship. He realizes that I am hurt, but he tells me that I am just tearing myself up over nothing. However, I have read some of their mail, and it has a lot of sexual connotation, plus signatures using old nicknames for one another and love always to one another. She lives 3000 miles away, so he does not consider this an affair since there has been no sex since he last saw her in 1976. I feel that he is emotionally tied to her and that our relationship has suffered. Of course, he tells me that he turned to her because I was preoccupied with my job, even though the week before I found out about the extent of their relationship he told me he believed we had the best marriage he knows of.

I love our life together and I love him. I have come to the conclusion that I have 2 options—stay and accept his relationship with her or leave. I have only one friend that I can talk to about this and even though he says their relationship is normal, he does not want it shared with our children or other family and friends. I do very well pretending all is well for a few weeks, then something happens and the wound reopens with corresponding pain. I have considered counseling and he says he would go, but he will not give her up even if the counselor thinks it is an affair. I don't see how counseling would be of much benefit for that reason.

Lately he has been more attentive and tried to share more with me, but I think he is just trying to prove to me that he can have us both. There are some parts of our marriage that have grown better due to this crisis, but I don't see how it can heal as long as he continues contact with her. She divorced a year ago and she prints all the communication between her and my husband in a notebook, because he says she figures he will dump her again and then she will have some part of him to keep. I am very depressed and don't know what to do, where to go from here? I don't know whether I should give him an ultimatum; he may never forgive me. If I put up with it, will it end on its own? Any suggestions you have will be appreciated.

Dear Reader,

This letter raises *many* issues that are quite complicated and confusing.
— "He also believes God brought them back together..."
This is a classic case of trying to absolve yourself from responsibility—and is one of the worst of the many kinds of rationalizations people use to justify their actions.
— "He tells me that I am just tearing myself up over nothing."
This is another classic case of trying to absolve yourself from responsibility by blaming someone else for their normal response to your actions.
— "He tells me that he turned to her because I was preoccupied with my job"
Yet another effort to place blame somewhere (*anywhere*) else, instead of accepting personal responsibility.
— "I have 2 options—stay and accept his relationship with her or leave."
This no-win trap is precisely what the other person *hopes* their spouse will think. This leaves them in the driver's seat—in control of whatever happens, avoiding any consequences of their actions.
— "He does not want it shared with our children or other family and friends."
Another instance of trying to control everything—so there's *protection* from having to deal with any consequences.

11

— "I do very well pretending all is well for a few weeks, then something happens and the wound reopens with corresponding pain."

When deep feelings are hidden or buried, they don't go away; they're simply buried—and re-surface at a later time. So this pattern is inevitable when things are not dealt with.

— "He will not give her up even if the counselor thinks it is an affair."

Another effort to be in control of everything, allowing no room for change or compromise.

— "I think he is just trying to prove to me that he can have us both. If I put up with it, will it end on its own? "

It's quite typical in this kind of situation that a person simply doesn't want to give up anything. They want what they see as the best of both worlds—regardless of the impact on others. Unfortunately, they're unlikely to end it on their own; they're often willing to remain in this situation until either the spouse or the third party insists on their making a choice.

— "I don't know whether I should give him an ultimatum; he may never forgive me."

No one else can determine whether or when some form of ultimatum is reasonable, certainly not unless or until there's a clear willingness to accept the consequences. So the fear that "he may never forgive me" is quite telling. (In fact, any effort to force a decision is best approached in terms of clear time frames, etc., rather than an ultimatum per se.)

In almost every instance described above, the overriding issue is to confront the fact that there's an effort to dictate and control everything and everybody (using blame, fear, intimidation, and any other means possible to justify/defend/rationalize the behavior)—while accepting no personal responsibility. So resisting the efforts to be controlled as to how you *think* (and beginning to see through the rationalizations) may be the first step toward resisting the efforts to control what you *do* about this situation.

2: Why People Have Affairs

Husband's affair

Dear Peggy, (This is a shortened version of a very long letter.)

My husband had (is having?) an affair with my "former" best friend of 21 years! He had never approved of her previously; however, I began feeling like there was something going on over a period of a few months. Then he helped her move, and everything began to fall apart. I later walked in on them in her bed, confirming it. When he helped her to move he basically never came home again. We have been married 7 years and have two young children. He later rented an apartment and she moved in with him!! It has been so blatant and painful. I have always been very, very much in love with him and I never believed he was the kind of man who would be unfaithful to me. I always trusted him and loved that I felt so comfortable with our trust... Also, it was such a shock to be so betrayed by her, she knew how much I love him...a friend I had known since she was a teenager!!! My best friend!!

It is as though he is a completely different person. He is beginning to be more reasonable, helpful, more kind. However his attitude changes back to cold and indifferent without me knowing what or when to expect it. He told me that he asked her to move out, that there is no intimate relationship with her, only a roommate situation, but it is very difficult (impossible) to believe.

We are talking more, he visits the kids occasionally but we do not talk about our problems, as he is avoiding the confrontation. He says he wants to take it slow. I wish he would talk to me. I cannot understand what I have done to be treated this way. We had a good marriage, some conflict, but we were doing so well, I have always been happy with him. I am devastated for the fact that my family and marriage has been torn apart, they are the most important part of my life.

Dear Reader,

This letter contains some of the key elements that create enormous pain and devastation when a spouse has an affair. First of all, the feelings of devastation are understandable—because this is a life-altering experience. As is so clearly expressed by this reader, it's more than just the affair (as if that weren't enough). It's also the loss of the world as she knew it. It's overwhelming to discover that your spouse is not who you thought he was; your marriage is not what you thought it was; and in this case, your friend is not who you thought she was. The bottom line is that your world is not the way you thought it was—and this can indeed be devastating.

While there is no way to "compare" the degree of pain involved in various kinds of affairs, most people recognize the double-whammy when the affair partner is also a friend. Dealing with the deception by both your spouse and your friend can be especially disturbing. The comment: "It is as though he is a completely different person" shows that her husband now seems like a stranger she doesn't really know. However, some of this kind of behavior is fairly predictable among people having affairs. There is often an effort to "compartmentalize" life—as if one part (the affair) has nothing to do with the other part (the marriage). This is a common way of avoiding confronting what's really happening.

A couple of other statements in this letter deserve comment. First, "He told me... there is no intimate relationship with her...but it is very difficult (impossible) to believe." While there's no way to know the truth in any specific instance, in general, it's safer to listen to your head than to your heart. Second, "I cannot understand what I have done to be treated this way." As hard as it is for a person to believe it when they're in the midst of the pain of these feelings, it seldom has anything to do with whatever they have (or haven't) done. The tendency to think it's "my fault" is extremely common—and wrong. It's painful enough to deal with this kind of loss without adding to it by blaming yourself.

* * * * * * * * * * * * *

Very confused in my marriage

Dear Peggy,

I'm a 36-year-old woman with 2 children, ages 10 and 4. I've been married for 13 years to my grammar school sweetheart. We've been dating since we were 14 or 15.

The past few years of our marriage have been terrible. Lack of communication, lack of respect, taking each other for granted, etc. Because of his business, he is never home (or home very late at night), leaving me to take full responsibility for the household; mind you I also work 3 days a week. It has taken a toll on us, along with financial difficulties—which we all know is the root of all evil.

Well, things have come to a boil, and I have been unfaithful to him. Something happened one night, while I was out drinking with the girls, with a friend of his. I was drunk and regret what happened. It meant nothing to me. But nevertheless a few weeks go by and I am out again and meet a guy in the bar and was hanging out talking with him, etc. Well, he walked me to my car and we began to kiss. That's all that happened with him. We then began to Email each other and through that I began to gain certain feelings for him. I see him driving or walking on the avenue, but nothing further has happened. Well my husband found out about all this and needless to say is destroyed, and so am I. Why do I continue to seek out the attention of other men? Is it because I lacked it for quite a few years? I do love my husband and want to get help to work it out, but what is going on with me?

Why People Have Affairs

Is it because I was with my husband since we were young and didn't have time to find myself. I am very dependent on him, always have been. I find this whole separation (which we are in now) very scary, but I feel we both need it to explore our feelings for each other and grow somehow. I definitely need to get counseling for myself to learn about myself. I feel like I'm going through an identity crisis at this point in my life. I was always his girlfriend, then his wife, then the mother of his children—and never found who I was. Everything I did was done for him or my kids, I was always put aside. But now I think I'm finally waking up and seeing what I've missed in my life. I love my children to death, they are my life and I will always continue to put them first in my life. I feel that I need and want time for myself now. Does this all make any sense to you? Well you know I could go on and on, but I'll end it here. I'll be eagerly awaiting your reply, and I appreciate all this.

Dear Reader,

This questioning and confusion as to "why" someone has an affair is all too common. Usually it's the spouse who is obsessed with why their partner had an affair. But, as in the letter above, the person having an affair often doesn't fully understand why they did it themselves. In fact, this is often the source of a great deal of turmoil when an affair is discovered: the spouse thinks that a failure to answer the question of "why" means the person is withholding the reason for their affair—when, in fact, people frequently don't have a great deal of clarity as to why. This is because there's never one *single*, simple "reason." It's a *combination* of factors, all working together. But, as I've said before, no matter why someone might "want" to have an affair, the essential ingredient in acting on that desire is a willingness to be dishonest and deceptive.

Having said that, I'll review some of the "reasons" mentioned in this letter because they're typical of the ones people try to come up with to explain their behavior.

— "Is it because I lacked it [attention] for quite a few years?"
There are always "unmet needs" in *any* marriage, so it's easy after-the-fact to identify whatever lack there might have been in the relationship that led to an affair.

— "Is it because I was with my husband since we were young and didn't have time to find myself?"
Early marriage may make it more difficult, but late marriage (after people are set in their ways and don't want to give up their independence) can be just as problematic.

— "I feel that I need and want time for myself now. Does this all make any sense to you?"
Yes, this makes lots of sense. But the way for anyone to "find themselves" is *not* by going from one relationship to another one; that just continues the pattern of not finding your *self*. Instead, it's better to seek more activities that are meaningful on an individual basis (outside the roles of wife or mother or

15

partner to some other man) and that are *not* hurtful to yourself and others in the way that inevitably happens with an affair. Certainly, a person deserves to develop a separate sense of themselves, but not at the expense of others. It's important to find a good balance.

* * * * * * * * * * * * *

Repeated affairs

Dear Peggy,

What is it in the basic personality of a person that makes them periodically go out and look for an affair? Is this more a sign of something obviously wrong within the marriage? Or could it be some glitch in the psyche of a person?

Would really be interested in hearing your opinions on the subject. Thanks!

Dear Reader,

The biggest question related to people having affairs is "Why" they do it. Whether it's a one-time experience or many affairs, there's no easy explanation for any specific person's behavior. This reader recognizes that there are many potential factors, including basic personality, something wrong within the marriage, etc. In fact, it's almost impossible to pinpoint precisely what is involved in leading a person to have affairs.

This letter represents the typical way of thinking about why people have affairs—that it's due to some *problem* or *lack*, either in the individual or the relationship. (However, these are only the things that "push" people into affairs.) There are also factors that "pull" people into affairs, including novelty and excitement. Finally, there are societal factors that also play a part. The reason any specific person has an affair is usually due to a combination of all these factors.

Therefore, it's probably more useful to focus on what can be done to change the behavior than to determine why it's happening in the first place. And the key to changing behavior is usually linked to increasing the level of honest communication—not just about affairs, but about all important issues in the relationship. The more people really *know* each other, the less likely they are to be willing to be deceptive or to act on whatever "reasons" are leading them to have affairs.

* * * * * * * * * * * * *

Why do I do this??

Dear Peggy,

I was in a marriage and very happy. I had my happy little family, and I swore that I would never have an affair or do anything to lose my husband. Well, after 2 years of marriage, my happiness disappeared, and I had an affair. Two of them. First with an ex-boyfriend, and then with a man that I had been friends with for about 3 months. Well, I ended up leaving my husband for this man I was having the affair with.

Now, I was having a lot of emotional problems when I started my affairs on my husband, and I tried to blame it all on that (i.e. I had a miscarriage with our

16

second child...would have been my fourth, I found out I had cervical cancer and kept having surgeries because it wouldn't go away, and our mutual best friend died.) Needless to say, I went a little nuts, and I blamed all of this for my infidelity and the fact that I uprooted my children from their happy home.

Well, here I am, a little over 2 years into this live-in relationship, and I am wanting to have an affair again. I can honestly say, that with my husband, I didn't love him the way a wife should. I was young, thought I was in love, and wanted a good life for my children. But this man, I can say that I love—and I know it's true. I don't want to be without him, we have talked marriage, and yet...I have been thinking about having an affair with an old friend.

A friend and I discussed this and she says it's the excitement that keeps making me want to go back to an affair. My Mom says I am acting like my Dad. My family also says if I have an affair, they will never forgive me, and if I leave this man, they will be extremely disappointed in me. And, I don't want to leave him...I just want to have my cake and eat it too!!

I don't know what to think. Is something wrong with me? I would appreciate any input that you may have as to my situation.

Dear Reader,

This letter does a good job of analyzing a situation that seems to have gotten out of hand. Unfortunately, there's too much emphasis on analyzing, pondering why, and wondering what to think. It's easy to put too much emphasis on understanding why we're the way we are instead of focusing on what to do about it—regardless of why.

For instance, while *attractions* to others are natural (and not a problem in and of themselves), deciding to *act* on those attractions can be devastating to everyone involved. In the final analysis, what matters is what a person decides to *do*.

Life has a way of creating consequences for all our actions. Sometimes it's not obvious or immediate, but there are consequences nonetheless. Usually, when the problem has been more openly discussed within the family (as described above), it leads to a certain accountability that helps a person be more responsible in their actions. It's when people are secretive and deceptive that the problems get more difficult. In fact, the more honest we are able to be in all our interactions (whether love relationships or others), the fewer consequences we will have to face throughout our lives.

* * * * * * * * * * * * *

Building up to an affair

Dear Peggy,

I hope you can help me. My husband sleeps with prostitutes. He doesn't all the time, only about 8 times in a four year marriage. He says all men do it, and compares himself to politicians/presidents, past and present. He is a lawyer. He says it is no big deal, and it releases tension, but has nothing to do with me. We have been separated, on and off, during the past three years. We have been through 5 marriage counselors/therapists, and he very easily explains his way out of this bad behavior. It almost seems like he is addicted, as an alcoholic, because he can act like a different person when he goes into his "acting out affair" mode. We have two children, and I have tried every bit of strength and resources I know of to keep this marriage up and running, but I am fading fast. He wants to come back again, (we are separated now), and promises to go to therapy again, and try to be closer to us, his family. The really weird thing is, he is very open with me, and can be very loving. After so many chances, and so many slip-ups, am I setting myself up for another failure?

I am still a fairly young woman, but this is aging me fast, and I feel the impact of all of this is hurting my children. But every time I try to break it off, he cries and cries, and tells me it has nothing to do with me or the children. But, on the other hand, he says it is a release from the pressures of being a father and a husband. (He is 10 years older and never was married.) Some of these prostitutes are horrid, not to mention the fact they've had an abundance of partners who may have had an abundance of diseases.

How much devotion does a wife have to have to try to keep her marriage together, even if this person apparently has a psychological problem? I feel like my life is a wreck for the next 15 years, till my kids are grown and I can fly away and escape all this pain... What can I do?

Dear Reader,

Perception is a fascinating thing—how two people can look at the exact same situation and see it so differently. In this case, the husband seems to be frustrated that his wife can't see his point of view, especially since he's so good at "explaining his way out of his bad behavior." Unfortunately, he can't seem to see his wife's point of view—and she's suffering the consequences of that failure. The common statement by those involved in affairs is that "it has nothing to do with you or the family." When my own husband was trying to explain his affairs, he also said they "had nothing to do with me." Perhaps from his point of view, they had nothing to do with me, but from my point of view they had everything to do with me. (Fortunately, he finally understood that his perception was not "reality.")

The common thinking behind this kind of attitude is based on rationalization. It's a way of compartmentalizing life and pretending that one part of life (the outside sex) has nothing to do with the other part (the wife and family). Of course, this is absurd, but it's a way of avoiding responsibility for actions that are hurtful to those who are supposedly loved. As for needing "a release of pressures of being a father and husband," doesn't every man and woman with children feel the pressures of that role? And yet there are many outlets for release of tension that don't involve hurting those you love.

Of course, convincing a spouse of their faulty thinking process can be difficult—especially when the spouse is a lawyer, as in the above letter (or a psychologist, which was the case with my husband). Even with the better argument, it's hard to *win* a discussion when it turns into a debate. So any successful effort toward clearer thinking needs to appeal to the heart as well as the head. If there's genuine caring on the spouse's part, it needs to be reflected in a willingness to stop hiding behind *excuses*—like "everybody does it," "it releases tension," even the "I can't help it because I'm addicted" excuse.

The letter-writer's final question, "What can I do?" is the question that her spouse needs to be asking himself: what can he do—before it's too late. As for what *she* can do, the practical concerns about kids are a reality for a person in this situation. If there's a feeling of being "trapped," it's all the more essential that there at least be a *plan* for the future. That way they can gradually make whatever changes might help to bring more peace and less pain during the process of working toward a better future—either with or without their spouse.

* * * * * * * * * * * * *

Husband wants what I don't give

Dear Peggy,

I have a disease and don't give my husband "what he thinks he needs." He feels it is acceptable for him to chat with single women in the rooms and if he meets one and they connect, and the timing and circumstances are right he may get "what he thinks he needs" and that is okay. I don't at all. I'm at a loss.

Dear Reader,

Most of us tend to think that a partner's interest in outside sex is due to some failure on our part to "meet their needs" and that not meeting their needs will "cause" our partner to get them met elsewhere. By thinking it's due to "unmet needs," we set ourselves up to take the blame when our partner has an affair—and to take the responsibility for keeping it from happening in the first place.

The fact is that we can't control another person's behavior by our actions; each of us is responsible for our own behavior. But since *all* marriages have problems from time to time, it's easy to point a finger to whatever identifiable problem exists in the relationship—and say *that's* why the affair happened. (However, if that particular problem hadn't existed, there would have been some other problem—and *that* one would have been identified as *the* reason.)

In my own situation, I tried to meet every possible need I could imagine. I tried to be the 'perfect' wife, mother, hostess, sex partner, cook, intellectual partner, etc.—everything aimed at "meeting his needs." When we finally talked about all his affairs, I asked, "Didn't it make any difference that I was trying so hard?" And he said, "Well, I just thought I was the luckiest guy in the world. I had this great wife who was doing all these terrific things—and I had my affairs too!"

I *finally* came to understand that no one person can meet all of another person's need all the time. So while "unmet needs" may be a quick and easy "excuse," it's not the reason people have affairs. It's only one factor among many others.

* * * * * * * * * * * * *

19

"Diagnosing" the cause of affairs?

Dear Peggy,

In reading your book, "Beyond Affairs," I was shocked to learn that your husband had affairs with about 15 women! I have never known anyone whose husband had the same amount of affairs as mine!

I am having a very, very difficult time understanding this. We have a great relationship outside of what I call his "evil twin." The psychiatrist says he has a need for acceptance with women, as a result of some experiences from his childhood. How can I ever separate this "childhood problem" from just plain old "feeling jilted?" What can I do? What do you suggest? I really need help!

Dear Reader,

I am not qualified to comment on the psychiatrist's explanation of the cause of this behavior. However, having received candid comments from thousands of people through the years about their experiences with therapy, diagnoses that call for going back to "childhood" issues to explain behavior have usually been more like taking 2 steps *backward* to try to take one step forward—very hard to ever make progress.

While it can be useful to understand all the factors that may have contributed, any particularly "insight" like this doesn't necessarily change anything. What usually makes the biggest difference is making a decision here and now to change—*and* being held accountable on a daily basis for behaviors aimed at that change.

However, with that general background, I want to use this letter as a vehicle for addressing the whole issue of using any specific diagnosis for a person who has had an affair—as if this establishes *the* reason the affair happened.

One of the most common diagnoses (especially when someone has multiple affairs) is that they have a "sexual addiction." (A "sex addict" is defined as a person who is addicted to the sexual experience and its surrounding behaviors.) Even though sexual addiction includes deviant sexual behavior that has nothing to do with affairs, the term has been used to include *any* person whose sex life is destructive and out of control. (Of course, there *are* sexual deviants in this society, but based on the large numbers of people having affairs, this is hardly "deviant" behavior.)

While the term "sexual addiction" may be relevant in a few cases (perhaps 7 percent according to the person who coined this phrase), it's unfortunate that many people are tempted to grasp at this simple explanation as the cause of affairs—whether or not it fits. However, despite the problem of inappropriately labeling someone who has affairs as a "sexaholic," any genuine effort to understand and deal with this issue may be helpful to some people, especially when it involves getting more perspective of the consequences of their behavior and working to deal with the problems it has caused.

Since this letter referred to my husband's multiple affairs, I can report that what he decided to do was to commit to honesty (which made him "accountable"), followed by actions to back up the commitment. As a result, without any therapy or outside "help," he *stopped* having affairs back in 1973 before telling me about them—and has been monogamous during all the years since that time. So the bottom line for any person who has been involved in secret sexual experiences (regardless of the label or diagnosis) is "What are you going to *do* about it?"

* * * * * * * * * * * *

Will upbringing cause affairs?

Dear Peggy,

Do you think that having a father who was very strict and distrusting while I was growing up may contribute to the likeliness of an affair today? I was never allowed to date, my mom had to lie for me so I could go out. Dad was very protective and I was very spoiled, but denied relationships. As a result I did a lot of sneaking around even though my mom knew about it and covered for me. He wouldn't even meet the guy I went to the Sr. prom with and always acted angry or hurt if he did find out I was going out. I have an older brother who was followed around by my dad and he did get into his share of trouble, but I feel as though I had to constantly prove to my dad that I was not like my brother. My brother consequently has had trouble with alcoholism and manic-depressive episodes, while I suffer from the issue with the affairs. Any thoughts on this?

Dear Reader,

The first thing that comes to mind is a saying from "Transactional Analysis: "The way you are may be your parents' fault; but if you stay that way, it's your own fault." So while family experiences during childhood may lead someone to be inclined toward some particular behavior, it does *not* determine behavior as an adult.

As for the issue of affairs, people virtually never have affairs for any *one* reason. So while family relationships might be one small factor in their thinking about affairs, there are many, many other factors that all combine to determine whether someone has affairs. As I've often pointed out, this includes factors that "push" them toward affairs (problems of one sort or another), things that "pull" them toward affairs (the excitement, novelty, etc.), and the societal factors that support affairs. (Despite the fact that society gives lip service to monogamy, we glorify affairs and maintain a secrecy that allows them to thrive.)

One of the hallmarks of maturity is recognizing and accepting responsibility for one's own life and behavior. So while it's helpful to understand our past, we are not bound by it. It doesn't "dictate" our future.

* * * * * * * * * * * *

A positive affair

Dear Peggy,

I met her online a year ago, we chatted for 5 months; then a business trip brought us together for one night. It turned out to be more magical than I ever

21

expected. We are both married, she for over 20 years Her husband is home 5 days out of the month and she wants more, and when he's home he complains and spends little time with her or her daughter. Worse, because of his job he moved her from her family in Arizona to Ohio where she is apart from family and friends. This has been going on for some 4 years. Additionally, he hasn't supported her efforts in trying to start a small business or go to college, to wit he stifled her dreams. I'm married too, over 20 years, a rocky one, my wife had a few affairs, one of which I caught her red-handed in my home. Through therapy we got past it, but I wonder if I haven't got past it now?

We have seen each other a half dozen times in the last 6 months, spent about 3 weeks together all told; we have made no promises. We both feel we love each other but also have a hard time dealing with the fantasy aspects of an online affair and meeting in romantic places under ideal situations we feel isn't reality. But isn't dating very much the same? I guess the reality of the kids and finances is what is keeping us from a hasty decision. One great positive thing has come out of this; she has gone back to school at my beckoning. Her husband refused to pay for it so she took a loan. I positively support her education. I have told her that even though we love each other, it may be impossible for me to leave because of the kids, and if she leaves or doesn't, at least she will be financially free. We morally support each other. We agree not to be pushy and we don't see each other but once every 2 to 3 months.

We have gone through all the online feelings of love and soul-mates (and after meeting many times the feelings of love and caring keep getting stronger); it has been a year now. I have emotionally moved further away from my wife, but I had problems that caused me to move away from her before I met this special woman. I feel the kids are getting older and we don't have similar interests anymore. I feel I may very well want to spend the rest of my years with this woman who I am so compatible with in all areas. My big concern is will the kids destroy the new relationship, will my ex use the kids as a weapon. We are going very slow, which I think is wise. My kids are 12, 13 and 15; hers are 14 and 17. Any ideas are appreciated.

Dear Reader,

This letter is an indication of how sometimes people involved in affairs are trying *very hard* to be rational about the situation and to protect others from being hurt. Yet despite the sensible efforts to proceed cautiously, there's an inherent risk (for *everyone*) whenever people are living "secret" lives.

The kind of limbo situation described above is extremely common; it's part of the human condition to "want it all," but life usually involves tradeoffs. And a failure to make a clear *choice* (and act on that choice) leaves everyone shortchanged.

This letter also indicates a common pattern of thinking that involves identifying the problems in the respective marriages (including a former affair by the letter-writer's wife in this case) as a way of justifying (or at least explaining) the affair. However, it's important to remember that there is no marriage that is without problems; so it's not reasonable to point to whatever specific problems exist in a particular marriage and assign a "cause and effect"—as if the affair wouldn't have happened if that particular problem hadn't existed.

The writer understands the fantasy nature of the relationship—that it's like dating. This is the normal course of new relationships, but those initial feelings aren't the same as the deeper love that can come from building a life together, which can in turn be a source of strength and support for facing the world at large. And as long as the source of support is sought outside the marriage, there's little hope for developing it *in* the marriage. So regardless of whatever problems might have contributed to the affair, continuing the secret relationship only creates *more* problems—and the marriage is likely to grow even more strained and distant. Unfortunately, holding onto a fantasy makes real-life even more difficult. So until there's a clear choice (and a commitment to pursuing that choice), there's likely to continue to be a lot of confusion and questioning about the future.

*   *   *   *   *   *   *   *   *   *   *   *

What needs aren't being met?

Dear Peggy,

Why is it that the first real question when a man falls in love with another woman is: What needs weren't being met in the marriage? It seems that that question refuses to look at the possibility that maybe he didn't have a loving relationship with his wife, and met someone he could be happy with. Why is it, that when two people get married, if one or the other isn't happy with the marriage and has the opportunity to be with someone he/she loves, does that factor seem to be overlooked or negated as if the love he/she has with the other person is "invalid," or just a "symptom" of trouble in the marriage, etc...

It seems that when a partner has an "affair," the relationship is viewed merely as a "sign" of a problem, rather than maybe that person may have married for the wrong reasons, or has realized that they don't thrive with that partner, or even like or enjoy them. Granted, a person should get a divorce if they are unhappy and want out...before they enter into another relationship, but what if they don't know how unhappy they are until they meet the person of a lifetime? Answer this for me please.

Dear Reader,

I have never said that a relationship is merely a sign of a problem. In fact, I totally reject the idea that affairs happen because of unmet needs in the marriage. Since *no* one person can fill *all* the needs of another person *all* the time—if unmet needs were *the* cause of affairs, virtually *everyone* would have affairs.

As for people "not knowing how unhappy they are until they meet the person of a lifetime"—this is an after-the-fact effort to defend/justify an affair.

23

People don't necessarily *realize* they are rationalizing, but that's the case nevertheless. Comparing the feelings of a *new* relationship with a long-term marriage often lead people to revise their feelings about their marriage. By comparison, they're likely to say that "while I love my spouse, I'm not *in love* with them." However, the "in love" feeling is only the initial stage of love that's based more on biological "chemistry" than anything else—and has very little to do with a deeper, lasting love.

The feelings toward a person in a new relationship *will* change over time. The specialness of a new person has much more to do with the fact that they're *new* than with the individual themselves. As for knowing whether someone is "the person of a lifetime," many people think when they marry that they've found such a person—but about 50 percent of all marriages end in divorce. It's impossible to know in the beginning whether or not someone fits this description; it can't be known unless/until you actually spend a lifetime together.

* * * * * * * * * * * * *

He said his affair was my fault

Dear Peggy,

My husband got a promotion which made us move out of state. This meant I would be leaving my entire family behind. A difficult move to say the least. I was very reluctant. Found out about the move when our second child was 3 months old, sibling was 2-1/2 years. He said he would be going to the new place with or without me. Half-heartedly, it seemed, he said he wanted us there. When I arrived in our new state I was lonely but doing what I could. Gave up my career to be a stay-at-home mom—this was My choice. He was not there for me emotionally the way I needed him. He was going out with friends till late at night occasionally and was difficult to locate when I called him at work. Turned out he had started an affair 5 months before we moved and continued it upon our arrival. By the time I figured things out, he had supposedly quit seeing the woman but was still in verbal contact with her.

We are in therapy together now. Trust is tough for me to regain. There are many reasons things are difficult: 1) He does not seem overly remorseful; 2) He says he was unhappy for 2 years and this woman filled his needs (he was unhappy during my pregnancy and during the first year of our son's life); 3) If I had been more supportive he wouldn't have Needed to do this...the woman approached Him and it "wasn't like he was looking for her!" Thus, it is my fault for not meeting his needs. How can I get him to own up to his responsibility for doing the wrong thing???

Also, I worry a lot about whether the odds are against us in trying to mend things. What are some indicators of couples that have survived?

Dear Reader,

This is a long letter, giving many specifics that have an impact on the overall situation, but I think it's reasonable to only try to reflect on the final comments.

1. "He does not seem overly remorseful."
   This is quite common. It may be a way of protecting against having to deal with the full impact of your actions. To avoid fully acknowledging the impact of what you've done allows some distancing that serves as a barrier against feelings of remorse.
2. "He says he was unhappy for 2 years and this woman filled his needs (he was unhappy during my pregnancy and during the first year of our son's life)."
   The period of pregnancy and infant care is stressful for both mothers and fathers—and again is quite normal. Focusing on whether you're *happy* during this significant period is usually relegated to people who resist/resent the tolls involved in parenting and want life to be unfettered by such responsibilities.
3. "If I had been more supportive he wouldn't have *needed* to do this..."
   This is closely related to the point above, and arises when people seem to need to be the center of attention.

As for "getting him to own up to his responsibility for doing the wrong thing?"—no one can *make* another person feel something they don't want to feel. We usually think in ways that help us feel better about ourselves, so we often rationalize that "it's not our fault" in order to feel OK about something we've done. Clear, rational thinking would allow anyone to know that it's not a spouse's responsibility to "meet all our needs." And if that were the criteria for a successful relationship, no marriages would be successful.

As for "some indicators of couples that have survived"—the main factors are those I frequently mention: answering all your questions, hanging in through the inevitable emotional impact, and severing contact with the third party. Obviously this is not magic; it's only what makes mending the relationship *possible*. The mending involves time, effort, and lots and lots of honest communication on an ongoing basis.

3: Online Affairs

Online affair with a married man

Dear Peggy,
I have been carrying on an online affair with a married man. We have no intentions of ever meeting, although we have talked on the phone. Is this wrong? Can it really be considered an extramarital affair? I think that it is all innocent, but sometimes I feel guilty for talking to him.

Dear Reader,

Even though they may not involve physical contact, online affairs still involve the same kinds of thinking and emotions as other affairs. On one hand, they usually involve novelty and excitement, and on the other hand they usually involve secrecy and deception.

Novelty and Excitement:
— People often present the freest and freshest aspects of their personalities online.
— Online interactions often provide an "escape" from the realities of day-to-day living.
— The fantasy world online can make the real world seem dull and boring.
— The sheer numbers of people create unlimited potential for "newness."

Secrecy and Deception:
— The secrecy involved in online affairs is part of their appeal—and part of their danger.
— The secretiveness increases the intensity of the feelings generated by this contact.
— By deceiving a primary partner, online affairs become high-risk, no matter what.
— Recovering from being deceived can be extremely difficult, even if no sex is involved

Here's a typical scenario for what happens in these kinds of situations:

You meet someone interesting Online.
You present the "best side" of your personality, and so do they.
You share confidences: hopes, fears, fantasies.
The intense sharing brings you closer and closer together.
You fantasize about being more than online friends.
You become infatuated with your "friend" and want more interaction.
You begin to feel like you're "in love."
You want to meet your online friend in person.
You feel like "soul-mates" or that you were "meant for each other."

You consider "risking it all" to see your online friend.
You either meet and engage in sex.
(Or you don't meet—and feel like "star-crossed lovers.")
Your online relationship eventually ends.
Your life has been changed in ways you never intended.
Some comments about this scenario:

You feel a loss, but it's the loss of a fantasy that was never real. Any new connection is going to be exciting, but it may not be the particular person who makes the difference. The excitement has more to do with the *kind* of relationship than to the specific feelings about a real person. So whether or not it's wrong, it's probably not a *smart* path to pursue—especially when looking down the road to see how it will probably end.

*　*　*　*　*　*　*　*　*　*　*　*

Meant to be?

Dear Peggy,

I am 25 and I have a 6-year-old daughter. My husband and I have been married for 6-1/2 years. We are having problems now and I feel that the best thing is for us to try separation and counseling. He feels that my mind is made up and that if we separate we will never get together again. We have been through so much together, but I feel that we have grown apart. He wants different things than I do, and I do not feel that he loves me anymore. He does not listen to me and when he does try to get me to talk, he changes the conversation. I recently got on a diet; I feel great, I work out and I am losing weight—I lost 30 pounds in a month. But he is not happy about it, he is not being supportive; every time I want to go and work out, he gets upset. I don't understand him anymore and I don't think he understands me. He keeps saying I am cruel and heartless. When we are together all we do is fight. I'm tired of all this fighting.

Since everything has gotten worse, we got on AOL and I got online one night and was talking to different people. Well I met this other guy and we talk regularly. He listens to me and understands me; we have a lot in common, and he has given me the friendship I have always longed for in my husband. I have grown very fond of him and I am starting to develop feelings for him, as so has he. He advises me to go to counseling and try to work things out with my husband, then take things from there. At this point in time I don't want to get married again if we don't work out; I think we need time for ourselves and then we can determine if we are meant to be. I feel that everyone in the world has a soul-mate out there; however, I don't think my husband is the one for me. I feel like if I stay with him I will never find the right person for me, and I will keep living an unhappy life. I am grateful for the good things he has done for us, but when there is no love, friendship, understanding and trust in a relationship, there is nothing else.

My friend believes just as I do; yes I understand he may have faults too, but no one in this world is perfect and we all have faults. I honestly am so confused. My husband says he cannot live without our daughter and me; then why does he act this way. We have been to counseling before, and it has gone back to the old ways. I can not keep going this way.

Through all of this there is this saying that sticks in the back of my mind and it goes something like this "If you want something very badly, set it free. If it comes back to you, it's yours forever; if it doesn't, it was never yours to begin with." I believe in that saying; that is why I believe that we need to be apart to see if we are meant to be. Could you please give me some insight on what I should do.

Dear Reader,

This situation accurately fits the typical scenario of online affairs described earlier. This letter illustrates the predictable pattern: "getting online and talking to different people...met this other guy...talk regularly...he listens to me and understands...lots in common...given me the friendship I've longed for...grown very fond of him...starting to develop feelings for him."

I encourage everyone who is, was or *might* be tempted to form an online friendship with someone of the opposite sex to note whether your situation is progressing along the lines of this typical scenario—so you can understand how it is likely to end and perhaps avoid learning the hard way.

Finally, the idea that "...everyone in the world has a soul-mate out there" or that any particular relationship was "meant to be" are just romantic illusions— not rooted in reality. There is no one *right* person above all others, and it's useless to spend time thinking/hoping that's the case. And, in any case, finding a person who may be a good fit for a long-term relationship is almost certainly not going to be found online.

* * * * * * * * * * * * *

Met an Online Flirt

Dear Peggy,

I've been chatting with a gentleman online whom I've met in person recently. He has met my boyfriend and has told me he is married. He gives me lots of compliments about how I look, my eyes, etc., a real sweet talker. He would like to take me out for dinner but I do not want him to get any ideas. He is a nice guy and I have met the rest of his band members. (Yes he is in a famous band and his brother is lead singer)—but I have told him that his sweet-talking will not change the way I feel for my boyfriend.

I would like to go to dinner with him. Would that be wrong? I have told my boyfriend of some of his comments and that I was being very cautious. He has no problem with it since he feels he is a nice guy. This may be minor but I love my boyfriend of 2-1/2 years, and the other guy has been married for 11 years. The other guy does make me feel special....though. I feel a bit guilty for the things he tells me...but it does sound nice.

29

Dear Reader,

This letter represents the "meeting in person" stage of an online relationship—which happens more often than might be expected. Of course, regardless of whether the meeting first takes place online or in person, there's a certain degree of fantasy/infatuation involved in any situation like the one described in this letter. And while it doesn't require that the person be famous, it certainly adds to the difficulty in thinking straight. I still recall how flattered I was at the attention I received when I was 25 and working for an older man who was sophisticated, successful, and well-known. He and I were both married, and I loved my husband very much, but I was captivated by his smooth ways and his constant compliments. It wasn't until years later that I could appreciate how narrowly I avoided making a serious mistake.

When we want to do something, it's always tempting to be a bit naïve or to rationalize about it; but a thoughtful assessment of the idea of going out to dinner with a sweet-talking married man is a question anyone can answer for themselves if they're prepared to be honest about the situation. It's not difficult to figure out that a married man may be interested in a great deal more than dinner. In hindsight, many people who wind up having affairs eventually recognize that they could have/should have known what they were getting into, but they simply blocked it out. A common lament that I've heard repeatedly over the years is, "I didn't intend to have an affair." There's every likelihood that this kind of situation will lead to damage and regrets—and almost no chance that it will work out well.

* * * * * * * * * * * * *

Falling in love online
(Here are 3 letters before my response.)

Dear Peggy, (letter #1 - from a woman)
What if you have fallen in love online and you and he are both happily married? When you and he started talking you were both just playing around, and then you realized that you had a connection and that you and he were best friends and soul-mates?

I love him and he tells me he loves me and he always says it before I can, and I know he means it. He is not the type to just say it, and I am the only woman besides his wife he has ever told that to. And I am not the type to just say "I love you" without meaning it... Am I nuts—or can you really fall in love with someone you have never met?

Dear Peggy, (letter #2 - from a man)
I want to know if I should pursue a relationship I got in online. I am married but I am really starting to fall head over heels for this woman. She is married also but she talks so sweet to me. What should I do??

Dear Peggy, (letter #3 - from a woman)
 I have met this great man online. He lives just ten minutes from me... We have been talking for months. He has recently told me he loves me. He says he no longer loves his wife, last year she decided she'd rather be with a woman instead. However, they still live together, due to their son... I am also married, sometimes happy, sometimes not. My husband drinks a bit too much, and I don't like it, and we fight a lot... When he's sober, things are ok...

 We plan on meeting one day next week, I'm a bit nervous due to the fact that there's a very strong sexual attraction... He says he doesn't care at all if we have sex, because he respects me, unlike my husband... He truly sounds and acts likes he does love me, and I am beginning to get real confused about what to do... What if we meet, and we do end up having sex? Any advice you can give me will be taken into consideration... Thank you.

Dear Reader,
 This is a very common issue—one that is growing all the time. I dare say it may reach epidemic proportions before people "wake up" and recognize that relationships formed on the Internet (that quickly develop into "love") are based on the fantasy of thinking you really *know* someone—and that they are somehow different and special.

 I'm constantly amazed at the degree to which people accept at face value whatever they are told by someone they meet online. For instance, just to focus on a few of the comments in the above letters:
— "He is NOT the type to just say it, and I am the only woman besides his wife he has ever told that to."
— "I am really starting to fall head over heels for this woman...(who) talks so sweet to me."
— "He says he no longer loves his wife...however, they still live together, due to their son."
— "He says he doesn't care at all if we have sex, because he respects me."

 If these statements sound somehow familiar, it's because they are such stereotypical "pick-up lines" as to have virtually no validity. Of course, it's *possible* that some parts of some of these comments are true in some instances, but by and large, it's typical/common to say whatever sounds good or works— regardless of whether or not it's true. And even to whatever degree part of it *might* be true at this fantasy stage, it's a pretty sure bet that none of it would hold up over time in the harsh light of reality.

 It's unreasonable to assume that a person you meet on the Internet is being completely honest and that you therefore know their "true nature." And even if what is shared is *relatively* true, there's no doubt a great deal of information that is withheld that would provide a much more accurate and complete picture of who they are as a person.

To respond directly to one of the above questions, "...can you really fall in love with someone you have never met?"—it's possible to fall in love with the *image* of a person you meet on the Internet, but you can't fall in love with the real person behind the image—because you don't really know the real person. So pursuing a relationship that begins online is to let emotions overrule reason. It's simply not a smart thing to do.

* * * * * * * * * * * * *

Can't get over breakup

Dear Peggy,

A couple of years ago I met a man online. He was 25 and I was 33 at that time. After a few months we met and hit it off. That began an affair that lasted until last month. He's single and I'm married but I never told him I was married. It wasn't hard to meet because we only lived an hour away from each other. Around Christmas 1997 I found myself falling deeply in love with this guy. I didn't tell him how I felt until 2 months later. He didn't have anything to say at the time but did say he needed time to think. After that day he basically stopped talking to me. He would write me Emails on occasion (he always called me 'babe' and always signed his letter "Love Hugs and Kisses"). We used to have set times to chat online or on the phone daily, but suddenly he got 'busy' with other things.

One night 6 weeks ago we had dinner together and he told me he didn't love me and that we should end our relationship. The thing is—I can't let go. I am so much in love with him. The pain I feel now is so deep, I cry every day. I want him back so badly. I found out through a chat room that he has been dating someone else—while we were still dating and sleeping together too. He claimed he never slept with anyone else up to the point of our breakup. I guess my question is this: Is it worthwhile to pursue him? I don't love my husband and haven't for many years. I stay because it's convenient. How do I stop this intense heartbreak? This man was (is) everything I ever dreamed of. I don't want to give up but at the same time I don't want to come across as desperate. Please give me some advice.

Dear Reader,

The most significant aspect of the above description is illustrated by the phrase that "this man was (is) everything I ever dreamed of." This whole situation sounds like a fantasy, not based on real people having a real relationship. The very fact that she did not reveal the fact that she was married illustrates the pretense involved in the relationship. Also, relationships that develop from an online contact are generally more likely to be based on fantasy than reality. Unfortunately, people tend to get carried away and think that it's somehow *special*.

The end of this fantasy can be especially difficult when the other person ends it before you're ready. In *any* relationship, it's hard to let go when the other person basically rejects you and ends it on their own time frame. Often, one person just moves through the fantasy faster than the other—and is ready to move on to the next fantasy. Putting too much stock in (or having too many expectations of) a relationship that begins online is almost guaranteed to lead to the kinds of feelings described above.

While it may be difficult for the woman who wrote this letter to see anything positive about her situation, it's actually much better that the other person clearly stated that he "didn't love her"—instead of stringing her along while she got more and more deeply involved. This can be a learning experience if it is used that way. Instead of spending time and energy trying to analyze the meaning behind every statement or action of the other person in this situation, that energy would be better spent trying to figure out how to avoid this kind of experience in the future.

* * * * * * * * * * * *

Hurt from Online Affairs
(Here are 3 letters before my response.)

Dear Peggy, (letter #1)

My husband is constantly on the computer. He has been talking to some women on AOL and every time I enter the room he would get upset. He acted like he had something to hide. He finally admitted to talking sexual to two of the women. I let him know that it bothered me, but he says he doesn't see anything wrong with it. And he is still doing it with one of the women. He says she approached him about it. I don't think that should matter. He has the power to tell her no that he doesn't want to talk about it. I couldn't get him to stop talking to her and come to bed. It is affecting my sexual relations with him; when we are making love, I keep thinking that he is thinking about her, not me.

Dear Peggy, (letter #2)

I recently found out that my husband of 18 years has been having online affairs. He went so far as to give our phone number and was talking to these people on the phone. Online, they talked not only of sex, but love, etc. I get different opinions. Some say he was definitely having an affair, others say just innocent pastime that was an apparent turn-on, like looking at a girly magazine. Which is it? All I know is how deceived and hurt I feel. He might as well have slept with each of these women. It feels like he did.

Dear Peggy, (letter #3)

I know that my husband of 25 years is having an online affair, and it has caused me so much pain. Our sex life is great, better than ever now that the kids are gone; however is he really making love to me or getting stimulated by her. I have only doubted him on a couple of occasions in all of our married years, but this time when I have entered the room when he is online with this woman, my sixth sense has kicked in and I really don't know how to handle this situation. I really sense that he does not think he is doing anything wrong. Thanks in advance for any input.

Dear Reader,

As these letters describe, online affairs (although not necessarily involving physical contact) can lead to problems in the relationship. These affairs often involve the same kinds of thinking and emotions as other affairs, including the secrecy, fantasy and excitement—as well as the denial and rationalization. Most people who become involved in online affairs do not appreciate the impact this has on their partner. They think as long as there's no actual sex involved, it shouldn't matter; but it often has the potential for being as devastating to the partner as a sexual affair. As I've said many times, most people whose partners have a sexual affair find that they recover from the fact that their partner had sex with someone else before they recover from the fact that they were deceived.

Anything that is deliberately hidden from a partner (whether it's the fact of being involved in an online affair or the specifics of the online interactions) presents a problem. Whenever someone doesn't want to stop something, it's common to rationalize that it's OK or that it's not really an affair. While people may disagree about the definition of an affair, there's no mistaking the impact of online affairs on the partner who is feeling hurt and threatened. In fact, when these hurt feelings are ignored or dismissed as unreasonable, it shows a lack of caring that is far more of a threat to the relationship than the affairs themselves.

* * * * * * * * * * * *

Meeting Online

Dear Peggy,

My marriage of almost 14 years is in a crisis situation....and probably my fault at this point. Any friends or family that I've discussed my problems with react stating it's about time I started thinking about myself. My husband is non-supportive, both emotionally and financially. If we didn't have a 10-year-old daughter to raise, I'd be gone...but I am committed to sticking with this marriage until she's grown.

To get to the point....I have met a man online....we want to meet...but may never because of the geography involved. We talk every day at work on the phone...have very intimate meetings online and truly care about each other. He too is married and has a son who is 8 who he intends never to leave. (His marriage is also in pretty bad shape.) I care deeply for him and he for me, as much as I'm able to tell....(it's hard for me to trust any man).

My question is this: Is it realistic to think we are in love? Can this only lead to hurt? Am I silly to think that we will someday meet? He tells me he doesn't want to hurt me...and is afraid I am too emotionally involved, yet he's very concerned if I am not online...worries I will meet someone else...so I feel he's just as emotionally involved as I am. I sometimes feel I'm really nuts to let myself get so involved... I sure would appreciate your comments. By the way, if it matters...we are both 42, not children!

Dear Reader,

This letter is like so many that I receive in that the writer already understands her situation ("I sometimes feel I'm really nuts to let myself get so involved.") This is a common problem that arises for most of us when what we *know* contradicts what we *wish*.

It might help (both in clarifying the situation and in deciding what to do about it) if we look more carefully at some of the statements. "It's about time I started thinking about myself" is a very positive goal because as women, we frequently put ourselves last. However, "I'm committed to stick with this marriage until [my daughter] is grown" may contradict "thinking about myself." Also, the fact that the other man also never intends to leave his son indicates that there's little chance for happiness (whether or not it's "realistic to think we are in love"). And whether or not a meeting ever takes place, there's likely to be some pleasure and some pain, but probably the pleasure will be short-term and the pain will be long-term—which does *not* address the issue of "doing something for myself."

So while no one can predict the outcome in any specific instance, it may be that the best aspect of this meeting online is simply to serve as a wake-up call to find a way to truly "do something good for myself." Pursuing this relationship is probably *not* the answer to that issue.

* * * * * * * * * * * * *

Love on AOL

Dear Peggy,

I know you probably are asked this a lot, and I really feel rather stupid for even writing it, but I am being torn apart. Can you fall in love with someone on AOL? I never in a million years thought anything like this would happen to me. I have never met this person, but we have communicated both on the phone and on here for quite some time, almost a year. We are both married and have children. I decided last week to end it, and I did. But now I feel like I am lost. I miss him so much and it is tearing me apart. Is what I felt really love? I don't know what I am trying to say. Thank you

Dear Reader,

It's clear that this is a difficult decision that has been made and I understand how a person can "feel like I am lost." It is not "stupid" to feel torn apart; it's normal to get carried away with a relationship that develops like this. Perhaps the loss will be easier to bear by continuing the effort to rationally assess what happened and the feelings about it.

As to the question: "Is what I felt really love?" the answer is "maybe." It's more likely to be infatuation than love. But even if it is some form of love, it's just the initial heady feelings of a "fantasy" new relationship, not the kind of real love that is tested by real-life responsibilities involved in a long-term relationship. Any new connection is going to be exciting, and it may not be the particular person who makes the difference. It has more to do with the

35

excitement generated by this star-crossed lovers kind of relationship than to the specific feelings about him as a real person. Perhaps recognizing that it's the loss of a fantasy relationship can help diminish the intensity of the feelings of loss.

Also, this kind of experience provides an opportunity to rethink all aspects of our lives and determine what we can do to feel more alive that is rooted in reality and does not come with such a high price. It's worth seeking to find some other avenue for igniting the positive alive feelings that are a big part of the sense of loss that is experienced when this kind of fantasy ends.

*   *   *   *   *   *   *   *   *   *   *   *   *

Online Affair

Dear Peggy,

I know this will probably sound much like many other letters, but I really do need some advice. I am 42 years old, my husband is 51. Two and a half years ago, he was diagnosed with prostate cancer that had already spread to his bone. The only treatment available to him is hormonal treatments that will not cure the cancer but hopefully stop it from spreading any further. The doctors say that this therapy is usually effective for 2-5 years before the cancer will spread again, even in the absence of male hormones in his body. A side effect of this type of treatment is loss of all sexual desire and the inability to have an erection. I love my husband very much; however, I am struggling with the reality of no sexuality in my life. We went to see a human sexuality counselor but her main recommendation is that I take care of my own needs as my husband has never had any interest in any type of oral sex. I have done this; however, for me it is not meeting my needs of the feeling of wanting to be desired and physically touched and held by someone.

Now the other problem. I have met a wonderful man online who is also struggling with the same issues. His wife has MS and has been physically unable to make love for about 3 years. Our correspondence started as just mutually supporting each other but has now become very sexual and exciting. He is able to make me feel desirable again and our fantasies give new meaning to "taking care of myself." However, I know that I am beginning to have feelings for him that I shouldn't. I know my husband suspects that I am talking to someone online, but I don't want to stop. I feel sexually alive for the first time in several years and I don't want to have to bury that part of me away again (as that is the only way I can deal with the lack of sexuality in my life). But...I don't want to hurt my husband either. Is their any realistic way I can continue my written relationship with my online friend while reassuring my husband that I am not going to leave him? There is very little chance of me and my friend getting together; we live on opposite sides of the country. I know in my head that I am opening myself up to be hurt, but the thought of losing my friend and our sexual connection (when there is no other outlet for that in my current life) hurts even more. Help!!!!!

36

Dear Reader,

This letter describes one of the few types of situations where people are tempted by an affair who would otherwise not consider an affair of any kind. It also highlights what many people have come to realize: the primary power of an affair is in the way it makes you feel about yourself (for instance, as mentioned above, feeling desirable again). Having said that, there is still the issue of how to handle conflicting needs: the need to "take care of myself" and the need to not "hurt my husband." Clearly the appropriate question is stated: "Is there any 'realistic' way I can continue my written relationship with my online friend while reassuring my husband that I am not going to leave him?" There is no responsible answer to this question in that no one (not even the person involved) can *realistically* predict the form and direction a relationship will take.

Unfortunately, most people who become more and more involved with someone else never expect it to go as far as it often goes. (For instance, this online relationship has already developed beyond its initial parameters. So there's certainly no way to reassure anyone that it won't continue to expand.) As for "not hurting my husband," any kind of relationship that is kept secret and hidden (and therefore involves deception) creates some hurt. So it's probably not a matter of *whether* he'll be hurt, but what *kind* of hurt it will be. This does not imply that choices should be made on the basis of guilt, just that decisions should be based on clear thinking (as this writer is trying to do) rather than on rationalizations. In fact, as often happens, this writer has already answered her own question in saying, "I know in my head that I am opening myself up to be hurt." All I can do is verify that she is probably correct.

* * * * * * * * * * * *

Online Romance

Dear Peggy,

I have been having an online romance for about 6 months and we're both married. He says he hasn't been in love with his wife for over 3 years, but I've been married over 18 years and I know I still love my husband and couldn't leave him. I know I should end this, but I don't want to lose the friendship we have developed online and I know he would be crushed if I stopped it. Is it possible to have just a friendship after saying we're in love? I do love him but the guilt and the pain of letting this go on are driving me crazy. What can I do?

Dear Reader,

It's always difficult to give up something that feels positive and satisfying. But, as with most things in life, there are tradeoffs. The woman who wrote this letter is already clear that she loves her husband and couldn't leave him, but continuing the other relationship always runs the risk that this could eventually happen. So while it may feel crushing to give up the online relationship, this needs to be compared to the crushed feeling that would result in giving up the marriage.

In light of the above considerations, whether it's possible "to have just a friendship after saying we're in love," may be an irrelevant question. Anything that is really *just a friendship* wouldn't need to be kept hidden from a spouse. Anything that tries to bridge between both love and friendship would probably be seen as a threat. And anything that must be hidden from a partner is a barrier to closeness, creating a vulnerability for all kinds of problems to develop. So the issue is probably much bigger than whether or not it's possible to have a friendship after saying you're in love.

Most marriages are in a constant state of change (either getting better or getting worse); they seldom remain the same. The condition of the marriage and the degree of commitment to the marriage are reflected more by actions than by words. So any decisions that are made about outside relationships have a direct impact on the improvement or detriment of the marriage. As with most things in life, you can have most *anything* you want, but you can't have *everything*. This may be the time to choose—and act on your choice—while you still can.

* * * * * * * * * * * * *

Beyond the average AOL affair

Dear Peggy, (This long letter illustrates the typical "course of events" of an affair.)

My wife of fifteen years fell in love with someone she met online. Perhaps calling it falling in love is an understatement. It's more like she found her soul-mate. Within a space of three weeks chatting with him on line, she met with him—thanks to destiny. She lives 2500 miles from him and it just so happened that he came for a convention to the city where I live. (He rarely goes on business trips.) Coincidentally, during the same exact time, I was out of town to be with my mother who was undergoing cancer therapy. (I rarely go out of town.) By that point, they have talked about anything and everything over AOL and over the phone, so this was no fantasy situation. In fact, the phone conversations made them closer. As far as I can gather, they were incredibly compatible in every possible area that one can think of—from politics to sex. Seeing one another did not dampen their emotions. And two days of fantastic sex followed. Two weeks later, she flew to see him with the excuse that she's visiting her father (which she, of course, did—but made a stop to see him, too.)

At that point, he started talking to her about getting together permanently. The complication on his end is that he's married with two teenage kids. Or should I say unhappily married? His wife, to put it lightly, is very thrifty. She also has no interest in sex. Hence his longing for another woman. He kept talking to my wife and talking to her about getting together. They even started figuring out the logistics of making a life for themselves. But the man rushed my wife and declared that he's going to tell his wife that he's leaving her, before my wife was fully ready to tell me the same. But 24 hours later, he changed his mind, revealing that his wife became suspicious of a possible affair and changed her attitude towards him. She started treating him as if they were on

38

their honeymoon. In the process, this man sent a terse good-bye to my wife, which devastated her. Shortly thereafter I found out what happened. Between my questions, my intuition, and my detective skills, I found out perhaps more than I should have known.

Since this breakup, things are problematic on all fronts. The man regrets the terse Email and has asked my wife to give him time. He still loves her—but also loves his own wife, especially now that she's loving to him. (Of course, the wife knows nothing about his affair.) My wife continues to have strong feelings for him, too. She just can't get him out of her mind. To complicates things further, she still loves me a great deal. She explained the situation that she loves both of us, but is terrified that she'll end up alone in the end. She's very confused and anxious to say the least.

As far as how I feel? I don't know. I've already been through shock, anger, anguish, and tears for the past three weeks. Now I'm trying to be as rational as I can. One part of me says that this is way too complicated for me. That I should just end it and move on. Another part of me says that I love my wife. We've been so close for years and have gone through so much. When she says that she loves me, I honestly believe that she's sincere. She wants to make things work (but still longs for him). Still another part of me wonders whether, in the long run, I'll be able to truly forgive her for the infidelity. And yet another part of me doesn't want to be alone and doesn't think that I'll be able to find a woman as good as my wife. She has been as perfect as she could be all these years.
So the questions that I have are:
— Should I wait for my wife to decide what she wants to do? In many respects it seems that she's waiting for the man to leave his wife so she can be with him and try things out. Otherwise, I suspect she fears she'll go through life wondering that she missed out on some great love. (Think "Bridges of Madison County.") Interestingly enough, I just learned that the Man saw this movie and was horrified by the thought that he might end up living an unfulfilled life like Meryl Streep.
— Should I just let her go? (Yet I don't know if I'll be able to take her back if things don't work out.) Should I just be patient, hoping that the guy never gets the guts to leave his wife, causing my wife to get over him with time?
— Is there anything that I should say or do to convince my wife to commit herself to me? (I feel their romance is idealized in many respects, causing me to have no real chance of competing.) My wife says it's real, magnetic love. She just can't get over it. Of course, I never read any of the Emails they exchanged. But by all accounts, they seem to be passionately intense. And it's not like this man is better than me. He's just different. I suggested that she let things rest, but she can't stop herself from sending him Emails, even though she knows how much it's hurting me.

I know that this is a lengthy and complex letter. But if you could shed any insight that might help my situation, I would greatly appreciate it.

Dear Reader,

I thought it was important to print this entire letter because it is such a good description of a typical story—not at all the *special* situation that the parties believe it to be. The only really special aspect of this is the reasonableness and thoughtfulness of the man who wrote the letter.

First, let's take a closer look at this quote from the above letter: "My wife of fifteen years fell in love with someone she met online. Perhaps calling it falling in love is an understatement. It's more like she found her soul-mate." It's common when people have an affair to think they've "found their soul-mate"— whether on the Internet or through some other avenue. However, there is nothing about the story described above that causes it to stand out as anything beyond the standard *formula* situation that I've seen repeatedly during the past 20 years that I've been hearing people's stories.

This letter-writer is accurate in understanding the idealized nature of the spouse's relationship with the third party. When people are in affairs, they present a side of themselves that's not representative of the whole person. It's a special version of their best aspects, free from the normal responsibilities involved in sharing a total life situation. The very nature of playing the role of *third party* instead of *spouse* means it's a fantasy relationship.

For instance, any number of people could have been the third party. As the man who wrote this letter accurately recognizes, they're not special or superior to the spouse, there're simply different. The specialness of the third party has far more to do with the role they're playing than with the particular person playing it. Since the roles and structure of family life create many restrictions and responsibilities, a person's affair is not so much a rejection of the mate as a rejection of these role restrictions.

As for the "Bridges of Madison County," you can be sure that had the housewife been married to the world-roving reporter all those years, she would have jumped at the chance to fulfill what was missing in her life (which would have been the quiet, caring, constant attention of a simple man who stayed at home like the husband in this movie). We tend to fantasize about what it would be like to have *whatever* we don't have.

In fact, only about 10 percent of the people who leave a spouse actually wind up marrying the third party. And if they do marry the third party, they frequently learn much later (after the third party takes on the role of spouse) that their specialness had more to do with their earlier role than with the person themselves. Many people have an illusion that this new person offers a new life, only to discover after a few years that all the old feelings and issues are there just as in the past. They didn't really change games at all, they only changed the players. Today's third party may be tomorrow's spouse who is unhappy in their marriage.

It would be helpful for the spouse to use this perspective in order to overcome being controlled by her emotions (to the point where she "can't stop herself") and to make a more rational assessment of the situation and of her power to change based on thinking more clearly about the long-term, not just being caught up in the moment.

* * * * * * * * * * * *

Online love

Dear Peggy,

I am in quite a situation. I am married, have been for 4 years now. Just recently I met a wonderful man online. He makes me feel so alive, so sexy. We have mutual feeling for each other and we have grown to the point of making love to each other over the phone. He has expressed to me that he has fallen in love with me. I don't want to hurt him or my husband (my husband is a wonderful man), but I don't want to give up this feeling of sexiness and aliveness I feel with my online lover. I am 24 years old and he makes me feel like a teenager again. I want to meet him, but at the same time, I have 2 children and a wonderful husband at home. Your advice, please!

Dear Reader,

The sentiments expressed in this letter are extremely common—and very unrealistic. Of course, any new connection is going to be exciting, but it's not the person who makes it exciting. The excitement has more to do with the nature of the online relationship and the different sense of ourselves to be gained through interactions in this fantasy environment. Online, people present a very limited part of themselves—and get reactions based on this distorted presentation. The intensity of the feelings of sexiness and aliveness expressed above have little to do with real feelings of love; they're just a reaction to the excitement generated by the newness and novelty of this kind of situation. Risking the loss of a real "wonderful husband at home" is a high price to pay for pursuing the fantasy of an online relationship.

* * * * * * * * * * * *

So Confused

Dear Peggy,

After being friends and chatting with a man I met online, we started having an affair about two months ago. He makes me feel wonderful most of the time, and then, wham, feel like I have been broad-sided by a Mack truck.....just the way he behaves towards me. I am reasonably certain he has other friends online, and I don't think I can handle that much more.

We are both married and in my case don't feel any obligation to my husband, as he has not wanted to have sex in a very long time.... Could this be why I am so vulnerable to this person—and although it may hurt, would I be wiser to end the whole thing now?

Dear Reader,

There isn't really much question as to whether it "would be wiser to end" this relationship—since this is a pretty clear description of a dead-end relationship where she is just being used. So the problem is not in understanding the situation; it's in acting on the understanding. I suspect that writing this letter is the first step toward taking action. (Often, when we try to write out a description of a situation in order to explain it to others, we get more clarity ourselves.) It seems that she has already answered her own question as to whether it would be wiser to end the whole thing now. All I can do is reinforce her own knowledge of what to do.

Having said that, however, that is not to say that it's particularly wise to stay in a dead-end marital relationship with a husband who doesn't want to have sex. So perhaps recognizing that the vulnerability may have contributed to pursuing the online experience can provide the motivation needed to pursue some other (more positive alternatives) to the current situation. The larger issue to be addressed is how to find a better life situation that doesn't involve creating additional problems.

* * * * * * * * * * * *

Realism in Relationships

Dear Peggy, (This is a condensed version of a much longer letter.)

My second marriage of nearly ten years has been blissful in the extreme. He is loving, compassionate, emotionally stable and secure in his personal goals. His personal interests are very different from mine and we enjoy sharing those differences in many ways. Recently, I have developed a relationship on AOL with a man who shares my intellectual and philosophical interests. He is also "happily" married with two children.

My husband and I have discussed my Internet activities and have determined that this way of "acting out" is much preferable to that of an actual affair, especially in this day and age. He and I are both confident that our relationship remains secure as long as we keep our lines of communications wide open and discuss with each other any emotional insecurities or concerns often and frequently. I cannot say that I am perfectly happy with the circumstance, but I have a need for intellectual repartee and philosophical debate that my current spouse does not share.

I don't presume to know what manner of communication that my online partner maintains with his spouse. I know that we have discussed many sexual matters and even fantasize about getting together. If I felt that either legal relationship were threatened, I believe I would be strong enough to break the new one off completely. Not without emotional repercussions of course; however, we must make choices that take into account all individuals feelings whether directly or indirectly involved. I would be interested in your opinion on this situation.

Dear Reader,

As a strong believer in the importance of honesty and its power to forge a special connection within a marriage, I'm impressed with the commitment to honesty expressed in this letter: "we keep our lines of communications wide open..." However, there's always a risk in relating to others outside the primary relationship if the others do *not* practice the same kind of honesty with their spouse. So a genuine interest in "taking into account all individuals whether directly or indirectly involved" does *not* fit with saying, "I don't presume to know what manner of communication that my online partner maintains with his spouse." Everyone's feelings are not being taken into account unless there's clear evidence of honesty among *all* parties involved, whether directly or indirectly involved.

This letter appears to contain another contradiction regarding the nature of the outside relationship: on one hand saying it fills the "need for intellectual repartee and philosophical debate" and on the other hand, "we have discussed many sexual matters and even fantasize about getting together." There seem to be a number of general inconsistencies in the situation described in the above letter. And I suspect the writer's own recognition of this may have led to the inquiry in the first place. But it's an issue for all of us in that every responsible person wants to find a way to meet their needs without hurting others. Sometimes this is possible and sometimes it's not. Each of us must make that judgment for ourselves—and live with the consequences of our decision.

* * * * * * * * * * * *

Online friendship with opposite sex

Dear Peggy,

I'm curious to know what you feel about spouses who have a supposed friendship online with the opposite sex. I found Email my spouse sent to someone, but the words written were more than words that would be said to a friend. They've been talking online for almost 2 months. Just curious to find out how other people feel about this.

Dear Reader,

All too often, an online "friendship" is the first step in an interaction that almost inevitably leads to *more*. There is a fairly predictable pattern to online relationships. Most people kid themselves that it won't get out of hand and that it's harmless. After it does get out of hand and develops beyond what was originally intended, it's often too late.

A person in this position is often hesitant to make a big deal out of a spouses' seemingly innocent activities. But understanding the progressive nature of online relationships provides an opportunity to avoid greater difficulties later. Fortunately, this reader is already alert to the potential problems. By raising the question now (hopefully before things have gone "too far"), perhaps the typical pattern can be avoided.

The safest way to see that online interactions don't damage the primary relationship is to make sure that no online interactions are secret. This means not saying anything to someone online that you aren't willing for your spouse to read. Whenever someone invokes privacy rights, it's probably because they have something to hide—even if they honestly don't think they have anything to hide.

By keeping any interactions secret, it increases the chances that they will eventually reach the point where hiding become essential.

The person involved in online interactions may have no intention of letting it become inappropriate—and may deny (even to themselves) that it is becoming inappropriate, even as it is getting out of hand. So it's reasonable not only to be curious, but to be concerned—and to openly discuss those concerns in an effort to avoid potential future problems.

* * * * * * * * * * *

My Online Affair
(Here are 2 letters before my response.)

Dear Peggy, (letter #1)
    This concerns another online friendship...turning into love... We have known each other for over a year. Although I know that online love can be highly suspect, I feel this one IS different. We started out simply as friends when we met online...my first week on! We started out as chat room buddies, then began corresponding fairly regularly; and as time went by, the conversations grew more personal and confiding. Sex has not been an issue and only lately has it even been hinted at; it is 2 people who have found comfort through friendship, each encouraging the other to commit to their own marriage (which his has been in trouble for 2 years—discussed only as friends at first).

    But something has happened recently; I know it is only due to my exhaustion in dealing with the faults in my own marriage concerning communication, which my husband seems unable to address, even in a most basic form. He says I ramble, but I tell him that is because I never get a response...searching for "anything" he will talk about...My AOL friend, however, is open for any topic, and I find myself totally captivated by his every word. It has recently had the added benefit of phone conversations...very lengthy and even more revealing... I know we are not living our lives together—therefore not something I can totally judge in its trueness, but we do share so much of "us."

    I guess I am looking for answers I must discover on my own....my marriage is what most would consider ok, but I want more! Am I wrong to expect a closeness that I can get from a friend I met online...and have kept for over a year...to match up to the closeness I want in my marriage? PS: not what I would look for physically, but now attracted to...which makes my feelings seem even more real!

Dear Peggy, (letter #2)
    I really need some good wholesome advice here. I have been married for 4-1/2 years and have two children. Right from the get-go our marriage started off on the wrong foot. The day after we were married I found out that he had an affair a few months back with an old girlfriend. I find it hard to forgive him. And I have been unhappy in the marriage for some time.

Online Affairs

I have met a wonderful man on the Internet and he is everything that I want in a man. He even perceives a good marriage the way I do. I want not only a lover but my best friend in a marriage. He says that he loves me and wants to be with me in spite of all the baggage that I carry. I wasn't completely honest with him at first, and now that he know the truth he still wants to be with me.

I am not sure what to do, he wants to meet with me so that we can pursue a relationship. I feel obligated to give him that much, but I also feel obligated to my husband and children. I do not know what to do! Please help me.

Dear Reader,

These readers illustrate what is almost universally true: that each person thinks their particular new relationship is different and special from others. Having heard thousands of stories in the past 20 years, I detect nothing different or special in the above descriptions. They fit a pattern that is all too common.

Mostly, it comes out of comparing a reality (marriage) to a fantasy (a relationship with a new person). They fail to see that it's the nature of the roles, not the people, that creates the difference—with the marriage invariably coming out lacking by comparison.

For instance, one of the common complaints is that the spouse doesn't talk but the new person does. However, if you talk to the current spouse of the new person, you usually find that the wonderful talker isn't such a wonderful talker within their own marriage. Usually, the spouse of the new person has the same complaints about the communication within their marriage that the letter-writer has about the communication within her own marriage.

Another common problem is the habit of comparing the feelings toward the new person during the first couple of years of the relationship with the feelings for a spouse after more time. Not only is the newness a big part of the attraction, but the new situation does not involve the daily nitty-gritty responsibilities of making a life together. If the roles were reversed (so that the new person is the one who has been the spouse for some time and the current spouse is the one who was met online), it's very likely that the feelings would be reversed. That's because the feelings tend to follow the circumstances of the relationship, regardless of the particular person playing each role.

It's important to understand that if a new relationship eventually becomes the full-time relationship/marriage, it usually develops the same kinds of problems that were inherent in the original marriage. The bottom line is that the initial feelings developed with a new person online simply can't be compared to the feelings that develop when sharing your daily lives on an ongoing basis over a period of years in the real world, dealing with all the normal daily issues of life. Unfortunately, many people continue to think they've found their "one true love/soul-mate"—and don't discover until too late that it was an illusion.

* * * * * * * * * * * * *

Online Relationships
(Here are 2 letters before my response.)

Dear Peggy, (letter #1)
My husband and I have been married for 4 years, I love him with all my heart and I know he feels the same way about me. Recently we have purchased a computer and he joined the chat line. I've read some of the things that he has written. When he described himself to the other chatters, he said he was looking for nice girls to talk to, which upset me because it made me feel like he was offering himself to them. Also, when I was reading one of his saved chat messages, he said that if there was a naked woman laying in front of him, he would go for it because his #%!* (male organ) did the thinking for him. When I confronted him about it, he said that it was just a joke, and he got mad at me for accusing him of doing something wrong. I'm confused and don't know what to think. He has never done anything to make me distrust him, and I don't want to distrust him because of something I read. What should I do?

Dear Peggy, (letter #2)
My husband is having online affairs... I feel betrayed, but he insists they aren't like cheating...We turn on the computer and his girlfriends Instant Message within 5 minutes... I'm very confused by the attention they give a man they don't really know. Do you feel they are the same as cheating?

Dear Reader,
Even though these letters are from the "uninvolved" partners, it might be helpful to hear from a woman who *did* become involved in an online relationship as to what she learned. Here's an excerpt from what she wrote me about her experience:

"I want to share my experience with an online relationship…so maybe others can learn from it. The emotions that I felt were as real as any that I have ever experienced. I even considered meeting this man...perhaps for a physical relationship. Fortunately, he became angry over my questioning his real life morals and the relationship ended per his request. Please caution people that these feelings and emotions are very real....and can lead us to do things we would not normally do. I did not realize that I had such strong involvement until it ended...and I literally wept for several days. Caution Online!!!!"

(end of letter from someone who has "been there")

* * * * * * * * * * * * *

Attempting to end it
Dear Peggy,
I am currently involved in an online affair. I am attempting to end it. My wife is not aware of the seriousness of the situation. My "lover" and I have not engaged in intercourse, but we have discussed the possibility. Now that I have

46

made the decision to end the affair, I feel horrible. I need help "rationalizing" this.

Dear Reader,

As I understand it, the "decision has been made to end the affair," but he's still "attempting" to end it. This gap between intention and action may account for a great deal of the "feeling horrible." It's a limbo place that's bound to feel uncomfortable. So taking the actual step to make a clean and complete break may greatly alleviate the horrible feelings. While dragging it out or "letting the other person down gradually" may *seem* like a thoughtful way to proceed, it just makes it more difficult for everyone. This is somewhat similar to the differences in how you might remove a Band-Aid. For instance, jerking the Band-Aid off quickly hurts for a moment, but peeling it back gently (trying to keep it from hurting) just makes the hurt last longer.

As for "not yet engaging in intercourse," this is another reason to finalize the break as soon as possible. The pattern of online affairs is for them to eventually escalate to intercourse or to an intensified desire for intercourse. So this reader would likely feel much more "horrible" if he had already escalated the relationship to that level.

As for needing help "rationalizing" this, I assume he means thinking "rationally" about it. (Rationalizing is the kind of unclear thinking we engage in when we are trying to justify something that would not otherwise be rational.) One way to think more clearly about the entire situation is to focus on how much worse it could be (or likely *will* be) if he delays acting on his intention to end this relationship. Waiting will not make it any easier, but will probably make it even more difficult.

* * * * * * * * * * * * *

He won't stop online affair

Dear Peggy:

My husband and I have been married for 15 years. He met a woman online and has been having an online relationship for several months. They met and had a physical relationship a month ago. I told my husband that in order for us to have a chance to repair our marriage that he would have to give up contact with this woman online. He still speaks to her several times a week and insists that they are just friends. Can this be true?

Dear Reader,

Of course, neither I nor anyone else can predict in any *specific* instance—but *in general*, backing away from a physical relationship to continue only as friends is unrealistic at best and dishonest at worst. It's not unusual for people to want to remain friends with those with whom they have been intimate, but in most instances there's a direct relationship between the degree of ongoing contact with the third party (whether or not it's physical) and the quality of the primary relationship. As long as the third party is still in the picture in any way, the primary relationship usually suffers.

Wanting to "have it all" is a time-honored goal in our country, but rarely does it work when it comes to relationships. In the best of all possible worlds, many people would like to have their freedom while also being in a committed relationship. (What this usually means is: "I want to be free, but I want you to be committed.") Any time there's real fairness and equality in a relationship— where each person has the same degree of freedom (and acts on it)—you're likely to find a relationship that is sexually exclusive.

While the above letter is supposedly not about *sex*, that's almost a technicality at this point—since sex has already been a part of the equation. Most couples can't pretend the sex never happened and treat the other person just as a friend. It's tough enough for couples to cope with opposite sex friendships their partners may develop, but dealing with a friendship that at any point has been a sexual relationship is highly unlikely. So since there was an earlier sexual relationship, it probably doesn't matter whether or not it's true that they're only friends at this point.

* * * * * * * * * * * *

Safe Cyber Affairs?
(Here are 2 letters —from both sides of this issue.)

Dear Peggy, (letter #1)

I have made several friends on the Internet and find that I am not the only one who has developed an online relationship with a man. I find this man to be very exciting and (having been married for 32 years and never strayed) I find myself now having an ongoing cyber relationship with the lovely man that I met online.

My question is how safe is this? I don't have any wish to meet my online (......), what do I call him? He is more than a friend He is also married, and loves and has been faithful to his wife (as I have been with my husband). I guess the thing that bothers me most is that I have no feelings of guilt about the relationship. Should I???

Dear Peggy, (letter #2)

My husband is having a self-confessed mid-life crisis. He is questioning whether or not he wants to stay in this relationship. I am trying to hang on and be supportive, but I am confused regarding the following.

My husband is not literally having an affair, but he does have an online relationship with a woman. I am confused because he has stated that he loves me and he makes plans regarding romantic things we can do together, but I know that he chats online and talks on the phone with this woman. I have looked at her "profile" as well as my husband's, and they both contain cute references to the other, e.g., computer: my link to my 'baby', name: timmy's angel, etc.

48

Is this a harmless flirtation? It sure doesn't feel like it to me. I have discussed this, a little bit, with my husband and he says that this has nothing to do with our problems; our relationship is apart from his friendship with this woman. Should I just hang on or should I issue an ultimatum? I wouldn't tell him to decide between me and one of his friends, but this feels like something else to me. What should I do? Confused and Lonely.

Dear Reader,

On the surface, cyber relationships *seem* to be harmless. Underneath, however, no matter which role a person is playing (whether the one involved or the one whose spouse is involved), there's a nagging sense that there's something *more* to it, something threatening.

The overwhelming evidence favors the idea that these cyber relationships are potentially extremely dangerous in the threat they may eventually pose for the marriage. Most relationships of this kind either escalate with one person or switch to a new person, creating an ongoing strain in the marriage either way. Regardless of what is *believed* (or even *intended*) about the nature of these relationships, they have a way of taking on a life of their own that defies good judgment and common sense.

Both writers have some sense that there may be something more they should be concerned about. For instance, the first writer talks about her lack of guilt. Somehow she knows that guilt would be a normal feeling if it weren't being rationalized away by good intentions and pure ideas about a friendship with a "lovely man." The guilt could easily be a result of a deeper knowing that it's not as innocuous as she wants it to be, especially if it's being kept secret from her husband. Knowing you are being deceptive is, in and of itself, a legitimate basis for feelings of guilt.

While there *appears* to be less actual deception in the circumstances described by the second writer, there's still the same rationalization where the husband dismisses the relationship as just friendship or harmless flirtation. The claims of "loving someone" don't seem sincere when there's simultaneously a willingness to hurt that person by engaging in a cyber relationship.

While I can't advise precisely how to handle these situations, I can confirm that the feelings of concern or confusion are warranted. Seemingly innocent cyber relationships are damaging (or outright killing) many, many marriages.

* * * * * * * * * * * *

Can online affair work out?

Dear Peggy,

My estranged husband has been carrying on an online affair since mid-February and has gone this weekend to meet her. He claims he has already decided he'll be moving in with her this August, that he still loves me and is attracted to me but is not 'in love' with me. I realize that affairs are carried on because of something lacking in the primary relationship, but was wondering how realistic it is for him to base his life plans on this online affair, which would require uprooting his whole life and starting over in another state.

Since online affairs are based so much on fantasy, I'm wondering if the reality could work out well for him or is unlikely to. I know that either of us will be going into any new relationship with the same problems we originally had, that we'll likely just have to cope with them in a new setting with a different person, if that even stands a decent chance of working out. Is it possible that such a superficial relationship could work out well for him in a short period of time, or is that just something he's hoping for and will likely end up disappointed or hurt by?

Dear Reader,

While the primary question raised in this letter is about the possibilities for the future of the online relationship, the phrase that jumped out at me was, "I realize that affairs are carried on because of something lacking in the primary relationship." Unfortunately, this is a common belief—but it's a very simplistic answer to a very complex question. There's "something lacking" in *every* relationship, but that doesn't begin to be a full explanation for why an affair happens.

As to whether it's possible for the relationship to work out, that's highly unlikely. There is a very common scenario as to how online affairs develop. Relationships that develop online have not proven to be long-lasting—and *most* people wind up being either disappointed or hurt in the long run. Obviously, there's always a *chance* it will work, but a smart person wouldn't bet on it.

* * * * * * * * * * * *

Met a man online

Dear Peggy,

I met a man online last year and it was a whirlwind affair. I was lonely and he said he was too. We met and my whole life changed for the better. He moved in with me after he retired and we set up house. He told me he was still married and I told him to either do something about it or leave me alone. He started the divorce and asked me to marry him when he was free. We bought a wedding ring set and life was wonderful. He lived with me for 7 months and we dated for 6 months before he moved in. Then one day I came home from work to find him gone. He left me a note saying he loved me and would return after he got some things straightened out with his kids. They were mad because he was divorcing their mom.

I went through the Email under his name on my computer and found a love letter to a lady in New York saying that he loved her and would see her in 4 days. Three days before he left me he got on his knees in front of me and professed such love for me. I have since found out that he was sleeping around town while he was living with me, and I have talked to his wife and kids...seems that everything he ever said to me was a lie. He had been flying all over the country sleeping with ladies and then coming here to me. His poor wife is in shock because she got a note after 36 years of marriage. All of my friends were shocked too. None of us could believe that he was so very good at lying to us all. Everyone he met he told how happy he was and how much he loved me.

I found out that he had met this other lady before he met me and never fell out of love with her. I had called the other lady and talked to her and told her some of the truths I had found out, and I also talked to him as well. The big problem I am having is that I cannot trust my judgment or people at all. I do know that none of this is my fault; I was fooled by a pro. How can I regain my self-worth and begin to trust again? I think that this hurts more than the betrayal of all this.

Dear Reader,

As for questioning your judgment (after such an experience as is described above)—it's not that people don't, in fact, *have* better judgment; it's that they often suspend their good judgment when caught up in the emotional feelings from connecting with someone like this through the Internet.

For instance, it's highly likely that a *rational* assessment of another person would pick up clues as to their true nature. But an assessment based on *emotionally* wanting to believe in another person simply clouds our ability to know what we *could* know if we were thinking more clearly.

However, in some cases (which the above description certainly fits—and as is noted in the letter), almost *anyone* can be fooled by a real "pro." This does *not* mean a person has poor judgment. And the good news is that going through this kind of experience will almost certainly cause an *improvement* in a person's judgment in the future.

* * * * * * * * * * * * *

Lying about online affairs

Dear Peggy,

I am a married woman, living apart from my hubby. One of the reasons we are not living together is the problems we had with our respective children, but the real problem for me is his online affairs. I've caught him in so many lies... I've sent Instant Messages and Emails to his girlfriends, and he gets really angry. He says I'll ruin his relationships with his friends. He says that it's harmless flirting and he's just having fun; but since AOL came into our lives, our marriage has gone straight down into the sewer. One of his girlfriends told me that he told her that he doesn't love me and he loves her and they are intimate... I know he cybers with her and with others, and I know he gets phone numbers and calls these women. The other day he said something about phone sex being better than cyber. When I asked him how he knew, he said, oh I can imagine... He doesn't fool me. Like I said, I've caught him in so many lies that I can tell immediately when he's lying...

My problem is that I still love him!! I know I can't compete with all these women online, and I realize that he must have been really unhappy in our marriage, because happily married men don't pursue other women, either online or off. But I keep trying. Believe me, I've tried everything! Am I insane to keep hanging in there??

Dear Reader,

This letter covers a *lot* of territory. I'll just comment on *some* of the statements:

— "living apart...problems...with our respective children...but the real problem for me is his online affairs."

These, of course, are not *separate* problems, but part of an underlying problem of a general inability to negotiate areas of conflict.

— "harmless flirting...one of his girlfriends."

This sounds like an oxymoron (contradictory words); if it's "harmless," she's not a "girlfriend;" and if she's a "girlfriend," it's not likely to be "harmless."

— "I can tell immediately when he's lying."

Being able to determine when someone is lying is useless unless it is used to *do* something about it.

— "happily married men don't pursue other women."

This is a widely-held but totally false belief. Of course, it may be more *likely* for an unhappily married man to be drawn to an affair, but being "happily married" is no guarantee against affairs.

— "I've tried everything!"

This sounds like a parent often sounds who feels hopeless in dealing with an irresponsible child. But usually the only things that have been tried are those without much risk of consequences—to either party. Since everything in life involves tradeoffs, both people in a marriage need to decide just which tradeoffs they're willing to make. Once they make their choices, then (for better or worse) they're stuck with the consequences.

* * * * * * * * * * * * *

Meeting in Person
(Here are 2 letters before my response.)

Dear Peggy, (letter #1)

After 3 (!) failed marriages, I'm trying very hard to start over. My problem is my insecurity about men. I simply don't trust them. My last two marriages failed because of my husband's infidelities—the last one moved out on Christmas Day two years ago with absolutely no warning. I believe in marriage and fidelity. When I love someone, it's with my entire being and with no thoughts of running around or cheating. That's why it came as such a surprise when the last one left. I never saw it coming; I thought he felt the same way.

Recently, I met a man online and we "clicked" immediately. As a matter of fact, we're planning to meet in person later this month. I want to get to know him better, and I didn't hold back or hide my past because I believe in honesty— and frankly, some people are turned off by a "multiple marriage" partner. He seemed ok with it. Never said much about it other than he felt bad that I'd been so mistreated.

So here's my problem: I have a very hard time trusting him. If he's offline for a few days, I imagine all sorts of things going on in his life and start telling myself that he's probably involved with someone and doesn't care about me at all. I know it's just my insecurities talking, but how does one become secure? How do I learn to trust a man again? It's ruining my life and I know it'll ruin this relationship if I let it. Can you give me some suggestions? I'm ready to try anything!

Dear Peggy, (letter #2)
I first got my computer in March and I went into a room and this guy gets on. We talked, and the more talking we did the more things we had in common: he travels for a living and is married, I'm married also with two children (he has none). We talked offline for the next two months; he called me from everywhere and at least 5 times a day. I went to meet him for the first time for about a half-hour, and I made a fool of myself. The next night we talked online and things didn't feel the same, but I knew we were perfect together. After that night, he blocked me from everything and the phone calls stopped.

A month and a half went by; I always thought of him. I was online, and he came on and said he was sorry for blocking me and not calling. I said it was ok and that was all. The next week he was in town, called me, and I jumped; we had a beautiful night together. He asked if I was ready for what we were about to do, and I said yes, I felt liked I belonged with him. And the things he said and the way he held me all night, I thought he was for real. I never heard from him again; he shut his AOL service down and that was all. I'm very upset and confused; I feel used and cheated. I don't know how to make myself feel better? I want to know if what we had was real and I'm not just another in a different state?

Dear Reader,
These 2 letters could well be a "before and after" of the same general situation. That's not to say that *every* online affair ends as the one in letter #2, but it's wise to be wary about trusting someone you meet online. There's no basis for trusting someone you really don't know.

Both letters indicate a desire for something real or solid or trusting, but unfortunately, the Internet is not the best place to find that. This is not to say that it's not *possible*, only that it's not *likely*. It's better to admit the reality of the uncertainty of these kinds of connections instead of hoping that somehow a particular experience will be different. I've heard many, many stories, and 99 percent of them lead to disappointment.

If a person (as stated in the first letter) is "ready to try anything," then this may be something they try; but the second letter is an all-too-common reflection of what can (and probably will) happen. In the final analysis, everyone must arrive at their own conclusion, both about what to do (as in letter #1) and about how to analyze it afterwards (as in letter #2). But it's good to learn as much as possible about a situation before arriving at a personal conclusion, whatever it may be.

* * * * * * * * * * * *

"He" was a She

Dear Peggy,

I met a man online over a year ago, and right away we felt comfortable with each other. I had never met a man so understanding and compassionate and I told him things I had never told anyone. He helped me through some very terrible times in my life—with a difficult marriage and other things that bothered me and made me very confused and unhappy. We shared so much and I was convinced I had met my soul-mate.

In other words, this person became my life. When he learned of the abusive nature of my marriage, he offered that should I ever decide to leave, he would provide a safe place for me and my children and time enough to think and decide where to go from there.

I admit, I fell in love, and he said he loved me, too.

A short time ago, he told me the truth. He was a woman. I was devastated and hurt dreadfully. I felt betrayed and foolish and humiliated and very distraught. This person still stood by me and tried to help me through this, but I finally reached the breaking point. My online friends told me to dump this person, and I did.

But...so much of the love remains. I have never felt attracted to another woman. Nor, this woman told me, had she ever had intimate relations with another female. (The reasons for her deception are not important here and so I will not go into that).

I am so angry. My friends are helping me greatly. Yet, I cannot forget this deep and loving relationship she and I had. I want it back and on the other hand it scares me to death. I don't know what to do. So, any input you can give me will help.

Dear Reader,

This is a significant letter for many reasons—not the least of which is the lesson to be learned about the risk of assuming that people really are whoever they say they are on the Internet. Many, many people think they've met their soul-mate on the Internet, only to find (sometimes much later) that it was all an illusion. And even in a situation like the one above where the trust in this other person was misplaced, there's still a certain trust being shown in *other* Internet relationships by virtue of saying "My online friends told me to dump this person, and I did." This indicates there's still an assumption that online relationships are like having *real* friends (in the sense of really *being there* over the long haul and having your long-term interests at heart). Nevertheless, while

54

the above situation is difficult, at least it's not downright dangerous in the way some Internet-related activities turn out to be.

But aside from the Internet-related issues, there are a number of other important points in the above letter that deserve attention. For instance, one of the main attractions in the above connection was the understanding and compassionate nature of the relationship. This is to be valued in *any* relationship—and doesn't need to be sought only in opposite-sex relationships. Another point is the description of the relationship: "I fell in love, and he said he loved me, too." This was said *as if* it couldn't have really been love since he turned out to be a woman. However, we tend to have a narrow definition of love as *only* being "romantic" or sexual love. The really deepest love is not necessarily related to sex or sexuality. In fact, I have had a dear friend for many years who *first* loves an individual as a "person"—regardless of which gender they happen to be. It's just that we have defined love in such narrow terms that we tend to "throw the baby out with the bath water" in rejecting love that doesn't come in the *package* of being romantic or sexual.

So while the concern expressed is about the fear of having a deep and loving relationship with this person now that their true gender is known, saying ("I want it back and on the other hand it scares me to death,") the more appropriate basis for the fear is the deception involved in the relationship, not in the fact that "He was a she." Any real love or real connection needs to be based on honesty—regardless of whether it's between the same sex or opposite sex.

I'm limited in any input I might offer because the letter gives no information about the deception itself, instead saying, "The reasons for her deception are not important here..." But my general perspective is that the deception itself (and whatever factors relate to the deception) are, in fact, the most important aspects to be considered.

* * * * * * * * * * * *

Chat out of Hand

Dear Peggy,

My husband began chatting with a woman half-way across the world about 6 months ago. He invited her to come and meet him secretly and (after she flew all this way) he for some reason confessed all this to me and hid from her the whole time she was here. I spoke with her, unknown to him, and she is deeply in love with him and did not know about our marriage. We have been married 15 years and I am so confused by all this. Is this behaviour a sign of some mental illness or is he just heartless and insensitive. He is acting so kindly towards me now, it is like a honeymoon. My heart breaks for this other woman, though. Please help.

Dear Reader,

This touching letter is indicative of the truly dangerous proliferation of situations like this arising from contact through the Internet. Most people never *intend* for it to get out of hand. When they begin contact, it's seen as *harmless*—

but it frequently escalates far more quickly and more intensely than they're prepared to deal with. And sometimes (as described in this letter) they don't fully wake up to what they've done until it has gone way beyond what they ever imagined.

Naturally, the wife feels this kind of behavior makes no sense. In fact, it's likely that a husband like the one described in this letter is also quite confused by his own actions. When there's this kind of failure to think of potential consequences *in advance*, it can create situations like this where everyone involved is shocked by the results.

Understanding this dynamic does not necessarily require psychoanalysis— because it's not necessarily related to any of the things mentioned above: mental illness or being heartless and insensitive. It's more just being *thoughtless*. While it's almost impossible to imagine how someone can be so unthinking, it's part of a fairly common ability to ignore or deny reality and rationalize that "no one will know," "no one will get hurt," etc. But of course, *everyone* gets hurt—as illustrated by the wife's feelings of compassion for the other woman who *also* got very hurt in all this.

It sounds like this experience was a wake-up call for everyone. Hopefully, the other woman will understand not to be trusting of relationships that begin through chats on the Internet. And hopefully, the husband will continue what sounds like a genuine effort to try to compensate for his irresponsible behavior.

Finally, there's hope that the learning gained from this can be used to build a stronger marital connection based on a commitment to having no more secrets (especially no more secret chats). It's also hoped that this experience can be a lesson for others in the dangers involved in pursuing online relationships.

4: Emotional Affairs

Emotionally attached

Dear Peggy,

What can you do when it's an emotional betrayal? Physical you can fight, at least it's concrete. But what if they aren't having sex but are so emotionally attached to someone of the opposite sex that they refuse to give them up—no matter what the cost to the relationship?

Dear Reader,

Unfortunately, we usually focus on the actual sex involved in relationships outside of marriage, but emotional involvement can pose a threat to the relationship that goes far beyond the threat in a sexual involvement that does *not* include emotional closeness. Of course, a combination of sexual and emotional involvement is the most difficult to address, but (as expressed in this letter), the emotional issue alone can be quite a challenge.

In trying to figure out "what you can do," it may help to understand what is involved in developing and sustaining an emotional attachment. The most important ingredient in an emotional attachment is the degree of honesty between two people. Sometimes a person feels safer to be totally honest with someone other than their spouse because the other person doesn't have the kind of personal investment in whatever feelings are shared as the spouse would have—and doesn't respond with the same kind of judgment based on those feelings. (A quick way to verify this for yourself is to think how often we share information with a stranger that we would not share with friends or family—because the stranger doesn't know us and therefore telling them won't have an impact on our life.)

If, however, there is ongoing interaction with someone with whom you have been extremely honest, it generates a feeling of closeness that stimulates even more sharing and more closeness, and on and on. Eventually, this relationship can become extremely close and an emotional attachment develops.

Naturally, it can feel threatening when a spouse develops this kind of relationship with someone else, especially someone of the opposite sex—and even more especially if there is not a lot of ongoing honest communication within the marriage. This is not to say that there should be any sense of blame for whatever lack of honest communication there might be in the marriage, but it's important to make an effort to increase the degree of honesty.

It's important that this honesty be *responsible* honesty, meaning that it is undertaken for the specific purpose of drawing you closer together. This usually means sharing honestly about *yourself* (your hopes, fears, dreams, frustrations, joys, sorrows, etc.,) in hopes that your spouse will gradually reciprocate. People are drawn closer together when they feel they really know each other. So, strange as it seems, married couples sometimes cease to know each other after years of withholding their private thoughts from one another. But it's never too late to work on turning that around. So while you may not be able to directly address the original problem of a close emotional attachment with someone else, you can work at strengthening the emotional attachment within the marriage— which is sure to benefit the marital relationship and also may diminish the outside attachment.

* * * * * * * * * * * * *

Emotional Involvement?

Dear Peggy,

My husband is emotionally involved with another woman and also sexually involved and has been for a couple of months. Is it possible to rebuild our marriage if we both want to do this? Also, do most extramarital affairs usually last when there is emotional involvement?

Dear Reader,

This is a short letter with some very important questions:

1. Is it possible to rebuild our marriage if we both want to do this?

Yes, recovering and rebuilding trust are a by-product of the time and effort spent working through this experience and establishing a new relationship for the future. In fact, the process involved in working it out can bring you closer than you were before. For instance, most of us had blind trust before something like this happens. This is an opportunity to establish trust based on really knowing another person at a deeper level.

2. Do most extramarital affairs usually last when there is emotional involvement?

An affair between two people who are emotionally involved (as well as sexually involved) may last longer than a sexual affair with no emotional attachment. But affairs in general, regardless of the particular nature of the relationship, usually have a life-span of from 6 months to 2 years if left undiscovered and undetected. It often takes that period of time for the fantasy phase to conclude—where people can more clearly assess the situation. However, if the sexual affair ends but the emotional attachment remains, this could drag out for a very long time.

* * * * * * * * * * * * *

Do I have a platonic affair?

Dear Peggy,

I am currently involved in a very unemotional marriage and considering a platonic companionship affair. My husband has been diagnosed as manic-

58

depressive. He has gone to counselors and is on medication, however I can't keep up with what state of mind he is in from day to day. I am also on minute amounts of medication to keep my anxiety attacks away.

My problem is this: I have chosen to stick around in the marriage and praying someday hubby will realize what he has around him—instead of going through life with fear and anger built up inside of him. He refuses to go to any more counseling appointments and says I'm the one with the problems, not him. (Our counselor disagrees totally.) He does not support, encourage, or like anything I do outside of the home with the kids or scouting or my job, does not like the way I do things at home, and expects all the work of the family to be on my shoulders. He completely looks down on me in everything I do and think and believe.

I have accepted this marriage and have come to the conclusion that if I stay in the relationship, I will have to live sacrificing my emotional happiness forever. Now I'm lonely and need to be loved and no one to turn to; my children are great inspirations to me; however, they should not be burdened with this.

Please send me some inspiration, guidance, or at least your thoughts about my situation. I'm at the end of my rope and very confused.

Dear Reader,

The pain of the above situation is obvious. Even though trying very hard to cope, there seems to be a feeling of being trapped. However, it's doubtful that the desired relief or happiness can be found through developing a platonic affair. First of all, there's no way to be sure any strong companionship relationship would remain platonic, even it that's the intention. Also, if there's a determination to "stick around in the marriage and praying someday hubby will realize what he has around him"—then turning to an outside relationship will probably work counter to having that happen.

There's a certain catch-22 in a situation like this when someone tries to hold onto a relationship like the one above while simultaneously hoping to develop another (better) one outside. In general, it's better to get clear about one thing at a time. In other words, there's a better chance of success by making a clear decision and then putting effort into making that decision work. For instance, if still "hoping things may someday change," then staying married and putting everything into making it better—but if/when believing that thing's *won't* change, then leaving and putting everything into making a new life.

Any decision involves tradeoffs, so it's usually better to acknowledge that up front instead of trying to do two contradictory things at once. Then, the process of getting very clear about the pros and cons of the alternatives can help in moving toward a firm decision and a commitment to acting on whatever decision is made. Almost any clear decision is likely to be better than remaining in limbo.

5: Suspicions of an Affair

I don't trust him anymore

Dear Peggy,

How can I tell for sure he is having an affair? My intuitions are yelling YES at me but how do I find out for sure? He won't give me straight answers and I don't trust the answers he gives anymore. How true is the women's intuition theory? I would appreciate your opinions and any thoughts you may have on this problem.

Dear Reader,

Many people have trouble deciding whether or not to trust their intuition. And while it's not sufficient in and of itself, it plays a central role in the list of "signs and symptoms" of an affair. In fact, this is one of the first indicators of a possible affair—this gut feeling that something is wrong. Most people reported having this feeling, although it varied in the way it appeared. For some it was a sudden feeling that resulted from a casual comment or incident, while for others it came as a growing feeling of uneasiness.

The first signals of an affair are seldom the stereotypical things like lipstick on the collar or strange phone calls; they're much more likely to be an intuitive sense that "something is different." The signals may be quite subtle, just slight shifts in certain behaviors; for instance being more distant, more preoccupied with job, home, or outside interests, more attentive to clothes and accessories, more focused on weight and appearance, more absent from home with time unaccounted for, more glued to the TV set than usual, more interested in trying new things sexually than before, less attentive, less willing to talk or spend time together, less available emotionally, less interested in family issues, less interested in sex than usual, and less involved in shared activities

Of course, even if you detect some of these signs in your partner's behavior, you can't assume it means they're having an affair; it's not that simple. Determining whether or not there's any significance to the changes in behavior depends on evaluating both the number of areas of change and the degree of change. For instance, changes in only a few areas would not be as significant as changes in many different areas. And very slight changes would not be as significant as more drastic ones.

But even if there has been a great deal of change in a large number of areas, this does not necessarily signal an affair. There are many reasons for such changes in behavior that have nothing to do with affairs, one of the most likely being an increased level of stress in the work environment. Other possible causes include concerns about health, aging, family, or finances.

So there's no one, two, three process for knowing when a partner has had an affair, but these are some of the factors that can reasonably be considered. In the final analysis, it calls for talking about it—very directly with your partner. So, to get back to the original question, intuition is only a signal to begin the process of getting more information in order to determine whether an affair is taking place.

* * * * * * * * * * * * *

Is he having an affair?

Dear Peggy,

The other day my husband and I went out for dinner... And I came straight out and asked him if he has ever slept with anyone else. And his answer to me was, "Don't put me on the spot like this..."

And nothing else was said... I knew he didn't want to talk about it and I didn't know if I wanted to know the truth for sure. What do you think... Is or was he ever having an affair?

Dear Reader,

The first question to be asked does *not* need to be directed toward the spouse; the first question is one that each person must first ask themselves: "Do you really want to know for sure?" Only when you can answer that question with an unequivocal "yes" are you in any position to hope to get a truthful response when asking your spouse.

People having affairs are already convinced that this can't be discussed, so the questioning needs to be absolutely clear, unwavering, and persistent to have any chance of getting an honest answer. (Even then, the initial response is likely to be denial.)

So when someone feels uncertain (like the person who wrote this letter, saying, "I didn't know if I wanted to know the truth for sure"), their spouse is sure to pick up this ambivalence, which just reinforces their basic mindset not to answer.

So it's a waste of time and energy to ask anyone (whether spouse, friends, family, or me) unless/until there's more certainty about wanting to know for sure. In the meantime, it's better to do a lot of private reflection about your own feelings, understandings, plans, intentions, etc.

Sometimes people resist knowing for sure because they tell themselves that if it turns out to be true, they would *have* to get a divorce (or they may tell themselves they *have* to stay married, perhaps for practical reasons). In either case, they're not prepared to face the truth.

They're more likely to be able to deal with the truth (whatever it turns out to be) when they don't feel compelled to have to react in one particular way. That means being clear that even if it's true, they're open to deciding what to do based on how they do (or don't) use this crisis to improve their relationship for the future—instead of predetermining what to do based on the past.

* * * * * * * * * * * * *

He gets angry at my questions

Dear Peggy,

My husband works 16+ hours per day. He goes in to work early and come home about 11 p.m. or later in the evenings. Here's my issue: when I ask him questions about how his day has been, he gets angry and upset, tells me he doesn't want to talk about it. Simple questions are asked and his response is I'm nagging. Since his job involves travel, he's gone more then he's here. At this point, he could be telling me anything. How do I know he's where he says he is. We never use his car to go anywhere, I haven't been in it in over 5 months. We see so little of each other now that we have very little to talk about and he won't talk about work. He won't even give me his car phone number; if I need to reach him, I have to page him.

I have strong feelings that there's someone else, but don't have any physical proof. I can't even talk to him about us or how I feel! ....he gets angry and blows me off. I need to know what to do....What should I do??? We have two children and I don't know where to turn?

Dear Reader,

This is a very painful position to be in, as I know from firsthand experience. But this kind of strong reaction to questioning is not uncommon—especially when someone has something to hide. This is often an effective way to stifle further conversation. While there are exceptions, of course, the intensity of the reaction often corresponds to the validity of the questions. For instance, as the suspicions of an affair grow stronger and the questions become more probing and more frequent, the denials of an affair are likely to become more vehement.

When the denial includes an attack on the person asking the questions, it's more likely that the suspicions are true. A harsh response may be an attempt to bring any additional questioning to a halt. When someone isn't trying to hide something, they are more likely to respond in a calm (perhaps even comforting and reassuring) way; but a person who has something to hide is more likely to react defensively and make accusations in return. It's the lack of confidence in their own integrity that usually causes this kind of overreaction. (When someone is absolutely clear about the honesty of their response to a question—whether it's about affairs or some other issue—they do not feel threatened and do not feel the need to be defensive or critical.)

Having said that, there's still no way to know absolutely whether or not there is someone else. But the first consideration in confronting these suspicions is being sure you really want to know. It's important to genuinely want the truth, rather than just reassurance. And it's important to be "prepared" to either stay married or get a divorce before forcing a confrontation. There are many factors to consider as to whether/when/how to force a confrontation. Each person has to live with the consequences of their choices about this, so it's important to go about any decisions or actions in a way that best fits your own personal situation. Hopefully, some of this general perspective can be helpful in that effort. And it might also help to talk through this dilemma with a trusted friend or family member—to ensure personal support through this struggle.

* * * * * * * * * * * * *

Suspect an Affair

Dear Peggy,

I believe my husband has had an affair with a coworker; I confronted him and he denied it, yet apologized for hurting me. I only have circumstantial evidence and want to believe him. I called the coworker and confronted her and she denied it. I love my husband, yet am afraid that they will continue in a relationship, and that I am being made a fool. My husband states over and over that nothing happened and that he loves me and doesn't want to lose me. We have been married for 18 years and I thought we had a good marriage and great sex. He now has told me that we were in a rut. What am I to think and how do I put all this behind us? And how can I ever trust him?

Dear Reader,

Many of the circumstances in this letter are typical of the problems that a person faces in this kind of situation: suspicions of an affair at work, denials when questioned, afraid of being made a fool, and how to go on and trust.

It's true that many affairs start at work, so it's not unreasonable to be concerned. The fact that there are denials doesn't really prove much either way. If there is *not* an affair, then, of course, there will be denials. But if there IS an affair, there will almost certainly still be denials. The norm among people involved in affairs is: "Never tell. If questioned, deny it. If caught, say as little as possible."

Dealing with the uncertainty is easier (and the actions taken will be more effective) by rejecting the idea that a spouse's affair "makes you a fool." Most affairs are NOT a reflection on the spouse—even though the person having the affair will often try to justify it by finding some fault with the marriage (like "being in a rut"). But there are far more factors involved than the condition of the marriage or any perceived shortcomings of the spouse. When all is said and done, it's usually the people having affairs that are behaving "foolishly."

There is no basis for "putting it behind" and "trusting" until all the questions and concerns are thoroughly discussed in an open and honest way. A spouse's resistance to talking through it doesn't necessarily mean there's an affair, but it does indicate an insensitivity to the feelings of anxiety and concern—which usually means there is some kind of problem that needs to be addressed, whether or not it relates to an affair.

* * * * * * * * * * * * *

Suspicions of an Affair

Denies Affair!

Dear Peggy,

How do you deal with a husband who has an ongoing affair but continues to deny it? I've been trying to cope for several years. He seems to think he can do anything he wants—even if it makes me very unhappy. Our sex life is none. But he tells me he is too old for sex. We have been married almost thirty-eight years. I am 57 years old and he is 61. Do you have any answers besides divorce?

Dear Reader,

This is obviously a frustrating situation. At least the writer recognizes the rationalizations involved in the things her husband in saying. Denying an affair is quite common and typical. It's an effort to avoid dealing with it. This kind of behavior is usually an effort to stop further discussion of the issue. So unless a person wants to give up and accept the status quo—or get a divorce without continuing the struggle—it's essential to continue to state the belief that an affair is taking place.

It sounds in this instance as if there is a one-two punch. First, he denies having an affair; second, it sounds as if his attitude is that even if he is having an affair, he somehow "deserves" it. It might help to at least strive for clarity around whether he's primarily denying it or whether the real message is that he just "doesn't care" whether his wife knows. The "not caring" about her unhappiness is in some ways more significant than the denial. As I said, the denial is predictable, but being uncaring about obvious distress caused by the suspicions may be a far more important issue.

As for the age factor, this sounds like another rationalization. While he may not feel capable of handling both outside sex in an affair and sex within the marriage, the idea of being "too old for sex" is not reasonable—unless there is some particular medical problem.

In most instances, people will be better able to live with whatever decision they make (as to whether or not to get a divorce) if they can get all the facts on which they need to base a decision. It's very hard to play a smart hand if you don't know what cards you are holding. So the first step may be to be very direct about the need for clarity about what's really going on now—in order to decide where to go from here.

* * * * * * * * * * * *

Suspect my spouse...again

Dear Peggy,

My husband had an affair a couple of years ago. We separated, came very close to getting divorced, but he came back apologizing and realizing what a mistake he had made. Since then it has been very hard to trust again, but we joined a church and have been going faithfully.

Now my husband has taken a job out of town while I am still in our home until it sells, and some weird things have been happening since Christmas. He received a package without a name on it, so he says, for Christmas, with some pretty expensive gifts, then he has a pager and has gotten some strange beeps, like 6969, etc. Then this past weekend when he was home he got paged, then the phone rang, I answered and the person hung-up, then another beep, then the phone again, all my husband said was uh huh, uh huh, then hung up. Then another page came and the phone rang again, this time I picked up the speaker phone and muted it and I heard a female ask if he could talk to her now, he said no. When I confronted him, he said he had no idea who this person was. It just doesn't sound right to me and I don't know how to handle this. Any advice?

Dear Reader,

This description includes not just one strange occurrence—but many. While this is not *proof* that something is going on, it reminds me of the saying that "where there's smoke, there's fire." (There does seem to be a lot of smoke.) To continue the "smoke/fire" analogy—just as it would be dangerous to ignore signs of smoke, it's likely that the above occurrences should not be ignored either.

While accusations and confrontations don't necessarily elicit the truth, it's usually a good idea to calmly express (in as rational, non-emotional way as possible) that you need more information or better explanations of these unusual events. If there is nothing to hide, it would seem that the husband would also want to understand why these strange things are happening—in order to try to stop them. (Usually, even if a single incident might be dismissed, people are generally curious enough to pursue finding out about repeated instances like this.)

Again, there's no dependable way to assess whether these events add up to something to be concerned about. But anytime something "just doesn't sound right," it warrants following up. Our gut instincts are often good indicators, especially if/when we're trying to rationalize some other explanation in order to avoid facing a difficult situation. In fact, repeated rationalizations about a partner's behavior (as a way of discounting obvious clues of an affair) may be the biggest clue of all.

A final word about the comment that the husband was "apologizing... and joined a church and...going faithfully:" while these are positive signs; they are not guarantees. I've received letters from many people in the church, including members of the clergy. No one is immune.

* * * * * * * * * * * * *

Why can't I trust?

Dear Peggy,

I feel I can not control my reactions sometime. I say the wrong thing and think the wrong thing. I know my husband loves me but I sometime feel he is having an affair. I know it's not true, but sometime my mind runs away with me. This is my second marriage and my first husband did have an affair for years before I found out about it. Why can't I forget it and go on with my life? I have a

*wonderful husband now who needs my trust, and I know if I don't give it to him
soon he may leave. Help me please!*

Dear Reader,

This letter reflects a common problem that follows learning of a spouse's
affair: the difficulty in trusting again—even with a different spouse. There are
two specific aspects of this situation that could help someone in this situation
better understand what's happening.

First, we tend to think that the trust issue is "resolved" whenever there's a
divorce following an affair. However, our ability to trust *anyone* has been
undermined unless and until we deal with the emotional impact of the affair.
The degree to which a person recovers and is able to trust again does not
necessarily depend on whether or not they stay married. It depends on getting
more understanding of the whole issue. This involves doing a lot of hard work
(usually involving reading, talking, reflecting on it)—either with or without the
person who had the affair.

Second, it's not just a question of not trusting the spouse (even a new
spouse); it's also a question of not trusting your own instincts. This is
understandable due to the experience of having been deceived in the past. One
of the most significant comments about the above situation may be: "my first
husband did have an affair for years *before I found out about it*." Once someone
finds out after years of being deceived, there's a tendency to feel foolish at
having been trusting and to feel afraid of having that happen again.

While we do need to "learn from our experiences," the lesson to be learned
from this experience is *not* that you can never trust again. It's that you need a
different kind of trust: one that is based on an ongoing commitment to honest
communication—not the old kind of trust based on assumption. We can't just
assume monogamy—even though, based on the wedding vows, we think we
should be able to assume it. We need to recognize the prevalence of affairs and
establish the kind of honesty in the relationship that builds real trust. Trust is not
something you *bestow* on someone. Trust is a by-product of maintaining the
kind of close connection (and real knowing of each other) that comes from
responsible honesty.

* * * * * * * * * * * * *

Husband denied affair

Dear Peggy,

*My husband denied that he is or has had an affair. Yet this same person has
moved 100 miles away, saying it's the best thing for us. He still comes home on
weekends, but lives in another town during the week. Wouldn't this mean that he
has had an affair—or maybe that he's headed for an affair?*

Dear Reader,

A husband moving 100 miles away and coming home on weekends doesn't *necessarily* indicate an affair, but it does signal a serious problem in that it shows a lack of joint decision-making and good communication.

There are many reasons for wanting a lot of time together, not the least of which is our long-standing ideal of togetherness as the symbol of a good relationship. But the kind of togetherness that is stifling to the individuals is not to be desired. One of the biggest threats to the vitality of many couples is the boredom that results from too much togetherness. But the trick is to find the right balance.

Healthy relationships require enough time together for the maintenance and growth of the couple and enough time apart for the maintenance and growth of the individuals. Each experience contributes to the other: you will appreciate your time together much more if you have independent experiences to share with your partner, and you'll appreciate your time apart if you have a strong bond that allows you to venture out with confidence.

While it's *possible* for a couple to maintain a good relationship while spending a lot of time apart, it's essential that there be a strong bond of trust (based on a lot of ongoing honesty) so that each person is comfortable with the situation instead of being filled with anxiety. It's not so much a question of the *actual* time together or time apart as it is a question of *why*—and whether *both* people prefer it. But if one person arbitrarily decides to increase the time apart, this can create very serious problems for the relationship—*regardless* of the risk or possibility of an affair.

* * * * * * * * * * * * *

Desperate

Dear Peggy:

My wife and I started dating while she was married to a verbally abusive, possessive man. She soon filed for divorce after we started dating and her divorce lasted 2-1/2 painful years. I was there for her emotionally and financially every step of the way. We were married in 1994. It was her second marriage and my first. She brought to our marriage 3 wonderful children that I get along with dearly. A little while ago she started undermining my authority with our children by contradicting anything that I did with them.

Last October she started a new job that requires her to travel a lot. In the beginning everything was going great. She would call every night and we would talk for a long time. Then a new man was hired by her in her company and travels with her and the rest of her crew on most trips. Now she doesn't call every night, and when she does call, it is only for a few seconds. She says that she is tired and is going to bed. The receipts that she brings home show that purchases at bars and restaurants are made long after she supposedly went to bed. Today I found out from 2 of my children that she always goes out to lunch with him. (My children work with their mother over the summers.) This man has purchased gifts for my 2 children as well.

For the past few months my wife has barely even talked to me. The only time she says I love you to me is in response to me saying it first. She doesn't clean up around the house at all and I do all of the housework as well. Should I be worried about these things or am I being paranoid? I adore my wife, and have never even questioned her about these things. Her first husband was a jealous man and I don't want her to think that of me, so up until now I have given her nothing but space. Please let me know what you think on this issue. It tears me up inside to think that she might be cheating.

Dear Reader,

Wondering if a spouse might be having an affair is a terrible way to live. (I know, because I lived that way for 7 years before confronting it.) And during that period of suspicion, I also felt the uneasiness while my husband was traveling—and tried to gauge his activities from the time/nature of his phone calls. He also went for quite a few years without saying "I love you." So while I can't know about anyone else's specific situation, I do have a firsthand understanding of some of the dynamics involved.

For instance, when my husband was traveling, I used to feel somewhat better on nights that he called me, thinking he must be safely in his room. Later, after finding out the truth, it turned out that many of those nights he called while another woman was waiting in the bathroom for him to finish his call to me. So any of these kinds of "detective-like" guesses are not dependable. This is *not* to say that anyone is actually having an affair, only that no one can know whether or not there is an affair based on phone calls.

In fact, this kind of "hoping for the best while fearing the worst" is extremely common. It's admirable that someone tries so hard to demonstrate that they are not like a previous partner (who, for instance, was verbally abusive), but sometimes going to the other extreme leads to being taken advantage of. For instance, "never questioning" actually makes it easier for a person to engage in secretive behavior. (I also had the posture of never questioning, thinking that it was important that he *think* I trusted him, even thought I didn't.) But that, too, is not effective.

The only realistic way to deal with suspicions and concerns is to get them out in the open. This is not to say that it should be done quickly or casually; but thoughtfully opening a conversation about dealing with possible attractions is something *all* couples need to do—*before* any specific suspicions develop. And even if it isn't done earlier, it's "better late than never."

Finally, any person who opens up this conversation needs to first be clear that they *want* the truth and are not just looking for reassurance. If someone is not clear about wanting the truth and being prepared to face the truth, they can be sure they will only get reassurance—but it may be false reassurance, which doesn't help to resolve this issue.

* * * * * * * * * * * * *

Feelings for ex-girlfriend?

Dear Peggy,

I am a 42-year-old female, happily married for over 22 years with 3 great kids. Life is good to us, my only problem is my feelings over a strange situation. My husband is on the same committee at work as his ex-girlfriend from 25 years ago, with whom he claims he never had intimate relations. I accepted that and over the years from time to time we all socialized together as we are from the same ethnic circle. Lately though I have noticed that she seems to be around more and she always makes me feel uncomfortable. She is not in a happy marriage and has no children. I understand that from time to time they must work together; however, I don't appreciate their friendliness. The last straw was the other day when we were at a social event at which my husband was honored and when we were leaving my husband kissed her good-bye on the lips.

Am I over-sensitive or is he just nuts? When I confronted him with this he told me that I am making much too much of this and that there was no malice intended, it was just a kiss good-bye. He gets very angry with me and tells me that I cannot restrict him and that he cannot live with restrictions. He feels like everything he does bothers me and that's not true; things he does with HER hurt me. We have a solid marriage besides this and we have a great sex life. What am I to do? My whole life is a shamble because all I do is worry about this. Please help me; am I crazy or what? I can't stand it.

Dear Reader,

I personally relate to the above letter because of my own experience with this concern about 30 years ago—which I can still recall. Here's the way I described my own experience with this kind of issue in our book, "Beyond Affairs:"

"I had trouble with the social kissing that was going on. The group we socialized with was into greeting each other with a kiss. I'd never been comfortable doing this myself—and I certainly wasn't comfortable with James doing it. My real fear was that he might be privately involved with another woman. Since I wasn't willing to say that to him, I focused on this social kissing as a way to get at my concerns. I'd say things like, 'Your kissing other women is embarrassing to me. It makes me look foolish.' I thought by telling him how I felt about his behavior in these public situations I could somehow influence his private actions. He invariably responded with statements like, 'That's ridiculous. Most of our friends do the same thing. You're the one who needs to change.'"

Well, some years later I learned that, in fact, the social kissing was not significant (in that he was not having an affair with any of the women he kissed socially in my presence)—but he *was* having affairs. I share this just to indicate that the social kiss *may* be an indication of an overall expansiveness with women based on having affairs, but it doesn't necessarily indicate that a particular woman he is seen kissing in public is someone with whom he's having an affair.

Obviously, it's reasonable to open a discussion about such concerns—but it's not the specific words in the response that may be indicative of the truth; it's the *attitude* of the response (whether it's reassuring or attacking). When the response is an attack (instead of an effort to be reassuring), it's likely to indicate the use of this common tactic for trying to cut off further questions or even further discussion.

* * * * * * * * * * * *

Not sure

Dear Peggy,

I am not sure if I should be upset with my husband or not? There are times that I feel stupid for being upset with him and that makes me feel bad. My husband is having an online long distance relationship with a woman many states away. He says that he is single and acts like I just don't exist. His profile says that he is single and has some very drawing comments in it. If he were single, then I could easily see where he would have someone latch on to him.

I am afraid that I might lose him. When he first started talking to this one girl it was mostly through Email. They have similar hobbies and had things to talk about. That didn't bother me too much. I don't care if he talks to other women. I have male friends so I don't see anything wrong with him having female friends.

Then she started wanting to call him or him call her. He didn't do it at first but then she started to doubt how he felt so he called her. They talked for about 40 minutes that first time. Then the next time it was 1-1/2 hrs and then this week he gave her our number and let her call him. The night that she called him they got on the phone at 12 midnight and talked until 3 a.m. I was heartbroken.

He tells me that he loves me, but I don't know if he does anymore or not. This is really making me feel bad about myself—and I don't need this. All I want to do is cry. I feel like there is a black cloud around me all the time and that I just don't want to be here anymore.

He says that nothing will ever come out of this. He tells me that he loves me and that I am his only one, but I don't know how to feel. I don't really believe him anymore. If he loved me he wouldn't hurt me like that. And at the same time I feel sorry for her. I don't like to see anyone hurt. I don't want to hurt either. And we have kids too. What about them?

I just don't know what to do. I don't know how I am supposed to feel. I love him and don't want to lose him. I feel like I need someone to talk to about it and I don't have anyone I can talk to. I need someone to tell me either I am worrying too much or not enough. Can you help me?

Dear Reader,

I'd like to begin with the last question as to whether "I am worrying too much or not enough." It's not the *degree* of worry that matters, it's what a person *does* about whatever worry they have. When actions based on the worry are as tentative as described above, it's not surprising that they have little impact—especially when a partner is completely rationalizing their behavior. It's very confusing when someone says they love you and then deliberately takes actions that are hurtful. They can only do that when they're rationalizing instead of thinking clearly.

What makes this even more difficult is that a person who is really into rationalizing may be kidding themselves as well as their partner. They may actually have convinced themselves that "nothing will ever come out of this," but that's either extremely naïve or a strong willingness to be deceptive. It's especially sad when someone takes advantage of the "goodness/niceness/give-them-the-benefit-of-the-doubt" attitude of their partner. When someone *says* they love their partner but consistently behaves in ways that are hurtful, the actions speak louder than the words.

All too often, people take advantage of a partner who is extremely thoughtful and sensitive. And sometimes a person may actually be *too* thoughtful in that they are willing to bear up under all their own pain while still trying to shield others from pain (as illustrated by the statement in this letter: "And at the same time I feel sorry for her. I don't like to see anyone hurt.") Often in partnerships, the more one is a Giver, the more the other becomes a Taker—until they have both gone way overboard in their respective positions. Any relationship is better when there is more balance—with more mutual caring, generosity, and concern for each other's well-being. The bottom line is that everyone has a responsibility to act in ways that both enhance their own well-being as well as the well-being of their partner. When either is sacrificed for the sake of the other, everyone eventually loses.

* * * * * * * * * * * * *

Afraid he'll cheat

Dear Peggy,

My husband and I have been married for two years, and we have two children. Up until our last child was born he was going to a bar 4 times a week. Now he goes at least once. I'm afraid he's going to the bar to meet another woman because when he goes to the bar he's out until 4 or 5 in the morning. I may not have a reason to be suspicious. But I still am. How can I find out if my suspicions are right?

Dear Reader,

Sometimes our fear stops us from doing or saying what we *know* is needed. (As I've said, I understand this because of my own years of being suspicious without speaking up about it.) Sometimes we aren't ready to "know for sure"—

so we keep questioning *ourselves* instead of questioning our spouse. When we *really* want to know, we're usually able to break through whatever fears or rationalizations may have prevented us from finding out.

While there's never a way to be absolutely sure about another person's behavior based on observing their actions, it's obvious (if someone is able to look objectively at a situation) when there are *serious* issues that need to be addressed. Whether or not a married man with two children is having an affair (or might start having an affair)—staying out at a bar at least once a week until 4 or 5 in the morning is a legitimate cause for serious concern about the relationship.

Anytime a person has suspicions or is concerned about their partner's behavior, their discomfort with being able to *talk* to their partner about it is indicative of a need to take action. So whether or not there's a "reason to be suspicious" about affairs, there's obviously a need to develop more honest communication.

* * * * * * * * * * * *

Suspicious and Jealous

Dear Peggy,

I have been with my husband for 18 years. We have 3 teenage children living at home. For the last few years we have been growing apart and pushing each other away, both physically and emotionally. But I always thought we'd eventually find our way back to each other. About 3 months ago out of the blue my husband suggested a divorce. He thought I wanted it as much as him. He told me he'd never loved me except as a friend and felt he couldn't give me emotionally what I wanted. He denied another woman. Needless to say I got extremely upset, depressed, and withdrawn. He told me he was afraid to try anymore. After numerous discussions he said he'd try. One week later I found a love letter he had written to a lover. When I confronted him, he cried and said he was sorry and wanted to work it out with me. He met her on the computer. He became very affectionate the next week and said he'd end it with her.

Well I snuck around and found his password for the computer and read his Email. He was telling me that things were going to work out and making love to me at night and then Emailing her in the morning asking her to meet him. When I let him know I knew what was going on, I became the bad guy for checking his Email. He was looking me in the eye and lying about her!! He finally after many tears decided it was "us" he wanted, but said it was unfair of me to not let him talk to her on the computer because they were now only "good friends." So against my better judgment I agreed because I love him so much. Last night when I put a pick in his coat pocket a program from my son's hockey fell out and scrawled across it was her phone number!! I don't want to share him!! Is it wrong of me (as he said) to say no more contact? I feel like he can't give her up. I don't know how to keep a handle on my suspicions and jealousy. I hate being like this always wondering.... Help.

73

Dear Reader,

Many aspects of this situation are extremely common, but they're also extremely difficult to deal with alone. It's hard to think straight when there are so many internal conflicting feelings and so many contradictions from a spouse.

As everyone on the Internet today knows, there are many opportunities for "meeting people on the computer"—and many times these meetings lead to relationships that threaten a marriage. To blame it on "growing apart" is a typical excuse for developing a friendship/relationship with someone else; but obviously, beginning a secret relationship (regardless of the particular nature of it) is a sure way to guarantee a couple will grow even *further* apart.

As for trying to make someone the "bad guy" for checking around and discovering the secret, that's a common tactic to deflect attention away from the discovery per se and blame someone else. And accusing a spouse of being wrong in objecting to continuing to be "good friends" with someone in circumstances like this is another effort to turn the tables and avoid their own responsibility for the whole situation. (A person wouldn't need to check up or to object to such a friendship if the secretive behavior hadn't warranted it in the first place.)

All the best information about successfully getting beyond the negative impact of a situation like this involves *no* further contact with the other person. It's perfectly reasonable to object to the relationship continuing (on *any* basis)—and it's perfectly reasonable to be suspicious, jealous, and to "check up" on someone when there's every reason to believe they're lying. (By the way, *most* spouses "know in their gut" when their partner is lying about something like this, so they're not likely to "keep a handle on their suspicions" unless/until their spouse shows some understanding of the suspicious environment they're creating by their actions and their attitude.)

* * * * * * * * * * * * *

Suspect wife having affair

Dear Peggy,

I am 54 years old have a huge gut feeling my wife is having an affair. We have been married for 33 years and she had two affairs before. But I did not have the gut feeling like I do now. On our 33rd anniversary I sent her 3 dozen roses and that evening had a candlelit dinner for her and then gave her a massage. During this time she never said she loved me. Just thanks. In the last year I have noticed that when we have sex she does a lot more things now then before. I am out of town a lot and when I leave she asks me if I am going to call her. I have questioned her about this, but she denies it just like the last two times. I have to catch her in a lie before she will respond with the truth. I am at my wits end and even thought about suicide.

Suspicions of an Affair

Dear Reader,

This letter illustrates just how serious it is (and how desperate it can feel) to know in your gut that something is happening—when the other person says it's *not*. This situation is extremely common—and its devastating impact is extremely common as well. Fortunately, even though most people in this situation have thoughts about suicide (including myself at one point when I suspected my husband but didn't know what to do about it), we know on some level that suicide is no answer at all.

Instead, I would hope that people in this position would take strength in knowing that they are thinking more clearly than they might imagine. For instance, it's perceptive to notice that what's *not* said also speaks volumes—like when someone fails to say I love you in this kind of situation. However, it doesn't necessarily mean they *don't*. For instance, my husband didn't say *I love you* for several years during the time he was having affairs. When I later pointed this out, he hadn't even been aware of it. His best guess was that he had simply shut down so much of his communication in order to protect his secret affairs that his expressions of love got shut down as well.

Unfortunately, when we don't know where we stand, we tend to notice and analyze every piece of behavior, looking for evidence to figure out what's going on— like noticing different things sexually and questioning about times of calling. Even though there's no guarantee of success (as illustrated by the denials described above when questioned about an affair), it's usually better to speak up about suspicions than to just play detective. And the more straightforward and clear a person can be in asking questions (whatever they may be), the better chance of getting some answers—or at least of verifying in their own mind that the other person is, in fact, lying. We can never control another person, but being clearer about the situation (at least within ourselves) allows us to make decisions as to how to proceed, with or without their cooperation.

* * * * * * * * * * * *

So jealous I can't breath

Dear Peggy,

Brief history: female, married 13 years, two kids and a lots of moves. Most years have been happy, have had some bumps in the road. but this time my heart is breaking and I feel like I'm on a train with no brakes. Problem: there is a girl my husband works with that has made me so jealous I can't breath. She calls all the time. If I answer the phone, she hangs up; same with the kids. If my husband answers the phone, he goes into the other room and whispers, and he locked out the Email—which I know they share letters. He says that she just needs a friend and he would like to be it because I don't always understand. What should I do? I love this guy so much that it hurts. This is the first time in two years that we see each other every day. I want to make this work. Do we need counseling? Please help me.

75

Dear Reader,

Jealousy/anxiety/concern (whatever you want to call it) is a perfectly reasonable emotion when confronted with a situation like the one described above. All the signals are there—not of an affair per se, but of *trouble*. (Anything that creates this kind of anxiety and distance between a couple is a cause for concern, despite the particular basis for it.)

Regardless of anyone's motives or intentions, it's fairly inevitable that there will be problems for the marriage whenever a person's relationship with someone of the opposite sex includes secret sharing. This is especially true if they believe their spouse "doesn't always understand"—which is one of the oldest rationalizations in the world for developing this kind of friendship outside the marriage. It's often only a matter of time until it becomes more than just friends.

So the sooner something is done to address this issue, the better. Of course, it means both people in the marriage wanting and being willing to do something to address it. It's not enough for only one person to "want to make it work;" both people need to be involved in working through this. Often, if a couple can not/will not do it on their own, it will be helpful to go to counseling or to seek some kind of professional help.

But no one else can really help unless both people accept that they need it and make the effort to get it. So the first step is breaking through a spouse's resistance to acknowledging that this is a serious problem that actually *needs* help—and realizing that avoiding facing it now means facing an even worse problem in the future.

* * * * * * * * * * * *

They were found naked

Dear Peggy,

I found my wife with a man about a year ago. She still claims nothing ever happened between them. He and I talked and he has admitted that they slept together numerous times. But I still wonder if she is telling the truth or he. They were found naked in his bed.

She tells me if we were to get back together it would never happen again. Is that an admission of guilt? Who should I believe and does she rate a second chance?

Dear Reader,

There's an old saying that "I'll believe it when I see it." The above description, however, illustrates that this saying is *not* necessarily true. The more accurate description is "I'll see it when I believe it." When we don't *want* to believe something, we use all kinds of mental gymnastics to deny reality.

While I can't possibly know for sure in the above case, any reasonable person would assume that the wife is not telling the truth. However, it's important for each person to deal with "the truth" in their own time; they should not be *forced* to face reality until they are prepared to deal with it.

As for the denial by the person having an affair—as I've said many times, the almost universal tendency is for people to deny it. There's an almost knee-jerk reaction to being questioned (or caught). And once the denial has happened, it's even more difficult to admit that they lied.

As for whether someone rates a second chance—that determination is best made based on their behavior *after* the facts are known. Just the fact that someone had an affair is not, in and of itself, an indicator of not rating a second chance. But failing to take responsibility for their actions (by failing to talk honestly about what happened and work to restore trust) makes a second chance less reasonable.

However, in every instance, the choice about any of these factors is totally up to the person involved—since they are the ones who have to live with the consequences of their decision. I can not provide prescriptions for any specific individual; I can only provide perspective aimed at helping them make their own determination, based on their own personal needs, wants, and priorities.

6: Confronting an Affair

Need Advice in Confronting Wife

Dear Peggy,
Found out recently that my wife had an affair, lasted 1-1/2 years. Met with the guy in my own home, after I left for work at 9:30 p.m. Ended when he moved out of state.

Would love to get into personal counseling to help sort this out before I tell her I know, but health insurance on new job is 3-4 weeks away. Want to confront the issue with her, but then again, not sure I'm ready yet. Not sure what to do, how to handle it. Want to get counseling for myself ASAP, then marriage counseling. Your advice????

Dear Reader,
First, I'd like to say that I receive a lot of letters from men whose wives had affairs. Many people do not realize how prevalent this is—or how many men try to work through it to stay in the marriage. In fact, during the past decade, a little more than a third of the people who have contacted me have been men whose wives had affairs.

As for this particular issue of how to know when you're "ready" to confront this issue (whether men or women doing the confronting), here are some general considerations. (Only when you can honestly answer "Yes" to both these questions are you prepared to confront your spouse.)

1. Do you really want to know?
   A person needs to be sure they really want to know before asking if their partner is having an affair. One of the biggest drawbacks to being ready to confront the suspicions is feeling unprepared to face it if the suspicions turn out to be true.
2. Do you feel open to either staying or leaving?
   An important consideration as to whether or not a person is ready to confront their suspicions is their willingness to remain open to either staying in the relationship or leaving it. If their decision is predetermined (whether the decision is to stay or to leave), then they're not fully prepared to deal with knowing about their partner's affair.

Once a person decides they're ready to confront, the next issue is how to do it. There is no way to guarantee the reaction to a confrontation, but there are some ways to improve the chances that it will lead to resolving the suspicions about an affair.

First, asking a partner if they're having an affair is a question that should not be blurted out without proper preparation. If the question comes as a complete surprise, it may prompt a knee-jerk denial.

Next, it's important to choose a time and a place where there will be no intrusions or distractions. It's also essential to establish real contact with the person; look them in the eye and tell them that you want an honest answer to the question you're about to ask. Make it clear that you do *not* want any false reassurance, that you only want the *truth*.

* * * * * * * * * * * * *

Getting the Truth about an Affair

Dear Peggy,

What would you think to be the best way to have my wife admit to an affair. In the face of much circumstantial evidence, she won't admit to anything. I would consider remaining in the marriage if I had the truth. Our counselor thinks she has had an affair (as do I), but nothing I've promised or threatened has done anything.

Dear Reader,

First of all, as I've mentioned before, it's absolutely essential that a person who is asking about a partner's affair is clear that they really *want* the truth. Tentative questions will inevitably produce denial. People involved in affairs are already convinced that it's too dangerous to admit an affair, so they must be absolutely clear about their partner's genuine desire to know the truth—no matter what it is. Therefore, in order to have the best hope of getting an honest answer, it's essential to be absolutely direct.

It's important to establish real contact with the person; look them in the eye and say something like this: "I need an honest answer to the question I'm about to ask you. I hope the answer is 'no,' but I need to know the truth. If the answer is 'yes,' that's not necessarily the end of the relationship. But if it's 'no' (and I find out later you were lying), I'm not sure we would be able to overcome that."

Of course, even making this kind of direct effort doesn't guarantee success in getting an honest answer; some people are accomplished liars and this won't have as much impact on them. It can be extremely frustrating to finally ask directly, and still feel the truth didn't come out. It's at this point that people come to the conclusion that the relationship is probably doomed, no matter what.

(I found it interesting that I had described the above confrontation scenario in my book, "The Monogamy Myth," originally published in 1989, long before the release of the movie, "Sex, Lies, and Videotape." However, there was a scene in that movie where the wife confronted her husband in almost the precise way I had described—and he still denied it. In the movie, they eventually divorced when she finally discovered the truth and verified that he had lied even when she had clearly stated that this was *the* critical variable in their chances of working through it. No two situations are exactly alike, but this fits with what I've seen happen during many years of working with this issue.)

80

Confronting an Affair

* * * * * * * * * * * *

Why is he angry and mean?
(Here are 2 letters before my response.)

Dear Peggy, (letter #1)

My husband of seven years left me and my two children and then I found out about her. He told me he wasn't in love with me anymore and he loves her. The affair lasted a year; I never knew. He says he wants a divorce and moved in with her two weeks after leaving. He is so cruel and mean to me verbally; he says horrible things to me. He never treated me in this manner before. I'm on the ground emotionally and he's kicking me. Why does he feel the need to be so nasty and mean to me? Saying things like "I don't like anything about you," "you're not my wife," "you were a controlling bitch." I told him I loved him still and he said it didn't matter. I'm devastated.

Dear Peggy, (letter #2)

My husband of nineteen years had an affair with a seventeen-year-old girl. This young girl was in my home many times as she was friends of the family. My problem lies here. Though he denies this, my heart tells me different. I am confused whether to stay in this marriage due to small children and my commitment to being a stay-at-home mother. However his constant lying and inability to tell me the truth about whether he had intercourse with this girl has consumed my ability to love him as my spouse. Furthermore, when I try to discuss this situation with him, he gets angry and criticizes me for continuing to question him. I believe it's because he really did have intercourse with her. I'm so confused!

Dear Reader,

Being irritable and criticizing everything about you or your effort to talk about this situation is usually a pretty good indication that you've hit a nerve. And when the denial includes an attack on the person asking the questions, it's more likely that the questions are on target.

A person who doesn't want to face the reality of what they've done is more likely to react defensively and even make accusations in return. It's part of a general tactic: "the best defense is a good offense." But the attacks really have very little to do with you as a person. This kind of overreaction is usually caused by their lack of confidence in their own integrity—and any criticism is just an effort to deflect attention from themselves.

When someone feels perfectly OK about who they are and what they've done, they don't feel the need to be angry or critical. In fact, when they aren't trying to hide something (sometimes even from themselves), they are more likely to respond in a calm (perhaps even comforting and reassuring) way. So, while there are exceptions, the intensity of the reaction often corresponds to the validity of the questions.

* * * * * * * * * * * *

I haven't confronted her...

Dear Peggy,

I found out two weeks ago that my wife was having an affair. While doing our taxes on the laptop at home I found some letters, and proceeded to read them. The letters were very erotic with references about their previous encounters over the last 8 months. I was devastated. We have been together 10 years and have been married for 5-1/2 years. Last summer she started going out with her girlfriends on the weekends and staying at their house overnight. I objected to this activity due to its single-life implications, but she literally reverted to a teenage rebellion, and told me she was going to do what she wanted regardless. It's of interest to note that she left home when she was 16 or 17 because her parents didn't want her dating this particular boy. Now I am wondering if this is in her character, rebellion without regard for those close to her.

I haven't yet confronted her with the letters or about my knowledge of the affair. I know that they at least still communicate because of the jokes she forwards to my office computer. (Some of them are sent to her from him and she forwards them to me, and I see his name.) I thought waiting awhile would be better to let her know of my discovery, that way I wouldn't be reacting with emotion, I would be responding with logic.

I haven't been sleeping well, working out, or caring about much since I found out. I haven't treated her any different either, so as not to give her any indication that I know about the affair. Oh, last but not least, if I am lucky she will give in to my requests for sex maybe once every 4 to 7 weeks, and then she wants a "quickie."

I know you have probably heard this story a million times before, but this is the first time for me, and it really hurts because I married my wife because I love her and am very much in love with her. Thanks for the ear.

Dear Reader,

This is a lonely, frightening situation to be in. I know the feeling of being afraid to confront, waiting for the right time, etc., and wondering "why." Instead of trying to analyze character problems (like rebellion, etc.) to explain affairs, I think the better effort is to determine when and how to confront the situation.

Each person needs to decide for themselves when they're ready to confront. I've already written about the need to be ready to face the truth (whatever it may be) and the need to be prepared to either stay in the marriage or leave.

One factor that also needs to be considered is the impact of continuing involvement, since any relationship that is ongoing tends to gradually escalate in intensity. As for hoping that waiting would allow for a more rational instead of emotional reaction, that too is very individual. But if the outside involvement escalates, the emotional reaction is likely to become greater, not less.

Sometimes, there's an understandable "approach-avoidance" in confronting a situation like this—which creates a certain limbo. The key is to determine at what point this limbo situation becomes the status quo. One toll of being in this kind of limbo is the sheer physical drain—like not sleeping well. Anyone who has been through this situation recognizes that there is a strong physical component (as well as the emotional one) which also needs to be considered. Of course, even confronting the situation does not immediately reduce any of these physical or emotional reactions; in fact, it may temporarily *increase* them.

So this calls for considering everything: the physical toll, any problems with the sexual relationship, the impact on the outside relationship by virtue of waiting... In the final analysis, this is a difficult balancing act that each person must do for themselves.

* * * * * * * * * * * * *

Dilemma

Dear Peggy,

My wife recently told me she was having an affair. When she told me, I was on the east coast and she was in California. I cannot believe she would tell me something that serious on the phone. When I came back home her gentleman friend was there, at my home among my things. I cannot believe how inconsiderate my wife has been. Why do you think she handled it the way she did? Thanks for your thoughts.

Dear Reader,

This is like a lot of the letters I receive in that the writer already knows the answer to the question being asked. In this case he has already clearly described "why...she handled it the way she did:" because she's "inconsiderate." A person who would tell something this serious on the phone (and then have the other man at the home when her husband returned) is obviously inconsiderate, to say the least.

Naturally, there may be other reasons as well, but it probably doesn't warrant his trying to figure it out. Any effort to try to understand this kind of behavior is almost as inappropriately *considerate* as her behavior was inappropriately *inconsiderate*. (In fact, another indication of his tendency to be nice about all this is reflected in the language used in referring to the other man as a "gentleman.") While this may just be a figure of speech, it's not an accurate description in light of the circumstances.

Unfortunately, some people take advantage of a person who is extremely nice. So while a nice person deserves to be treated with more consideration, that may not happen unless and until they are somewhat more insistent on being treated with the respect they deserve.

In any event, it would seem that a more critical question in a situation like this is "why she had the affair in the first place" instead of "why she handled it the way she did." So a person in this situation might more effectively use their energy by focusing on how to deal with the situation rather than analyzing the way they learned of it.

* * * * * * * * * * * * *

Finally told the truth

Dear Peggy,

I had suspected and confronted my husband at the time, but he always lied, he did this for 10 years! I was pregnant at the time with my third child. He had been going out drinking, and this woman from work would go to the bar and park right beside his car, go in and buy drinks for him and his buddies, then she would go out to her car and wait till he came out, then she would call him over to her car and give him oral sex. This happened 3 times, he says. Then he said it was over.

This is something that happened almost 10 years ago, but I finally got the truth about a month ago and I'm not dealing with it very well. I have never done or ever would do something like this to him, and I just don't understand. He says it was not an affair and that it meant nothing, that it probably happened because he was drunk. We would have these all-night marathons, where I would confront him and he would always lie, for 10 years! I think he finally told me the truth because I would never let it go, and it was getting to the point where it was and had been damaging to our marriage. It was amazing though how he would say things like, I'll take a lie detector test, I never had intercourse. To me the oral sex was just as bad, and how do I know for sure there was no intercourse? It's soo hard to believe that I even have the entire truth, though I want to believe I do. I made him tell ALL the details and questioned him like an attorney.

He has been a good husband and father for the last 10 years. I'm at the point of not knowing what to do. I always said I would leave if I ever found out such a thing. I'm very confused. He keeps being soo nice and trying to help me, but I don't know if I'll ever be happy with him if I stay, and then I'm considering our children. They don't know; it would kill them if they did. They love their father and have always been close to him.

I was soo hurt, about a week after I learned the truth, I found out her phone number and called her husband and told him. What a monster this made me, to hurt someone else that way. But all I could think about at the time was hurting HER, not thinking about him. They called my husband at work and she lied like crazy on the phone, never letting my husband answer. Her husband got soo frustrated, he threw the phone and called them both Liars. I have never done anything that bad in my life and now I feel soo sorry for telling him.

Dear Reader,

This letter presents a vivid picture of the lasting impact of secrecy and deception. Doubts and suspicions don't just go away with time. They may go underground for awhile, but they're sure to come up again. The denial of an affair (hoping it will finally go away) is quite common—as is splitting hairs by saying oral sex is not really an affair. Naturally, it makes no sense to draw this kind of distinction, but it's a very common kind of thinking used by people to somehow justify or explain away their behavior.

It's quite common for people to proclaim (in advance) that they would "leave if they ever found out..." about a partner's affair. But, of course, nobody actually knows what they'll do unless they are faced with this situation. And one month is an extremely short period of time within which to try to deal with the emotions. No long-term decision about the future can reasonably be made while still trying to integrate the new knowledge about the reality of the situation (regardless of how long it may have been suspected). It takes time and patience (and lots of talking through the situation) in order to go on. Any decision needs to be based on the prospects for the future of the relationship, not on the actions in the past.

Another indication of how emotions can lead people to do things they regret is reflected in the feelings described above about hurting the other woman's husband by telling him about the relationship. It's understandable to want to lash out, but it usually means not only hurting someone else, but actually feeling worse instead of better—because of the realization that you have done this.

At this point, there's an opportunity for both people in the marriage to use the learnings from their mistakes in dealing with this crisis to build a stronger relationship based on a commitment to honesty in the future. Nothing can change the past, but learning from the past can change the future.

7: Coping with the Pain

Marriage on the Rocks

Dear Peggy,

Seventeen years of unconditional trust has been shattered by an affair that my wife has had. It started in chat rooms and turned into the real deal. I love her a great deal; and forgave her and we tried to work though this problem together for the last two months. The problem is this: I captured their letters and read things about the way she felt about this man at the time, that I should have never known. I just couldn't get those things out of my head. It was driving me crazy, and worse, her as well. I worried myself to death about what she was doing while she was out of sight. I truly want to trust her, but just don't know how to stop thinking about the way she said she felt for this man, even though it is over and she says she made a mistake.

She left a month ago, and I am now dealing with a great deal of depression and stress. I would like to seek out counsel, but really don't know where to start. It takes all my resources to survive and I don't have the money to get the help I need. I do have insurance, but at the moment I can't even afford the deductible. I have lost 45 pounds all at once, I can't sleep at night, I can't eat....and I can't concentrate on my job. I am reaching out for help but I just don't know where to turn...

Dear Reader,

This letter clearly demonstrates an important impact of affairs that is often overlooked: that the initial reaction when people first face the reality that their partner has had an affair is likely to be a physical one. They tend to feel disoriented, lightheaded, and weak in the stomach. Anyone who hasn't "been there" can't appreciate the overwhelming physical effects of this knowledge. Most people (including myself) describe feelings of a pit in the stomach, a shortness of breath, a metallic taste in the mouth, a hot feeling behind the ears, weakness and fatigue, an inability to sleep, and a significant weight loss. The first order of business after learning of a partner's affair is simple physical survival. The immediate challenge for most people is simply getting through each day. In many instances, people feel so weak and depressed that they find it difficult to function. Unfortunately, this happens just as they need a great deal of energy to cope with the issues they face.

They can't begin to recover until they get enough physical strength and vitality to sustain them through this period of emotional devastation. Most people fail to appreciate the importance of taking care of the basics: exercise, nutrition, and relaxation. Exercise is one of the best sources of energy—and one of the more effective ways to deal with overwhelming emotions. Nutrition is another basic problem for people who are dealing with the stress of an affair. While it may be inevitable that there will be some problems with eating, a person needs to be conscious of the importance of nutrition in order to have the energy they need to simply get through the day, and hopefully avoid getting sick. Relaxation is another important factor in dealing with the stress of this situation by finding some natural ways of relieving their tension, such as meditation, relaxation tapes, religious services, or simple things like watching sunsets or water scenes if that's available. So the first order of business is to take care of yourself physically—which will then allow you to better deal with the emotional and practical issues involved.

* * * * * * * * * * * * *

Devastated by wife's affair

Dear Peggy,

I am devastated by my wife's affair that happened some years ago, but I can not get it out of my mind. It is painful to this day. Is there a way to get it out of my mind?

Dear Reader,

Devastated is the single most common word people use to describe their feelings about a partner's affair. The idea that the feelings of devastation can last for *years* seems unbelievable to someone who hasn't faced this situation. However, it's been my observation through the years that people usually can't get it out of their minds unless they feel the issue has been fully dealt with. That means that they have gotten some understandings that help them make sense of what has happened.

It usually begins with wanting/needing answers to some of their questions about what happened. Even if the answers aren't satisfactory (or the facts are very painful), almost nothing seems to be as difficult to deal with as "Not Knowing!" In the absence of knowing, most people can't get it out of their mind—which is understandable because their mind is trying to fill in the blanks about all the questions and uncertainties as to what happened/why/what can be done about it, etc.

The man who wrote this letter doesn't say whether or not he and his wife are still together. While it's easy for most people to understand how hard it might be to get it out of your mind if you're still with the other person, many people who have been divorced for many years still have trouble dealing with it. Overcoming the pain has more to do with whether you're able to get more understanding and perspective about affairs in general (and hopefully about your own experience in particular). Without getting the kind of information that helps make sense of something that seems crazy, the pain just continues and the thoughts continue to run around in your head.

So it's important to realize that there's no length of time by which it will spontaneously cease to be a problem. No matter how long it has been, it's still important to read and talk and use as much rational effort as possible to offset the mental and emotional turmoil that doesn't simply go away on its own.

* * * * * * * * * * * * *

Shock and Devastation

Dear Peggy,

I've recently discovered that my husband of 5 years had two affairs (the first during our first year of marriage and the second right after the birth of our second child—at the end of our fourth year of marriage). We have been together for 12 years total and I thought we had a great, honest relationship. All of my friends were jealous of our great relationship. The discovery devastated and shocked me. I'm ashamed to tell my family. The first was with a coworker and the second was an online affair. I love him soo much, but cannot see myself getting over the devastation. I don't believe in staying in a marriage because of children. I think that the right thing to do is to divorce him, but I love him soo much that it hurts... My life is shattered, all of my dreams destroyed. How do I overcome the sense of devastation, betrayal, shame and hurt???

Dear Reader,

This particular letter exemplifies the feelings and dilemmas facing a person who finds out about a partner's affair. First of all, during the early stages of being faced with these feelings of shock and devastation, most people are not prepared to make a clear decision as to whether to stay married or get a divorce. Since the strong emotions can block the ability to see *any* hope for the future (no matter what a person decides to do)—they need to spend some time getting more information and understanding before trying to make a decision.

This process needs to begin with understanding that affairs are not *just* a sign of personal failure (either of the individuals or of the relationship). This involves understanding that we hold many false beliefs and assumptions about affairs—what I've come to call the "monogamy myth." The monogamy myth is the belief that monogamy is the norm in our society, that it is supported by society as a whole, and that you can *assume* monogamy without having to discuss it. The reason it's important to get this understanding is that the effect of believing that *most* marriages are monogamous is that if an affair happens, it's seen *strictly* as a personal failure—leading to personal blame, personal shame, wounded pride, and almost universal feelings of devastation.

Once there's been an affair, things are never the same—but that doesn't mean they have to be worse. This crisis can be used to establish a different kind of relationship based on ongoing honest communication. It takes a lot of time and effort on the part of both people to rebuild the marriage and establish trust—but it *can* be done.

* * * * * * * * * * * * *

My Husband and my Friend
(Here are 2 letters before my response.)

Dear Peggy, (letter #1)

I have just found out, by reading my husband's (of 30 years) Email, that he had a one-time intimate meeting with my best friend. Through the Email (and confronting both my best friend and my soul-mate), I have found out that my husband wanted the relationship to continue, but my friend was afraid to hurt me... Needless to say, they never wanted me to find out, and their hopes to not hurt me didn't work. I am devastated, scared, confused, and oh, so lonely.

I not only feel betrayed by my husband, but even more so by my friend. She knew me better than anyone, and we had often spoken of infidelity, me saying that I could never find it in my heart to forgive and therefore my marriage would be over...never once thinking it could happen to me. In addition to being my best friend, we also worked together in the same office for the past 20 years. Our lives are intertwined, with company friends, parties, lunches, get-togethers, as well as she being an important part of my family life. All my family, my children, and my friends out of work include her as a member of my family— and will therefore wonder where she is now. I have been able to maintain a 'working' relationship at work, and we talk about "the weather," but I feel so gypped out of everything.

As I told her, if my marriage is over, I'll never be able to forgive her, and if it's not, I can't imagine keeping her in my life as a personal friend. But I do miss that relationship so much. My husband and I have decided to try to work things out. He tells me he loves me and due to personal health-related problems, he erred in judgement...is heartily sorry, takes full responsibility and blame, and begs me to forgive him because he can't live without me. I want to believe him, because, as stupid as it sounds, I so truly do love him. I am praying every day for forgiveness for both of them, but the pain keeps surfacing...it's so unbearable at times. I try to keep on a happy face, because I'm tired of hearing that "I'm sorry"...then I have to respond and say, I know you're sorry...it just hurts. So I cry in solitude. I don't know what to do, I'm already tired of the whole situation, and I've only known about it for 3 weeks (it happened 3 months ago). They both swore it was one time, and I do believe that, but indications are that my husband wanted more...that hurts tremendously. I need direction. Please help.

Dear Peggy, (letter #2)

I found out three days ago that my wife of 3-1/2 years had an affair with a former coworker, who was a "friend" with whom we socialized often. I'm sure my reaction to the news was typical, but my wife wasn't completely honest. I only found out because I overheard her on the telephone with him. When I confronted her, she admitted only to some "heavy petting." Later in the day, as we discussed it, I had to drag out of her the fact that she actually slept with him.

Then, yesterday, sensing she still had more to tell, I finally got out of her that she had slept with him on three occasions over a three week period.

She keeps telling me how sorry she is, and that she feels horribly guilty about it. I want to believe her because I know I still love her. Although it has been only three days, I know I can forgive her for her indiscretion, but I'm having a very difficult time reconciling her claims of repentance with the fact that she may never have told me the full truth if I hadn't forced it out of her. It almost seems like she's more sorry she got caught than sorry for what she did. If it had been a one-time thing, I might be more inclined to understand how guilty she feels. But, she went back three times over an extended period of time. If she really knew what she was doing was wrong, why did she keep going back?

It's obvious to me that something was not right with our marriage. I look back now and I see instances where I wasn't there for her when she needed me. I can see that I pushed her away sometimes, and I know I have to take some responsibility for putting her in the position where she could make this mistake.

Since I found out, I've been an emotional mess. I alternate between anger, frustration, fear, guilt, jealousy, hatred, love, compassion, disgust, and every other emotion on the spectrum. While I know this is natural, and that I will probably feel this way for awhile, I don't want to keep feeling this way. I want to stay with my wife and make our marriage stronger than ever. But this emotional roller coaster is eating me up. What can I do to lessen the pain or to get myself to concentrate on the good that will come out of this? I want to be positive, constructive and fair to my wife. I want us to be the happy couple we were on our wedding day. We will be seeing a marriage counselor shortly, but the pain these last two days has been unbearable. What can I do?

Dear Reader,

The raw pain and suffering from the initial impact of learning of a partner's affair is clearly evidenced in these two letters. In the first letter, it has been 3 weeks since learning of the affair—and in the second letter, it has been only 3 days. During the period immediately following the discovery of a partner's affair, the biggest challenge is simply dealing with the emotional shock and the physical impact.

The desire to figure things out and decide what to do (both about the marriage and about the friendship) may *seem* like burning issues that require immediate resolution (or at least immediate attention)—but it takes *time* to be *able* to think clearly enough to make any critical decisions or take any definitive action. Realistically, no one is in any shape to deal with the affair until the emotions subside enough to *begin* to be able to think clearly about all this.

So the best way to ensure being able to handle all these important decisions in an effective way is to *first* focus on attending to the physical and emotional toll taken by learning this information. Only after there has been enough time to somewhat assimilate the shock of this new information is it possible to make the kinds of decisions discussed in the above letters.

Naturally, it's hard to be patient at a time like this. Since the situation is so painful, there's a desire to do something (anything) to try to alleviate the pain. But doing the *wrong* thing (which is very likely when under such stress) can wind up making matters even worse.

* * * * * * * * * * * *

Husband's affairs

Dear Peggy,

I found out three months ago that my husband has been having an affair for over a year with someone in another city. We went to counseling to try to work things out, but the bottom line was that he wants out of our marriage to pursue this other relationship. We have been separated for over a month now, but he has made no attempts to file for divorce. When I ask him what he wants to do, reconcile or file, he responds that I should file. By the way, there is a small child to consider. I have recently found out that this other women has broken off the relationship because she found out about several online affairs and at least one local affair that he is also engaging in. He has promised, for her, to get counseling, because he wants to continue their relationship. I wanted to go back to counseling with him, but he says that only one of us wants to stay married. I have already forgiven him for the initial indiscretion, but the evidence of the others is too much to take. I feel like I have no choice but to file for divorce. This has also been extremely hard on our young child. Not knowing what is going to happen between Mom and Dad has resulted in a lot of acting out, regressing, and aggression. Any light that you can shed on this situation, or any advice that you can give me, would be immensely helpful.

Dear Reader,

Strange but true, men in this position often avoid taking action that clearly gives up either the marriage and family *or* the affair. They seem to want to maintain both options and avoid responsibility for taking action, putting the wife in the position of being the one who actually files for divorce. Sometimes, an ultimatum by either the spouse or the other woman will force them to act. (But ultimatums can be dangerous—because the reaction can never be fully predicted.) Especially when there are concerns about the impact on a child, it's better to take controlled, deliberate actions rather than ones that escalate an already volatile situation.

This letter represents a very thoughtful, rational approach to carefully considering all the factors involved in resolving this situation. This effort deserves ongoing in-person support that goes beyond the scope of this brief response.

So even when both partners don't go to counseling together, counseling might be helpful for one in clarifying and sorting through the options and potential impact. (Naturally, the choice of counselor is extremely important so as to avoid wasting time with a long-term approach that delves into childhood issues or general problems in the marriage.) However, professional guidance in considering all aspects of the situation, especially as it relates to a child, might allow for a problem-solving approach that could provide the kind of clarity needed to make the best decision in light of all the circumstances.

* * * * * * * * * * * * *

Mid-life crisis and extramarital affairs

Dear Peggy,

My husband has had (is having) an affair which he says is emotional, almost obsessive. He claims that they have never had sex, but he can't tell me that he doesn't love her. He says that he's not sure what the feelings he has for her are, but that he knows that he can't put them away without trying to understand them.

In looking back over the past several months there were certainly hints in his conversations that something was going on, but I was saved having to guess when the woman's husband sent me and my oldest son letters indicating that something was going on, including asking that great question, "Is it really over between you two or was he lying to all." Needless to say I was stunned, devastated and heartbroken. My husband said at that time he was willing to give her up because he wasn't prepared to put his family at risk, and although he would miss her friendship the family was most important. That was 4 months ago; now I'm hearing that he never agreed to stop seeing her or talking to her. I also get the feeling that the most important thing to him any more is himself and how happy he is. He feels that he only has 20 years left (he just turned 45) and he wants to know when there will be time for him. Seems to me he's certainly taking really good care of himself, to the exclusion of everything else. By the way we've been married 21 years and have 3 kids.

Is there any hope in situations like this? There seem to be so many problems: his involvement with her, his chasing the happy wagon and then trying to repair our relationship, that I am simply overwhelmed. He refuses to go to counseling. He says he needs to concentrate on the positives in our relationship and I feel like I'm living a lie. I feel so empty inside that it's difficult to describe.

How do you go on when your partner tells you he knows you have issues of infidelity and betrayal but they aren't his issues. How do you get on the same page to repair the relationship? I guess the real question is, do you think he wants to fix it? I really don't know anymore. I am very confused.

How do you go on when trust is destroyed and you can't even come to an understanding of what the problems are that are facing your relationship? Am I just kidding myself?

Dear Reader,

It's clear that this letter-writer doesn't understand her husband's behavior, but there's plenty of evidence that he doesn't understand it himself. For instance, the statement that "the family was most important" doesn't fit with saying he "can't put away [his feelings for her] without trying to understand them." When

93

people are confused in this way, they tend to rationalize that there's some legitimate excuse for what they want to do—like understanding their feelings for someone else.

However, statements like this are common among people who want it all—and who are willing to rationalize that somehow it should be possible. It's similar to the way a child might hope that somehow they won't have to deal with the natural consequences of their behavior. They hope others will accommodate in ways that will let them do whatever they want without consequences. Unfortunately, this is not possible (even if others *want* to do this kind of accommodating)—because there are natural consequences to the choices we make.

Denying responsibility for any of the issues that are created in this situation is an effort to shift the blame for the consequences to someone else. This denial of responsibility is evident in the comments that "he needs to concentrate on the positives in our relationship" while the "issues of infidelity and betrayal aren't his issues." This kind of attitude turns things upside down in an effort to make any problems someone else's fault.

Despite all this confusion and manipulation, it can be helpful to recognize that this attitude is a result of some feelings (pain/fear/unhappiness/lack of fulfillment, sense of mortality/etc.) that warrant compassion and understanding. However, recognizing the basis for the difficulty doesn't mean trying to rescue him or protect him from facing the consequences. We know that in general whenever anyone helps a person avoid the natural consequences of their actions, they're not likely to change. We also know that we cannot *force* someone else to change.

Finally, we know that gaining insight doesn't automatically change anything. So all this effort to better understand the situation doesn't resolve anything. It just provides a better basis from which to consider what actions to take. But since the final point in the letter expressed a desire to "come to an understanding of what the problems are that are facing the relationship," I hope these comments can help toward that effort. In this situation, as in all individual situations, only the particular person who is dealing with it can decide what to do. This is appropriate because they are the ones who will have to live with the consequences of whatever actions they take.

* * * * * * * * * * * *

Roller-coaster Ride

Dear Peggy,

After 10 months of riding the roller-coaster from hell...up, down, nauseating curves, jumping the tracks (I just knew I was going to die)...it seems the train is about to dock at last!! I can't say the marriage itself was really the problem...it was our lifestyle that caused the problem within the marriage. Everybody going different directions all the time, etc. Since my husband's affair we have greatly changed our lifestyle. I feel absolutely wonderful, both physically and mentally.

Coping with the Pain

I have more energy than I can remember having in a long time, and am completely mentally alert. I now have both the time and ambition to do the things that I enjoy personally, and we both have time to do the things we enjoy together. The problem??? Now that I finally feel as though I have a life once again that does not always include being a wife, mother, or employee....it seems as though the marriage itself in no longer strong.

We have worked through this crisis together, but now it feels as though I am sharing my life with my best friend as opposed to my husband. I went out with the girls the other night and I noticed afterward that I had not really thought about him while I was away, did not really miss him, was not really anxious to get home. In the past, it would have been quite the opposite. I don't know if that can be attributed to the fact that before we seldom had time together and I did miss him often... Now that we see each other so much, I suppose that it could just be normal not to feel the loss of his presence when we are not together. In any sense, it frightens me sometimes because I am not sure how strong my feelings are for him any more. Sometimes I really believe that if it weren't for the entire family unit...(home, kids, etc.) that at this point I could easily walk away from the marriage and not miss it that much. Just curious about your thoughts on this.

Dear Reader,

This letter raises a concern that many women experience when the nature of our relationship with our husband undergoes a significant change—whether or not the change is related to affairs. I've conducted life-planning workshops for many years and have seen how lifestyle changes can challenge our views of love and of what makes for a strong marriage. I also personally identify with the experience of going from being focused (obsessed?) with my roles (as wife, mother, worker, etc.,) to feeling the freedom that comes from finding the person behind the roles. This feeling is so unfamiliar for most of us as women that we assume something is wrong when we don't miss our husbands. (Ironically, one of the by-products of an affair is that it brings this issue out in the open where it can be dealt with in such a way as to relieve the earlier fears about affairs that may have caused us to feel somewhat insecure or anxious about being away from our husbands.)

When a marriage shifts to a deeper relationship (based on *really* knowing each other and becoming best friends), we tend to think that something is lost. In fact, it's just the normal change from one stage of love to another. Some couples never successfully make this transition; but ironically, it can happen when a couple put in the time and effort to work together to deal with a crisis like an affair. If you make it through to the other side, you can finally relax with each other in a way that you couldn't do before.

For instance, I now absolutely love time alone. And even when I spent an extended time away from my husband to attend to a family illness in another state, I never really missed him. When I commented on this to a friend whose

95

own husband died several years ago, she gently reminded me that my enjoyment of time without my husband is based on knowing that it's not full-time and forever—knowing I can still be with him whenever I want. So it may be that feeling more comfortable (and less in need of constantly being together) is indicative of a more mature, lasting love. Since this is an unfamiliar feeling, we think something is wrong—when, in fact, it *may* be a very positive sign.

* * * * * * * * * * * *

Will I Overcome The Pain?

Dear Peggy,

I am thirty-three years old and have been married thirteen years. We have two wonderful children. Sounds like the all-American family, huh? Well, my husband has told me that since the first few years of our marriage he has been unfaithful to me! Before this whole thing came out in the open, no one would have suspected that he would be anything less than perfect. He is a very hard worker, fairly successful in his work, and a very good father. I always felt confident that he cared for me very deeply and that he would never do anything to jeopardize our relationship. When he told me about his relationships with these other women, he says he told me because he loved me and wanted us to have an honest and loving relationship. He wants very much to stay married to me and wants us to "forget the past and go on with our lives." I still love him and want this to work out, but I wonder if it's possible to ever overcome the pain.

Dear Reader,

I understand how it feels to learn that your husband (and your life) are not what they appear to be. After eighteen years of marriage (to my childhood sweetheart), my husband told me he'd had affairs for the previous seven years. So I know the struggle to overcome the pain, and I want to encourage others to believe that the day can come when they won't hurt as they hurt in the beginning. It seems hard to believe, but it is possible.

However, it doesn't happen by trying to "forget the past and go on with our lives." It requires getting more understanding and perspective—both about your own situation and about affairs in general. Without this kind of effort, the painful emotions may never go away, whether or not people stay married. But when both parties are committed to putting in the time and effort required to deal with this experience in a constructive way, it is possible to finally overcome the pain—and even to build a stronger relationship than before. While I would never have voluntarily chosen to go through this crisis in order to develop a better relationship, perhaps it helps to know that this result is possible.

* * * * * * * * * * * *

The Hurt

Dear Peggy,

I am sure that you have heard this a thousand times...but how do I live with the pain of my husband's affair??!!! We are both 31...been married for 11 years and for the past 3 years he has had an affair with someone he met through the computer! Naturally, once I found all the proof I needed, I kicked him out and filed for divorce! Now he is back and doing everything in his power to earn my trust back!

My problem is working through the pain and anger!! We have gone to counseling and our counselor said that we are in a good place and that we are handling the entire situation better than most couples would be able too. I just cannot seem to let go of the hurt and anger! I have no doubt that my husband is sorry and truly believes that he would never do such a thing again. I just don't know how to let go or if I even should let go. I think that the fear of being hurt again is overwhelming me and that if I stay distanced from him that it is my form of protection. Any comments or feedback??

Dear Reader,

The situation described in this letter is representative of many people in this position. We often make a rational decision (to stay together and try to work this out) while we continue to have an emotional struggle. That's because there's usually a gap between our intellectual understanding of a situation and our ability to deal with it emotionally. The insight shown in the statements about "the fear of being hurt" and staying distanced being "a form of protection" reflect this gap in coming to terms with the emotional impact of this experience. Again, this is perfectly understandable.

While deciding to let go of the hurt and anger is a good first step (and probably what the counselor means by handling the situation better than most), it's clear that emotionally letting go of the pain takes a lot longer. It will gradually disappear as trust is built, and that takes time—and work. Continuing the process of establishing trust through ongoing honest communication can eventually lead to overcoming the fear of being hurt again—and allow the letting go to happen. It simply can't be forced; it must evolve as a by-product of the time and effort spent dealing with all this in a productive way.

* * * * * * * * * * * * *

When an affair ends

Dear Peggy,
How do you get back to normal after the affair?

Dear Reader,

This is a common desire—for things to get back to *normal*. However, the supposedly normal situation that existed prior to the affair was one in which the affair happened. So it's not really desirable to go back, even if it were possible.

An affair is a significant event that forever changes a relationship, but not necessarily for the worse. It's not the affair (or any other significant life event) that determines the future; it's how we *react* to the event—what we *do* in response to the event.

97

So the question is not how to get back, but how to go forward. And only the people involved can determine that. If the affair creates anger, hurt and resentment that is never dealt with or learned from, it can lead to limited prospects for a good future together. But if it is used as a catalyst to developing ongoing honest communication and a trust that's built on that honesty (rather than on blind faith), then the results will be quite different. It's up to each person (and each couple) to decide which it will be.

* * * * * * * * * * * * *

How long does it take to get over?

Dear Peggy,

It has been two years since my husband had an affair with one of his coworkers. At one time I also considered her to be a friend of mine, and treated her as such, although because of the work relationship, he had contact with her much more often. She continues to live about a mile away from us. They have completely broken off, and both have ill feelings about the other. Luckily, she was laid off, so my husband no longer sees her, except by chance, as I do. It continues to bother me that she has never expressed an iota of remorse to me. She has not even come close to taking responsibility for her actions!

At any rate, after some counseling, we were doing just great; however, it continues to haunt me that it even happened. Is this normal? Will the pain ever go away? I think that it is probably worse, as there are triggers everywhere I turn, forcing me to think of what happened. My husband has made it clear that he will regret this until he dies. He takes responsibility for his actions, although he also realizes that this woman is extremely manipulative. I know that to be true. Of course she owes us money too.

Can you give me, and others, some advice on how to get past this? I am trying to be patient, but I want it to go away soon! Of course there are many, many details to complete this story, but I'm sure that you've heard most of them before. Waiting for your response. Thanks.

Dear Reader,

The questions raised at the close of this letter are *the* most prevalent questions I hear (as the letter-writer recognizes), especially the lament, "I want it to go away soon!" Understandably, neither partner wants to drag this out; they want it to be over *now*! But it just doesn't work that way. It requires committing a lot of time to working through this experience and establishing a new relationship for the future. This can't be done in days, weeks, or months; it usually takes years. But when both parties are committed to putting in the time and effort required to deal with this experience in a constructive way, it is possible to finally overcome the pain. It doesn't happen by trying to "forget the past and go on with our lives."

This letter describes an effort to be patient, which is good, because it does take enormous patience. And being patient during the process of rebuilding the trust can be more tolerable when there's an appreciation of the fact that the effort is not *just* to get over the past but to create a *better* future in the process. I know from my own experience that this can happen. In the meantime, the slowness of the process can be handled easier by accepting that it will be slow, thus avoiding the frustration of having unreasonable expectations about how long it will take to get beyond all this.

* * * * * * * * * * *

Lied to for 7 years

Dear Peggy,

My husband of 18 years, (my high school sweetheart and soul-mate) had an affair. When I found out, I was devastated. I couldn't believe how two people who got along as well as we did could end up in a situation like this. He said it was with someone I didn't know across the city and he called her on the phone in front of me and said to her, "It is over." I never felt like he was sorry for the affair, which he claims was very shallow, and over the next 2 to 3 years he purposely said things to hurt me or make the love that I thought was so real, nonexistent. I never got over his affair, feeling deep hurt and pain each day for over 7 years. Then one night a month ago, I got the truth out of him. The affair was actually with his office girl who he saw each day at the office and he said he was in love with her. Well, he "loved us both—wanted us both." This went on for at least another 2 years or more with him seeing her off and on over those years sexually. He said he couldn't tell me who the person really was because of the working situation... What could he do? Fire her?

I am extremely angry with him and now understand why I never got over this affair even after 7 years. He lied to me about who it was with, the emotional attachment that occurred and how long it carried on—and the fact that he went back to her when he knew I was devastated at home.

I cannot begin to tell you the anger that I feel at this time. I suffered so much during those years, including physical ailments such as chronic headaches. I have had emotional and physical pain resulting from his affair. Oh, by the way, did I mention that he was also with the other woman that he had originally said the affair was with, but he did not love her.

I feel like I am reliving the entire affair again. My husband feels that since it was over 4 years ago, that I should just forget it now. That makes me even angrier. I feel the only way I can deal with this now is to have an affair of my own. Why do I feel this way? What are your feelings about "just forgetting it" since it was over 4 years ago?

Dear Reader,

"Just forgetting it" is the most typical desire of the person who has had an affair. And not being able to just forget it is the inevitable plight of the spouse. Having heard from thousands of people, it seems that just forgetting it isn't realistically possible (even if both people *want* to forget it). Any effort to bury it without thoroughly discussing it simply doesn't work. It doesn't matter how much time passes, it doesn't just go away; it sits there between the two people and creates an emotional barrier that prevents them from being as close as they would like to be. In most cases, an unwillingness to deal with an affair (regardless of when it happens) may leave the marriage intact but it's likely to be a deadened, meaningless connection instead of what most people want out of marriage.

While it may be small comfort to know that this behavior is common, the pattern of telling some lies, some partial truths, some half-truths, etc., is almost universal. Finding out the truth is very much like peeling an onion, with one layer coming off at a time. Unfortunately, there's a failure to recognize that each new revelation leads to repeatedly triggering the raw emotions of pain and devastation. So the longer the process of telling the truth is drawn out (and the more layers are uncovered over time), the longer it takes to begin the healing process.

An affair doesn't necessarily *feel* like it's over until all the truth is out and dealt with. And while feelings of having a "revenge" affair are understandable, it does nothing toward helping to forget. In fact, it's likely to do just the opposite, further delaying any chances of healing. So the best hope for recovery depends on both parties understanding that the standard attitude of "say as little as possible" about the affairs is exactly the opposite of what needs to happen. *Forgetting* is not the critical issue; the goal is to get to the point where remembering no longer triggers such painful emotions. That's what healing is all about—getting enough understanding and perspective so that you can have control of your emotions instead of your emotions having control of you.

* * * * * * * * * * * *

My husband had an affair

Dear Peggy,

It has been 7 months and I am still crying. How can I stop thinking about what he did to me. I still love him very much. I tell him that all the time. He says it's over and it only happened once. But for me, once was too much. I don't want to leave him. I just can't stop thinking about what he did. It was with my "close friend." That hurts even worse.

Dear Reader,

This problem of "thinking about what he did" is quite common. It takes time to get to the point of diminishing those automatic images. This means rebuilding the primary connection and replacing those painful images with some new, more positive ones *together*. This will gradually allow the painful ones to recede into the background.

There's really no way to stop thinking in the sense of preventing the images from coming in the first place. But each time they come, there can be an effort to deliberately move away from dwelling on them (as opposed to the tendency to be obsessed with them). For those who have tried meditation, this process works much the same way as meditation. It's important to be gentle with yourself—accepting that the thoughts will come, but noticing when they do and moving away from them as soon as possible.

* * * * * * * * * * * *

Getting over the anger

Dear Peggy,

It's been a year now since my husband told me about his affair with a woman at work. We have been trying to work it out since. The problem I have is trying to get over the anger that I feel towards him. I love my husband dearly and I know I'm hurting him with my anger. I'm fine for a couple months and then it starts in again. How can I deal with these feelings toward him?

Dear Reader,

Much of the anger comes from feeling, "why did this have to happen to me?" It helps the healing process to actively seek information about affairs. Recovery comes from clear thinking—getting more information, understanding, and perspective about affairs in general. This will help you see your situation in a broader context, which in turn allows you to come to grips with your feelings.

It doesn't work to bury your anger inside and hope it will magically disappear. You need to express your feelings—but that's not the same as "acting them out."

Here's a brief list of some of the keys to dealing with your anger in a productive way:

— Acknowledge your anger in clear terms to your partner. It will only complicate matters to attempt to maintain a brave front.

— Be prepared for your feelings to change rather quickly, both in type and in strength.

— Acknowledge the validity of all your feelings, whether they're turned inward (self-pity, depression) or turned outward (anger, resentment). All your feelings play a part in your efforts to come to grips with this experience.

— Whatever you feel is OK, but remember—you don't have to act on your feelings.

— Resist the urge to lash out and punish your partner. Any satisfaction you might gain will be short-lived.

— Express your feelings in ways that lighten the load of carrying them around—that help you feel better, not worse.

* * * * * * * * * * * *

He won't discuss his affair

Dear Peggy,

I found out 5 years ago that my husband had an 8-month-long affair with an also-married coworker. This was someone whom I had been friendly with. She is an alcoholic, very unattractive and a real mess. I have been extremely angry and hurt and I don't understand at all why anyone, let alone my husband, would have become involved with this woman. He won't discuss this with me. He becomes angry and almost violent at the mention of this affair. He has blamed it on me, saying that if I would have pleased him, this would never have happened. I should also tell you that during this time, he was drinking heavily. I am ill and was on some pretty heavy medication at the time this all occurred. So, I think it is very unfair of him to say I wasn't pleasing him.

I am a very faithful person and this hurt is something I just can't seem to let go of. I feel so much hatred towards this woman and him for what he has put me and my children through. He went one time to counseling and as far as he is concerned, that is all he needed. This anger, hatred, and pain is eating my soul. I don't even know who I am anymore. Any advice to help me regain my sanity will be appreciated.

Dear Reader,

This letter is loaded with common issues. I'll go through them one at a time with some comments.

— Having an affair with an unattractive person.

This always seems mysterious in that we tend to think the third party must be something special. But often they're quite ordinary. An affair has less to do with the nature of the particular third party than with the role they play in allowing the person having an affair to feel special about *themselves* by virtue of the attention showered on them.

— Blaming it on the spouse for not *pleasing* him.

This is simply an easy excuse. It's ludicrous to think that any one person can meet all of another person's needs. As I've said before, no marital partner can meet all of their spouse's needs, so it's easy to point to whatever need is "unmet" and blame that for an affair.

— Unwillingness to discuss the affair and getting angry when it is being mentioned.

This too is extremely common. Naturally, it's uncomfortable to accept responsibility for the pain caused by an affair. Getting angry is a typical way of avoiding this responsibility.

— Going to counseling once and needing no more.

Understanding and dealing with affairs is a long-term process. While it doesn't have to be done through counseling, it can't be done quickly.

— Not knowing "who I am anymore."

This confusion is common because your world has been turned upside down and nothing is as you thought it was. But there's nothing wrong with you; a spouse's actions in having an affair are a reflection of them, not of you.

* * * * * * * * * * * *

Lingering pain of wife's affair

Dear Peggy,

It's been more than 20 years since my wife's affair occurred, however the pain and sorrow remain in my heart. My wife explains the event as an error in youthful judgement, and that the other man took advantage of her romantic inexperience. All of this is understandable, however I carry such anger and resentment. At times I feel as if I'm going to explode with rage. When will the torment of this history stop? It's damaged the relationship and we are now considering divorce as the final resolution.

Dear Reader,

Many people fail to realize that recovering from the "emotional impact" of a partner's affair is an extremely long-term, difficult thing to do. It's not unusual to fail to recover (even after 20 years)—whether or not a couple stays married. Recovering depends on talking as much as is needed to be able to make some kind of sense of it. This usually means getting answers to all questions and having a partner who is willing to hang in through the long process of dealing with the feelings.

What's usually needed is more than simply explaining the factors that led to the affair. There's also a need to demonstrate a genuine understanding of the pain this caused and make every effort to show comfort and compassion for that pain. While the past can't be changed, the real need is for a sense of recognition of the degree of the pain and a genuine sense of regret and remorse for the suffering caused by the actions—no matter *why* they happened.

As the above letter illustrates, just the passage of time does not lead to healing. In order to deal with the deep emotions that result from this experience, it's essential to talk through what happened, its impact on the relationship, and what is needed to rebuild a new connection by virtue of honestly addressing everything related to this experience.

It's natural for the person who had an affair to want to just forget it, especially after so long a time—but it's unlikely ever to be forgotten if the pain and suffering have never been properly acknowledged and addressed. While it's certainly preferable to deal with the repercussions of an affair in a more timely way, at this point it's probably a case of "better late than never."

* * * * * * * * * * * * *

Extra, Extra, Extra

Dear Peggy,

Even after you have "forgiven," how do you forget? We live in a different state now and it has been 8 years since this happened, but it still hurts and I feel this woman will in some way always be part of my marriage... Let me briefly tell you the story:

Eight years ago my husband was in practice for himself, he is a doctor... He was to play golf that Saturday morning and I and my two young daughters were going to help my parents move... We had traded cars for the day, as he had a larger vehicle that would be more convenient to use for my purposes... Well I went to fill up with gas after he had left for the golf course... the gas station was next to his office. I noticed my car and the car of one of his nurses (she was single) parked behind the office... I had some extra sunscreen so I thought I would just run it into him!!! Plus I was curious what was going on since he was to be at the golf course already!!

So I left my two children in the car and used the key to the back door that no one knew I had... (thank God I didn't take my girls in with me)... all was quiet in the office, so I went back to another exam area, no one around... so I opened a door to one of the exam rooms that had a bed in it (for patients that may need to rest before going home)... There with horror I witnessed the nurse on top of my husband, having sex... (I still shake just remembering)... The look on their faces was equally as priceless... there was a big fight, they jumped up and got dressed... I said a few choice things and left... They had been involved in a relationship before we met... then we met and fell in love, got married and had a child... He did not fire her, so for the next two years I was in contact with her when I went to the office; (I did not work there). I loved my husband, plus I had the future of my children to think of... I could not stand sending my daughter off for weekend visits if we divorced... so I stayed!!! I could have embarrassed him and her and possibly have done damage to his career in such a small town... but my girls and their future were in my foremost thoughts.

We eventually moved for other reasons... but this woman is still out there. He called her sister when his Mother died because they knew each other... well of course the sister called her! They showed up at the funeral! My husband has tried to make amends over the years... he still gets angry if I bring it up... But the act of opening that door and the scene on the other side is seared into my mind... I forgave him, stayed with him... even was decent to the other woman... Sometimes I feel like a fool, but I wish I could get the memory of that day out of my mind... This woman is married now and has a daughter of her own, but she is still out there and would be quick to jump at the chance to take my husband away if she thought it were possible... I really believe that!

How do I go on with this memory... I think I have gone above and beyond the call of duty and responsibility... but it still hurts deeply...

Dear Reader,

I want to address the critical question in this letter, which is right in the very beginning: "Even after you have *forgiven,* how do you forget?" While there are many other issues involved, this is a huge one for most people. And, of course, it's even more difficult to forget if you personally witnessed things as described above. Most people have images in their heads, but in this case there's a literal image based on the actual scene.

The bottom line is that someone in this situation should not be expected (either by themselves, their spouses, or others) to *forget.* Nothing short of amnesia or a lobotomy will make that happen. But it is possible to remember—*without* the intense pain of the initial experience. This can *only* happen over time, as there is an accumulation of positive experiences, memories, and images to help offset the painful ones—*and* as there is a build-up of honesty, trust and commitment between the husband and wife.

Coping with the Pain

When someone feels they *should* be able to forget, it only makes it that much more difficult—because they tend to feel that they're somehow failing if they haven't succeeded in forgetting. But under circumstances like this, there's no need to be hard on yourself about not being able to forget. As I said, the goal needs to be aimed at learning to live with the memory in a diminished form so that it doesn't trigger the same pain. There's every reason to believe it can be done, but it's unfortunate when someone (like the husband described above), still gets angry if she brings it up. A person in this woman's position needs/deserves the support that can come from talking through it instead of having to deal with it alone.

As for the final concern—that "this woman is still out there and would be quick to jump at the chance to take my husband away," I understand how that feels. When my husband ended his last affair, the final words the other woman said to him were, "Let me know if you *ever* break up with Peggy." But it's important to avoid becoming so distracted by fears about the future that it prevents you from moving on with your life. In fact, you can hear the strength and determination in the above letter, showing a strong person. And surviving an experience like this can make you even stronger, thereby helping make it possible to handle whatever life brings in the future.

* * * * * * * * * * * * *

Embarrassed

Dear Peggy,

My husband is a teacher at a local school and had an affair with a teacher he works with. I found out about it 5 months ago. The affair had lasted for about a year and a half. We're in therapy together now and doing well. I have all the common symptoms of others who are dealing with this issue. I also have another symptom: I'm embarrassed to see anyone. I feel as if everybody knows. I also have this desire to tell people when they comment on my recent weight loss. I tend to stay closer to home now and avoid people. Should I tell or continue to act as if nothing is wrong?

Dear Reader,

There is no absolute answer as to whether a particular individual *should* tell. But there are some general thoughts that can help in considering whether to tell. First of all, quite often the secrecy surrounding a partner's affair serves to compound the difficulty in dealing with it. Part of this is because if something feels too awful to talk about, it's likely to feel too awful to get over. Also, there's a terrible sense of isolation when it's kept secret, trying to act as if nothing is wrong—when nothing could be further from the truth. (I know that sense of isolation because I didn't tell anyone during the many years of my suspicion and anxiety about my husband's affairs.)

However, in considering telling, it's important to do whatever talking is done in a way that shows you are not sharing this out of being pitiful or looking for sympathy. Rather you are simply refusing to hide something that is *not* your

105

fault and *not* a reflection on you personally. This openness often causes others to re-think their own attitudes. People may expect you to feel embarrassed and ashamed; when you don't, it causes them to stop and wonder why. (This is especially true if you're still married, because it shows that you also understand this is not *just* a personal failure of your particular spouse or your particular marriage.)

So while there's potentially great benefit in talking about this, it's more likely to be beneficial when there's clarity about what you want/expect once you do the telling. The clearer a person can be about what reaction they want, the more likely they are to get it. For instance, if all they need is to avoid keeping the secret and avoid being alone, it's important to say so. If they want to be distracted by other activities, that, too, needs to be expressed. If they want ideas or opinions about the situation, it's good to be specific in asking for ideas. And if they *don't* want advice, it's important to be clear in letting others know that as well. Without this kind of clarity, many people just don't know how to respond, and they may respond in a way that makes things worse instead of better. But by taking charge of the telling and the responses that are desired, there can be a relief from carrying around this secret and using so much energy in pretending.

* * * * * * * * * * * *

Will an affair help me forget?

Dear Peggy,

My husband had an affair and I found out about it... We talked it over and decided to work things out... Even though I try to put it out of my mind... I can't help thinking about him with this other woman... And now I have been harboring bad feelings and I'm thinking of having an affair myself. I know it's not right, but will this help me forget the hurt I feel or will it make it worse?

Dear Reader,

Deciding to work things out is only an *intention*. Unless there's a joint *effort* to deal with the fallout from the affair, it's unreasonable to think someone can simply put it out of their mind. As I've said before, thoughts like this can't be buried because they're simply buried alive—and continue to come back over and over until they're dealt with.

In general, it's important to talk through all the thoughts and feelings about this issue—even the difficult ones like harboring bad feelings and thinking of having an affair yourself. When someone tries to work through their feelings alone, they're unlikely to think clearly—and wind up doing something (like having an affair themselves) that will almost certainly makes things even worse. Not only will it not make someone forget the hurt; it's likely to generate even more hurt for both people.

But simply deciding to avoid having an affair is not enough; it's important to deal with the issues that led to having those feelings in the first place. Which brings us right back to the need to jointly work together to talk through and work through all the emotional issues that were created by a partner's affair.

106

Coping with the Pain

* * * * * * * * * * * * *

The pain is overwhelming

Dear Peggy,

I have been married for 19 years. A year and a half ago I found out about my wife's affair. She still works with the guy but not in the same place. She swears she never talks to him, and I do believe her now. (I also have friends that work there that would tell me if she talked to him.)

Anyway, I feel our marriage has improved ten-fold, but I just don't feel it will ever be good enough for what my wife has done to this family. The pain I have felt and still do is something I hate. I still have images of them together even after all this time, and will wake sweating real bad at night. I resent that she still works with him and feel disrespected because she does, but her job is something I don't want her to quit; I feel that would be the ultimate control type thing that she blames me for doing this in the first place.

I know I have lost respect for her also. I feel she owes me something and know I should not feel like that if this is to work. The hatred I feel for the other man yet is so bad I just feel I have to deal with this parasite in my own way and will never be better until I do. (I also know this is wrong, but I can't help it; I really feel like that about it.)

These are terrible feelings and I just am sick and tired of feeling like this. I feel I have lost my wife no matter how close we seem to be, it is still so empty and lonely, like something is missing. Is this a lost cause or will I someday learn to put it all away? I ask you that and then I ask myself, Do I want to put it away?... I'm not sure. The pain and disrespect I still feel can be overwhelming!!

Dear Reader,

The emotional pain in the above letter is obvious and real. At the same time, there's a complimentary rational understanding of the almost certain negative impact of acting on each emotion. This is a perfectly natural part of the process.

Even though it may *feel* hopeless, it's not. Not, that is, if we allow our rational side to eventually overcome our emotions. The key question, as stated above, is: "Do I *want* to put it away?" The bottom line is (as George Carlin says in one of his comedy routines): "you've gotta wanna." The feelings won't just magically go away one day if we don't really *want* to get beyond them and actively work to get beyond them.

This is a process—one that won't happen overnight. It takes *time*. But time alone won't help; it's important to actively work toward focusing on the rational understandings in order to eventually overcome the power of the painful emotions.

On a practical basis, one fact as described above ("she still works with him") makes this process *much* more difficult. It's not a matter of *control* but of practical reality—that continuing to have any kind of contact serves to inflame the already raw emotions. It's not just that a person *should* sever contact; it's simply a fact that in most instances this is a critical determinant of the degree to

107

which the emotions can subside. So it's important to do everything possible to focus on thinking as rationally as possible—and to support this effort though actions that reinforce this process instead of undermining it.

* * * * * * * * * * * *

Online and Off-line Affair

Dear Peggy,

My husband had an online affair with a gal for a couple months, then on an out-of-town business trip, he met this gal in her home town. Supposedly they just met and had drinks, but of course there were plans made for his return trip through her town. These plans supposedly never came to be, because he had a case of conscience.

However, they continued talking online and by phone for several more months until I opened the phone bill one day and put two and two together and called him on it.

At first it was denial, denial, then he finally admitted what had been going on. He says that he will never talk to her or converse with her online again; (that it didn't mean that much to him). My problem is that I am so devastated still (after 7 months) that I can barely function at times. All it takes is a little argument between us and all my insecurities and fears about the whole affair thing just overwhelm me, and I get really depressed and cry a lot.

When all of this online chat etc., was going on, I thought things were going so well, better than they had in a very long time for us...so when I found out about it, it really devastated me.

What will it take for me to get through this? Sometimes I just hurt so bad, I can't stand myself. (Any words of wisdom will be appreciated.)

Dear Reader,

This letter describes many of the common problems a person faces in coping with a partner's affair (regardless of the particular nature of the affair: emotional, sexual, or online). These typical problems include: being devastated, having insecurities and fears, being depressed, feeling hurt, and wondering how to get through it.

Understandably, people often believe there's no hope for overcoming the pain of their partner's affair. But the first step to recovery is believing it's possible. I know from my own experience that it *is* possible to recover from a mate's affair. I understand how it feels in the beginning when you're overwhelmed with fear and pain. When I first became suspicious that my husband was having affairs, I didn't think I'd be able to survive if it were true. My emotions were very much in control with almost no perspective to offset them. I honestly felt at that time that my life was ruined.

But as my understanding of affairs grew, so did my ability to deal with it. It felt a little like a see-saw, as I gradually shifted from being controlled by my emotions to being able to rationally understand what had happened. This process involved years of talking about my experience (both with my husband

and with others) and reading everything I could find about the subject of affairs. Gradually, its grip on me loosened and then slipped away one day when I didn't even notice. There was no great moment of truth when I knew I was over the hump. It was a very slow process of turning it inside out and upside down until I had control of it instead of it having control over me.

8: What about the Children?

Should I tell the kids?
(Here are 2 letters before my response.)

Dear Peggy, (letter #1)

After months of my husband denying an affair, he finally admitted to a long-term (years) relationship with one of his employees. I asked him to leave immediately. Prior to his admitting the affair he requested on many occasions to please "let him go." Our four kids (ages 17, 15, 12, and 10 were told that daddy was moving out because we have many problems that we can't work out at this time. I insisted that we shouldn't tell the kids about his relationship because they know the woman and because they know that this woman has also "dated" two of my brothers and my husband's brother. The two oldest kids do understand what we mean by "dating." My entire family (as well as his) also know that she has had sex with these other members of the family, and it was often a source of comic gossip in the past.

He has been gone for a month now and has been wonderful to the kids. He has been the father he should have been, but never was. The dilemma is this... the oldest is aware of the situation and is angry but continues to see and work with his dad at least 4 times a week. The other three kids still don't know, but seem to be getting more and more confused that we can't live together because they believe that there really is no big problem—because we never fought and our life really wasn't bad. I now feel that it is time to tell the kids that "daddy has a girlfriend." My husband doesn't want to. After much heart and soul searching I really believe that my kids will be able to cope better when they understand that there is a reason for the separation. I know it will be a shock to them, but isn't it better to have a concrete reason?

Dear Peggy, (letter #2)

My husband had an affair, it's over, but in a fight I blurted out to my daughter about it....I feel bad now, but again, think she should know.

Dear Reader,

Well-intentioned parents often try to protect children by withholding information from them indefinitely. The reality is, children are far more perceptive and aware than most adults are able to acknowledge. They are especially good at picking up cues we give out when we're trying to hide something. Our words say everything's OK, but our non-verbals say something's wrong. The anxiety children feel when they pick up these inconsistencies can be worse than their knowing the truth we're trying to protect them from.

Unfortunately, there are no absolute rules that define when a child is ready to deal with a certain kind of information. In general, when kids know there's something wrong and don't know what it is, they tend to imagine that it has something to do with them. They're also not likely to be as shocked as we think they would be—because kids today are far more aware of such issues than in previous generations.

In our own case, we decided to tell our children because we were working to establish a stronger basis of honesty with each other—and we wanted to expand our honesty with each other to include more honesty with our children. They were 11 and 13 when we told them about my husband's affairs, and I do believe that as they grew into adults, the strongest lesson they carried with them from this experience was the importance of honesty.

Each person and couple, of course, needs to decide for themselves just when (and more importantly how) to tell their kids. But it's probably unrealistic to think that something this significant (with this much impact) can simply be hidden forever. So telling them in a planned way may be preferable to unintentionally "blurting it out" as mentioned above. However, it's not so much how they are told as how you deal with their knowing. It's important to "be there" to respond to questions and to support them in their own efforts to deal with the situation.

* * * * * * * * * * * * *

Staying for the Sake of the Children?
(Here are excerpts from 4 letters before my response.)

Dear Peggy, (excerpt #1)

My husband has had 2 affairs, 10 years apart. At this point in time I would like to give him that divorce!!! Unfortunately, we have 3 children. The two older ones are sick of hearing us fight—although they do not want us to split up. The youngest is an 8-year-old son who idolizes his father and does not want mommy and daddy to split up. What would be best for the youngest of our children? I feel nothing for this man any more. Is it worth staying in this relationship? I am at a confused point in life... Any help would be appreciated.

Dear Peggy, (excerpt #2)

About a year ago I started to have an affair. My husband knows about the affair and would like me to come home to try again. He says that I'm causing severe emotional problems for our children and that they will never recover. He also said the other day that he is moving to another state and taking our younger child with him, but leaving our 15-year-old with me. I'm confused. I wonder if I should go home for the sake of the children. I know what the right thing to do is... Why can't I do it? I don't want to live the rest of my life alone. Sometimes I think I'm crazy.

What about the Children?

Dear Peggy, (excerpt #3)

I found out about my husband's affairs, but I kept this info to myself until I could bear it no longer. My children are used to a certain lifestyle. To remove them from this and expect them to get by on minimal child support and a minimum-wage mom seems unfair, since they are not to blame. The only thing that keeps me going is the children. I hold them dearly to my heart and use them for my strength. But I still cry.

Dear Peggy, (excerpt #4)

I found out about my husband's affair the same day he left the home. I don't know if I can ever forgive him for this but I have to try. I know you can't stay married for the kids but they do deserve to know that we tried to make it work.

Dear Reader,

The above excerpts illustrate the critical factor that *children* play in any effort to deal with affairs—regardless of which role a person plays. It's not unusual for people to decide to stay married "for the sake of the children." While we often think of mothers making this decision, it's equally true for fathers who fear they may lose their children forever if they get a divorce.

Sometimes this concern for the children leads to a decision to stay married that works out well for everyone. But sometimes the person having an affair becomes so absorbed by their outside relationship that they cease to care about anything else, including the children. (This, of course, also presents an exceptionally difficult situation for the spouse. They are placed in the position of dealing with their own feelings of rejection while attending to their children's sense of rejection by the other parent.)

While staying together for the sake of the children is a time-honored idea, there are times when staying together may *not* be in the children's best interests. Some women decide that the strain between them and their husbands makes life too difficult for the children if they continue to stay together. This is in keeping with the research done by Judith S. Wallerstein whose study of children of divorce led her to say:

"To recognize that divorce is an arduous, long-lasting family trauma is not to argue against it. Divorce is a useful and necessary social remedy. And the fact is that most divorces with children are not impulsive... Most worry about the effects of divorce on their children. There is considerable evidence that a conflict-ridden marriage is not in the best interests of the children. There is evidence, too, that children benefit from dissolution of such marriages."

It may be that the more important issue is not whether or not there is a divorce—but how the parents handle the divorce and their relationship with the children during the years that follow. For instance, sometimes the animosity between the parents during the years following a divorce creates a constant state of stress and tension for the children. And on the other hand, sometimes the anger, resentment, and general dissatisfaction in a deadened or difficult marriage can create a constant state of stress and tension for the children.

So in the final analysis, the particular arrangement may not be as critical as the attitude of the parents in carrying it out. Putting the well-being of the children first should be a high priority in these situations—and it's not always obvious as to precisely what *action* will accomplish this. But it is abundantly clear what *attitude* will make a difference: one that *really* considers the best interests of the children.

* * * * * * * * * * *

Extramarital affair resulted in child

Dear Peggy, (This is a shortened version of a longer letter.)

I have not seen this discussed. The other woman went after my husband and purposely got pregnant. After some time I was able to truly forgive him, but he cannot seem to forgive himself and this is preventing us from fully repairing. I know his guilt is tremendous but he will not accept anyone's help, professionally or otherwise. His excuse...he was mad at me!

I feel no compassion for this child at all, though I know it is not his fault. His presence in our home would be nothing but chaos for me and our children, who do not know at this time. I do feel they will need to be told in time but am not sure when the right time will be. Otherwise, I think it is very likely that someday he could come looking for his "family." I admit to not wanting my husband to see this child, and our only involvement is child support. Truly my life is not the same and never will be!

And my husband feels tremendous guilt. When the guilt is so severe, does it ever end? What helps a person accept their own responsibility for the affair—and an illegitimate child—and then move on?

Dear Reader,

When we think of the children in relation to a partner's affair, we're usually thinking of our own children. However, there are times when a child results from an affair. When this happens, most people (no matter how much they're hurting) don't want to hurt an innocent child. So this situation obviously calls for different kinds of thinking and behavior. (I'll reflect on the behavior part before discussing the thinking/feeling issue of guilt.)

As for "what to do," I can only pass on what I've heard in the past from people who have faced this kind of situation. For most, the attitude was to try to deal with the third party and child similar to the way they would deal with an ex-spouse and the child from a former marriage. For some, they were unable to accommodate to this situation and tried to *force* a choice. On the other end of the spectrum, one woman even took her husband's (and the other woman's) child to raise—after the other woman didn't want the child once she didn't get the husband. Clearly, when children are involved, there are no clear/easy answers, and nothing about this whole ordeal is black and white or written in stone. So anyone dealing with this issue need not depend on finding a reliable outside source for guidance in how to handle it. Rather, they can become a resource to others as they find their own way.

As for "how to deal with the guilt" and the fact that "life will never be the same"—these are the realities and challenges of any life crisis (like being responsible for the death of someone else in an automobile accident). When we're faced with consequences of our actions that can not be erased or undone, it calls for digging deep inside and discovering some way to become better people by virtue of this experience. So the first step is letting go of thinking "if only..." and looking toward "what can I do to demonstrate that I've learned an important lesson" from this experience. And, further, how can I take this learning and use it to help others. The answers to those questions will be personal and individual, but it's worth the effort—both for your own sake and for the sake of others who have been affected (or could be affected) by this kind of experience.

* * * * * * * * * * * *

Child by Lover

Dear Peggy, (This letter has been edited due to its length.)

Here's a situation that I now understand happens more often than anyone likes to admit. Bear with me as I explain a complicated situation. My marriage was on the rocks and I could not get my husband to therapy for over 3 years. Depressed, no longer in love with my husband and feeling emotionally neglected and needy, I resorted to having an affair to fill the needs that were not being met in my dysfunctional marriage...

I decided, after much thought, to get separated from my husband. For a year, my lover and I had a strong, real relationship that was fraught with its own problems, not the least of them the discovery that my lover was manic-depressive and needed serious medical attention. During this time I became pregnant by my lover. There was no question: I would keep the child...

Knowing I needed stability and to focus all my strength and energy on my pregnancy and the birth of my child, I ended the relationship and decided to be a single parent. My lover and I calmly discussed maintaining friendship and allowing contact between him and the baby. My husband kept telling me the baby didn't matter and that he still loved me. I felt affection for him, felt guilty, worried about our daughter and my unborn son. I tentatively went back to counseling with my husband and we decided not to divorce. We decided to raise the baby as his own, allowing for some contact between the child and my ex-lover, since we wanted to avoid animosity and because my ex-lover wanted very much to be a part of his son's life...

My lover has seen the baby (now 3 months old) twice and is clearly in love with the child and still professes his love for me. We are all trying to deal as best we can in a very difficult situation. No one is getting exactly what they want. My husband is doing a remarkable thing, but our marriage may not recover. For my ex-lover, every day he doesn't see his son is painful for him.

And honestly, I've tried very, very hard, but I have not yet been able to get back to loving my husband. Many of the serious problems that existed before I even had the affair are still very much there.

Right now, my focus is on providing a stable environment for the children. I have a wonderful friendship and connection with my ex-lover, which I'm afraid may get in the way. But for the baby's sake and out of compassion, I cannot imagine cutting my ex-lover off completely. Nor do I really want to. Can you give any advice as to how I can deal with these mixed feelings I'm having? I'm caught in the middle!

Dear Reader,

Even though this letter has been significantly shortened, it's still clear that this is a very complicated situation. As stated in the first sentence, this situation "happens more often than anyone likes to admit."

Part of the frustration no doubt comes from feeling that there *should* be some better way of resolving this kind of situation. But if ever there were a situation for which there is no ideal solution, this is it. It may help to realize that with really complex situations like this, there is probably no way to have everything work out best for everybody.

It seems extraordinarily reasonable that the path now being taken is probably the best one possible: "my focus is on providing a stable environment for the children." While it may be difficult and/or stressful to some degree for everyone, the children deserve to have the least stress possible—with *all* the adults doing whatever they can to minimize the stress for the children.

One perspective that might be helpful is to realize that this period when the children are growing up is a finite period. While the current situation probably feels like it will last forever; once kids are grown and you look back on that time, you realize that it has passed with amazing swiftness. (I know from firsthand experience that when my own kids were small, I couldn't imagine a time when they would be grown—but surprisingly that time comes sooner than you think. In fact, my kids are now in their 30s, and those days of their youth seem a very long time ago.)

There will be better times and worse times; but at any given moment, we do well to simply do the best we can *at that time*, knowing that things may be better/easier at some point in the future. The bottom line is to realize that having mixed feelings about the situation is entirely reasonable. There is no simple advice and there are no easy answers as to how to handle it; it's an ongoing process of continuing to think as clearly as possible about all the complicated factors.

* * * * * * * * * * * * *

What about the Children?

She's pregnant

Dear Peggy,

My husband had an affair for 2 years. I knew nothing about it until I caught him talking with her and about 2 hours later she called me and told me. Well, I confronted my husband and he admitted it. To make matters worse, she is pregnant. He has broke it off with her and says he loves me very much. If she goes on with this pregnancy, he wants to stay in touch with her. I don't know how much of this I can take. What should I do? The lady is 4 weeks along in her pregnancy. This is tearing me apart; I love my husband so much. I didn't know what else he could do to hurt me and me still love him—and then he told me he had an affair about 5 years ago. I thought our marriage was on the right road. We have been married for 9 years...

Dear Reader,

Of all the particular situations related to affairs, having a child result from the affair is surely one of the more difficult. I've seen this kind of situation develop in many different ways. Here are some of the various scenarios:

—the other woman *says* she's pregnant, but isn't; it's just a ploy

—the other woman does have the child and wants ongoing contact with the man

—the other woman has the child and only wants financial support from the man

—the other woman has the child but wants no contact/support from the man

When there is continuing contact, this is likely to create an ongoing issue for the rest of their lives. Some couples who stay married try to maintain as much separateness from the child as possible, perhaps fighting legally to avoid involvement. Other couples who stay married actually participate in the parenting of the child, feeling that the child is innocent and deserves to know both parents.

The impact on the marriage seems to relate not so much to which path is chosen as to whether or not both the husband and wife *agree* on the path. As with most ordeals in life, if they pull together to face it and deal with it in a united way, they can actually strengthen their bond. But if they are in disagreement as to how to handle it, it's likely to pull them apart.

The other factor, of course, is that in the very early stages of contemplating this situation, most people don't know precisely how they're going to feel until the baby is born. So until that time, there's usually not a great deal that can be done as far as getting real clarity about how to proceed in the future. There's a natural sense of urgency to get this settled, but a hasty decision as to how it will be handled may or may not still be relevant as more time passes, more aspects are considered, and the full reality of the situation sets in. So patience, thoughtful consideration of all aspects, and ongoing honest communication about the whole situation is probably the most reasonable course to follow.

9: Dealing with the Third Party

Obsessed With the Other Woman

Dear Peggy,

Yes, my husband had an affair. And yes, I'm angry and hurt. But I'm even angrier at the other woman! As I sit here writing this, I cannot tell you how very much it hurts to think about her. I called her after I found out about the affair. I wanted to destroy her, but I did not go to her husband—only because I didn't want him to hurt the way I have been hurting. However, I'm obsessed with her and just can't get her out of my mind. She has ruined my life. And I don't know what I can do about it.

Dear Reader,

Most people have a hard time dealing with their feelings about the third party because they tend to think that an affair wouldn't have happened at all if it hadn't been for that particular person. But the specific third party doesn't warrant our obsession with them because, in fact, they're not "special." Any number of people could have been the third party. The very nature of being the *third party* (instead of the *spouse*) means it's a fantasy relationship without the daily concerns and responsibilities required in making a life together in marriage.

Obsessing on any particular third party gives them far more importance than they deserve. In my own case, my husband had affairs with about 15 different women. In some ways that seems overwhelming to deal with; but on the other hand, it allowed me to avoid focusing on any one person. Instead, I was able to see that their importance was only in the role they played, not in who played it. This perspective might be helpful in dealing with the strong emotions about the third party.

* * * * * * * * * * * *

4-year affair

Dear Peggy,

My husband has been having an affair for 4 years. We've been married 12 years and have 2 children. Needless to say I feel betrayed and devastated. It has torn my world apart. He wants to stay and work this out. I haven't been able to make a decision about staying in this relationship. My real problem is, I see the other woman almost every day. I get so angry when I see her. How could she do this to my family? I know that my husband has run into her a few times. He tells me that it is over, but I'm not so sure. I'm scared to move ahead with her so close by. We have been going for counseling, but it doesn't seem to be helping me right now. I am in my home town and feel like I should move away to get away from her. Please help!

119

Dear Reader,

The third party is often the focus of a great deal of anger and pain—especially when there is ongoing interaction with them. This kind of interaction can be like pulling the scab off a wound so that it never heals. So whenever it stands in the way of a couple's rebuilding their marriage, it's a legitimate issue that calls for a willingness (by both partners) to do whatever it takes to change the situation.

Unless there are extenuating circumstances (like the third party being a relative or there being a child by the third party), it's reasonable to try to create a situation that allows for severing all contact with the third party. Some people have gone to extraordinary lengths to allow this contact to cease—including changing jobs, moving to other towns, etc. It may not be that these actions per se make the difference—but that a spouse's *willingness* to take such actions demonstrates the kind of commitment to the marriage that can go a long way toward the rebuilding process.

Another point in the above letter deserves attention: when counseling "doesn't seem to be helping," it's important to try to find a different counselor. Counseling can be extremely helpful or it can be an additional problem to deal with; so it's important to find counseling that fits your needs—especially the need to deal directly with the issue of the affair, not just general marital therapy. Any decision about staying in the marriage should not be made hastily—so as to prevent second-guessing or wondering whether there should have been a greater effort to stay. However, it's also important not to just sit around waiting, but to be actively working toward determining whether the relationship can be improved. So it's perfectly reasonable to pursue any potential course of action, including moving away.

* * * * * * * * * * * *

Hate the Other Woman

Dear Peggy,

I have been divorced for two years and I still have a lot of anger toward the woman that my former spouse left me for. While I know she is not the person to whom my feelings should be directed, I simply cannot shake the thoughts that she is evil. I have nightmares about her where she and I are fighting. She has never been around my children in the four years that she and my former spouse have been together, even after the divorce. I often wonder why? They have never married. I am in a happy relationship and have come to some resolution, more or less, with my former spouse—but I am pretty sure that if I ever saw her again, I would pour a pitcher of ice water over here head!! Why can't I let this go? How do I?

Dear Reader,

The first thought I have upon reading about this situation is that the woman who wrote this letter displays a clear *understanding* of the situation, but her *emotions* have simply not yet caught up. We tend to think there's something wrong when our emotions don't just fall in line with what we understand to be true. (For instance, in this case there's an understanding that "she is not the person to whom my feelings should be directed," but there's still the emotion that "she is evil.") It's not easy to drop the "if only..." and "what if.." kind of thinking that leads to dwelling on past experiences and reliving them long after they have ended.

Unfortunately, our brain doesn't discriminate between actually experiencing an event and only thinking about it. So the best motivation for letting go of the emotional obsession is to recognize the damaging impact on your own body. It causes a repetition of all the pain that was felt originally—just as if it were happening all over again. And unresolved anger can just eat you up inside. So whenever the angry feelings involuntarily come to mind, it's possible to deliberately, voluntarily focus on some positives—like the fact that this has been resolved with the former spouse and the children are not being involved. It's a little like the old question of whether the glass is half empty or half full. Our feelings tend to follow our focus. So more of an effort to focus on the present and the future (instead of the past) can go a long way toward diminishing the strength of the negative feelings about the third party.

* * * * * * * * * * * * *

Anger after the affairs

Dear Peggy,

About a month ago, I discovered that my wife had a series of affairs for the last 18 months. I went through the "devastated" and "blame myself" periods, but we have decided to stay married and work things out. The one question that I do not see addressed is rage. Real rage. I have driven by the house of the last man she had sex with several times. I do not know what I would do if I saw him. I have so much anger at him and my wife and I am having a hard time with that now. I scare myself sometimes. Will this ever go away or is this a normal phase in the healing process?

Dear Reader,

The third party often becomes the target for a lot of the anger and rage people feel, especially during the early period of dealing with affairs. But a person's assessment of the third party is often exaggerated, causing them to think the third party either has some exceptional qualities that they are lacking— or that the third party is some kind of terrible ogre. In most instances, there is nothing particularly unique about the third party, either positive or negative.

Of course, sometimes the rage felt toward the third party serves to reduce the rage felt toward the spouse. But eventually, it's important to work to get beyond the feelings of rage. Those strong emotions can keep you stuck and unable to make progress in rebuilding the marriage.

As for whether it's a "normal phase," people react differently; it's normal for some people, but not for others. One of the factors is whether the initial reaction is one of "How *could* you," (which usually reflects more pain and less anger) or

121

one of "How *dare* you," (which usually reflects more anger than pain). Naturally, the anger results from pain, so this isn't a clear distinction.

One of the best books on anger is a classic titled "The Dance of Anger" by Harriet Lerner, Ph.D. While it is clearly directed toward helping *women* understand and deal with their feelings of anger, it can be helpful in a general kind of way for anyone wanting to get a better understanding of this emotion and how to deal with it.

* * * * * * * * * * * *

Still confused

Dear Peggy,

My husband had an affair with my best friend. It has been 5 months since the discovery. At first we didn't tell anyone and things went on like before...too much like before. My husband still called her and asked her to meet him. I found out about 2 months ago that he was still calling her. We had it out and still decided to try and work things out. He has not had any specific contact with her except when he calls my office to talk to me. She is the secretary at the office where I work. She and I have also had our peace and remain friends despite the affair. My dilemma is will it be possible to maintain my marriage to my husband and my friendship to her?

My husband and I are currently in counseling, and things seem to be going well, I am just concerned with the fact that they have to talk when she answers the phone. It was a very short-term affair lasting only 3 times and during a very stressful time for both of our families. We want to be back to being friends and playing cards, barbecues, etc. Am I absolutely crazy? I am so confused and mixed up. By the way, my best friend's husband is also my husband's cousin and best friend. My what a tangled web we weave.

Dear Reader,

There are those who might read the above letter and think she's crazy to consider remaining friends with the woman her husband had an affair with. But this is not as foolish as it might appear. In fact, when there's an effort to remain friends after an affair, it's usually in a situation where circumstances are likely to lead to some kind of contact (like being relatives, life-long friends, or having children from the affair). When ongoing contact is inevitable, some people prefer to *try* to make that contact less stressful by reestablishing the original friendship.

While this is not normally the way these situations are resolved, it is *possible*—if everyone involved agrees they want to work together to make it work. And those few who *choose* to handle it in the way described in this letter certainly deserve respect and support, not criticism. Each person has the right to decide for themselves how *they* can best deal with the fallout from an affair.

* * * * * * * * * * * *

Dealing with the Third Party

The Other Woman

Dear Peggy,

I just want to ask you one question. I am not sure I have ever heard of this happening to anyone else, although it probably does. My husband had an affair when we were only married for two years. I was 7 months pregnant with our second child and he began seeing a girl. Her parents had been friends with my parents for years. Her father helped us get our first furniture, through credit at a major store. I had never met her before, but I knew her brother from school. She is 5 years younger than my husband and me. I saw her many times after he met her. My problem is that I don't, after 19 years, remember what she looks like. He ran into her again about 8 or 9 years later and it started up again. She would come by our home. She would call our house. She would follow me when I was in my car. So why won't my mind let me remember what she looks like?

We have since moved from our hometown to another state. I fear that she is here; I get phone calls. (Yes, I do have caller ID.) But the phone rings and no one answers me. We got Email once from someone and it was for my husband; I fear it was her. But how can I remember what she looks like without staring at her and giving her the satisfaction of my attention. What am I doing wrong? Did I actually lose him when he met her? Is he with me because of our ten-year-old son? I ask, but he assures me I am wrong. I just really would like to remember what she looks like, I want to know if she is around. I would like an opinion of someone who won't think I am a fool for letting this get to me. Thanks for your time.

Dear Reader,

This letter is like many in that people don't know whether their situation is different or whether it has ever happened to anyone else. First of all, no one is "a fool" for being concerned about the stability of their relationship with the one they love. It might be somewhat foolish *not* to have any concerns. But it is very important to try to assess the concerns in a realistic way and not become obsessed with some particular aspect. In this case, it may be reasonable to be concerned about someone who has had a recurring relationship with a spouse, but focusing specifically on remembering what she looks like may not be the most effective use of energy.

The inability to remember what she looks like may indicate a desire to block her out of both your mind and your life, which is understandable. Many of us have a kind of approach-avoidance attitude toward things we fear—for instance, wanting to know what she looks like but not wanting to stare at her. This kind of thinking just keeps things in limbo and prevents any resolution. It's usually better to take action that would end that kind of dilemma. This would involve either deciding that it doesn't matter what she looks like or doing whatever it takes to find out.

* * * * * * * * * * * *

123

Harassment by other woman

Dear Peggy,

My husband had a 6-year affair with a woman who harassed me during and after their affair. I had no idea he was involved with her when she was flipping me off, cursing at me as she would drive by me in her car. I never told her husband for fear of what he might do to mine. However, she shows no signs of permanently stopping this harassment. A few weeks or months will go by with no sign of her, and then there she will be—flipping me off, or grinning like a jack-o-lantern and waving vigorously at me as though she were thrilled to see me! She also drives past my house or through my neighborhood to show her contempt for me. I have filed a police report and a prosecuting attorney sent her a letter warning her to stop, but she continues, even waiting on my route to work to grin and wave!! She is a nut!!

I desperately want to tell her husband, who knows nothing about any of this. How do men typically react in this type of situation? Would telling him place my foolish husband in mortal danger? This has cost me so much emotionally and physically. It has taken such a psychic toll on me. I need some direction here.

Dear Reader,

Since the specific question relates to whether or not to tell the husband of the other woman, that's *usually* not a good idea—*even if* there are no extenuating circumstances such as this kind of harassment or this kind of fear of a physical attack. (I must say, personally, that when my own husband had affairs many years ago, he carefully avoided having affairs with women who were married— precisely because of this realistic concern about possible physical retaliation by an irate husband.)

However, since the consideration of telling the other woman's husband is due to her ongoing harassment, the bigger issue is a desire for the other woman to stop the harassment. The common wisdom (with which I agree) is that the best course of action is to make absolutely *no response* (and *no reaction*) to any effort of the third party to maintain contact in any way. This would also include making *no* contact with anyone associated with the third party—except, of course, in possible legal, criminal ways when things progress to that point.

So the third party may continue to be an irritation, no matter what—but it might not feel quite so distressful if it's viewed as something that only serves to make you *stronger* as a couple. An attitude of "It's you and me against the world" can be very powerful in withstanding *anything*.

10: Staying or Leaving

Should I give up?

Dear Peggy,

About a year ago my wife almost left our marriage of 21 years for another man. I had no idea that there might be someone else until about 6 months prior to her telling me that she had strong feelings for another man. I had suspected something was going on because of how bad she was treating me, and I had done nothing wrong and just about everything right. I had asked her several times during a six-month period if something was going on, but she continued to deny it. Finally she broke down and told me when I threatened to leave her. She said it was a mistake and said she wanted to stay with me and try and make it work. I said only if we would get marriage counseling. She doesn't want to go. She said it is senseless because she says everything is ok now. Now I feel as though I want to give up and get on with my life. What should I do?

Dear Reader,

The above letter describes the most common pattern (whether among men or women having affairs)—that they first deny it when questioned and only admit it if/when they absolutely *must*. It's also common to then want to "go on" and "put it behind" without having to deal with it head-on—either with their spouse or through counseling.

However, it's perfectly reasonable for a person in the position of the man who wrote the above letter to insist that their partner deal with the aftermath of the affair. First of all, the idea that "she wanted to stay with me and try and make it work" is incompatible with her saying she "doesn't want to go" to marriage counseling. This is obviously an instance where the actions don't fit the words. And, it really isn't the role of the one who *had* the affair to determine whether or not "*everything is ok*." It's only OK when the spouse who is trying to recover from their partner's affair decides it's OK.

While it's frustrating to have a spouse who is unwilling to work through the issues related to their affair, it's unlikely to be a satisfying resolution to simply "give up and get on with my life." It's very hard to get on with life when something like this is so completely unresolved. It's usually preferable to be able to feel that you've done everything possible before giving up—so you don't look back with regret, saying *if only...* Whereas everyone has to make their own decisions as to when/how long to try to get their partner to see/accept the need to work through something like this, *in general*, it's better to make every reasonable effort to do so. In that way, a person is more likely to be able to really get on with life—regardless of whether that future life involves continuing in the marriage or leaving it.

* * * * * * * * * * * *

I'm trapped

Dear Peggy,

After 20 years of marriage, my husband had an emotional and sexual affair with a coworker. (And he still works with her) The sexual affair is over, he says he still loves me and we are in counseling, but I know he still feels deeply for her and I'm afraid that what he really wants with me is the Package (our kids, home, and respectable life). What will happen in a few more years when the kids are grown and gone?

I feel trapped. Although I recognize that I need to grow and change into a better, more mature person, I think I could do that better without him. Every time I look at him, the unbearable pain, betrayal and loss cloud everything else I am trying to accomplish. The trapped part comes in when I think about my children...they are not very stable themselves right now. They love their dad and have remained close to him. A divorce would devastate them. So I feel like I must choose between my own welfare and that of my kids.

I feel such loss that I doubt I can ever regain my trust and respect for him. Neither of us had ever had sex with anybody else before this...and naive as that may sound in today's world, it made me feel special and cherished by him. It also made the sex act feel very personal, bonding, and sacred to me in our relationship. That is all lost forever with the loss of exclusivity. Now, I feel like a whore when we have sex. Believe it or not, our sex life was great right up until I found out about the affair. Now, all I want to do is find a way to avoid sex with him and the bitter disappointment it leads to in me.

My head says keep trying to work it out for the kids, but my heart looks at all these strikes against us. I have to ask... Can you really ever put Humpty Dumpty back together again?

Dear Reader,

This letter touches on a number of very important points.

1. When someone is still working with a person with whom they had an emotional and sexual affair, it makes it extremely difficult (and unlikely) that there can be any real healing or recovery. Avoiding all contact with the third party is a critical factor in giving the marriage a good chance to work.

2. Feeling they must choose between their own welfare and that of the kids is a common and very difficult spot. It's not unusual for people to decide to stay married for the sake of the children. However, this time-honored idea has come to be questioned in recent years. While divorce does appear to have a long-lasting impact on children, so does staying in a marriage that is filled with tension and anxiety. Each person must assess their own situation and determine which is *really* best for the children.

126

3. When neither member of a couple has ever had sex with anybody else before an affair, it *does* tend to create a special protected feeling. (I understand this personally because that was also my experience. My husband and I had learned about sex together as teenagers and had never had sex with anyone else until he had an affair.) However, even when this is not the case, there is always some particular aspect of an affair that seems especially difficult. So if it hadn't been this particular loss (spoiling the specialness), it would probably have been something else that felt just as painful.

4. "Putting Humpty Dumpty back together" *can* be done—but not without a lot of time and effort on the part of *both* parties in working to establish a different kind of relationship based on developing trust through a commitment to ongoing honest communication.

* * * * * * * * * * * * *

Numb to Affairs, Still in Love

Dear Peggy,

After years of anesthetizing myself to my husband's flirtations (some of which became minor affairs or one-time sex play sessions), I find that it's closed me off to him and to intimacy. Of course! But I still love him, and I know he loves me. We just disappoint each other. He complains that I'm not loving enough, that I no longer adore him the way I used to, and am not willing to make love often enough. I tell him that while I take responsibility for my own closeness issues, his flirtations and sexual affairs have not made it easy to trust him. Sexual attraction, for me, is based on trust. I don't feel respected. Sexual attraction, for me, is based on respect.

I do feel love coming from my husband in many areas, and we have a great, undeniably strong bond. It's uncanny. But our relationship is about to end because of our mutual unwillingness to trust and care for the other in the way that we know is possible in a good marriage. Yet, I'm afraid that entering counseling is going to force me into a situation of having to make commitments to be a lot more loving (sexually) than I'm willing to be right now. I'm not sure I can find a therapist who would understand my reticence. I'm afraid I'll be stuck in a counseling situation where we're forced to make promises to be nicer to each other. I think that this is too superficial an approach. There are many complex layers to this problem, and to our stories, but I wonder what the next step might be for us, or for me, anyway. I believe we both feel ambivalent about living together now, but don't feel ready to split.

Dear Reader,

The description of this situation shows a degree of thoughtfulness and fairness that might be difficult for some people to understand. It shows there is, in fact, (at least on her part) a strong bond. For instance, saying "we just disappoint each other" or referring to "our mutual unwillingness to trust and care for the other..." shows a remarkable sense of fairness and consideration, lacking the kind of one-sided "blaming" that is so often present in these situations.

This letter also represents a remarkable ability to think clearly, which I can only reinforce. She is quite clear about the legitimate reasons she no longer adores him "the way I used to..." And she's also clear in recognizing the need to find a therapist who will not take a superficial "be nice" approach. A good therapist can be a great help, and a bad one can make things even worse. It's important to *interview* therapists until the right one is found.

Finally, regarding the ambivalence, while it's frustrating to feel uncertain about the future, the best approach is the one indicated here—recognizing that "there are many complex layers to this problem" and actively seeking ways to bring clarity to the situation in order to make the best decisions possible.

* * * * * * * * * * * * *

Settling for Stability

Dear Peggy,

I have been married for 8+ years to a good, stable, devoted man and have two children (6 and 3 years old). Over the last several years, I have been feeling increasingly unsettled in this relationship from a personal perspective. Currently, I am at a point where I feel affection for him, but I really want to be either 1) on my own or 2) with someone else. I feel no distinct interest in intimacy, but participate just to keep things going. I don't really want to try planning one-on-one time now because I've always been the one to suggest and plan these interludes in the past. I feel that I married him for the wrong reason (to escape an overprotective home environment) and I now wish that I had taken a different route in my life. However, I am very comfortable with him (at least 90 percent of the time) and we have two small children.

I have met a man who (based on similar upbringing, interests, etc.) brings a sense of connection to my life (both mentally and physically). We are wonderful together. My question is this: What is the merit of trying to undo a hasty decision just to satisfy a need to start over? Especially once children are involved? Should the "older and more experienced" you be listened to—or does it traditionally work better to make do with what you have (since you really don't have it "bad," just empty)? Help!

Dear Reader,

I hesitated to respond to this issue because it's unclear whether the primary problem here is an affair. However, on more careful thought, quite often an affair is mistaken as the central issue when it is simply a catalyst to facing up to other issues in life that have been ignored until this happens. So it might be helpful to look at how these two issues interact.

First of all, an affair may serve as a wake-up call to *other* changes that should have been considered instead. The awareness of a need to take a different route in life doesn't necessarily mean that the new route should involve switching to a new man, however wonderful it may seem. With every situation (whether the one we choose when we're young or the one we think we "should have taken" once we're older), there are positives and negatives. Unfortunately, we tend to focus only on the negative aspects of our current situation compared to the positive aspects of some other alternative—when, in fact, this is an unreasonable comparison.

Almost everyone has some alternative scenario in their heads of how their lives might have been. For me, it was the fact of being "local girl singer" and expecting to become a professional singer. While I was exceptionally talented as a child, I was not exceptional as an adult—and it's questionable that I could have made it in the entertainment business. And even if I had succeeded, the down side of the life of many/most entertainers is a life I would not relish. So when the older and more experienced side of me looks realistically at the life I chose instead of taking a different path, I think the decisions I made when I was young worked out well.

It's good to rethink important life decisions on an ongoing basis throughout life so we don't come to the end and say "if only..." However, it's unlikely that an affair is more than a reminder that we need to do this. It's probably not the best way to start over. Sitting down and carefully thinking about all aspects of life (without considering the other man) may allow for a more sensible, practical, and ultimately more satisfying decision about whether or not to start over.

* * * * * * * * * * * *

Affair with an employee

Dear Peggy,

Recently, I found out that my husband had an affair with an employee of his. He tells me that I am the only woman that he has and will ever love, so how could he have an affair? I had suspected this was going on for about the last 6 months and he always denied it.

I found out in a very humiliating way. I went out to the lake and found out that the two of them were spending the weekend together. It was not a really good scene because I had my 2 children with me at the time. He says that he loves me and wants to work things out, but she is still working with him at his business. I feel that if he really loved me and wanted to work things out that he would fire her and not have any dealings with her.

My daughter made a scene yesterday with this woman and he is upset with me because he feels as if I have put everything in her head. My daughter is 15 years old and is devastated by the turn of events.

I have been with this man for about 20 years, and I am just not sure what to do. Should I leave and go on with my life? Should I try to work things out with him? I am so afraid that I might do the wrong thing, do you have any advice?

Dear Reader,

This one letter refers to *many* of the issues faced by people in this situation: 1) wondering how he could have an affair, 2) affair taking place with someone

129

at work, 3) denying it, 4) saying he really loves his wife, 5) child being upset, 6) not being sure what to do, and 6) looking for advice.

1) *Why?* is always the first (and most pressing) question when an affair comes to light. There is never *one* simple reason. It's a combination of factors and can't be understood by looking *only* at an individual's own marriage. Societal factors also play a part.

2) Many affairs begin through work contacts. The ongoing closeness that can develop at work leads people to share more and get closer, sometimes leading to an affair even when that was not initially the intention.

3) Denial is almost universal. The common attitude among people having affairs is: "Never tell; If questioned, deny it; If caught, say as little as possible."

4) The idea that a man "won't have an affair if he loves his wife" is one of many myths. While it's difficult for a wife to comprehend, this is often the case.

5) Affairs have an impact on a lot of people, and dealing with the impact on the children is especially difficult. In most instances, the long-term impact on the children is primarily influenced by the way the hurt spouse deals with it. So in the midst of personal struggles, it's still important to recognize that the children will probably only deal with it as well as the hurt parent.

6) It's important not to *do* anything too quickly. While the emotions are so intense, it's very hard to think straight enough to make a decision that is this important.

7) While it's helpful to get as much input and perspective as possible, *no one* can tell anyone else what they "should" do. Each person has to live with the consequences of their decision—so they should be the one to make it.

* * * * * * * * * * * * *

Best friend/more?

Dear Peggy

To make a long story as short as possible I met this guy 5 years ago, one week before he moved to a different state. We talked a little before he left but nothing much. We have talked on the phone and seen each other a couple times a year. I consider him my best friend; he is the only person I have ever been totally open with.

Almost 4 months ago I got married to a great man. I was a single mother and he loved my daughter and me very much. We only knew each other for 6 months before we got married. We are having a hard time making this marriage work. I keep telling myself (and I know he does too) that it's always like this in the beginning, but it is hard. See, he knows all about my best friend and is extremely jealous of him. At one time we were more than friends, but realistically it didn't work because we live so far from each other and we didn't want to ruin our friendship. The feelings that my friend and I share are strong but we know the situation.

I love my husband very much but sometimes it feels hopeless, and I wish I had maybe seen what really could have happened with my best friend and me. I know this was a crappy situation to get married under, but I really feel like my husband and I could make it work. It just seems we don't want the same things out of life, and then I think about how my best friend and I have similar goals and opinions. I am sorry if this rambles, but I am a very confused woman. If you have any suggestion or opinion I would really appreciate it.

Dear Reader,

While the confusion is clear, the process of trying to write out your thoughts in a clear enough way for others to understand them can be a useful effort, in and of itself. Actually, the basis of the confusion is understandable in light of the obvious contradictions described above: on one hand, "I got married to a great man"..."I love my husband very much." On the other hand, "The feelings that my friend and I share are strong" and "my best friend and I have similar goals and opinions."

It might be helpful to focus on the fact that it's much easier to have strong feelings and to share similar goals and opinions with someone with whom you don't share serious life responsibilities—like children, finances, etc. Comparing the two kinds of relationships is like comparing apples and oranges. One is grounded in reality and the other is a sort of fantasy of what might have been (or what still could be)—neither of which is likely to be very realistic. Wondering what really could have happened with the friend is a typical way of second-guessing decisions, wondering if somehow the grass is greener on the other side of the fence. In fact, it seldom is—because all relationships have strengths and weaknesses. It's just that it's much easier to see the drawbacks in a current relationship that in a potential alternative.

We need to constantly remind ourselves that we can have most *anything* we want, but not *everything*. It's important to consider what's really important, then give up whatever interferes with that priority. Trying to have it all may lead to having *nothing*. Only the person involved in a particular situation can make the decision as to what to do, but it's encouraging that this person is thinking seriously about the situation and recognizing the need to get more clarity for herself about the contradictory thinking she's been doing. This process can significantly help in dealing with the confusion.

* * * * * * * * * * * *

Confused

Dear Peggy,

I have been married for 17 years. I am 36 years old. I have a 19-year-old and a 14 and 13-year-old (and a 2-year-old granddaughter), and I love them all very much. My husband is a good man and I would never want to hurt him for the world, but lately it has been getting harder to put aside my feelings for a friend I have known for 23 years. We used to date as kids, then I met my husband and got married.

But through the years this friend has been in and out of my life, and it's been recently that I feel like my feelings have grown stronger for him, at least I think so. Because I am not sure how to tell if that is what it is or maybe he's just an excuse for me to leave—not because my husband is mean, I just feel like I have outgrown him and ready to move on. I have learned how to depend on myself, so I guess my question is: how do I know if it's the friend I want to be with or just a way out on my own?

Dear Reader,

First of all, one member of a couple often feels they've outgrown the other. This usually means they've simply grown apart due to a failure to communicate about how each of them is changing through the years. Everybody changes; we don't stay the same as we were when we got married. But it's seldom the changes per se that create distance; it's usually the lack of talking to each other about the changes taking place in your thinking as to what you want out of life.

Having said that, it's also true that at some point it seems more reasonable to question whether it's really something else that's calling you away. And the comments above are very astute in recognizing that the stronger feelings that have grown recently toward the long-time friend are likely only a symptom of a need to be on her own rather than a need to be with him. It's quite common to revert back to an earlier time or earlier relationship when we're in the process of re-thinking our lives. But it's usually quite difficult to think clearly about what we really want unless we take time to do it on our own.

So while I can't know in a given situation what the desire to move on really means, in this instance it sounds as if she already senses that she really wants to be on her own, but switching to the other friend just seems safer or more convenient (or simply more *known*) than going out completely on her own. It's helpful to do some careful thinking (and planning) about major life changes prior to taking any significant step. Even the simple process of writing down her thoughts may have been helpful in clarifying the issue somewhat in her own mind.

* * * * * * * * * * * * *

Why won't they stop?

Dear Peggy,

I have been married for 5 years. For at least 8 months my husband has been having a fling with a coworker, and I have been through the wringer on this one. I went to her and asked her to back off; she said no. I asked him to please work with me on the marriage, he said for him it is over. I feel I haven't had a choice in this. I have been in therapy and although it helps, it doesn't take the pain away or the anger. His job knows what is going on. I just want a chance; I know it probably sounds silly, but I want to save my marriage. I love this man and I know he loves me in some way. He told me he loves me and cares about me but not "in love" with me; what is that?

We have children and they do know about her and are afraid of getting a new mom. I don't know what to do. We have a house that we bought but it's not a reason for me to stay in this relationship. He thinks we can stay together as

132

roommates; my feeling is that he wants someone here to clean up after him. She tells me that they love each other and he tells me that there are feelings for each other, but he doesn't want to live with her. How could another woman who knows what kind of pain I've been in continue this? How could he? I know it sounds like I'm playing the victim here but I am devastated. Please help me understand.

Dear Reader,

A person having an affair often says they love their spouse but are not *in love* with them. I've addressed this many, many times: it's simply that there are different stages of love. Those initial *in love* feelings are just the first stage, and they don't last over a long period of time. Nevertheless, it's especially difficult when a spouse says they don't want the marriage—*but* goes on to say "he doesn't want to live with her [the other woman]." Ironically, it's typical for a person to want to avoid having to choose—because they don't like the consequences associated with either choice.

As for wanting to understand how her husband and the other woman can be so uncaring about her pain—most people involved in affairs simply block out an awareness of the pain being caused, while focusing on whatever pleasure is involved. By focusing so much more on the pleasure than the pain, they're able to continue to feel OK about themselves. It would be much more difficult to continue an affair if the people involved actually focused on the pain.

So even though it may feel unfair that the husband and the other woman are unwilling to do anything to alleviate the pain, it's important to try to stay focused on thinking clearly instead of getting bogged down in emotions. Of course, this is easier said than done, but it's an effort worth making. While feeling like a victim is completely understandable, it undermines our efforts to handle difficult situations. There's nothing silly about wanting to save a marriage; in fact, it's important to appreciate the strength (not indicative of being a victim) that is required for a person to undertake this effort.

* * * * * * * * * * * * *

Should I stay or should I go?

Dear Peggy,

I have been married now for 17 years to a great guy, and a wonderful father of 3. We have had our problems during this time, he was an abusive alcoholic for the early part of our marriage. I stood by him. He sought counseling and is a new man, but our marriage never was what it should have been. I have had several affairs, but never have the courage to leave. I am worried about the children, but my husband and I don't even sleep together, and haven't in 6 years. I feel like I am in a business relationship. I have met a wonderful man, but can't commit to him obviously, so should I stay or should I go?

Dear Reader,

It's extremely difficult to cope with such feelings of uncertainty. Until a firm decision is made, a person is likely to be completely preoccupied with the question of whether to stay or to leave. Sometimes a person gets so tired of trying to figure out what to do that they wish someone else would make the decision for them—but, of course, no one can make such an important decision for someone else.

Some people are critical of the idea of considering practical factors in deciding whether to stay married or get a divorce. But *everything* deserves to be considered. It's especially important to realize that any decision will involve tradeoffs. There's no one path that has all the benefits without any drawbacks. So it comes down to individual assessment of the situation—not just for now but for the future.

Since there will be a long-term impact on many aspects of life, it's important that any decision take into consideration what's best long-term. None of this is easy and there are no guarantees. But a thoughtful consideration of all the factors involved and clearly making a decision can lead to taking whatever actions allow for moving on in life. For instance, a decision to go would lead to taking steps to end the marriage—while a decision to stay would lead to specifically working to improve the marriage. Either decision may be preferable to remaining indefinitely in limbo.

* * * * * * * * * * * * *

Why can't I leave?

Dear Peggy,

I need help!!! I've been married for 17 years and have four children with a good man. He is a good provider, but a terrible husband. I have my faults also; for instance, I have had several affairs. I feel I'm looking for something that my marriage is missing, so I try to find it in other men. My husband is very self-centered, controlling, abusive and not compassionate at all. I want to leave him but I don't want to hurt the children. I've seen the effects of divorce and what it can do to children. I want them to get a good education without any disruptions. I just can't seem to leave. I've come close, but always find a reason to come back—financial or kids wanting their dad. I don't work so I'm taking a few classes so I can get a job. I don't love him and I haven't for 10 years or so. Do you think I'll ever be able to get up enough courage to leave? Do I have the affairs because I don't love him? I have so many questions. Should I put my happiness on hold until the kids are gone? I have learned to cope and make people think that everything is fine. Thank you for listening.

Dear Reader,

This letter represents the dilemma felt by many people (both men and women) in marriages where something is missing. (Just for the record, there's likely to be something missing in most marriages; the question is whether the positive aspects outweigh the negatives.)

Obviously, in the above case, she isn't sure at this point. And certainly she is the only one who can decide when/whether to finally leave. As for the question about getting up enough courage to leave, I don't know that it so much takes courage as clarity. With real clarity about wanting to leave (after assessing all the pros and cons), it really doesn't take much courage to act. But without that kind of clarity, leaving wouldn't be courageous; it would just be a risk.

As for whether someone has affairs because they don't love their spouse—the reasons for affairs are always more complex that any one reason. So while this may play a part in her inclination toward having affairs, it's not necessarily the reason. Many people who don't love their spouse don't have affairs and many people who do love their spouse do have affairs—so it's never as simple as that.

Finally, as for putting happiness on hold until the kids are grown—this is a common dilemma for many parents, and one with no clear answer. It's probably helpful to honestly (and realistically) assess whether divorce will actually allow for the happiness that is desired. As with all choices in life, divorce may bring some measure of happiness, but there will also be aspects that cause unhappiness. That's because things aren't black and white; either staying married *or* getting a divorce will be fraught with difficulties that interfere with happiness. Actually, happiness is more a by-product of people's attitudes about their situations than a reflection of the actual situation. So the questions asked are good to ponder, but not to be answered too quickly.

P.S. The one word "abusive" used in the description of the husband above is not clearly defined here, so I can't comment on it directly. But, of course, physical abuse is an extremely serious issue that would take precedence over all others.

* * * * * * * * * * * *

What's wrong...?

Dear Peggy,

I have been with my wife for 7 years, married 6 months. In the past, as we lived together, I discovered she tended to have affairs. I for a while kept to myself out of fear for being alone and without my son (since I lost 2 sons from a previous marriage, and we now have a great relationship). I started to get tough and ask why she does this and what was wrong? No answer. But she would change for awhile, and months latter another phone number and constant wanting to go out with the girls ("yeah right"). Well...she wanted a wedding, and her parents gave her one. I was not sure about this... And here I am again in the same boat...her cousin confirmed she was at it again...this time I threaten divorce and leaving. She keeps trying, but for how long?

My wife is very attractive and is very vain...selfish and immature. We do discuss these issues and she has gone to counseling. But like school and

135

employment, she constantly gives up and changes her mind about everything in her life. Does she have a personality problem? And what can I do?

The only thing that matters is her looks, her secrets, her material things. She won't open up to me but she insists she loves me but doesn't know what is wrong with her... Please help with more information.

Dear Reader,

This is clearly a very frustrating situation. In some ways, it would be easier to deal with this situation if there were absolutely *no* signs of effort at improving things. But the fact that there's a short-lived effort (with counseling, etc., and then giving up) has a way of maintaining hope. No one can know for sure, but the question arises whether the hope provided by these small efforts is in fact false hope. When there's such an intense desire to find hope in a situation, it can lead to difficulty in seeing the "writing on the wall."

As with many situations, this *may* be one where all that can be done is to work for the best while preparing for the worst. In other words, as long as there's any realistic hope of change (especially given the goal of maintaining contact with children), it's understandable to do everything possible to see if things can work out. But *at the same time*, it's important that people be actively working on a back-up plan—one that will be implemented if/when there's no hope left for anything else. Actually, people are more likely to change in reaction to change they observe in you than they are to change by any direct efforts at trying to force them to change. In the final analysis, each of us can only control our own actions—and hope that these actions will have an impact on others.

* * * * * * * * * * * * *

A Soap Opera

Dear Peggy, (This letter has been edited due to its length.)

Close to three years ago, I went down the wrong path and entered into an affair with a dear friend. What began as an adventure, turned into what I thought was true love. Over time, through continual nurturing of the extramarital relationship, my relationship with my husband was neglected. I began to focus on my husband's weaknesses and my lover's strengths. The affair continued for 18 months. We talked about the day our kids would be in college and we would be free to leave our respective spouses and finally live the fairytale life we knew we would enjoy. Then his wife discovered an unfinished letter he had written to me. She called me at work and told me the affair was over and she wouldn't confront my husband if I promised to stay away from her husband. Of course, I did not stay away. In fact, we had arranged to meet that next weekend, which we went ahead and did. He told me we would have to be more careful for awhile, but he couldn't bear to lose me.

That entire summer was a soap opera. I told my lover at one point that I just couldn't continue the deceit and wanted to end it. He went home to his wife and confessed the affair was still going on. She called my husband that evening. I had already told him about the affair, but he believed it was over. My lover ended up leaving his wife and coming over to see me the next day to try to convince me to leave my husband. However, before I could even talk to my husband about this turn of events, my lover called me at work and told me he was returning to his family and that "he couldn't love me anymore." The affair started up again less than a week later with a phone call from him. He left his wife again later in the summer, but again returned to her a few days later.

Then in early November, I decided to leave myself. I talked this over with my husband, telling him I needed time to myself to see what it would be like to live without him. Then my lover told me he had decided to stay with his wife and for me to go home and forget him. He said he liked his life the way it was; his income, his wife's income, his standing in the community, his lifestyle. I was, of course, devastated. I called my husband and asked if I could come home. He had certain conditions. My lover told my husband he had no intention to ever contact me again.

Then, a few weeks ago I heard from my lover, claiming to be curious about how I was coping. He told me he was happy but not an hour went by that he didn't think of me. He said he wanted to renew our 'friendship' without the physical side to it. I admit I was happy to hear from him. But the guilt is starting to eat away at me. Although, I am not cheating on my husband in the traditional sense, I feel that I am deceiving him. And I'm not sure I can have a platonic relationship with my former lover. I'm curious about what my reaction would be upon seeing him again, but it scares me to think what might happen if either of our spouses finds out the contact has started up again. I've felt so lost without him, I would like to have him back in my life. But is it worth the risk?

Dear Reader,

This letter already makes its own best observation about the situation, saying it's "like a soap opera." The only difference is that this is *real life*. Anyone reading this description can easily see that almost no statements, plans, intentions, etc., regarding this relationship could be depended on; they changed like the wind. So the legitimacy of placing *any* confidence in any particular path or outcome of pursuing this (even as a platonic relationship) would, based on the track record, be totally unfounded.

Also, the idea of moving a formerly sexual affair to a platonic friendship is very unrealistic. Even if it were possible, the pain to the respective spouses would be cruel and unusual punishment. The patience shown by the spouses in this situation has already been beyond what could normally be expected. As for whether "having him back in my life is worth the risk"—a smart gambling person would never bet on this risk paying off. The only hope would be to avoid losing absolutely everything in the gamble.

* * * * * * * * * * * * *

Surrender

Dear Peggy,

I had an affair with a man for almost two years. Both of us were married at the time. Both of us living in situations where our spouses just didn't want to change the negative situations at hand.

My situation was living in a lonely marriage where my husband had no time for me or our relationship. Putting our two daughters in the number one slot of his list didn't hurt me, except when he didn't come through for them. His problem: a year-long cocaine addiction, which now he is seeking help and in recovery for. Let me tell you that this is not the first time he has had a problem, but it is the first time he has sought professional help, after years of me asking him to seek drug and/or marital counseling.

I surrendered to the fact that I am powerless over his addiction, and am seeing him grow. However, my lover and I have long since broken off our affair. (He is now divorced). I miss my lover terribly, and can't seem to get him out of my mind. I told him that I could not give my heart to him anymore unless it was completely. It hurts, but it gets easier every day. He has since found another woman, and forgotten about me.

Although I try to find love with my husband, I am still untrusting, cautious and unfulfilled by him. Love-making is very infrequent, yet fulfilling when we are intimate.

Do I continue to stay in a marriage where I feel no reward or intimacy, even though he is trying to help himself? He has dedicated a lot more time to our daughters, our home (fixing things up) and his personal training to enter triathlons this summer. I continue to be the lowest priority.

Dear Reader,

The question of whether to stay in the marriage is unanswerable by someone outside the actual situation. Only time (and effort) will tell whether or not the relationship will become more satisfying in the future. However, I can offer some perspective that might help see the benefit in making a more effective effort to determine whether or not that is likely to happen.

First of all, no relationship stands still in its degree of satisfaction. It's always getting better or getting worse. So this is the most important consideration in looking toward the future. The description above sounds like it's more toward the getting better end of the scale. In that case, there are some ways of thinking and behaving that can make a difference.

Some things that might help include:

— understanding that part of the dissatisfaction may be due to comparing the marriage to a life with the former lover—or some other life situation. This, of course, is an unreasonable comparison because when an outside relationship takes on the day-to-day problems inherent in any long-term primary relationship, it loses much of it's specialness.

— understanding that feelings of distrust or caution are inevitable, given the amount of secrecy that has existed in the relationship. Hiding something like an affair is a major secret that creates distance—in addition to the caution (and therefore distance) created by his earlier drug problems, etc.

— understanding that it's important not to depend on another person to fulfill you (by being preoccupied with where you place on their priority list.) It's more helpful to consider where you place *them* on *your* priority list—since there's usually a strong connection. All to often, women hold to a general principle of "wanting to be wanted" without considering the other side.

Also, there's usually a delicate balance that exists between couples where one is seeking more time/attention from the other. Unfortunately, efforts to *get* that time/attention usually serve to simply push the other person further away. So letting up on pursuing attention often frees the other person to genuinely feel interested and actually *want* more time together or mutual involvement in life.

While not all marriages can/should be saved, most people who get a divorce don't stop to think that any future relationship is likely to have many of the same issues (or some different, but still difficult issues) after a period of time has passed—and sometimes it's better to try to improve what you have than to start all over. But of course, each person must make this decision for themselves.

* * * * * * * * * * * * *

My husband's affair

Dear Peggy,

Five months ago, I discovered my husband's 9-month affair with a coworker. This coworker became a friend of mine during the affair. The other woman is married too. I confronted her first, giving her the option of telling her husband before I did. My husband became angry that I did this. I should have kept it between the two of us. We separated for a week. While we were separated my husband and his lover co-habited at a friend's house. He returned saying he wanted his wife and his family and hoped I would let him return. I did.

During the next 2 weeks he kept in contact with her—by phone and seeing her after work. I discovered an audio tape in his car (of them together) and I played the entire tape. When my husband discovered that I had the tape and provided a copy to his lover's spouse for their divorce case, he was angry to say the least. However, on this same day I discovered that she was not only having an affair with my husband, but also with another friend's boyfriend. I told my husband this. He did not believe me. When I provided him with the evidence of this other affair, he felt he had to confront her with it. This was on Friday. He went to meet her when she got off work. He told me he would return home after he confronted her. I didn't see him again until Sunday afternoon. I didn't find out until a few weeks later that he confronted her, then slept with her again and spent the night with her at her friend's home where she was staying.

He still says he wants to be with me. He promised he would go to counseling, but to this day has not. I have just this week discovered that he has

139

not yet broken all contact. I know that they still talk on the phone. I do not know if they are seeing each other.

I confronted him with this and told him that I had had enough. I did not want to listen to his empty promises any longer. Again, he says that he is where he wants to be, he is committed to our marriage. I don't see it. He has suddenly become more attentive and affectionate. I do not know where to go now. He doesn't think counseling will help. Is there any hope? I love this man, but I do not want to live this way any longer. He is out of town for a few days, and I plan on giving him the opportunity to be honest and open up with communication. I am lost. I don't know which way to go. Both of us have been married before (with children from those marriages). And now I'm at home with our 20 month-old, trying to hold everything together.

Dear Reader,

There are so many different issues in the above letter that it's hard to know where to start. The bottom line is that when a person (like the husband described above) *says* he is "committed to our marriage," but shows nothing in his behavior that would back that up, his actions speak louder than his words. (Obviously, it's just empty words unless the behavior demonstrates what is being said.) So regardless of how someone decides to proceed at this point, it's probably wise to *only* go by what the other person *does*, not what they *say*.

Another critical issue, of course, is when there are children involved, especially in cases like this where there is a blended family. The significance of this is illustrated by the statement about trying to hold everything together. Naturally, each person needs to determine for themselves what decisions to make about their future—and practical factors certainly play a role. But the commitment to trying to hold things together needs to include an evaluation of the quality of what is being held together.

Also, even when there's no evidence of past efforts to build a good marriage, any decision needs to be based on the prospects for building a good marriage in the future. So it's important to evaluate whether there's evidence (based on actions, not words) of a real effort toward that end. At some point, promises need to be demonstrated by actions if there's to be any hope for improvement.

Finally, it's probably helpful to look at a person's actions regarding *others* as well. When a person makes a decision (like sleeping with the lover even after knowing they're having other affairs), this may be an indication of a lack of responsibility in general—not just in relation to the marriage. But regardless of any particular circumstances, each person needs to weigh the overall situation for themselves in deciding what to do—and when to do it.

* * * * * * * * * * * * *

Anxiety about moving on...

Dear Peggy,

My husband had an affair 2.5 years ago which lasted off and on for over a year. I went into counseling immediately because I was devastated by his betrayal. In the beginning he derived an enormous sense of power from his affair—he had both women hanging on. But over time, as he started to see the reality of the other woman, he realized what he had done to himself and to me and to our relationship, and he became very depressed and anxious. About 9 months ago we separated, and since then his depression and anxiety has only gotten worse. He only entered counseling after we separated, and I find myself totally frustrated with his lack of progress. I want to move on with my life, but I feel the only alternative available to me is the one thing I never wanted: a divorce. I am finding it impossible to close the book on what was (for me at least) a very good marriage of 15 years (prior to the affair). Can you offer me any help in dealing with a partner who is ill and who cannot work on marital problems? Sometimes I see myself old and gray and still separated...

Dear Reader,

This letter describes a situation that is all too common: a man doesn't realize how much his wife's support means to him until he loses it. Many men are much more dependent on their wives than they realize. It's only when this support is threatened that there's a realization of how much they actually need their wife. Of course, the other side of this is that many wives thrive on being needed—so there's often some collusion in this situation.

However, the writer of the above letter sounds very thoughtful (in being concerned about her husband's well-being) *and* very wise in recognizing her need to take care of herself and move on with her life.

An affair certainly qualifies as a life crisis, and any kind of crisis can serve as a wake-up call, leading *both* people to rethink their lives and their hopes for the future. Actually, a crisis *can* be an opportunity to get in touch with what's really important and to *improve* life overall (either together or separately). There is some hope that a marriage (that was a "very good marriage of 15 years prior to the affair"), can be rebuilt and become even better, but it all depends on what happens at this point. Unfortunately, being depressed, not getting help and not actively working to improve the situation all indicate living in the past instead of an effort to build toward a new future. So it's understandable for someone to look toward moving on alone if there's no evidence of working at moving on together.

Of course, this still leaves the problem of determining when to make this decision—which involves considering both the practical factors as well as the emotional ones. However, a dedicated effort to get about the business of moving on (either alone or together) is usually better for everyone concerned than continuing to live in limbo.

* * * * * * * * * * * *

Second husband had affair

Dear Peggy,

Recently, I learned that my second husband has been cheating on me for over a year. At the beginning, I handled it pretty well. I even had the girl over to

141

my house to talk to her. It has only been two weeks and my husband and I thought it was best to separate. I told him that I would forgive him and we could try to make it work. I was willing to forgive for the reasons that he gave me. I don't think that he expected me to react this way. It hurts more now because we had problems and he turned to another woman; and I feel that he is in love with her, just by talking to both of them. He said he wanted to do it and is afraid that he may do it again.

Everyone I talked to thinks that I am crazy for even wanting to stay with someone who cheats on you. He says I always tried to be his mother. I feel that I have helped him too much and now he doesn't need me anymore; but I just loved him so much that I wanted to help him. Could you please give me some advice? I would really appreciate it.

Dear Reader,

While this letter asks for advice (and it can be helpful to get as much perspective as possible from others), it's essential that each person make their *own* decisions.

It's especially difficult to think clearly when, "Everyone...thinks that I am crazy for even wanting to stay..." Unfortunately, no one knows what they would do if faced with the situation of a partner's affair. It's easy to give simplistic, knee-jerk advice and to say someone is crazy for whatever choice they make— but it's very different when it's *you*! When someone is faced with this kind of situation, they need to be able to confide in others, but they need to be clear that no one else can (or should) tell them what to do.

I want to be clear that I'm *not* saying someone should stay and try to work it out; I'm only saying that each person should make their own decision. Also, whatever decision is made will probably be more responsible and easier to live with if it is not made too hastily. The timing of a decision and the reason for whatever decision is made are almost as important as the decision itself. It simply takes time to think through everything and become clear enough to make a good decision. In the meantime, others need to respect the decision, regardless of whether they agree or understand.

* * * * * * * * * * * * *

Wandering husband

Dear Peggy,

I am quite confused and need desperate help. My husband and I have been married almost five years. We were both with someone else when we met and left those people behind to be together. I am 47 he is 49. We both left the relationship without much. I lost my job. He quit his. I now have worked for the same company for 5 years, he with his for two. We have bought property, and we have just bought a home two months ago, his first. He has also taken on a temporary job that involves travel. He has been gone for 95 days and we have traveled back and forth a couple of times. Things seemed fine until last weekend; he came home and couldn't wait to go back. Even admitted it. I have just found out this week that he has somewhat decided to stay, and today I find out from him that he's interested (slightly) in someone else. My husband and I have always been joined at the hip. We do everything together, cook, clean, grocery shop; he has always spoiled me and more than taken good care of me. I have always kept myself up, I am 5'6" 118 pounds, light brown hair. I have never said no to sex; in fact, he rejects it sometimes. I am told I do not look my age; the men I attract, unfortunately are old enough to be my children. (This is not an ego boost.)

I love my husband very much, and I am trying to be supportive and patient. His parents live here in the same town. They are very angry with him as they do not understand; his brother is very angry at him also. I have asked his brother to please talk to him and help him understand. He tells me he does not know what to do, or what he wants. And we've only talked on the phone about this problem. My husband is a very caring man. And I gave up a lot to be with him. I would do this all again because it has been the best five years of marriage I have had. (I have been married twice before and he once.)

It's very hard to go to work. I have a twelve-year-old son I can't even cook for. I feel very guilty. But I need some answers. Do I become bitter and tell him to take a flying leap, or do I wait it out to see what if... I know I want him back. He has not pursued this woman; he does not know if she is interested. He says he's still wearing his wedding ring. So far I think he's being honest. But I am in limbo, How do I make him decide one way or another? Please help. I have been on my own before, and I can do it again. I don't want to lose this. Is there some way to make him come to his senses. Do I cut off communication for awhile, or will that fuel the fire? Help!

Dear Reader,

There are a lot of questions in this letter such as: "Do I become bitter, and tell him to take a flying leap, or do I wait it out to see what if?" and "How do I make him decide one way or another?" Unfortunately, these ideas are presented as being either/or, black/white—but this is all far too complicated for such simplistic, absolute answers.

There are some obvious signs that indicate that this puzzling kind of behavior shouldn't be *too* unexpected. For instance, when a relationship begins as one where "we left those people behind to be together," it's not too surprising that there might not be a lot of dependability about someone sticking around if something else looks more enticing at the moment. And far from being a *positive* sign, being "joined at the hip" can actually lead to a desire for more distance, thus moving away. Also, it's not usually helpful to ask others (friends or relatives) to talk to him and help him understand.

Finally, as for asking: "Do I cut off communication for a while..." any resolution of confusing situations like this requires clear communication between the two primary parties—without guessing or manipulating. It's always better to know precisely where you stand than to wonder (and hope) that things will get better.

* * * * * * * * * * * * *

Back and forth

Dear Peggy,

I've been separated from my husband almost two years now. In the meantime, I met someone else. I never enjoyed sex until I met him. I love being with him, being close, and he makes me laugh. I've been back and forth between him and my husband. Both of them want me, and I can't let go of either one of them. In the meantime, I lost my livelihood and have been living out of a suitcase running in both directions. My husband is in the military and we move around. I'm wondering if maybe I should just go off on my own because I was financially independent until we moved away from California. I've been depressed since that move 4 years ago. I always felt I could have a better life with my husband because we think more alike in terms of the future. How important is that as compared to loving being with someone a lot? There's nothing like it that I've ever experienced. People say that you can rekindle the spark of the spouse, but I am really beginning to doubt that. How can you create feelings that are not in your heart, even though you love someone very much? I have forgiven him for ignoring me and taking me for granted for ten years, and he has forgiven me about the affair. I just don't get excited around my husband, but I can spend the rest of my life with him. Am I just thinking too negatively? I feel that the love and intimacy like I have with the other man is the basic glue for a couple. What do you think?

Dear Reader,

I immediately gravitated to the one section in this letter that was *not* related to choosing between the two men. Hidden in the middle of this letter is an important insight for anyone who is ambivalent about choosing between partners: "I'm wondering if maybe I should just go off on my own because I was financially independent until we moved away from California. I've been depressed since that move 4 years ago."

Before addressing that particular issue, though, I want to make a few comments about this whole idea of choosing. Almost everyone has a tendency to second-guess themselves when trying to choose. The closer they get to one choice, the more they focus on what they're giving up that would be available with the *other* choice. Then if/when they shift toward the other choice, they again start wondering about what they're giving up in making *that* decision. As I constantly remind people, *every* choice has tradeoffs. The key is to decide which tradeoffs are the most important to you personally. Trying to hold onto *everything* at once (not wanting to give up *anything*) makes a clear choice almost impossible.

In most instances, getting some distance from the tug-of-way between two choices (by going off on your own) allows for a degree of clarity that isn't

144

possible when caught up in the issue. Also, being independent opens up the possibility of finding that a break from any relationship might be preferable. Basically, when a choice is this difficult to make, it's likely that neither choice would be a really satisfying one. So it may be that people have a kind of knowing (like the comment about going off on her own) as to what to do—but they get distracted by the ongoing struggle and never get clarity around whether or not there's something there to pay attention to. Each person needs to assess these kinds of instincts for themselves and rationally analyze whether it would, in fact, serve them well to follow that sense of what they *might* do.

* * * * * * * * * * * * *

Better to move on?

Dear Peggy,

I have a lack of sexual desire for my husband; and although I am no expert, I believe it IS one of the basic cores of a strong relationship in that it breeds fidelity, friendship and trust. When you have great sex and pure love with someone at the same time, it is unlike anything I've ever imagined. So why do you advise all of these women to stay in marriages (with no children involved) that are lacking in being sexually fulfilled emotionally and physically? I am very confused by this attitude of once you marry it's for life! I cannot imagine having this feeling with my husband. Maybe I found something that most people don't. What do you think? This has been ongoing for a year and a half and it's always an awesome, indescribable experience—and I have spent a lot of time with this man, too, during my separation. Please explain why you feel you should stick in there and try to make it work and create these feelings of sexual desire? I truly believe it's there or it isn't.

Dear Reader,

I do not believe (nor do I recommend) that all women stay in marriages where they are sexually unfulfilled. (In fact, I strongly recommend a book called "Marriage Shock" by Dalma Heyn, which addresses the need to improve the lot of women in marriage so that the well-being of wives is not sacrificed for the sake of the institution of marriage.) So the comments I make that seem to side with the idea of staying married are actually only pointing out what is often ignored: that comparing the sexual excitement in a new relationship to that in a long-term one is quite superficial and shortsighted. A person is only buying time until the new relationship becomes old—with many of the same problems that were inherent in the previous relationship.

While a good sexual relationship is extremely important, I have not seen evidence that it "breeds fidelity, friendship and trust." In fact, in general, it's the other way around: fidelity, friendship, and trust can breed great sex—because the best ongoing sex is one that emerges out of a deep knowing of each other that allows for the kind of closeness that comes from trusting each other enough to be totally vulnerable and open. The excitement of sex in a long-lasting relationship comes from having developed a connection based on honesty, commitment, and full openness to another person.

For instance, trust that's based on a deep knowing is very different from that which is typical of new relationships. In relatively new relationships, there's often a *feeling* of complete trust—which may or may not prove to be justified when you get to know the other person at a deeper level. And as your trust increases (based on a deeper knowing of each other), you see that your initial trust was superficial in that it was based on limited information.

Since most of the letters I receive are from people who are having serious problems with honesty and trust in their primary relationship, it's understandable that it interferes with their sexual relationship. So unless someone intends to change partners every few years, solving the sexual relationship issues by simply changing partners is a very temporary solution.

That's why I try to help people understand the "changing nature of love," so they can realize that the pure sexual excitement in a new relationship will eventually wither unless it is replaced with a connection that is based on a genuine bonding on a deeper level. This connection, in turn, will allow the sexual relationship to be far more than just the sex act per se. With this understanding, more people might choose to develop the honesty/trust/vulnerability with their current long-term partner instead of waiting a few years until the new partner becomes more long-term and requires the same kind of shift as is currently needed in the old relationship. In other words, I try to present the long view of life instead of the Instamatic snapshot, hoping people can be more thoughtful in making whatever decisions will serve them best in the long run, not just for the moment.

* * * * * * * * * * * *

I fell in love

Dear Peggy,

I am having an affair. I fell in love with him. I know it's wrong and I want to stop. I have tried, but he convinces me to stay. The look in his eyes when he says he loves me is overwhelming. Neither of us plans to leave our spouses. How can I break up with him and truly do it? Please... I am going out of my mind... one day I want him... the next day I want to commit to my husband.

Dear Reader,

As with many letters like this, I always hope that the process of writing the letter indicates a willingness to break through the fantasy about *love* in this kind of situation (which is usually more about infatuation and newness than anything else) by examining the reality of the situation. For instance, the statements that "it's wrong" and that "neither of us plans to leave our spouses" show how hopeless this is. But at this point the rational understanding of the situation is being overpowered by the emotional reaction.

The internal struggle is exemplified by the description: "one day I want him..." (no doubt when being controlled by emotions) and "the next day I want to commit to my husband" (no doubt when doing more clear thinking). So this makes the course fairly obvious: to try to stop the power of the emotions anytime they get in control by deliberately, consciously focusing on the reality of the situation.

It's also very helpful in situations like this (where we *want* to make a change but feel like it's too overwhelming) to confide in someone who will *support* the change. This doesn't mean having someone act as a conscience or try to lecture or convince (or in any way take responsibility for the change). It simply means being in the position of being *accountable* to someone who knows the struggle and is willing to support the clear thinking. As with AA groups or other support groups, this idea is based on having someone to turn to for help in avoiding doing something the person is trying to stop (in a case like this, avoid contacting the third party). The feelings are not likely to diminish as long as they are being fed by ongoing contact of any kind. So severing the contact is the first goal if there's a genuine desire to get over the attachment.

* * * * * * * * * * * *

Can't deal with this

Dear Peggy,

I am a twenty-two-year-old college student that lives with my fiancé of four years. I recently found out that he had a work affair with another woman. He had been very miserable for about two months and blamed it on me and my faults. I would cry every day, thinking there was something wrong with me. Well come to find out, it was his guilt from the affair. He didn't tell me about the affair until I caught him coming home from her house. He then was going to leave me for her, and now wants me. For about a month now he has been willing to do anything for me. I feel that all the gifts in the world will not help. He has even agreed to go to counseling. My question to you is because I have lost all hope, faith and trust in this man, how can I ever feel right about the relationship or being with him when all I see when I look at him is him being with her? I feel betrayed and they say that with time things will get easier, but for me all that has happened is it has gotten worse. Please help me understand why someone that says they love you so much could ever break your heart and spirit by cheating on you?

Dear Reader,

It's extremely common for the person having an affair to find fault with their partner and lead them to believe there's something wrong with them. This can be positively crazy-making and just compounds the pain when the truth is eventually revealed. Also common is the scenario by which a person is caught rather than voluntarily admitting an affair. This, too, makes it more difficult. Then once the affair is revealed, any ambivalence of the person who had the affair (as to whether they want to go with the other person or maintain the primary relationship) is another blow.

So it's quite understandable that all this is not easily erased by gifts or any more substantive efforts like offering counseling. But a combination of things *can* make a difference, including counseling, reading lots of good material about affairs, and talking about all aspects of affairs—as well as focusing together on how any future attractions will be handled. This, of course, takes time. So it doesn't necessarily get easier with time to deal with what happened unless that time is spent actively establishing a new basis of honest communication that can eventually lead to rebuilding trust. (As for questioning whether someone can really love you if they have an affair, as strange as it seems, this is quite common—especially among men. Men are better at compartmentalizing the different aspects of their lives.)

But any decision about whether to stay together or whether to trust again needs to be made based on considering the possibilities for the future of the relationship instead of just focusing on the painful things mentioned above. So the real challenge in situations like this is not just making sense of the past and recovering from what happened; it's whether or not this crisis can be used as a motivator to develop a different kind of relationship in the future.

* * * * * * * * * * * * *

Angry and Hurt

Dear Peggy,

I have been with my husband for 17 years, and we have 3 wonderful children. We've been having problems communicating and are always angry with each other. For the last month and a half he tells me we must try and make this work and that he loves me very much. Three weeks later he tells me he's out of love with me—and I got it out of him that he's been speaking with this other woman who works near his job. It went as far as them hanging out and kissing, but he swears no sexual act has happened and won't happen. I asked him if he can stop seeing this woman, and he said yes. I asked him will he stop seeing her, he said he doesn't know. He said he doesn't love her, but she's fun to be with. At this point I was outraged and kicked him out, but then cooled down and said he could stay until he finds another place to stay—but he said no, he'll go. (He's staying with relatives.) And there's no hope for us. He said he's tired of the fighting and the pain we both inflict on each other, but he also said he doesn't know what will happen in the future. He swears he's not seeing this other woman. I still love him dearly and want us to work things out. Should I give him his space and become his friend and try to build something from that—or do you think it's hopeless and he can really fall out of love in a matter of weeks?

Dear Reader,

It's no wonder the woman who wrote this letter is feeling confused. Nothing about the situation described is very clear or rational. When someone doesn't seem to know what they want—and doesn't seem to be able to be honest about whatever they *do* know about their real feelings, it's almost impossible to know how to proceed. In most instances, it's better to avoid trying to second-guess the potential impact on someone who is so vague and so unwilling to commit to any particular set of actions.

When someone behaves in this unreliable way, it can be helpful for the spouse to focus on her own feelings and try to get as much clarity as possible about just what *she* wants. Even when, as stated above, she "loves him dearly and wants us to work things out," there's still no guarantee that *whatever* she does to try to work it out will actually work unless there's a willingness on the part of *both* people to try to make it work. So giving him space or trying to become his friend may only allow him to delay getting around to making a firm decision one way or the other. In the meantime, it's reasonable to be hopeful that he will change—but to be prepared if he doesn't.

*   *   *   *   *   *   *   *   *   *   *   *   *

HELP???

Dear Peggy,

Ten years ago my husband left me for a girl that was 18 years younger than himself. At the time he had just turned 40. After 6 months and a lot of begging from me (I wanted him back home, we had small children), he came back home to us. I swore to forgive him; (there is no point in saying I would forget).

He just turned 50, and—here we go again. I went under his screen name to see if I had any Email and while I was online at 3 different points women came on to talk to him. The first 2 denied having anything to do with him—however the third one apologized to me, saying that he had told her he was a divorced 42-year-old man. At this point in time I would like to give him that divorce!!! Unfortunately, we have a child under 10 years old and two teenagers. The youngest one idolizes his father, and does not want mommy and daddy to split up. I feel nothing for this man any more. Is it worth staying in this relationship? What would be best for the youngest of our children? The 2 older ones are sick of hearing us fight—although they do not want us to split up. I am at a confused point in life.

Dear Reader,

This letter reflects some very important issues: 1) what about someone going back to having affairs after a "second chance?" and 2) what about staying together for the sake of the children?

Neither of these issues can be adequately addressed in isolation (without including the person who had the affairs). The above letter does not indicate whether the revelations from online were discussed with the husband. Also, as I consistently point out, any decision about whether or not to stay married (even for the sake of the children) needs to be based on the prospects for the future of the marriage, not just on the past.

Obviously, promises aren't sufficient to know that things could be different. But a full (and ongoing) discussion of all the issues is an essential aspect of determining whether or not there can be any kind of future for the marriage/family. While experts differ in their analysis of both the short-term and the long-term impact of divorce on children, they universally agree that a really bad marriage/family life is not preferable to a "good divorce." Naturally, "good divorce" sounds like a strange phrase, but it's the name of an excellent book by Constance Ahrons that addresses this issue.

As with most situations like this, a hasty decision (either way, whether quickly divorcing or being resigned to staying "for the kids") is probably not going to lead to long-term satisfaction. As difficult as it is to talk through all these issues, it's better than trying to decide in the absence of more information.

*   *   *   *   *   *   *   *   *   *   *   *   *

Lost and confused...

Dear Peggy,

Here's my problem. I have been with my hubby for 16 years. I have four children. I told him several months ago I was done and basically told him for the hundredth time how I feel. He then (as a last resort effort), told me about an affair that he had off and on over the first ten years of our marriage. I suspected it then and lived in hell for all those years (him constantly being insecure with me), when the whole time it was him.

About a year ago I fell for a friend of mine and told my husband I had a crush on him. I was feeling this way because I have no feeling for him (my husband)... I want out so bad, but I am scared for starters, and he won't leave. He just simply won't. No matter how many times we discuss it, he stays...and I have to get mad to make him listen—and he still does not! I am lost and confused. Any suggestions?

Dear Reader,

Many people find themselves in this kind of situation—where they don't want to stay but are afraid to go. It seems that the affair per se is not the burning issue at this point, although, of course, it may well be part of the reason there is "no feeling for him (my husband)..."

However, it appears that the current issue is how to get someone else to "take action" (as indicated by the comment that "he won't leave"). Unfortunately, one person can't *make* another person do anything. We can only take responsibility for our *own* actions. For instance, when one person wants to part, it's often their responsibility to take the necessary actions—in this case being the one to decide to leave. But the most telling comment is probably the one: "I am scared for starters."

This kind of fear and uncertainty is totally understandable. Part of it may be due to the lack of clarity about the unknown future if action is taken. Having a *crush* on someone really has no legitimate bearing on what to do or not do. Any decision to take action is best considered based *not* on going from one person to another, but in becoming your own person first. And if someone is not prepared to do that, then it's reasonable to focus their time and energy on doing whatever it takes to *get* prepared to be on their own.

150

Feelings of desperation can interfere with clear thinking and make it almost impossible to rationally evaluate the situation. It also makes it very difficult to work toward resolving whatever issues might make things better in the meantime. So it's helpful to try very hard to offset the emotions (fear, anger, etc.) with as much rational thinking as possible. This can be supported by lots of reading and finding people to talk with who are willing to help in this clarification process—*without* giving advice.

* * * * * * * * * * * *

Help—Age Difference

Dear Peggy,

I am a 54-year-old woman...my second husband is 46 years old...we have been married for 10 years. I didn't think we would make it that long, mostly because of our age difference and the step-children involved—and money problems as well. I have had a lot going against my marriage, but it's lasted for this long. The reason I am writing is that I just recently found out my husband has had a 6-month affair with a pretty woman, 42 years old (more his age and more to his taste I am sure). He lied and lied, but I had that feeling and I trusted my gut feeling...so I left a little tape recorder hidden and taped his/her conversation and caught him where he couldn't lie out of it. Well...he told me of the affair and said he didn't love her; it was just for fun...fun. I was gone for 4-5 months, away taking care of my dying father with cancer...that's when he met her...in a chat room, and they met in real. I was deeply hurt and was ready to leave him....but he said he wanted to try and make our marriage work...if I could get over her. I told him I needed time, but what it really is that I am dealing with is: I don't trust him (not that I trusted him that much before...had bad relationships with men is why).

Did I do the right thing...? Should I have divorced him...? Never trust him again. I am just waiting to see...I guess...people, relatives say I should leave him. I would be lost and I am confused...I am tired, and gotten very old acting. I don't feel like he really loves me, even though he sometimes (rarely) says that he does...his interests are totally different than mine; its like he goes his way and I do what I want to do, which is I hardly do anything... He has no respect for me or my age...I am at a loss...scared of losing...being by myself... Age does make a difference!...I knew it when I married him....I know now I shouldn't have married him. Ask me if I love him?...that's a hard question. What's love at my age?...or what's love got to do with it...love/hate is a thin line...and I guess its a love/hate relationship. I think I am going to be a loser here...matter of time... What you think?

Dear Reader,

My heart goes out to those who feel as the woman who wrote this letter— that they're old and helpless in the face of such disappointment in their lives. I still remember that when my husband told me about his affairs, my first reaction was to think I really had to find a way to work this out. And a *part* of my

151

thinking was that I was *too old* to think in terms of starting over after investing so much of my life in this marriage. Well, at the time I had those thoughts—I was only *37 years old*! Now I'm in my 60s—and I don't filter everything through my age in the way I did at an earlier stage of my life. It's usually when we feel helpless and not in charge of our lives (regardless of the particular age) that we feel old.

I know (especially because of age-related physical issues) that age *does* make a difference—but it doesn't make the difference we *think* it does when we give it the power to control our image of ourselves. So while there are many issues presented in the above letter, most of them seem to be tied to this feeling of being too old. The image we hold of ourselves is the one we present to the world—and people tend to treat us the way we present ourselves to be treated. However, whether or not others change their perception of us, we're much better off (especially as women) if we focus on strengthening our sense of self and valuing ourselves as total human beings instead of basing our worth on our particular age or marital status.

* * * * * * * * * * * * *

Do I stay or start over?

Dear Peggy,

My wife had an affair 5 years ago and I cannot get over the feeling of mistrust of her. I thought that I could forgive her, but in reality I still get physically sick when I think of how she lied and manipulated my trust in order to keep her affair going. She never offered any information about the affair, and it is only because I discovered proof of the affair (I found a letter sent to her with intimate content) that she admitted that she had been seeing someone else. But she has never admitted that she had sex, only that she went to motels (I found one of the receipts) to talk and have drinks with the man. By the way, the man was an ex-lover from college days, and they ran into each other at their 30-year high school reunion, and things developed from their reunited meeting that night. As you can read, we are not kids and we have been married well over 20 years and have two lovely kids (no problems), both going to excellent schools and doing well in their lives. I might add that my wife has had her own practice counseling families, mainly couples, for marriage and other personal issues for the past 20 years (and certainly understands the reality of what she has done) but has failed to make me understand why she would put our family at risk for her personal satisfaction without first leaving me.

She now tells me that through the reunited experience she had with her ex-lover she has gained much appreciation of me and that it cemented in her mind that I was the only man for her. Since from the beginning she has lied about this affair and everything connected to it, what I do believe is that she has found out that her lover was not the catch she thought he would be and he has no intention of leaving his wife. When I first realized the extent of the affair, I considered leaving my wife; however, after painful months of talking it out with my wife, I decided to stay because, 1. I did not want to split up the family and, 2. I thought that I had the capacity to forgive and forget. I still do not want to split up the family, but I have discovered that I do not have the fortitude to forgive her for the virus she alone has planted in our marriage. My question is, do I go on living my life realizing that my wife has admittedly been a weak person (and in spite of all the education and life's experiences still could fall into another relationship as illustrated above) or do I make the leap and look for a partner that I can trust to live out my days?

Dear Reader,

Such a thoughtful letter. Some of the obvious problems in working through this kind of situation in order to continue the marriage include: "She never offered any information about the affair." "She has lied about this affair and everything connected to it." "She has never admitted that she had sex...only...went to motels...to talk and have drinks with the man..."

As I've often said, marriages can survive without talking through an affair—but they're likely to be deadened, meaningless relationships. This is all the more difficult in the face of feeling there was a lie about the basic *fact* of there having been an affair. Of course, I can't possible know for sure whether or not there was a sexual affair in this particular situation. But, *in general*, this is reflective of the mindset that is so common among people having affairs: "Never tell. If questioned, deny it. If caught, say as little as possible." People seldom tell the whole truth (even when caught); they tell as little as possible.

These factors maintain the feelings expressed in the very first sentence: "I cannot get over the feeling of mistrust of her." And the lack of trust naturally continues to erode the relationship, leaving it somewhat empty and hollow—which then leads to thoughts of leaving and "looking for a partner that I can trust to live out my days."

Unfortunately, it's not that simple. First of all, there will never be any "guarantee" that another partner will be one that can be trusted to forever remain faithful. I don't mean this to be pessimistic, only realistic—in that most people *intend* to be monogamous when they marry. And any assurances that might be given in the beginning can not be guaranteed to last forever. Everything depends on being able to *maintain* ongoing honest communication about attractions, potential temptations, etc., in order to *avoid* an affair.

So since the key to preventing a future affair (whether with a person who has already had an affair or with a new partner) depends on committing to and practicing this kind of ongoing honest communication, this effort is essential—regardless of whether there's a decision to stay or to go.

Of course, the other significant factor involved in a situation like the one above is the legitimate concern about splitting up the family. Each person needs to weigh this for themselves as they consider everything involved in such a decision. Certainly, the *potential* for being able to work through something like this is there for any couple who *both* decide to work on it—regardless of what has happened in the past.

Finally, it's revealing to note that the wife described in this letter is a counselor herself. This simply highlights the fact that people often fail to be able to act in accordance with their understandings. I know from many years of hearing all kinds of stories from all kinds of people that you can *not* determine what someone is likely to do based on their knowledge about marriage or personal relationships.

The bottom line is that any decision involves some risk and uncertainty. So it's important not to leap to any particular decision too quickly, but to devote lots of time and energy to carefully considering all the factors involved before making a final decision. In fact, the *process* used in making the decision has a significant impact on the long-term satisfaction with the decision (whatever it turns out to be).

11: Rebuilding the Marriage/Trust

My husband had an affair

Dear Peggy,

Please help me!!! I found out in February that my husband was having an affair, when I confronted him with this he did not deny it. I asked him if he was in love with her and he told me yes. He then moved out for a month (then returned home for a month), but during that month, he left for a hunting trip for two weeks and spent them with her. He lied and told me that he did not see her. But then on Memorial Day weekend he told me he was going to see her again. I then told him that it was over and that I was getting a divorce. He left and the following Monday he came back home. I told him to leave and that it was over, he begged me to take him back. After a few days I gave in and let him come back home. He told me that it was over for good between him and the other woman and that he was afraid that he would lose me forever and he just couldn't bear the thought of that and that he was in love with me and always has been but he was just confused before. She left him a good-bye letter and returned all the things that he had given her.

My problem is that I cannot trust him, so I am asking for your help. I need to know if I would ever trust and believe in him again. I love this man with all my heart, but I just don't know what to think any more!!??!! Please help me!!!

Dear Reader,

Even though trust has been shattered, it does not mean it can never be rebuilt. It is possible, but it can't be done quickly. Rebuilding trust after an affair is a slow and difficult process. It calls for a great deal of honest communication on an ongoing basis. Real honesty implies more than just "not lying." It means "not withholding relevant information." So it's important that there be a willingness to answer whatever questions arise and to hang in during the inevitable emotional difficulty caused by the actions. All this will take time and effort. Trust is not something a person can just "bestow" because they want to (or because the other person wants them to). Trust is earned by actions over time; it's a by-product of the things that are done (or not done)—not just what someone says.

As to whether or not to invest the effort in doing this rebuilding, that calls for a day-by-day assessment. While it may be slow, it's essential that there be some evidence of a gradual increase in trust for it to be reasonable to truly trust again. By gradually increasing trust, there's hope of eventually regaining even more trust than before.

155

So it's pretty difficult to know at the time of the initial discovery of the affair whether or not trust can be restored. That will only be determined by devoting lots of time and energy to getting to know each other in depth so that the trust can come out of that knowing, not just wondering.

*   *   *   *   *   *   *   *   *   *   *   *   *

Telling all the details?

Dear Peggy,

My husband found out about my affair just two months ago. He insisted on knowing all the details of the affair including dates and times I met him and everything we did. My husband said it was better for him to know the details, and that it would help him to know exactly what took place rather than to always wonder. It was the most difficult thing I ever had to do, but I believed him and thought he was entitled to know if that's what he wanted. I don't think in the long run that this has helped. In fact, I think it has been a roadblock to our getting beyond the affair itself. Do you think I made a mistake by telling my husband all the details?

Dear Reader,

The importance of answering the questions (whatever they may be) is in keeping with the best thinking on how to deal with affairs—because unanswered questions create enormous problems, including:

— inability to trust honesty in the future if no honesty about the past
— feeling of being treated like a child when someone knows something you want to know, but won't tell you
— imbalance of power and equality in the relationship by virtue of being unwilling to tell.

Now, having said this, there still is no guarantee that telling will make things OK. Even when, as happened above, telling *seems* to have created a "roadblock to our getting beyond the affair itself," it's likely that *not telling* would have been even worse. (This is similar to taking medicine that doesn't *seem* to have cured the problem, when, in fact, there's no way to know just how bad the problem might have been *without* the medicine.)

So it may be a little like "damned if you do, damned if you don't." *Still*, the best bet is on telling. The sense that telling didn't help may be based on a false belief that this can be quickly overcome. I've never known *anyone* (including myself) who completely recovered from the emotional impact of a spouse's affair in less than 2 years—even with the best efforts by everyone concerned.

So while second-guessing the telling is understandable, it's probably still better than the alternative might have been. Time, patience, and continued efforts toward honest communication are still the most likely to pay off in the long run.

*   *   *   *   *   *   *   *   *   *   *   *   *

Can I get through this?

Dear Peggy,

My husband of 3 years had an online affair for a month before I found out. I have never felt so betrayed. He knew how I felt about this matter, because we had discussed it before we went online. We both have been married before and hurt before. We knew this would be different because we are Christians. I'm not throwing a holier than thou attitude, but I can't believe he did this. He said he only did it for fun, will never do it again, will never lie again, and will do anything to prove his love for me. I'm not mad anymore. I just don't feel safe, special, or that I know him anymore. I don't know how to work it out.

Dear Reader,

I personally understand the statement: "I don't feel safe, special, or that I know him anymore." It almost drove me crazy trying to understand how my husband could have had affairs. We had been childhood sweethearts; he had never had sex with anyone else but me (even before we married), he was a pre-ministerial student when we married and attended Yale Divinity School before transferring into psychology. And we had been married 11 years when he began having affairs.

I want to offer encouragement that it is possible to overcome this and to once again feel safe. In fact, the process involved in working it out can bring you closer than you were before. Most of us didn't really know our partner before this experience. Afterwards, there's an opportunity to develop a different kind of relationship, the kind that's only possible through rock-bottom, responsible honesty. Of course, this calls for a great deal of honest communication on an ongoing basis, not just a promise that they will "never do it again."

It will take a long time to fully recover from this experience and establish a new relationship for the future. This can't be done in days, weeks, or months; it usually take a couple of years. Be patient and persistent. With time and effort, your relationship can eventually be better than before.

* * * * * * * * * * * *

Should I get pregnant despite the affair?

Dear Peggy,

My husband of nine years had an affair 3 years ago. We separated at that time, but eventually got back together. Periodically, I found out that he kept in contact with the other woman, who lives several states away. We decided we would "work through" this, and decided a year ago to have another child. I miscarried in June, and we have been trying to conceive since then, with fertility drugs due to reproductive problems.

I found out a month ago that my husband still Emails this woman, and I asked him to separate. He asked for us to go through counseling, which I agreed to—which is going quite well. Problem is, my husband and Dr. are pressuring me to get pregnant, the Dr. because of the drugs I must take. I would love another child, and love my husband, but feel like I am taking a big risk getting pregnant right now. I know that my husband has not seen this woman in three years, and I have seen the Email he was sending; it is not personal or involved. He has given me his password and told me to sign on whenever I'd like. He does not check his mail without me being present, but I hate having to go through that. Just wondering, what is your opinion on this?

Dear Reader,

A child is an awesome responsibility—and this reader is to be congratulated for taking the idea of getting pregnant so seriously. By writing this letter, she already demonstrates an awareness (fear?) that she can't count on her husband to do/be what is needed as a committed husband/father. It's not completely clear as to whether he finally gave up contact with the ex-lover (including no more Emails); but if not, this would reflect poorly on his caring about the health and well-being of his wife. Also, the Dr. seems to be colluding in making it more difficult for her to act on her own sense of the situation. If the Dr. doesn't know about the former affair and later contact, this might make a difference.

Another factor may be whether the counselor knows of his continued contact with the former third party. A counselor who is knowledgeable about the dynamics of rebuilding trust following an affair would recognize that the ability to trust a commitment to the relationship and their future together is understandably affected by a failure to severe all contact (whether Email or some other form).

Clearly, there's a need for more support for the effort to think clearly about this overall situation. While a baby can be a wonderful addition to a solid relationship, it can further strain one that is already shaky. It's pretty well-recognized that having a baby is not a solution for other marital problems. So while I can't advise just what someone should do about a situation like this, I'm quite clear that there needs to be more solid input from informed, unbiased people who care—and less pressure from husband and/or professionals in undermining the ability to trust your own judgment.

*   *   *   *   *   *   *   *   *   *   *   *   *

What's happening here?

Dear Peggy,

I have been married 7 years with 2 kids. My wife recently had an affair with a coworker. She states that the affair is over, but the two continue to see each other at work and communicate via computer mail. She becomes somewhat angry and wants to avoid any further discussion of the affair. Do you feel that the affair is still happening? If not physically, emotionally? What should I do? I just don't like the continued contact between them or her reluctance to really discuss the continued contact. She states that they are just friends and coworkers. I feel that something is still happening. Your thoughts and advice please!

Dear Reader,

Regardless of whether or not something is still happening (either physically or emotionally), it's completely reasonable (and smart) to discuss the continued contact. Continuing contact works against recovery. It keeps things *stuck* because the contact is an ongoing source of anxiety and concern that interferes with recovery. But even more important is that an unwillingness to severe all contact shows a lack of caring about the husband's feelings of discomfort. And the reluctance to even discuss the continued contact is an additional indication of a lack of concern for his feelings and for what is needed to restore trust and rebuild the relationship.

In any particular situation, there are exceptions. But in general, a situation where there is continuing contact with the third party (even though the affair has definitely ended) makes it unlikely that the marriage will recover to a point where it can be a really strong, vital relationship. So if the marriage is truly valued, every effort will be made to completely cut off any contact with the third party (regardless of the difficulty related to changing jobs, etc.).

* * * * * * * * * * * *

Lies about having an affair

Dear Peggy,

I can't get past the lies my husband told. He was in this affair for months before it became sexual. When his girlfriend started harassing me and telling me about the affair, she called my work, stalked my movements, wrote me letters. And through it all, my husband denied knowing who was making the calls or writing me the letters. Lied over and over again. I have been able to get over the sex, but I can't get over the lies. I am extremely honest and just can't conceive the reasons for lies.

How can you trust someone who can lie to your face over and over again. How do you know if they ever tell the truth. I don't want to be so fooled again. I tell him I'll never believe him again and seem to look for ways to catch him in some sort of story. I want so bad to be able to trust him again. I can forgive but not forget.

Dear Reader,

When a person has adopted lying as a way of life (which often happens when someone is having an affair) it's often hard to quit "cold turkey"—even when there's a genuine desire to do so. Part of the reason for this is that a person who has lied to others has usually first lied to themselves. They have rationalized their behavior and told themselves whatever was required in order to deal with the discrepancy between who they were and who they pretended to be.

For them to become trustworthy involves going through the process of becoming comfortable with this new, unfamiliar way of behaving. When someone is having an affair (or keeping any significant secret), it probably feels *safer* to lie than to tell the truth; but once they commit to rebuilding the trust that has been broken, they need to see that it's now both safer and smarter to tell the truth.

So while it may seem unfair for the person who has been hurt by the earlier lies to be supportive of their partner's efforts to tell the truth (especially when the truth hurts), it's critical to avoid punishing them when they do tell the truth. (Since most of us do or say whatever "works," if they feel it's not working to tell the truth, they won't be motivated to continue trying to break the habit of lying.)

The bottom line: All habits can be changed when there's a genuine desire to do so and when there's support from others during that process.

* * * * * * * * * * * * *

Am I just as guilty?
(Here are 2 letters before my response.)

Dear Peggy, (letter #1)

I recently found out that my wife of 8 years had an affair. Even though I am deeply hurt, I still love her very much. However, the affair isn't the only thing that is bothering me, it's how I found out about it... I read her diary. Before last weekend, I had never read her diary, and I never intended on reading it at that time. I was looking for something I lost and I moved her diary to see if it was behind it (she keeps it under the bed). When I did, a piece of paper fell out, so I opened the diary to put the paper back.

When I did, I glanced down at one of her entries. That's how I found out about the affair. What's worse is that I felt so hurt and angry I went back and read the whole thing. Now I feel terrible. I know that what I did is a major violation of trust. Even though I feel I had the right to know about the affair, the words she puts down in her diary are her own and I had no right to look at them. Right now I am very confused. I really want to talk to her about the affair, but I know if I do she will know how I found out. I guess my question is: If I do decide to discuss the affair with her, how will this affect the discussion? Aren't I just as guilty as her?

Dear Peggy, (letter #2)

I caught my wife of 22 years making out like a teenager on my couch with my best friend. After I gained my composure, I found out that they had met 2 times before in a park secretly. There was no kissing, but she tells me she needed someone to talk to. This 'former' best friend of mine had offered to meet with her because my wife was complaining at a bar about me during one of our Saturday night outings. When we talk, she doesn't want to refer to her relationship as an affair. I think she is in self-denial. Incidentally, I had thought there was something going on when she came home drunk one evening covered with perfume. She denied meeting anyone; however, this turned out to be one of the meeting nights. Alcohol has played a part in every one of their meetings. She simply wants to play this off as a bad mistake. I have read quite a bit on extramarital affairs and I believe we have quite a bit of work to do. She hasn't really opened up in any of our counseling sessions. Every time I talk about the betrayal, lying, and hurt, she responds by saying I have lied to her several times in the past. I have never had a relationship with anyone. Any help would be appreciated.

Dear Reader,

In letter #2, the writer's spouse is trying to lay a guilt trip on him by equating the deception involved in having an affair with whatever lies *both* people have probably told each other through the years. However, unless he has failed to acknowledge some pretty significant lying that might have taken place, it's ludicrous for the spouse to try to say in essence that they both have done the same thing. While all deception can be destructive to varying degrees, having an affair is a far more damaging lie and/or deception than most other things that happen in a committed relationship.

In letter #1, the writer is "laying the guilt trip" on *himself*. This may be positive in that it shows a recognition of the importance of honesty in a relationship and recognition that what he did was a violation of trust. However, equating reading a diary with having an affair is simply not reasonable. Part of the guilt feelings may come from the fact that it's extremely unlikely that the discovery of the writing in the diary was as benign as it is described. Nevertheless, while in *principle*, any deception is harmful to a marriage, it is not true that ALL deceptions are equal in their potential for damaging the relationship.

In both instances described in these letters, there's clearly a lack of trust on the part of everyone involved. Any effort to deal with the affairs or to recover and learn from this experience depends on getting beyond the blaming and comparing blame—to focusing on how to begin taking responsibility for being honest from this moment on. Crisis situations like this can be used as an opportunity to begin to develop real honesty. But this can't happen until there's a willingness to drop the guilt trips and try to actually *do* whatever is called for to rectify the situation. The past is over, and can't be changed. Being sorry (on either person's part) is not enough. The question is, "What are you going to do about it?"

*   *   *   *   *   *   *   *   *   *   *   *

Husband is distant

Dear Peggy,

My husband and I have been married for almost 10 years. Five months ago, I confirmed my suspicions that he was having an affair. It lasted 16 months and was with a coworker. We decided to stay together to try to work things out. We have two young children that provide us additional incentive to try.

Five months later, I have come a long way. I have accepted things that I can't change and have forgiven him as much as I can. He won't go to counseling but has agreed to work through issues in a rather formal manner at home, with the guidance of several self-help books.

The problem is that he is still so distant. I have begun to feel close to him again. I know I love him and want to remain married to him. But he says he is not sure if he could ever be in love with me again. The harder I try to get close to him, the more he resists. He says the feelings for me have not come back and I know the feelings won't return until he tries to reach out to me or to let me in. He is willing to try up to a point, but won't give of himself emotionally yet. Is it as hopeless as it seems?

Dear Reader,

The situation is not hopeless—certainly not after only 5 months. It takes much longer for most people to recover from the impact of the discovery of an affair. We usually expect it to take some time for the person whose partner had an affair, but this can also be true for the one who had an affair themselves. There may be many understandable reasons for their conflicting feelings, awkwardness, and own sense of hopelessness that they can ever *live it down* and go on to have a good marriage.

As for the comment about not being sure about ever being in love with his wife again, this reflects a lack of understanding of just what it means to be in love. Unfortunately, all too often there's a false assumption that the euphoric, first-flush, excitement of Romantic Love is what it means to be in love—but that's just the first stage, not the be-all, end-all of love. Love changes; it does *not* stay the same.

Neither *forcing* nor *resisting* are effective as ways of recovering loving feelings. Since these feelings naturally develops as a by-product of a multitude of daily little caring actions taken by both people, it's important not to let any slight impulse pass without acting on it. It doesn't need to be anything big or significant, just paying attention to any positive feelings and saying or doing something that reflects that moment. At some point, both the actions and the feelings can begin to feel natural and familiar—and become a way of life. In fact, believing it's *possible* to recover the loving feelings is a good first step, followed by living every day in a way that allows those feelings to develop and grow.

* * * * * * * * * * * *

Wants 36-year marriage to succeed

Dear Peggy,

Hope you can help us succeed. I discovered 10 months ago that my wife of 36 years was having an affair. I believe it to be short-term (6 months). It started as an emotional situation for both of them and lead to 3 instances for sexual self-gratification. We since have decided to re-commit and work it out. We are both retired and seem to be doing okay so far. We have had many a discussion in trying to understand, and I've admitted to my role in pushing her into the situation. Basically, I thought I was giving her space to do whatever without complaining, but she took it as a rejection of her and an indication I no longer cared or loved her. We didn't do enough things together.

Rebuilding the Marriage/Trust

I have since realized she has great difficulty in handling rejection of any kind (with me or others) and has built up many walls to hide the pain and hurt. She still can reflect on high school days when she wasn't allowed in the so-called elite group. So here's my concern as I try to get on with the next step within myself. It is very difficult to raise my concerns with her in order to understand more fully—because she gets depressed and goes in a well for awhile, and then I feel sad because I caused it.

Oh, the pain, anguish, loss of moral values and self-esteem, confidence, etc., still comes and goes—but every day the intensity seems to getting a lot less and I've told her so. Maybe I'm wrong, but I feel there are two issues that I need her input on so as to get on with the healing faster, yet also feel she will lose it. Early in the process, she sent a generic note to Mr. X at his place of work—basically stating it was over, no more contact, and we are committed to work it out—not signed. Ok so far, a first step on her part.

Concern 1: Some 4 months ago, I learned nobody knew this Mr. X at the place of work; and since then I have kept to myself, hoping it would go away without dealing with it. It hasn't and I seem to be becoming more consumed by it and now suspect it was somebody we both know. In my mind, I think the matter of trust needs to be addressed somehow.

Concern 2 (corollary to 1 above): I cannot help but wonder what thoughts she still has regarding this man that gave her emotional support; does she miss or still need his input. She has successfully evaded any response when I ask if I'm providing the support she needs (whether in comparing him and me or comparing today versus 6 months ago). Maybe I'm being unfair, but I can no longer just take things for granted.

I'm at a loss as to what to do but am still willing to keep my commitment as long as there is hope. Am I being too impatient?

Dear Reader,

This is a touching inside-look at a 36-year marriage. Obviously, there's a great deal of investment (and love) involved—and a willingness to do whatever it takes to rebuild. The final question, "Am I being too impatient?" is especially difficult. While it *does* take time and patience, time and patience *alone* are not enough. This means the 2 specific concerns listed above are on target.

Concern 1: This reflects the typical reality that questions don't just go away without being addressed. *If* a person has questions to which they want answers and the other person is not willing to give those answers, it's very difficult to establish trust. The basic feeling is: "If I can't trust them to be honest about the past, how can I trust they'll be honest about the future?" So it's reasonable to ask for clarification of whatever questions continue to be a barrier to moving on.

Concern 2: This, too, is a reasonable concern because there's no real resolution of anything by trying to "take things for granted." This concern, as mentioned above, is related to the first concern. In both instances, there's a need for more information—both as to facts and as to feelings. It's perfectly

163

predictable that the person who had an affair wants to say as little as possible and to expose as few details as possible. However, this is just the opposite of what is usually needed to rebuild a marriage.

So the concerns are not unfair; they are legitimate—and the approach does *not* reflect impatience. In fact, it appears that the degree of support and understanding that is being offered is not being met with a comparable measure of effort. So it may actually require *less* patience and more of a strong appeal for mutual consideration.

* * * * * * * * * * * * *

How do I cope?

Dear Peggy,

I am the guilty party. I had an affair 2 years ago. Although it has been long over, my wife found out about it only recently. She is very hurt, angry, disappointed and confused. We have 2 terrific kids. What made matters worse, I blamed her family for my doing such a terrible thing. I was wrong. I exaggerated the impact of their involvement. I since have apologized to my in-laws, and through the kindness of their hearts they seem ready to forgive me. My wife, on the other hand, is not ready. I remind her that I love her very much and that this person is totally out of my life. She found out about this 2 weeks ago. She is very angry still.

My other big problem is that I can't get over the fact that I hurt all these good people. I don't know how to deal with myself in this situation. My wife accuses me of not understanding the impact of what I have done, but the truth is, I am struggling mightily not to let this terrible thing I have done devastate me. How can I deal with these two issues? I feel if my wife would let me do nice things for her, I will be able to cope. But she refuses to let me do anything nice for her. And when I do, she resents me even more. Let me remind you: this affair has been over for 2 years. Please help.

Dear Reader,

The biggest factor involved in situations like this is the *huge* difference in perspective based on the *time* involved. For him, it's been over for 2 years—so he's had 2 years to digest what happened, reflect on it, deal with it within himself, etc. However, his wife found out only 2 *weeks* ago. So even though it actually took place 2 years ago—for *her*, it's as if it just happened. So it's important to keep this perspective in trying to deal with it.

With that background, there are some other significant issues reflected in the above letter. Some of the positives are: the personal acceptance of responsibility instead of continuing to blame others, the understanding attitude by the in-laws, the regret at hurting people, and the desire to do nice things for the wife that is loved.

On the other hand, it's understandable that the wife is very hurt, angry, disappointed and confused. She's no doubt still in shock, trying to simply survive the impact of the initial information. So it's unreasonable to think that she might be ready to forgive. Forgiveness is something that is earned based on building up a history of actions showing that forgiveness is deserved. So it may simply be a matter of continuing to do as many positive things as possible (despite the resistance), thereby demonstrating a commitment to continued efforts.

In the meantime, the focus needs to be on the challenge that lies ahead: of gradually working through this in order to rebuild the marriage and the trust. And this simply doesn't happen quickly. It usually takes a couple of *years*, not weeks. So time, effort and patience can eventually succeed. It's tough, but it's worth it—and it's the only path to complete healing for everyone involved.

* * * * * * * * * * * * *

Regaining Beliefs

Dear Peggy,

I caught my wife of 16 years in an extramarital affair. I accused her first. She denied it. Then I trapped her using AOL. She stated that it was only an AOL affair. No Sex. A week later, I found out the truth. A guy in town, 2 to 3 times over the past month.

She broke it off, and we are both seeking counseling. She wants to stay. I love her, but do I put myself through agony. We have two children, 10 and 13. If I can know that I will regain my trust and belief in my wife, I will be willing to stay and work it out.

Dear Reader,

This letter expresses a common thought: that the willingness to stay and work it out depends on *knowing* "that I will regain my trust and belief in my wife..." Unfortunately, this kind of *certainty* is impossible. While it's important to believe that recovery is *possible* (and to make a serious effort toward recovery), it's unrealistic to think there can be any *guarantee* that the effort will pay off. It simply doesn't work that way.

Ironically, it's risky to think that *anything* (either a vow or a crisis like this or a serious effort to rebuild or a desire to avoid this in the future) can make a couple immune to this issue. While most people want some absolute guarantee of monogamy, this is an issue that's never settled "once and for all".

Of course, there are no guarantees about anything related to relationships. For instance, many people say they won't get married until they're *positive* that their marriage will last; others (who have been divorced) say they'll never marry *again* unless they can be *sure* the next marriage will last. Unfortunately, people may not do the necessary ongoing work and make the necessary ongoing effort to give the marriage the best chance of lasting if they're hoping for some magic way to assure it will last *without* this kind of ongoing work.

This consistent effort is even more critical when dealing with affairs. Unless a couple commit to establishing and maintaining a very close bond/connection through ongoing honest communication, it's very difficult to succeed in reaching the goal for which they're wishing there were some *guarantee*.

* * * * * * * * * * * * *

Affair by my husband

Dear Peggy,

It is not that I am so upset about the affair, it is more that I am so upset that he lies to me about it and continues to lie about it and other things. He is like a Dr. Jekyll and Mr. Hyde in that he is so mean and then he is so nice to the other woman. I do not know if he is still having the affair, but I do know he has a secret place somewhere because he has a key on his key chain that he cannot and will not explain. He used to have a secret mail box, but I found out about it and he cancelled it. I think he has a storage room and is keeping files and other things in there—so in case he dies, it will be kept from me and given to his son.

I think sometimes that he hates me and does things just to upset me. I know he has done that in the past. I am not perfect, but am considered attractive and pleasant. I have many friends and attend a church where I am happy and active. I am 73 and so is he. He is not well and has many problems, but he was well enough to take a woman as a secretary and travel with her and introduce her to his business friends as an aide and treat me very badly. Since he is not well, divorce is not an option, but he slanders me and lies to me and swears and says unkind things to me. I never know what he is going to do next. I am trying to be gracious and not be bitter or resentful. I could probably do better if he admitted his ways and then said he was sorry. How can anyone trust someone who lies and then lies about his lies?

Dear Reader,

The most striking thing about this letter is the integrity that shines through, despite the painful situation. Age does not automatically bring this kind of wisdom, but it does bring a certain perspective and *can* bring a certain degree of grace under fire—as indicated by the statement: "I am trying to be gracious and not be bitter or resentful."

While I don't subscribe to the philosophy that things happen for a *reason* (in order for people to learn some particular lesson); I *do* think that once things *happen*, it's possible to *respond* in such a way as to find some kind of meaning. In a case like the one above (where there may be no good resolution), the strength of character that is required to cope with the situation may be worth its weight in gold. I've done life-planning workshops for many years, and when people thoughtfully reflect on their lives, those who feel the *best* about their lives are the ones who feel the best about *themselves* (based on their sense of personal integrity)—not the ones who had it easy, without facing such challenges.

Let me emphasize that having integrity does not equate with simply being *nice*. (People often take advantage of a person who seems too nice.) In fact, being a person of integrity requires a great deal of courage—because it goes beyond simply avoiding being self-serving or having ulterior motives or hidden agendas. It also requires "saying what needs to be said," regardless of the difficulty involved. So when people with a high degree of integrity (like the woman who wrote this letter) are caught up in situations where they are being abused or taken advantage of, it does *not* undermine their integrity to stand up and speak out for themselves. In fact, it's part of the process of insisting on the respect that is deserved by virtue of being a person of integrity.

Regarding questions as to why someone would behave as the husband described above: "I think sometimes that he hates me and does things just to upset me." Often when someone has been this hurtful for this long, they no longer even know why they behave this way; it has simply become a *habit*. And well-engrained habits don't tend to just suddenly change without some outside pressure—which is just one more reason for a person to stand up for themselves against such treatment. And, finally, as for "how anyone can trust someone who lies and then lies about his lies?"—obviously, that kind of person *can't* be trusted.

* * * * * * * * * * * *

Living in the past

Dear Peggy, (The following is an excerpt from a much longer letter.)

My husband and I have been married for 10 years. Two months after finding out I was pregnant with our fourth child he had an affair. He apparently began an affair (which I did not immediately suspect) with someone he had met at a bar while having drinks with several coworkers after work (who were also friends of mine and frequently visited our home). This went on for approximately 1-1/2 months. He did not come home till he decided to, he refused to talk to me about our relationship when I pleaded with him, he refused to work on our marriage, and he didn't seem to care anymore that he had children that loved him dearly. His attitude got progressively worse.

He had a suitcase packed and ready to go if I chose to throw him out. He then proceeded to tell me everything he did in the past, which I am still very hurt and upset over... bars, strip clubs, stags, etc. He was living the lifestyle of a married single guy..."have your cake and eat it too." All was hidden from me and even disguised as..."I have no desire to do those things" or "you should feel lucky to have a husband like me because I don't do those things." He simply led me to believe in this fictitious character that I so much wanted to be married to. Unfortunately, he was lying to himself as well as me.

My dilemma is (finally), after being lied to over and over again (throughout ALL the years I was married to him), how can I believe he is being truthful now? He has totally changed and devoted his life to honesty. He is now the trustworthy, compassionate, loving and caring person I have dreamed of having in my life. He is extremely remorseful for everything he has done and tells me that every chance he gets. It has been almost a year since everything has come out and he will still answer my questions, even though we have gone over them over and over and over again. He occasionally becomes frustrated but never loses hope. He begs me to focus on our future together and tells me we have

167

something to look forward to because he is so in love with me. I can't seem to move on from the past, although I do love him and want to make our marriage work (most of the time). Because I feel he is lying about what really *happened, I still feel as though I'm being betrayed as I have in the past. I have always discredited my inner feelings and accepted what he said as being the truth. I don't want to subject myself to that ever again.*

I am desperate! I know I am putting a bigger wedge between us by obsessing over the past, but I am still so devastated over it. I guess if I didn't convince myself with the words he told me in the past about being an innocent *person...I wouldn't feel as shattered. However, I do realize that the real issue is not necessarily whether or not he had sex with her or others but that he overstepped the boundaries of our supposed commitment. Unfortunately, I cannot address that aspect until I feel fully satisfied of the sex part of it. My other concern is our children. The older ones are aware of what has happened (limited) and are feeling the strains of our relationship. I don't want them to grow up as a maladjusted adults because of this. I don't know what to do.*

Dear Reader,

Many of the issues in this letter are common (and very difficult) for people trying to reconcile their previous understanding of their spouse with the new information about their affairs. So I'll touch on some of the key points:

1. He wanted to "have your cake and eat it too."

This is often the case, especially with men having affairs. As described above, when someone wants the positive aspects of the marriage (but also wants the fun of outside sex), it's common that "he was lying to himself as well as me." In order to feel OK about themselves, people having affairs often ignore or deny the reality of the risks/potential pain they are causing by their actions. It's not that they deliberately set out to bring pain to their partners; they simply focus *only* on the pleasure of the affairs and deny or ignore the potential consequences. Naturally, this is extremely difficult for a spouse to understand— because they're trying to apply rational thinking to behavior that simply isn't rational.

2. He "begs me to focus on our future together."

Naturally, the person who has had affairs doesn't want to have to deal with the fallout from their behavior. They may even believe it's best for everyone to move on. (They certainly feel it would be best for themselves.) But trying to move on without completely dealing with the fall-out is like trying to bury it, which is, as I've said before, simply burying it alive; it will continue to come back over and over until it's finally dealt with. *Or* it will simply sit between the two people, creating a barrier to gaining the closeness that could help avoid a deadened, meaningless marriage.

3. "I have always discredited my inner feelings and accepted what he said as being the truth."

Learning the truth about a partner's affairs *does* become a wake-up call to most people to realize that they *can* usually trust their instincts about whether or not they're being told the truth. But, unfortunately, learning that their instincts were right in the past (when they had been discredited) may make it *more* difficult to avoid being even more suspicious in the future, whether or not it is warranted. Basically, while it's generally not wise to just accept whatever someone says as the truth, it *is* a good idea to test their truthfulness by basing trust on actions (both in words and deeds) rather than based on someone simply saying, "trust me."

4. "...the real issue is not necessarily...sex...but that he overstepped the boundaries of our supposed commitment."

It's true that most people recover from the fact that their partner had sex with someone else before they recover from the fact that they were *deceived*. It's the deception that makes it difficult to go on and trust in the future.

5. "I don't want them [the kids] to grow up as a maladjusted adults because of this."

The message/lesson that kids come away with has more to do with the way the parents handle this crisis than with the specifics of the crisis itself. While it's tough on everyone, it's *possible* to use this as an opportunity to instill in kids the importance of honesty—and the problems that come from lack of honesty, regardless of the particular situation. This is a lesson that can serve them well in the future, and is one of the possible good things that can come out of this generally bad experience.

* * * * * * * * * * * *

Some words left unknown

Dear Peggy,

I found out through a very stable course of conversations that my husband had "quickie" affairs with 2 females, but there was more. Anyway, I managed to make him confess to 2 incidents (which he said were because of the fact we were so young when we started dating and he just wanted to see what he may be missing...) and he was intoxicated....with a bad influence...he indulged. Well, that is somewhat understandable...yet I am at the anger stage...and he awaits my recovery. Still there is more....but he won't tell me. I told him to confess all....as I know there were a few other times...(not so much sex...and affairs, but others who got him off). He swears there were no others. I am just dealing with what I know now as true...but as if with a sickening medicine...shouldn't I request the rest? He won't tell...he has it all...he knows...he hates his mistakes...and they have all but destroyed me. I am a super wife...and I know it's not my fault. None of these things are ongoing...but I want the whole truth?????? Is that wrong????? Why does he refuse to give me his trust in this way? As if I can establish such a trust again???? Wonder why I am stuck in the anger stage?????

Dear Reader,

It's fairly clear why someone would be stuck in the anger stage (or stuck at any stage), given the above scenario. For instance, the very idea that "he awaits my recovery" (all the while refusing to answer questions) is like waiting for a miracle. One of the most critical factors as to whether trust can be rebuilt is whether the person who had an affair is willing to answer questions. While there are many arguments they may use as to why they think it's better not to answer questions, overwhelmingly, nothing is worse than "not knowing." While nobody should be forced to hear information they don't *want* to know, every person in this position *deserves* honest answers to their questions.

There is nothing *wrong* with wanting the whole truth. In fact, when you don't know the facts, you tend to imagine the absolute worst. (Instead of being concerned only about a specific person or place or song or whatever, you're concerned about *every* person or place or song or whatever.) And if your questions are never answered, they continue to haunt you for the rest of your life—and the anger is likely to continue.

*　*　*　*　*　*　*　*　*　*　*　*　*

I had an affair

Dear Peggy,

I am the one who had the affair. I am 41 (as is my husband) and we have been married for 15 years. We have two children...both girls...ages 7 and 4. When I started the affair, I was feeling neglected and uninteresting. My lover thought I was wonderful and he made me feel very special. The affair ended when my husband found out...and I have made a commitment to make my marriage work. The problem is with the way my husband is handling it. He doesn't want to talk about it...he doesn't want to deal with it. I have tried to talk about it with him, but he just says, "It's over...move on." I keep worrying that he will eventually explode. He will not go to counseling with me, so I am going alone. I don't know if it's helping, but I will do whatever he says at this point. How do I go on?

Dear Reader,

This situation is a reversal of the more common situation; usually the person who had the affair doesn't want to talk and says, "it's over...move on." (When the person who had an affair doesn't want to talk, it's reasonable for the spouse to request/insist/pressure them to talk—because if the spouse *wants* to talk, they deserve to get answers to their questions.) However, when it's the hurt partner who doesn't want to talk, it's reasonable for them *not* to be pressured to talk. This is because the person who is trying to deal with their partner's affair has the right to do whatever they want/need in order to deal with it.

It's important to keep in mind that just because someone doesn't want to talk about it *now*, doesn't mean they will *never* want to talk about it—so it's essential that they know you are willing/ready to talk whenever they might want that to happen. When a person (like the husband above) has been dealt this kind of blow, they need to feel as "in control" of their own decisions as possible—rather than having someone else tell them what they should do.

While I have a very strong belief that it's better for everyone involved for this issue to be completely discussed, I don't think it can be forced upon someone like this who is resisting it. In fact, any efforts to force a discussion may turn into a power-struggle that would make it even more difficult for them to acknowledge it if/when they *do* decide they're willing/able to discuss it.

While I understand how difficult it is for a person in the position of the woman who wrote the above letter—it's *always* difficult to deal with the aftermath of an affair, whether or not a couple talks about it. She indicates that: "I will do whatever he says..."—and this is probably all that can be done. In the meantime, she can only hang in and continue to be patient and understanding, letting him know that she is available for him in any way that might be helpful.

* * * * * * * * * * * *

Will I Ever Know the Truth?

Dear Peggy,

I have been with my husband for 6 years. We have been married for 2-1/2 years and have 3 kids. Before our marriage, I had suspected him of fooling around with a coworker and had confronted him several times on the issue. He has always maintained his innocence, while at the same time not offering me an explanation for certain things... (I always feel that people know when someone is being dishonest.) I had left him once before our wedding, then found out I was pregnant—with twins! We ended up staying together, getting married and have had another child, but we are having some major problems now—and I know part of it is because I can't let go of this feeling that he did fool around, lied about it and never got caught. I have a real hard time with people that get away with things and pull one over on you. He says I just have a chip on my shoulder about men. I don't know if I will ever believe that he did not fool around with this person—and if that's the case, how will we ever get our life together?

He also is a workaholic, is never home and is out several nights a week until 3 or 4 a.m. playing pool for extra money—because his regular job doesn't pay the bills and he won't look for another one. Concerned? You bet. Up until a few months ago, I was a full-time stay-at-home mother. I finally got a job so we could have regular health insurance for our kids (his job doesn't offer it). He is 36 years old and I feel he just does not want the responsibility of a family. He offers no help whatsoever with the house or the kids. They never see him. His whole existence is working, playing pool and sleeping. Bottom line is, almost every time we argue, the subject of this ex coworker comes up in one way or another. He says it's old news and I need to get over it already. I feel like he never levels with me about anything, and therefore I cannot trust him. What advice can you offer me???

Dear Reader,

Regarding the initial question, "Will I ever know the truth?"—in general people won't know the truth unless they persist in their efforts to get the truth. The other person almost never *volunteers* anything—and will almost always resist (or deflect) any questions. This is in keeping with the common way of handling affairs—or anything someone is doing (or has done) that they want to keep secret. In addition, the above behavior is typical in that one common way of deflecting questions is to "attack" the questioner for asking the questions in the first place.

As for whether questions about the past are old news, it's not really *old* by virtue of the *new* current behavior—like staying out until 3 or 4 a.m. several nights a week. It's totally reasonable to be concerned and to not trust someone who is so uninvolved with the family—and who doesn't seem to *care* that they're not involved. Being a workaholic is a convenient excuse, but people's priorities are usually reflected in the way they spend their time.

Having said all this, it still comes down to the reality that no one can control another person. All anyone can do is to make it clear that they do not accept their unreasonable statements or actions. It's better to focus energy on what you can change about your *own* behavior—and see whether or not this makes a difference. Such changes as getting a job and looking to the future (whether with or without the other person) is a practical way of proceeding in a very difficult situation.

Most people (like the writer of the above letter) *know* when things are totally out of whack. But when there seems to be no good alternative, it's easy to feel trapped. Even when there's nothing that can be done *at this moment*, it can be helpful to be working toward trying to achieve more balance in the relationship (by at least not enabling a partner's irresponsibility)—while preparing to be able to leave eventually if things never improve.

12: Aftermath and Perspective

Where do I go from here?

Dear Peggy,

I'm a 30-year-old female. I met my husband 7 years ago, and we just recently wed 9 months ago. Never had problems of infidelity during all those years. Well, 2 months ago things started to drastically change. He started a new job. He told me that the guys asked him out for a Friday night "guys thing." It was fine with me. Well, it's been every Friday since then. On the third week, I went to the billiards where they hung out and it wasn't all guys. There were 2 girls and 2 guys...my husband being one of them. He looked excited to see me and introduced me to the girls. One worked in his office and the other was her friend. They seemed to be nice and even commented on how often my husband talks about us. I didn't feel threatened in any way. My husband told me that the girl from the office liked the other guy and he just met her friend that night. Well, it may have started out that way, but he has left me and is with her friend. We've never been apart. Never broken up before, we always worked through our problems somehow.

Now I'm going through a divorce and I feel lost. I feel like I lost my identity. I have been going out a lot...and now am realizing that I'm overdoing the drinking and staying out all night. I just don't want to be alone. The last time I was sexually active was with my husband one month ago...the day before he left. I can't picture myself with anyone else. I keep telling myself...it's going to be okay. I have good days...then I have bad ones. Where do I go from here?

Dear Reader,

As inadequate as it may seem, the only place to "go from here" is to keep putting one foot in front of the other—making sure not to stumble and fall (as can happen when overdoing the drinking and staying out all night). Any devastating loss and sense of abandonment is likely to make a person vulnerable to "looking for love in all the wrong places," but it might help to realize that sometimes the most *alone* someone can be is in the midst of a crowd. It's often better to go ahead and bite the bullet by actually *being* alone and dealing with the feelings. They aren't likely to magically go away just because they're being buried under activity or contact with others. They will still resurface and continue to interfere with getting on with life.

It also helps to realize that recovering from such a blow can not happen quickly. There will continue to be good days mixed with bad days for quite awhile. Simply understanding that this is normal can help; that way there's not the intense disappointment when there's a bad day—because there's a realization that that's just the way the process works.

So it's important to allow enough time to pass to be able to deal with this new life situation. In the meantime, spending time deliberately focusing on something else (perhaps something or someone to whom we can contribute instead of something or someone who can help *us*) can help to diminish the intensity of the pain of the moment.

* * * * * * * * * * * * *

Never before

Dear Peggy,

I have been friends with a man for 13 years and while our relationship has been sexual, we can be fulfilled just spending time talking to one another. Neither one of us has ever felt this way about another person.

Approximately three years ago our spouses found out about our relationship and we had no contact for about two years. This past Fall we began talking to one another again and found out that our feelings had not changed. We do not think that we can live like this forever nor are we naive enough to believe that this same euphoria would last if we were together always. What we do believe is that we could keep our relationship interesting enough and be honest enough with one another to make it work.

I guess I would just like to hear your comments because you always seem to say that relationships that start as affairs are headed for disaster.

Dear Reader,

It's not that *all* relationships that start as affairs are headed for disaster, it's that *most* relationships that start as affairs do not last and *most* people wind up being hurt—as well as hurting others.

This seems to be the most glaring omission in the above description—the lack of focus on the impact on the *marriage* by continuing the outside relationship. The comment about believing "we could keep our relationship interesting enough and be honest enough with one another to make it work..." was about the *other man*. What about the spouses? It's unlikely that both parties in the outside relationship can keep their *marital* relationship interesting enough and be honest enough...to "make it work"—as long as the outside relationship continues. At some point, something (maybe everything) doesn't "work."

While there are a few cases where these kinds of arrangements have worked over many years, they're unusual, the exception to the rule—which is why we hear about them. In real life, it's wishful thinking to try to maintain a long-term outside relationship *and* a marriage.

This letter comments on the fact that the "feelings had not changed" after a couple of years apart, but that's not necessarily significant—as is reflected in the recognition that there's a euphoric aspect to the outside relationship. In some ways the only way to avoid destroying the positive image/memory of the relationship is to end it while it's still good. Like many things in life, it can become something to reflect on later in life with some pleasure/satisfaction. Whereas if it continues until some likely incident or major disruption, the life-long reflection will be negative. No one can predict the future, but when considering life-altering situations like this, it's helpful to take the long view of life—not just think for the moment.

* * * * * * * * * * *

No further down the road...

Dear Peggy,   (This is a condensed version of a very long letter.)

My wife and I have been married now for 30 years. (We were high school sweethearts.) I got AOL on the computer and she took a great interest in the Internet. She had a very good friend who loved the chat rooms and she showed her the ropes. She told me that she only talked to women and her girlfriends, but she didn't understand why I would be upset at her talking to men; after all, "they don't really know who you are and it's all innocent fun." She would get on the computer before I went to bed and stay till long after I was asleep. This continued for six months.

Then one day AOL changed the format to signing on AOL. No longer did you have to type in your password. Bring up your screen name and hit enter. Wow, super! I'm getting ready to log on that night and it dawns on me, "Why not bring up her screen name and take a peak?" I did and quickly found out she was a cyber slut! I printed out a few juicy 'Instant Messages' that I almost instantly received, and laid them on the keyboard; and I grabbed some clothes and booked! I was devastated...this just blasted me to the moon. My heart was absolutely broken.

Now, two months later, I find I still have feelings for her and question whether I should try again. She wants me to; 30 years is a lot of waste. She says she has completely changed. She is so embarrassed and realizes that she has a problem—maybe a split personality, or whatever. She claims she has killed that other person and please just give her one more chance. Should I or am I being completely stupid? How many times do you forgive? When is enough, enough? Oddly, I still care a tremendous amount for her. My problem: I haven't healed and I'm having a very emotional hard time. I'm smoking like a fiend, drinking like a fish, still having contact with her every couple of days or so and after all this time, no further down the road than where I started. I'm confused, hurt, in pain and don't know how to act.

I met an old friend from high school (female) who I've taken out a few times, very platonic, everything on the up and up, no physical contact or intentions. I don't know how to deal with this. Should I continue? Should I quit seeing her? I'm scared of any emotional or physical connections. Our divorce is not yet final (finally filed just this week). I don't know what to do.

Dear Reader,

There's probably no more difficult place to be than in this limbo situation where there's so much uncertainty. The above letter illustrates many contradictory ideas—all of which are perfectly normal and understandable when in this place. But nothing is likely to bring about clarity until there's a definite, deliberate effort to focus most of the energy one way or the other.

For instance, the uncertainty shows up in many statements: "I find I still have feelings for her and question whether I should try again."—"I met an old friend from high school (female) who I've taken out a few times."—"Our divorce is not yet final..." Coping with such disparate thoughts/actions only creates stress, not clarity. At a time like this, it's usually helpful to dig deep down inside (being as honest with yourself as possible) as to what you *know* in a sensing way about what is best. "Trying again..." needs to be based on a personal desire to try, not on the fact that "She wants me to."

If, after great soul-searching, a person knows they can't "set the past aside and move on" unless they try again, then that's an OK thing to do. (And if that's the decision, it would be important to focus on that—not see other people as well.) But if a person comes to a point of acceptance that they've already done all they can do to try to make a relationship work, then they can pursue the divorce with a clearer mind—knowing it won't be easy, but that it's the right thing to do.

No one can answer this dilemma for another person. But continuously second-guessing yourself just maintains the limbo situation. So it's helpful for someone to get the best clarity possible within themselves and then pursue whichever direction they think is best. Sometimes there's no *good* solution; it's a matter of avoiding whichever one they think is likely to be worse. But making a decision (whichever one it is) is likely to be preferable to continuing to stay stuck in such a difficult place.

* * * * * * * * * * * *

I just don't get it
(Here are 2 letters before my response.)

Dear Peggy, (letter #1)

My husband of 10 years had an affair with a casual acquaintance of ours that lasted approximately 8 months. During that time, he treated me very poorly and insisted on a separation, stating his want to get back the "fire" that we once had as his reasoning for wanting the separation. Yeah right! My question is this. Why does he love me now? Why can't he live without me now? Why is it that now I'm everything to him. Right up until the moment that I found out about his love affair and confronted him, he was very involved with the OW. They saw each other every day, spoke on the phone for hours at a time, and even had a secret pager code going between the two of them. There are so many terrible things that he has done, it would take me pages and pages to describe them all.

My question is this. How does one go from being so heavily involved with another woman one minute to completely loving his wife the next? I just don't get it!

Dear Peggy, (letter #2)

My ex-fiancé and I broke up about two months ago and for the first month and two weeks I begged and cried to him to come back to me, and he always said he couldn't because he didn't love me the way he should. So I moved out of state so I could start a new life and got a different boyfriend. Well he called me tonight and asked me back; he was crying saying that he really screwed up and that he wanted to be back with me and he still had my engagement ring if I wanted it. Then we got on the conversation about the reasons he broke up with me, which the reasons were he missed being single and he missed being with his friends 24/7 and tonight he told the real reason he broke up with me. He said that all the problems I was having with my family were bringing him down and he thought that that was the best way to handle it. But he broke my heart and I'm scared that if I go back to him he'll do it again? What do you think I should do? Should I trust him again and go back out with him? Please give me some advice. I need to find my right path and I would like to know that if I go back it would be the right path!

Dear Reader,

The most immediate reaction to the confusing actions of the kind of men described in these letters is the total unpredictability of what they might do in the future. There appears to be no ability to focus on anything except "the moment" and whatever they want at any given point. So there's unlikely to be any clear, rational reason for whatever changes they make; it's more likely that it's simply a matter of "wanting what they want when they want it."

Another common dynamic among people who change their minds rather abruptly is that they're more likely to want something when it either becomes unavailable or at risk of being lost. That pattern usually involves wanting it *only* as long as they're not sure they'll get it (or keep it). Then, the minute they're assured of having whatever they've said they want—they may no longer want it.

As long as actions are based only on short-term desires, there's no assurance of predicting future actions. So any effort to determine likely future behavior needs to include looking for evidence of an ability and willingness to choose one thing over another—*and* to be consistent over time.

A good first step for people who abruptly change their minds is to be able to identify and express their long-term priorities. Then it's important to get some clear understandings and agreements about what behavior will demonstrate those priorities.

* * * * * * * * * * * * *

177

Life-altering affair

Dear Peggy,

Our life-altering affair discovery happened 7 years ago after 21 years of marriage. I was finally able to pass the anniversary date of the discovery, without pain, last year. But with all the news coverage and detail about the Clinton Crisis, the pain, anger, and fears were all stirred up for me. We put a lot of work into salvaging our lives and I must try every day to not bring the subject up. I believe there is a time frame when you can ask and he MUST answer all questions with however much detail you want...otherwise your imagination will make it much more than it was.

I believe that it is absolutely necessary that the couple separate until the cheater is sure about who he wants. Being without his family and seeing her in all her moods can clear up his fantasies. You can let him know how much you love him but he must also know that you are strong enough to go on if you have to. In our case, I did not want our 12 and 16-year-olds to know the full reason why Dad was moving out. I believed that we would end up together, and I didn't want my pain to color their feelings for their Dad. I was right, but a year after it happened my daughter (13) asked me point blank about it. I was truthful to her at that time and answered all her questions. That approach worked out well for us. I let my husband know that this was the only mistake that he would be forgiven for, after he expressed his regret and has been making amends.

I take issue with couples who say that their marriage is "better" after the affair...it is different, changed, but we are happy. I will always miss the innocent blind trust that I placed in him the moment we were engaged. I know that he misses the freedom he has lost because he must always be aware that I am comfortable with where he is and who he is with...which he willingly shares with me before I ask. I have taken a lot of steps and moved forward as best I can. The only thing I would like, in order to completely close this episode in our lives, would be an apology from the other woman. As someone who did her no harm, I feel I deserve it.

Dear Reader,

First of all, the term "life-altering experience" is one I have used for many years to describe the experience of dealing with a partner's affair. It's the only term that really fits due to the widespread impact on *all* aspects of life, not just on the marital relationship—like, for instance, the impact on children.

There are, however, several other points in the above letter that I'd like to reflect on:

1. Since the subject of affairs is one that will come up repeatedly due to the prevalence of affairs in our society (the Clinton situation being one significant example), it's essential to understand that recovery is *not* achieved by avoiding "bringing the subject up." The goal of recovery is to get to the point where the pain, anger, and fears are not stirred up—even when this issue is discussed. In fact, whenever I hear couples say they've recovered and no longer talk about the

178

affair—I know they haven't *fully* recovered. Because once you completely deal with this issue (and reach the point where your rational understanding overrides the emotions) you can talk about it *without* triggering the painful emotions. So if talking can still trigger painful emotions, complete recovery has not taken place. Also, the number of years is not the key to full recovery. While it *does* take time (usually at least 2 years), time alone does not necessarily bring recovery—no matter how much time passes.

2. The whole question of whether or not a marriage can be "better" after an affair is an important one. While it's certainly *possible* for a marriage to become better following an affair (as happened in my own marriage and in the marriages of many couples I've dealt with through the years), any potential improvement is *not* due to the affairs! It's due to the enormous amount of work we did together to recover and rebuild following the affairs. So it's important to understand that an affair is *not* an effective way to build a better marriage. (An affair is a crisis, pure and simple.) It's what a couple does in response to the crisis that determines the future condition (or even future existence) of the marriage.

3. Wanting an "apology from the other woman" is understandable, but neither realistic nor necessary in order to "completely close this episode." In fact, continuing to focus on the third party is to give them more importance than they deserve. It helps tremendously to understand that the third party's importance primarily depends on the role they played, not on the person themselves. They're not particularly important on an individual basis, and to look to them to somehow make things right or better is just wishful thinking—based on the idea that it's possible to have some kind of ideal resolution of this whole situation. Realistically, life isn't fair and we don't necessarily get what we deserve—either for better or for worse.

* * * * * * * * * * *

After 22 years...

Dear Peggy,

Two months ago I found out my husband had been unfaithful to me after 22 years of marriage. He promised it was over, but I found out it continued for another month. Again, he says it is over, that he does not want to jeopardize our marriage any more than he already has. There were 4 sexual encounters between him and the other woman. I feel so confused on why it happened. He says he does not understand how or why it happened. We are going to counseling, but sometimes I feel he is only going for me. We do have very candid talks about the affair, but he says they upset me too much, and he would rather not talk about it anymore. I want to be able to trust in him again, and to feel secure in my marriage, but she works at the same place he does, so I know they will have some contact with each other. I really just want to know if you think this was "a mistake" and that maybe he really does not understand why it happened, but because he does not understand why, isn't there a better chance of it happening again?

Dear Reader,

Here are some general thoughts about some of the points in this letter:

1. Affairs happen in all kinds of marriages and at all different stages. In the years I've been working with this issue, I've heard from people who were recently married as well as from people who were married as long as 42 years. There's no prediction as to when it might happen.

2. The first information that is shared by the person who had an affair is almost never *complete* information; it's just the first step in disclosing.

3. While it can be extremely frustrating not to get a clear answer as to why an affair happened, it's perhaps more honest when a person acknowledges that they don't really know than to give some simple (usually incomplete, after-the-fact) reason/excuse for why it happened.

4. Not wanting to talk about it (partly because it "upsets" too much) is understandable. But in this situation, talking is the lesser of the evils. *Not* talking about it diminishes the chances of working through it.

5. Working in the same place and continuing contact with the third party makes it much more difficult to recover. Most marriages that fully recover involve severing all contact with the third party, despite whatever sacrifices this might entail.

6. This is a crisis that provides an opportunity to learn from what happened and to use the learnings to be better prepared to avoid future affairs. Whether or not an affair happens again has more to do with establishing and maintaining ongoing honest communication about attractions, temptations, suspicions, etc., than with what happened in the past.

* * * * * * * * * * * * *

No soul, no trust, no hope

Dear Peggy,

My husband, supposedly had a 6-week, 4-incident affair last year. About 8 months prior to that time I had a "mental overload" and unfortunately attempted suicide due to a severe major depression episode I was experiencing. I can not seem to let this go. We have been to a marriage counselor and I have been seeing a psychiatrist and a psychologist for a couple of years. I am still numb over this and when I think of it, it causes me deep pain. I have never felt this betrayed in my life. It has made my trust level in him morbid. I am not even concerned in regards to a repeat performance. I start to think if he could do this (knowing how sick I was) he is capable of almost anything). I have read several books about affairs but non truly touch on this topic of losing your soul and trust in your relationship.

Dear Reader,

It is extremely fortunate that there is such a strong effort being made to deal with the situation described above (through seeking counseling and reading). Anyone in this position needs and deserves a great deal of support in dealing with this kind of situation. Extremely strong reactions (like those described above) are more understandable when we fully appreciate the significance of this experience.

For instance, the final comment provides an important insight: the issue of affairs is more than losing the trust in your relationship; it feels like losing your soul (losing your sense of yourself in the world: who you are, who your partner is, what your whole world is about). The intensity of the pain is quite understandable when it's seen in the context of this larger view. (This is the perspective I try to present in my book, "The Monogamy Myth." By understanding the issue of affairs within this broader context, each person can come back to their personal experience better prepared to deal with it.)

Another key point in the above letter is the word "supposedly." This shows uncertainty as to whether the true time-frame and nature of the affair is really known. In fact, the body may "know" what the mind may refuse to acknowledge on a conscious level—so it's possible for depression and/or feelings of suicide to be related to the sense of fear or anxiety or uncertainty created from the weirdness of sensing something like an affair even though there's no evidence of it at the time. As I've mentioned before, I personally experienced this disconnect. During the years when my husband was having affairs (before I knew for sure), I was so distraught at the isolation/distance I felt (which was due to his protecting the secrecy of his affairs), that I too contemplated suicide. Once I knew the whole truth, I was able to begin recovering.

I've heard this kind of desperation enough to recognize that the "knowing while not *really* knowing" has the power to lead to a feeling of "losing your soul." But by understanding this dynamic, it's possible to learn to trust ourselves and our internal knowing so that we're able to address whatever problems we face in the future much more quickly and more competently. It helps to remind ourselves of the saying: "That which doesn't kill me makes me stronger." So having lived through the worst, there's hope for gradually gaining strength and confidence in your ability to deal with whatever happens in the future.

13: Married Person Having an Affair

What do I do now?

Dear Peggy,

I'm going to be 23 this November and I've been married for 4 years. My husband and I married for the "old fashioned" reason....we were in love. I have always had high moral beliefs, my thoughts on extramarital affairs were those of disgust. I thought anyone who was willing to have an affair should at least have the courage to end their first relationship before it went that far.

Unfortunately, 3 weeks ago I broke all my own rules. I started going back to school 4 months ago and this extremely handsome man in my class began flirting with me. (He's married too.) We ended up on the same study team, which means we will be working on homework together outside of class for the next 2 years. A few weeks ago, he confessed his feelings towards me and since then several of our meetings have led us straight to bed.

I can't believe I, of all people, have let it go this far. I am at a loss as to what to do now. My marriage has been unstable for a little over a year and this can't possibly help it out in any way. I have been thinking about asking my husband for a divorce, but I'm afraid I can't make it on my own. Plus, we have a 2-year-old to think about.

I am pretty sure that this extra relationship is based purely on sex; I don't think there is anything more to it than that (so I know I wouldn't end up with this other man), but with all the other problems my husband and I have been having, I'm pretty sure this is the beginning of the end. Any advice for what I should do now?

Dear Reader,

This letter is a clear illustration of the fact that "anyone is vulnerable" and "no one is immune" from an affair. It's almost as if thinking "it can't happen to me" can make a person even *more* vulnerable—because they aren't on guard. It's only when it's too late that they stop and really think about what they did—as described in this letter.

So the first learning from this experience is to recognize that our typical assumptions that the person who has an affair is weak, insecure, uncaring, or a generally bad person—isn't based in reality. In fact, all kinds of people have affairs, not just certain types.

The second learning is to recognize that nothing will change the past, but there's a good opportunity now to change the future. This involves continuing the process of thinking rationally and clearly about the inevitable consequences of continuing this kind of path—and doing something to change it. Since *all* marriages have some kinds of problems (and all marriages go through a transition phase, especially when children are involved), any outside involvement just makes it even more difficult to resolve whatever problems might exist in the relationship.

While an affair is not a good way to get a clear grasp of what a person wants out of life, an affair often helps identify what they *don't* want. It can be used as a kind of wake-up call to take a good look at what's happening in their life and what practical (rather than fantasy) steps might be taken to make things better. Usually, making things better involves doing some serious long-term thinking about life and making plans toward something better—not chasing some temporary, momentary escape (where the price may be far too high).

As to whether this is "the beginning of the end," it can either turn out that way or it can be the beginning of working toward a long-term loving relationship that's based on more than just sex or even a *romantic* kind of love. As I've said before, marriages aren't necessarily unstable or doomed when the first romantic flush of love wanes. It's a natural stage of love that can be nurtured into the next stage that is far deeper and more meaningful. This calls for a degree of maturity and thought. So, there's no specific advice that can be given as to what actions to take, but doing this kind of reflection and consideration of the practical factors involved is a good first step.

* * * * * * * * * * * * *

I'd like to stop...

Dear Peggy,

I am a married woman currently involved in an extramarital affair with a married man. It began with talking on the Internet and has lead to an ongoing all-out affair. The problem is that I really and truly would like to stop it, but my feelings are so strong for him and not my husband that it is making it almost impossible. My marriage was not good at all before all of this started, of course. I would not have even agreed to meet him if I had a marriage that satisfied me.

My lover says that his marriage is great. He has said it from the beginning and has also said that he would never leave. I have noticed lately that my feelings for him seem to be a bit more intense than his for me. I say that because it seems that I am constantly thinking of him and writing and letting him know. He says his feelings are the same or more, but actions speak much louder than words. That is what I have always believed.

I do not know how I got so wrapped up in this thing but it is all I can do not to think of him and what he is doing when we do not talk. Please give me some pointers on what I could do to get myself out of this. Also, how can I look to my husband for the same emotional support that I got from this other man? Please help me.

Dear Reader,

This letter describes the classic struggle a person can have in trying to *act* in accordance with their *thinking*. There seems to be a pretty clear understanding that the affair is a "dead-end relationship." At least the other man is being candid in acknowledging that his marriage is great and he would never leave. (Actually, this is quite common among men having affairs—whether or not they admit it.) While this *should* make it easier to walk away, sometimes the unattainable seems all the more appealing (think Romeo and Juliet).

One of the reasons that her "feelings for him seem to be a bit more intense than his..." may be the fact that he feels he has a good marriage while she feels that her marriage "was not good at all." (This too is common—in that women are more likely to say their affair is due to some problem/shortcoming/disappointment with their marriage.)

The irony, of course, is that there's almost no chance of improving the marriage unless/until the contact is severed with the other man. So any effort to look to the husband for emotional support can only reasonably happen when a person is no longer looking to the third party for emotional support. Once there is *no* contact and *no* support from the third party, there's likely to be more motivation for figuring out how to seek emotional support from the husband— and for being willing to do whatever it takes to make the husband aware of just what is needed/wanted.

As for "how to get myself out of this"—the magic word is *myself.* No one else can do it for you. And the very first step in being able to do it is to genuinely, wholeheartedly *want* to do it. This is likely to happen only when there is a full acceptance of the uselessness of postponing the inevitable. One of the reasons we put off doing something that is distasteful to us is that we hope to somehow avoid ever having to do it; whereas if we fully accept that it's eventually going to happen, we're more likely to want to "get it over with," however painful. The delay and the staying in limbo does not lessen the pain; it just drags it out longer. So it's important to consistently remind yourself of that reality when your emotions interfere with rational thinking about the whole situation.

* * * * * * * * * * * *

Best friends who also have sex

Dear Peggy,

I'm a married female who has been having an affair with a married man for 3 years now. It is both a sexual and emotional attachment for both of us and gets stronger every year. A description might be best friends who also have sex. It may sound strange, but both of us manage to give the other pretty good advice on dealing with our spouses. We discuss everything. I would also say that both of our spouses are clueless about the affair and would describe our marriages as very good.

I can't seem to end the affair although I've tried 3 times. I know it's wrong and I hate myself for being so weak. Do you have any advice on how to distance yourself emotionally, so you can end an affair?

Dear Reader,

When long-term affairs develop to the point where the people use each other as sounding boards for their "real" lives, it can become a special little cocoon that is very difficult to give up—sometimes even more difficult than a more passion-focused affair.

As for the spouses being "clueless," that's highly unlikely. That thinking is part of the rationalization that most people having affairs develop as a way of feeling OK about what they're doing. Even when marriage partners don't specifically suspect an affair, they sense the emotional distance that is an essential part of maintaining this kind of secret from their spouses.

It's common for the person having the affair to think their marriage is "very good" because *they* are feeling fine about things. (It's doubtful that their spouses feel the same way about the marriages.)

As to how to distance yourself emotionally in order to end an affair, naturally it's hard to just turn off emotions. (It's like saying "don't think of pink elephants;" the process of trying *not* to feel something simply serves to feed the feeling.) But anyone can distance themselves physically. And this can be the first step toward diminishing the strength of the emotional connection—since the feelings of closeness are reinforced by constantly confiding in each other.

* * * * * * * * * * * * *

No sexual desire for spouse
(Here are excerpts from 3 letters before my response.)

Dear Peggy, (excerpt #1)

I am married with 3 children and I had an affair with a man who was married also. I felt unhappy in my marriage and so did he. My husband and I rarely had sex before the affair because I am not sexually attracted to him at all. I actually dread sex with my husband. I give in so that he won't be mad at me. I feel grossed out during sex with him and I want to get it over with. I can't just leave him. We have 3 small children together. I don't work and I would have nowhere to go. There is one positive side of my marriage. We are good friends and have a lot in common. I do love him as a person, but not sexually. I am afraid that I will go back and have another affair. I am still talking to guys on the Internet, and it will be any day before I do it again. All I want is to start over. This time fall in love first, with someone I am sexually attracted to. Then have a family and never ever stray. I know I am STUCK in my marriage and I am in pain. Any advice? Thank you.

Dear Peggy, (excerpt #2)

I have not had an affair but I have thought about it on several occasions. Our relationship has changed and I find myself no longer attracted to him sexually. Sexually, I am no longer fulfilled but scared to say anything to my husband because I know he will think there is someone else. That is a can of worms I don't want to open! There is a man that I know and we have become good friends. Nothing intimate has happened but I find myself strangely drawn to him and I have often imagined a relationship with him.

I love my husband and I have committed most of my life to him, and the last thing I want to accomplish is hurting my husband. If you have any suggestions as to how I can "rekindle the fire" in my marriage, it would be greatly appreciated.

Dear Peggy, (excerpt #3)

I was involved in an affair for over two years. Both of us are married. His wife discovered the affair almost a year ago, but the affair continued for at least another 6 months. It finally ended when I told my lover that I was tired of sneaking around and lying. I was willing to leave my husband to be with him but he chose to stay with his wife and family. I was devastated for quite awhile. Throughout this time, my husband's love never wavered. He continues to love me; in fact, his love for me seems to have increased because of his fear over losing me.

Over time, I have adjusted to my life without my lover. I realize my feelings for him were more intense than his for me. I was disappointed he chose to stay with his wife. I want to work things out with my husband. Obviously, our marriage wasn't perfect before the affair. Now, my husband expects me to feel sexually attracted to him and wants the same passion from me that I showed with my lover. I don't have those feelings for my husband.

I think of him more as an old, dear friend. Is this normal? He won't accept this type of relationship and it is very frustrating for him to feel this great passion for me and not have it returned. How do I deal with this? Is there a way to get these feelings back for my husband?

Dear Reader,

It's normal for there to be problems like this in a long-term marital relationship. In a "new" relationship, the sheer excitement of it may give rise to sexual feelings. In a long-term relationship, sexual feelings are often an outgrowth of loving feelings. If someone doesn't have "loving feelings" at this point, they also may not feel like having sex; or if they do have sex, they may not be very passionate.

I don't think sexy tricks and gimmicks help at all, but there are a couple of things that might help recover the loving feelings. First of all, try to be aware of any spontaneous positive feeling (however slight)—and act on it immediately. This doesn't mean jumping in bed or even being sexual. But even when not feeling particularly sexual, there are moments when some little incident will trigger a positive feeling. If at any point your partner just says something, or does something, or looks a certain way, or smells a certain way—or anything that triggers memories of more loving times, don't hold back. Let yourself touch, or hug, or just say something nice.

Also, physical activity helps a person's general feelings, their sexual feelings, and their "generous" feelings (which are connected to feeling sensual). So anything that makes you feel more *alive* (which frequently happens with more physical activity) can help stimulate feelings that are more expansive and expressive in all aspects of life, including sexual.

Loving or sexual or passionate feelings need to be nurtured. Just waiting for them to return isn't likely to happen; they won't just magically appear one day. You need to help them by noticing even the tiniest flutter of feeling. It's also important to have been sexually attracted to your spouse—at some point. This way you have a memory of what it was like once upon a time.

No relationship will ever maintain the kind of sexual excitement that is based on the newness inherent in an affair—no matter who the other person is. So unless someone is prepared to spend their lives going from one affair (or one partner) to another, this same issue will be repeated over and over again. If a couple once had the excitement in their relationship, they have just as good a chance of recovering it as they would if they started over with a new partner— since inevitably the new partner at some point ceases to be "new," and the excitement of the newness no longer applies.

One of the *most* significant factors that can increase sexual desire is feeling "connected" by virtue of having a really honest relationship—where nothing is withheld. This is because holding back in *any* area of life has an effect on holding back in others. No feelings (including sexual) can flow as freely unless *all* feelings flow freely. So whatever secrecy there was/still is regarding the affair may be having an impact on the degree of openness felt toward the marital partner. This is not something that can be resolved quickly or easily, but it's good to be aware of it in order to better understand and deal with the whole situation.

Also, we often feel more sexual desire for someone who is unattainable or who we're concerned about "losing." So trying to see your husband through the eyes of a new person who doesn't know him as an "old, dear friend" may help appreciate him as a *man*, not just in the role of *husband*.

For more perspective on the changing nature of love, here's an excerpt from our book, "Making Love Stay:"

"Romantic love is just the first stage of love, and it either evolves into a deeper, richer love or it withers. It's necessary to move beyond the initial romantic stage of love to achieve the richness that's possible in a loving relationship. Lasting love is not a less desirable state; it's just different. It has its own unique form of intensity and excitement, both of which emerge from a deeper knowledge of yourself and your partner."

Married Person Having an Affair

* * * * * * * * * * * * * *

A Younger Man

Dear Peggy,

Last spring, I met a young man by chance and we were very physically attracted to one another. We seemed to 'mesh' well together in conversation and intellect. He is not married, but we had no intention of furthering our conversation after our initial meeting, until we kept running into one another. Finally we found we were not only intellectually compatible, but also physically compatible. As many times as we admitted to each other that this is a huge risk, and we cannot speak again, neither of us had the 'strength' to stop the affair. I am now away from the place where we met, but we still communicate on the telephone. I feel a 'need' to speak to this man, and a definite 'want' to speak with him. My attachment is growing much more emotional toward him, and I find myself daydreaming about him very often.

My husband is a wonderful man, and if he knew that I had feelings such as this for another man, it would crush him. Occasionally, it is difficult for me to be interested sexually toward my husband, as I find myself wishing he was someone else. I need to get my 'life' back on track, and stop these emotions from taking over my thoughts. Do you have any comments about my situation?

Dear Reader,

I'll begin by focusing on your relationship with your husband. (This might be a helpful approach for anyone in this position—to specifically, deliberately focus more on their primary relationship as a way of countering the "automatic" focus on the outside relationship.) As for the lack of sexual interest in the primary partner, this is not surprising when caught up in the euphoria of a "new love," whether emotional, physical or both. These new feelings are powerful and can block out rational thinking—as well as sexual feelings for the primary partner.

The longer there's a lack of sexual desire (or even much physical contact), the more strain and awkwardness is likely to develop—making the recovery of sexual intimacy even more difficult. While it's usually best to avoid "pretending" or "faking," it can be helpful to move toward "acting as if" the sexual feelings are already present as a way of stimulating them to come.

This letter shows an awareness that something needs to be done to change the current direction, which calls for making a conscious effort to stop so much daydreaming. Like meditation, it may not be possible to avoid *beginning* a daydream, but the dreaming can be stopped instead of fueled. So the first step in shifting back to reality is to do less dreaming and more rational thinking.

The above comments sound like most people in situations like this: at some level there's an awareness that this is getting out of control, but on the other hand there's a rationalization that somehow it won't lead to dire consequences. In most cases, this kind of situation is damaging to the primary relationship whether or not the spouse ever finds out—because when someone is obsessing about another person, it breaks the connection in more ways than just sexually. So if there's a genuine desire to stay in the marriage, the sooner there's a deliberate effort along the lines discussed here, the better.

* * * * * * * * * * * *

Friendship to affair....

Dear Peggy,

I married at 23 to the first man I've ever dated, was a virgin... Four years ago I had an affair. It ended, but I realized how sex could be and is not with my husband...I have tried to focus on just my husband and working on our relationship.

I met a man two years ago who I am just friends with, we are very close and I can talk to him about anything and he is very supportive of me. He has confessed to wanting more and so do I, but how can I just up and leave my husband and two children. I do love my husband but only as a friend...I don't have strong feelings for him sexually and haven't for years...I'm pretty sure I found my soul-mate in this other person if there is such a thing, but I wouldn't want to leap into that either, I would like time to be alone and figure what I want. Am I being selfish?

Dear Reader,

Many of us as women never stop to figure out what we really want. We simply float along, assuming we'll get married and have kids, then wake up one day and wonder if we chose this path. I identify with this personally. While I'm very pleased with my life overall and would not change the way it has gone, I do realize that I never actually "chose" any of my major directions for the first 37 years of my life. But since then I've been much more deliberate about thinking through what I want. This is not necessarily "selfish;" in fact, getting clarity around our desires may help us realize that we would choose the same things all over again.

As for finding a *soul-mate*, leaving a marriage to pursue a soul-mate is an unrealistic way of thinking. No rational assessment of life can be made while jumping from one man to another. Doing so can wind up being a life-long pattern, never finding whatever is missing. It's a little like running all over the place searching for something—only to find that it's been right there within you all along. So finding a clear sense of who you are as a woman is a step toward accepting responsibility for your decisions—and for their consequences. It's usually much more difficult to think clearly about what we really want unless we take time to do it on our own.

* * * * * * * * * * * *

I Wish I Knew

Dear Peggy,

My wife and I have been married for 27 years. For the last 15 years I have traveled extensively developing my business (we own this company) and we have "drifted apart." We both still claim to "love" each other; (we have 2 children, 25 and 21, and they are well-balanced, well-focused, happy young people). My wife discovered her "Spiritual path" about 4 years ago and this has been sensational for her. She has become a vegetarian, does not touch any alcohol, and sex is not high on her list of priorities....however, she is calm, happy and totally obsessed by her guru.

I need socializing in my life; I crave our lovemaking to be here again; and I enjoy eating meat from time to time... I am so worried... I need my "basics." She is at peace with her life... What can I do????? Have an affair??? That will take care of the sex—and perhaps the "going out to fun places"....but...is this right/wrong/normal???? Please tell me what you think. I appreciate your comments.

Dear Reader,

Although a situation like this goes far beyond the issue of affairs, I assume that the sex/affair factor is a central part; so I will make some general comments.

First of all, it's normal for two people who are part of a couple to choose different areas of focus as their lives progress. So it's normal for the wife to want the things she is now choosing—and it's normal for the husband to want the things he values. It's not the choices per se that cause the feelings of "growing apart;" it's the distance that's created when the choices come without both partners having shared their thoughts and feelings as the changes/choices are being made.

Since there's some truth to the saying that opposites attract, it's quite possible that we would be attracted to someone new who made the choices an old partner is now making. A new person might seem fascinating by virtue of these differences. But the old partner often simply seems different or strange because we're comparing the way they have become to the way they once were. In addition, none of us particularly likes changes not of our own choosing—especially when it means we have to make adjustments to accommodate those changes.

As for the changes related specifically to sex, for women it's often the case that strong feelings of a sexual connection with their partner are closely aligned with feelings of a strong connection/involvement in other, non-sexual aspects of life. (When the overall connection is weak, so is the sexual connection.) Therefore, it's possible that being more involved/connected in other areas of life can rekindle involvement/connections in a sexual way as well. Of course, it takes both people sharing their deepest hopes, fears, and desires to forge this kind of connection. But it might be worth making this kind of effort—especially if the alternative is simply to have an "affair." While an affair may solve one problem, it's almost sure to create others.

* * * * * * * * * * * * *

Loving Two Women

Dear Peggy,

I am a very confused man. Married to someone who I love and who accepts me for who I am. I am also in love with another woman, who loves me unconditionally and accepts me for who I am.

I can share so much with both people. I share much more with the other woman. And I don't know why this is. For example, I went to Mexico recently, and ended up in a house of ill repute, paying for a prostitute. I told the other woman about this, but of course I hid it from my wife. I have shared with the other woman many of my past indiscretions, that I hope my wife would never find out about.

My problem is that I have always been looking for something better than what I have. I have always thought I was unhappy. But now I want to stop all of that because I do feel that what I have always been looking for was right in front of my face. And I just never realized it. I just learned this when I went on a trip and spent time with the other woman. Leaving her was difficult, and I realized how lucky I was.

The biggest problem is that I believe that both my wife and the other woman bring to me a complete happiness that I could not have with one or the other. I need both of these women, in the same way: to share, to love physically. For me it seems so possible. I don't want to lose my children, I don't want to lose her. Do I have to make a choice? I know I probably sound very selfish to you. I guess what I am asking is whether it's possible to love two women in the same way? And is it possible to live that kind of life?

Dear Reader,

The first statement in this letter sets the proper tone for all the rest of it: "I am a very confused man"—so it provides some hope that he can think more rationally than is currently happening.

For instance, the fact that he "shares more with the other woman..." about things he wouldn't share with his wife is quite understandable—and doesn't carry any special significance as to the quality or closeness of the outside relationship. It's always easier (and safer) to share with someone when there's not as much at stake and not as much invested. (If the current other woman were the wife, it's unlikely that he would share with her any more than he shares with his current wife.)

Now, to the specific questions as to whether he can have both these women or whether he has to make a choice: Obviously, people can do a lot of things— *if* they're willing to disregard the impact on others. Living this kind of life (secretly, deceptively) is quite different from deciding (on a fair and equal basis) to include other significant love partners. Some couples choose to have a sexually open marriage because they jointly decide they want to include others. But more often, people establish two sets of rules: one for their own lifestyle and a different one for their spouse.

If a person truly loves someone, they're unlikely to be willing to benefit at the other's expense. And it's unlikely that this kind of situation could continue for any extended period of time without there being a "price to pay" by one or both women involved. Thinking otherwise is the classic rationalization used when people want to "have it all"—with no consequences. There are very few free rides in life; most significant decisions have consequences. So anyone can have/do whatever they want—as long as they're willing to accept the consequences.

* * * * * * * * * * * *

I want both

Dear Peggy,

One can have extramarital affairs and still love his mate. He may just need more sex than she is willing to give, or the variety of activities that he desires, such as oral sex, or more than two or three times week. I'm tired too, but I have a greater need for sex than my partner does. I like experimentation but she doesn't as much; there's more than missionary and doggie style that helps add variety and excitement to a relationship. If I don't feel too old for more variety and frequency, then why doesn't she? I thought women were supposed to reach their peak at a later age than men? Sex makes me feel young and desired.

Dear Reader,

This letter covers a *lot* of issues: having affairs and still loving your mate; different needs and desire for frequency and variety; age and sexual potency; and sex helping self-esteem. On the surface, it would look like a simple case of incompatibility, but things are seldom as they appear on the surface. Since many of the issues are ones that other couples face, I'll make some general observations.

First of all, contrary to traditional thinking, it *is* "possible" to love your mate and still want to have affairs. However, if you also value, respect and are *honest* with your mate, then you probably won't *act* on that desire. It's normal to be attracted to others, but acting on the attraction shows a willingness to be dishonest that can lead to all kinds of problems in the marriage, regardless of whether the affair is ever discovered.

As for differences in preferences around sex, sometimes the differences are not really about sex at all. The lack of interest can be due to lots of other factors, most notably a lack of trust or a build-up of resentment over feeling there's some inequity in the relationship. Of course, sex drives do vary; but if a couple genuinely wants to find ways to work through the differences to find a mutually satisfying sex life, it can be done.

Sexual compatibility may not just come naturally, but there's nothing wrong with getting some professional guidance in learning better ways of dealing with different sexual preferences—if the differences really are simply sexual. In fact, this is one of the most straightforward issues to deal with—far simpler than the more complicated feelings of fairness, equality, concern, understanding, and

193

commitment. If those things are present in a relationship, no purely sexual differences will stand in the way of finding a way to satisfy both partner's needs.

* * * * * * * * * * * *

Marital crisis

Dear Peggy,

I am having an affair with another woman, this has been going on for over a year. My wife found out but now thinks it is over with. The other woman thinks I have left my wife. I cannot decide who I love and of course this has led to many problems. I know I am being unfair to all. I just cannot make up my mind as to what to do. I need help in sorting out my feelings.

Dear Reader,

The above is a classic approach-avoidance situation—which is quite common when people feel unable to make a decision. What happens is that the closer we get to a particular decision, the more we think about what we're giving up by choosing it instead of the alternative. Then when we shift toward the other decision, the same tendency happens again—this time focusing more on what would be lost by giving up the first consideration. It's true in almost all aspects of life that there are tradeoffs. You can't have *everything*; you have to get clarity about what you're willing to give up in order to have something that you want more.

Sometimes an effective way of handling this is to actually make two written lists so the two alternatives can be more easily compared. However, it's important not to assume that the longest list *wins*. It's necessary to weigh the two lists in terms of the *significance* of the items on each list.

If this seems too cold and calculated, another technique is to project 5 or 10 years down the road, envisioning life in terms of each of the two alternatives. Sometimes we get so caught up in the moment that we take a short-sighted view of the situation and fail to account for the more important long term.

Finally, when there's too much of a struggle to decide between two choices, it may be that the choices should not have been limited to those two in the first place—that what's really going on has more to do with some general sense of lack of satisfaction with *either* choice. So this whole process is an opportunity to get to know yourself better and be clearer about the choices you're making—and why you're making them. And no matter what choice results in the end, you're likely to know yourself better by virtue of having been thoughtful in the whole decision-making process.

* * * * * * * * * * * *

Affairs are Confusing

Dear Peggy,

I really wonder if I need to see a psychiatrist. I was involved with another man while I was married. It lasted for a year, but has since ended. But now I am involved with another man (however, we have not had sexual intercourse). I know I must be crazy to take the chances I have taken with my marriage the past

194

Married Person Having an Affair

2-3 years. I just don't understand why I can't be satisfied with my husband. He is a wonderful man... that loves me dearly... and treats me like a queen. I have what every other woman wants!! Can you give me any idea why I would take such a chance. I have two kids and have been married 12 years... and now I have to wonder if they are the only reason I stay with him. I really don't believe that... but I'm running out of rational explanations for my behavior. I've always thought that I loved my husband very much... but I just wasn't "in love" with him. As I write this to you now... I feel love for my husband. But... I can't help but wonder if my "love" for him is really something much less.

How can I continue to do this if I love him? Is it possible that my need for excitement... thrills... and the unknown are so much greater then my love for him? Is it possible that I really don't love him at all? Right now I just feel like a self-centered woman... who thinks only of myself. Also, I have noticed that I am much more pleasant... and happy... and content with life when I am involved with another man. And when I'm not, I'm pretty much miserable... and that definitely reflects in my marriage. So...when I'm having an affair... my marriage seems to be reaping the benefits also.

Well... I can go on forever... and I know you can't "diagnose" me or give me a "quick fix" on what little information I've given you. I feel pretty sure my childhood (lack of a father figure) has a lot to do with my behavior... and there are many other factors to consider. My main question is... is this just a phase that I'm going through... like a mid-life crises? Will I ever be happy with just my husband again? Or... will it take some therapy to figure out why I behave the way I do... and if it will continue forever? Or... is it possible that I just don't truly "love" my husband anymore? I know what I'm doing is wrong... and dangerous... so you don't have to give me the third-degree in your response... I feel bad enough about it (when I really think about what I'm doing). Thanks for listening.

Dear Reader,

While this letter is packed with questions, I'm glad to see that there's a recognition of the fact that neither I (nor *anyone*) can reasonably diagnose such a complex situation. In fact, I'm concerned about her own effort to diagnose herself by trying to identify a label—like mid-life crisis, lack of father figure in childhood, etc. And I'm also concerned about thinking it requires therapy to figure out why she behaves this way.

In fact, there's probably no need to go beyond the insight already expressed: "I'm running out of rational explanations for my behavior." Very little about having secret affairs has to do with rational behavior. Since much of the behavior is based on rationalization, this can be a good starting point for looking at some of the irrational beliefs that might be contributing to the situation:

1. "How can I continue to do this if I love [my husband]?"

Many people assume that if someone loves their spouse, they won't have an affair. That's not necessarily the case—because there are different kinds of love.

195

As I've said repeatedly, the *love* in an affair is different from the love in a long-term relationship. In an affair, there's a first-flush of euphoria that's typical of all new relationships. It doesn't last. That's because love is not static; it changes over time.

2. "When I'm having an affair... my marriage seems to be reaping the benefits also."

People having affairs try to find ways to rationalize that their behavior is not only *not* doing harm, but may, in fact, even be benefiting the primary relationship. However, the secretiveness and deception undermine the primary relationship—regardless of whether or not the spouse ever finds out.

3. "My main question is... is this just a phase that I'm going through... like a mid-life crises?"

This kind of thinking reflects an attitude based on thinking that our life experiences just "happen to us"—rather than being something we do. Since most people don't feel like they *choose* to have an affair, it's as if it's beyond their control.

In the final analysis, this reader is not really asking these questions because of a lack of *knowing*. She clearly shows that she understands what she's doing (and the risk involved): "when I really think about what I'm doing, I know what I'm doing is wrong...and dangerous." So if she just keeps that thought constantly in her awareness, she can change her behavior. It's only when we suppress our awareness of such realities that we do things we *wish* we weren't doing.

* * * * * * * * * * * * *

Very Confused

Dear Peggy,

I'm married, but not happy at all. I have been attracted to a male friend for years and not too long ago we started having an affair. He is not married but has expressed very unhappy feelings about my marriage. He wants me at times, but then he starts thinking and then breaks it off, then the same thing over and over. We spend a great night together. Then he doesn't call or talk to me for days. He doesn't want me to leave my husband for him but he doesn't want me to be married either. Should I just break it off with him even if I do get divorced? Or is it his way of saying he wants me to get divorced?

Dear Reader,

An unavoidable first reaction to the description of the man above is that he may want the fun without any commitment. While I can't know about this particular situation, it's unlikely that any significant life decision should be made based on what this other man *might* want. There's no indication of serious consideration of her feelings in all this—just what "he wants..." (And unfortunately, she is trying to figure out what *he* wants as well—when the better course of action would be to figure out what *she* wants.)

It's usually smart to make one decision at a time. In a situation like the one above, a woman might better disregard *any* consideration of the other man and *first* determine what she wants regarding her own marriage: Does she want to stay married or get a divorce? If she wants to stay married, then obviously all her energy needs to be focused on making that work. If she wants to get a divorce, then it would make sense to take steps to begin that process.

If there's a decision to divorce, then it's usually wise to think/live/experience life independently before immediately hooking up with someone else. Too many women spend their lives going from one man to the next, hoping to find "The One" who will make them happy. A reasonable course of action for any person is to first learn how to be happy on your own—and *then* seek someone to share your happiness. Otherwise, the grass may always seem greener on the other side—no matter what man (or men) are currently part of your life.

* * * * * * * * * * * * *

Southern Gentleman

Dear Peggy,

I have been married for 18 years. This is the first time I have had an affair. My husband is a good provider, father, and sexual partner, so I don't understand the affair myself. I met a southern man and he is so exciting. He compliments me, takes me out dancing, loves to cook together and hardly ever sits around the house. My husband is a couch potato. I know it's wrong but I love the best of both lives. At times I would love to leave my husband and go be with "Mark" but I could never hurt my husband and kids that way. I know I should stop the affair but I love this man and there is no doubt he loves me. He wants to get married. Any advice you could give would be appreciated.

Dear Reader,

The first thing that strikes me about the above letter is the common statement when someone is having an affair: "I could never hurt my husband and kids..." This is, of course, precisely what is likely to happen. However, most people having affairs are in denial about the very real consequences. Overwhelmingly, people focus most of their attention on the *positive* aspects of the affair—things like those described above: exciting, getting compliments., dancing, etc.

Speaking of dancing, many women see this as a special treat—one that men sometimes fail to fully appreciate. It's definitely a part of the attraction. For instance, my husband doesn't care for dancing, but he regularly went dancing with the women he had affairs with—because it was all part of the seduction.

It's almost always unreasonable and unfair to compare the attention from a man with whom you're having an affair and the attention from your husband. The nature of an affair (or any new relationship) is not like the long-term, real-life relationship in a marriage. For instance, had the woman above been married to the man in the affair for many years, his behavior would likely be more like her husband's—and if her husband were the new man who had just come into her life, he'd be likely to behave more like the man (or any man) having an affair. It goes with the territory—not dependent upon the particular person.

Having the best of both worlds is a common desire, but almost never possible. It may work in the short term, but be disastrous in the long term. At some point everyone has to make a choice—and live with the consequences of that choice.

* * * * * * * * * * * *

To Tell or not To Tell
(Here are 2 letters before my response.)

Dear Peggy, (letter #1)

My question is whether to tell or not to tell my husband about the affair I had. It is over now, and although he has seen and felt the impact, it is not known that the affair actually took place. I think the reason for the affair, in part, was the lack of emotional bond between him and me. I guess I am wondering if it is possible to mend my marriage, in the true sense, without hurting him with the knowledge of the affair and without risking a divorce, thus spreading what I see as my own pain to the people that I care about the most.

Dear Peggy, (letter #2)

I had an affair with one of my husband's friends. Now I feel awful about it. But my husband still does not know. It will never happen again. I love my husband very much and I can't believe I was weak enough to have an affair. Should I be honest and tell my husband or let it go?

Dear Reader,

Every person must make the decision about "whether or not to tell" for themselves. There are some factors to consider that might not at first be obvious. While there's an understandable caution about the potential risk of telling about an affair, there's also a risk if it's *not* disclosed. In marriages where affairs are kept secret, certain topics of discussion are avoided because the deceiving partner fears being discovered and the other is reluctant to appear suspicious. This causes many relationships to be dominated by dishonesty and deception. It's doubtful that a couple can keep something like this hidden for the rest of their lives without a terrible strain developing. A large part of the high divorce rate may be due to the alienation caused by the dishonesty inherent in affairs, even if the affairs are never confronted. So it may be that there is no escape from the pain, regardless of whether the affair is kept hidden or exposed.

This is not meant to diminish the pain of finding out. But one of the advantages of volunteering the information about an affair instead of waiting until it's unexpectedly discovered is that it allows a degree of preparation that can significantly reduce the pain of finding out. However, the person doing the telling has a responsibility to take steps to increase the likelihood that the disclosure will lead to building a closer relationship rather than tearing it apart. First of all, they need to be motivated by a desire to improve the relationship, not a desire to unload their feelings of guilt. They also need to be prepared to hang in and work through their partner's reactions to the information, regardless of what those reactions may be.

So it's not a simple matter of whether or not to tell. It's a matter of why, when, and how. Perhaps the most responsible course is one that doesn't rule out telling *at some point*, and uses that thinking to consistently improve the honesty and commitment to the relationship in such a way as to make it possible to eventually tell. In the meantime, this will have the benefit of strengthening the relationship, regardless of whether it leads to telling about the affair.

* * * * * * * * * * * * *

Do I have to tell on myself?

Dear Peggy,
I recently took a business trip with my boss. We were together for 5 days and on the last night, after a night of dinner and drinks, we slept together. We both acknowledged that this would never happen again and decided to keep this to ourselves. Telling my husband will only cause hurtful feelings. Do I have to say anything or can I keep this to myself?

Dear Reader,
While it's important to address the issue of whether or not to tell what has already happened, the more immediate issue to be addressed is understanding the problem involved with *continuing* to add to the secrecy by continuing to work together or see the other person in any ongoing way (albeit not sexual). So before focusing on whether to tell a spouse, it's important to strongly consider the risk/danger/ongoing deception of having *any* contact with the third party.

As for telling, many people assume that if an affair is never disclosed and never discovered, then no harm is done to the marriage. But, of course, the secrecy *does* create ongoing harm. However, telling is not a black-or-white issue. It's more reasonable to think in terms of always working toward telling at some point. Mainly, it's important to reject the idea that you can never tell.

* * * * * * * * * * * * *

Should you tell?

Dear Peggy,
Should you ever tell of an old affair? It's over and in the past; why tell?

Dear Reader:
This is similar to the above letter—except in this case it's "old news"—not a current situation. Unfortunately, there's a common belief that "if the affair is over and in the past, no harm is done by not telling your spouse about it." However, all the comments about the damage of secrecy still apply—and the message about whether or not to tell is also the same: never say never!

* * * * * * * * * * * * *

25 Years Ago

Dear Peggy,

I am at my wits end. After years of having accepted my wife's assertion 25 years ago that nothing happened during a very wild night, I now see the facts from that night do not support her story. Rather, it seems she may have indeed had sex that night with two different men. When I asked her about it she said she didn't remember, yet she DID remember several very insignificant details from that night during the time I suspect she was having sex with them. She also remembers very specifically seeing me in the hallway as she left the bedroom with one of the men and went into the living room with the other man.

Is it really possible that although she clearly remembers insignificant details, such as who was sitting where on the bed, that she cannot remember whether or not she had sex with one or both of those men that night? I told her it doesn't matter what she did then, but it matters very much that she appears to be hiding behind her "I don't know" and "I don't remember" responses to my direct questions about what actually happened. I just can't live with the denial. Please help.

Dear Reader,

I'm a great believer in honesty and in a willingness to answer questions. Unfortunately, getting "reasonable, consistent, believable" answers is often not possible—because after-the-fact (especially after so many years), it's almost impossible for people to *know* precisely what they said or did—or why they said or did it.

For instance, when my husband tried to remember facts related to his affairs, he didn't even know the answer to a fact related to actual time—like when he began his first affair. He was a whole *year* off. He honestly thought it was a year before it was; all he knew was that it began at a professional conference that took place each year at Labor Day. He also didn't know exactly how many affairs he had; (we never could be sure he remembered or accurately counted them all up). But it was his willingness to try to answer the questions (even when there were no clear answers) that made all the difference.

Sometimes, a person may have shifted things around in their heads so much to make them fit into a reality they can live with, that they really don't have good clarity around a lot of the details. The details simply aren't as important to them as they now are to you—so they may be trying to dredge up clarity when there simply *isn't* any, especially when it comes to feelings. And when someone is this confused about the facts, they often fall back on saying whatever they think might *work* in more nearly being an answer that will satisfy the questions enough to *stop* the questions—which is usually their primary goal.

So a better judge of the significance of any denials of being able to remember more details may be found in the *attitude* behind the denials. Does there seem to be a genuine wish to be able to remember or does it seem to be a handy excuse? While it's understandable to assume this is a deliberate *hiding*, given the above explanation of the process of remembering, it may be that she genuinely can't recall after all this time. So the statement that she "appears to be hiding" behind her responses may or may not be an accurate perception.

* * * * * * * * * * * * *

Coping with my affair

Dear Peggy,

I am a 35-year-old female. For the last few years I had been struggling with a marriage that never felt right. I was always the loyal wife and never even had many friends. As time went on, the problems in the marriage grew more intense. There was a great lack of communication, lack of respect which lead to abusive behavior on my husband's part (both physical and mental abuse took place). I felt like the loneliest person alive. Eventually, I made a friend. A person who lived in my same neighborhood. We began a friendship which ended up in an affair. The affair lasted 2 months. Eventually, it all came out in the open right after the affair had already ended. It all happened so fast that the person who I was involved with and I never really had a chance to properly discuss it. It was just an abrupt discontinuation of the affair.

My husband and I are still together and it has been a struggle. I have made no attempt to contact this other person and don't have any urges or intentions of doing so. My question is that this person still lives a few houses down with his family and we still live here. I wish I could relocate to another neighborhood but it is not possible at this point. The wife of this person has demonstrated behavior which seems to me to be obsessive. I understand her anger and if I could change what happened I would do so without a doubt. However, 6 months have passed and I make it a point to stay out of sight, but this woman has been stalking me, making hang-up calls and is constantly watching out for me. It got to the point that I had to involve the authorities. She calmed down for about a period of two weeks but has started up the behavior again. I am a person with a nursing background education and know how to recognize obsessive behavior.

I know I was wrong but how can I make her understand it is over. I feel like her behavior is getting out of hand and fear for my life. What's worse is that her behavior started at least one year before the affair ever took place. Back then, she didn't have a reason. Unfortunately, today I can't say the same. I can't understand how this happened or why it took place. What I do know is that this woman's worst fear became a reality. I truly regret what took place and very much resent this other man for ever approaching and pursuing me, but most of all I resent myself. I find it difficult with each day to forgive myself or even accept my mistake. I don't know how I'll ever be able to overcome this.

Dear Reader,

This letter illustrates how easy it is for someone to take actions as a result of one set of problems—only to create a *different* set of problems. I must quickly add, however, that the early reference to physical and mental abuse indicates an *extremely* serious problem—that needed to have been addressed *directly.* (It's a wonder the fear of retaliation isn't coming from the husband instead of the wife of the other man.)

But I'll try to address some of the many issues presented, including a friendship turning into an affair, "properly" discussing the end of the affair, the obsessive behavior of the other wife, and the desire to "make her understand it is over."

First of all, the woman who wrote this letter understandably regrets having had the affair. It was, of course, a very poor way of dealing with her loneliness. While she never expected the "friendship" to turn into an affair, this is extremely common. And it probably *could* have been detected—if there had been a genuine desire to recognize what was happening at an earlier point. In fact, it's a good bet that the other wife *did* recognize the potential for an affair back when it was *only* a friendship. The fact that her obsessive behavior began long before the affair began *may* indicate that she detected the possibility of an affair before the people involved recognized what was happening.

As for regrets at not having "a chance to properly discuss it" with the other man—it's really too late for that to matter at this point. It would seem that there was not good clarity/discussion all along at every step of the way—and at this point it's not reasonable to think of going back and getting clarity about what happened. It's only a *primary* relationship that needs/deserves the effort to "clean up" the past—*not* an affair. So staying away is almost certainly the best thing to do.

As for wondering "how to make [the other man's wife] understand it is over," there's probably nothing that can be said or done to alleviate her fear/concern. All too often saying *anything* winds up only making matters worse. It's *usually* better to say nothing—because *any* contact is likely to just reinforce the obsessiveness over this whole situation. Also, most people are likely to feel that "involving the authorities" is only adding insult to injury—that they have a *right* to their obsessive behavior.

I can't possibly give any specific advice as to what might be the best course of action. But, obviously, "relocating to another neighborhood" would resolve a lot of the issues. (And based on the statement about actual "fear for my life," it might be worth doing *whatever* it takes to make that happen.)

On the other hand, because of the fear, *if* there's no way to avoid being thrown into the same environment, it may feel like it's essential to say/do something. So—if the obsessiveness continues and there is a decision to try to say something to the wife—it may be safer to *write* than to speak. And whatever is expressed needs to be *totally* geared toward reassuring the wife (with *no* effort to explain/defend/complain about any of it). It needs to be *only* a note of genuine regret and apology for the pain that has been caused.

As for "how I'll ever be able to overcome this," much of the healing from this kind of experience simply requires time. It take time to assimilate such painful experiences and find ways to grow stronger by virtue of dealing with them. So while there may be regret over what happened, there can be pride in handling the fallout in a responsible way. And since we often learn more from our mistakes than our successes, we can use whatever crises we face as an opportunity to learn something that allows us to be better people in the future.

* * * * * * * * * * * * *

Ending an Affair

Dear Peggy,

What is the best way to end an affair? When I found out (after she called the house because he hadn't been calling her), he then called her and told her that it was over in my presence. She screamed at him and accused him of treating her "like a piece of meat." The call only lasted a couple of minutes and there was really no conversation or explanation. Should we just let it go at that?

I am so hurt and disappointed and am suffering with all of the symptoms you have written about in your books. We are seeing a therapist whose attitude seems to me to be that we're just waiting for me to "get over it." My husband swears he loves me and our children and grandchildren—and never intended anything permanent with her, (it just got out of hand and was primarily a phone relationship), and he wanted to end it long ago but just didn't have the guts because he was afraid of what she would do. But I feel that I want her to know that. I don't want her to go around thinking that the only reason he stopped was because I stopped it. Should he or I write to her, call her, ignore her or what???? Please help me.

Dear Reader,

First of all, it's extremely positive when a third party is informed directly that the affair is over. And it's an extra bonus for the spouse to be able to hear it firsthand. (I personally had that experience when my husband called to inform a woman he had had an affair with that he was "out of circulation." He did it in my presence, which left me no doubts as to just what he said, etc.) Certainly, it's better that the husband was the one to inform the third party of the end of the affair. It would be unlikely for the third party to be able to hear anything the wife in this situation would say directly to her because that would surely be interpreted as coming only from the wife without the husband's full support.

Nevertheless, it's understandable to want the third party to "know the score" in hopes that it will prevent "thinking that the only reason he stopped was because I stopped it." Based on the description of the third party in this letter, it seems unlikely that any effort to clarify things with her would succeed. The nature of perception is that we bring our own belief system to whatever is said or done. So any effort to clarify the situation would probably not be interpreted by the third party in the way it is intended. The result of additional contact would be likely to leave things even more unclear and create even more of a desire to get it cleared up.

It's a good guess that nothing is actually lost by not having additional contact with the third party. *Any* additional contact could potentially stimulate some kind of action (based on the husband's comment about not having the guts to end the affair earlier because "he was afraid of what she would do"). There's an old saying that "whatever you feed is what will grow." So feeding the contact with her could serve to cause it to continue. In this instance, probably "no news is good news." If the third party is never heard from again, that would likely be a good outcome.

Finally, the therapist's attitude of just waiting for a person to "get over it," shows the importance of finding a therapist who has a better understanding of how to deal with the issue of extramarital affairs. The therapist's attitude described above is useless at best and harmful at worst. Most people, both professionals and those dealing with it personally, need to get more information, understanding and perspective about the whole issue of affairs.

14: Single Third Party in an Affair

Being the Other Woman
(Here are 3 letters before my response.)

Dear Peggy, (letter #1)

I have been involved with a married man for over a year now. We are very much in love, but he can't leave his wife due to his immigration status. Am I right to believe that things will change once he is legally able to leave her or am I being played for a fool? I really love him but 2 years seems like such a long time to put my life on hold, waiting for his loveless marriage to end.

Dear Peggy, (letter #2)

I am currently involved in an affair with a married man. We have been seeing each other for 7 months and I am totally in love with him. I know it is wrong, but I don't know what to do. He has no plan for divorce, but says he cares for me but is in no position to get a divorce yet...but promises me he is going to do it, he just doesn't know when. I wish I had the strength to let go of him; I have tried but we always end up back together. Any advice?

Dear Peggy, (letter #3, condensed)

I am the other woman. Recently, his wife caught us. She is not certain of the nature of our relationship. And it took all I had to keep from telling her that we are deeply in love. I did not tell her the truth because that needs to come from him, not from me. She is on the brink of leaving. But she probably won't leave. My boyfriend has cheated on his wife several times over the term of their 9-year marriage. One relationship resulted in a child. His wife knows about most of his indiscretions; yet she still stays with him. And he will not divorce because of the children.

I want a life with him. I hope that she will soon leave and leave him no choice but to make a life without the benefit of living with his children every day. He and I are very much in love. But if he wants to play the role of the loving, devoted husband in order to keep his wife from leaving, then I have to respect that. I want so much out of life. If I were him or her, I would let this go and allow myself to find true happiness in another partner. What do you think?

Dear Reader,

The *reasons* given for why these particular Married Men can't leave their wives and be with their "true loves" are:

1. due to his immigration status
2. he is in no position to get a divorce "yet"
3. he will not divorce because of the children

I've heard at least 100 others similar reasons/excuses to explain why men can't leave their wives, but the bottom line is that people in this position usually want *both* the family *and* the affair. They don't want to have to choose and give up either one. So the other woman is left waiting, hoping, longing for the day when things will be different. Yes, it might one day happen...but so might winning the lottery; it's just not reasonable to count on it. The sooner the other woman recognizes this pattern and the price she is paying for this hope-against-hope, the sooner she may be able to get on with her life.

As for "true love," in these situations it's usually an illusion that is part of the fantasy surrounding an affair. There's a certain make-believe quality to a good affair, whereas marriage is for real. Many find out too late that ending a burdensome marriage to pursue an affair as their primary relationship doesn't really solve anything. When the affair becomes a full-time thing, it frequently takes on the same qualities the marriage had. The whole issue has more to do with the difference between affairs and marriage than with the particular people involved.

* * * * * * * * * * * * *

Feelings of the other woman

Dear Peggy,

What about the other woman? How does she feel? What happens to her if the affair is terminated? Affairs aren't moral, but there are people involved in them, and they need support too. There needs to be some emphasis on them as well, identifying them as being normal beings, instead of some sort of gold-digging prostitute. I would think that the affair would be incredibly stressful for them too.

Dear Reader,

In order to fully address the entire issue of extramarital affairs, we need more insight into the roles played by *everyone* involved. We do need to combat the simplistic notion that "bad" people have affairs and "good" people don't. *Anyone* is vulnerable to having an affair—and *no* couple is completely immune. The primary culprit in all this is the dishonesty and deception that are an inherent part of having secret affairs. So more open discussion of this issue can go a long way toward preventing the pain that almost inevitably befalls everyone involved in affairs—including the other woman.

* * * * * * * * * * * * *

I Am the Other Woman

Dear Peggy,

I have been seeing a 43-year-old man for 5 months now who is married. During my last visit with him, he told me he was happily married and that I would never have him. This, however, has not stopped him from wanting to see me and continue our relationship. He would be happy to have me as his affair for the rest of his life. I am the fourth woman he has had an affair with.

Single Third Party in an Affair

Can a man be happily married and have an affair? I know that I have to let go; unfortunately for me, I fell in love before he gave me this information about his happy marital status. I do want to let go, but I really do want an answer to my question. How can someone be happily married and seek outside women as he does? Is this possible?

Dear Reader,

As unreasonable as it may sound, yes, it is possible for a man to be happily married and still have an affair. Most women believe: "if my partner loves me, then he won't have an affair." That's a belief based on rational thinking, but there's very little rational thinking involved in having an affair. Affairs thrive on rationalization and denial. The stereotypical example of this is the common statement: "What she doesn't know won't hurt her." This is more common among men because it's somewhat easier for men to compartmentalize their lives and say that one part (their wife and family) has nothing to do with the other (their affairs).

When I suspected my own husband of having affairs (30 years ago), I tried in every way to be the *perfect* wife, thinking he wouldn't want anyone else if I did everything possible to make him happy. But most men don't think in terms of either/or; they want both: the love and stability of wife and family—and the fun and excitement of an affair. (This is usually somewhat different for a woman having an affair. She's more likely to feel a need to *choose* and not try to have both for any extended period of time.) But if women try to apply this same thinking to men's behavior, they're failing to realize that men don't necessary feel that way. Most men who are perfectly honest admit that in their ideal world they would have both. (This reflects the old-fashioned double-standard thinking of most men in that they think they should be able to handle both—but would not want their wives to do the same.)

* * * * * * * * * * * * *

Marry me or I'm out of here...

Dear Peggy,

I am an African American woman, well-educated and currently in pursuit of my bachelor's degree in nursing, in which I expect to graduate next year. I have been involved with a man who I feel could very well possibly be my soul-mate. The only problem is that he is married and is currently going through a divorce in which the relationship has ended approximately 2 years ago. Anyway, we have been courting for a year and a half and enjoy being in each other's company, and he stands behind me 100 percent. We also make beautiful love, the kind that puts the sleeper on you! Anyway, I gave him an ultimatum, either he is going to marry me next year or I'm out of here while I'm still a young tender. Well, he gave me a date—but so far we have not made any wedding plans. How do I approach the situation without being pushy? And if he doesn't marry me by next year, should I give up on the fact that he might want to remarry again?

207

Dear Reader,

The first point I want to address is the reference in the above letter to the fact that this man "could very well possibly be my soul-mate" One aspect of feeling someone is a soul-mate is that it clouds *all* perception of that person. For instance, if someone really "stands behind you 100 percent," there's not likely to be a concern about "how to approach the situation"—*any* situation. As for not being pushy, it's hard to see how it's pushy to follow up on an ultimatum. (Of course, it's best to only give an ultimatum when there is a clear commitment to following through on it. Otherwise, it's meaningless.)

While I'm not cynical about the development of loving relationships, I'm very realistic about them based on hearing so many stories of people who wait and hope things will work out—while ignoring warning signs to the contrary. While I can never know in any given situation (and would not predict the outcome of the one described above), *in general* there needs to be a great deal more openness, trust and ability to communicate than is usually described in the letters I receive.

Since it's usually better for people to avoid mistakes than to learn from their mistakes, I try to share some perspective that will help people analyze their own situations more clearly and make their own decisions. Usually, people *know* what's likely to be the outcome of the questions/situations they describe in their letters, but they resist acting on their own knowing. While certainly there are risks in taking certain actions, there are also risks in *not* taking some actions. So each person needs to be as accurate as possible in comparing one set of risks against the other—and make their own decisions.

* * * * * * * * * * * *

Why risk getting caught?

Dear Peggy,

I have been involved in a deep and meaningful affair for a few years now. Recently however, her husband found out, and she felt compelled to end the affair. A few weeks after it was over, we met (and it was planned) at a store and talked for awhile, but she soon had to go to meet her husband for a lunch date. She asked me to follow her there and go into the restaurant at the same time they were having lunch (but not at their table, and certainly without her husband knowing who I was or the fact I was there). She has also invited me to other social events where he was, wanting me to be close by, where she can see me and I can see her. What is on this woman's mind? What would motivate her to risk being caught? What can she gain by me being there?

Dear Reader,

These are interesting questions: "What is on this woman's mind? What would motivate her to risk being caught? What can she gain by me being there?" Since I'm not a mind-reader, I can't know for sure what's on her mind. The most reasonable, sensible, and potentially effective thing to do in a situation like this is to ask *her* these questions. Usually when people do things that are not rational, it's because they're in a kind of undecided, limbo state where they don't know just what they want—and they want to keep all their options open at all times. Keeping an affair partner nearby when with the spouse may serve to reassure that the affair partner will still be there if and when she turns to them. Basically, there's nothing in this for a person in the position of the man who wrote this letter, and there's no point in going along with this kind of thing just because the other person is unreasonable enough to ask it.

As I've said before, these are general comments about this *kind* of situation—not an assessment of what's going with this specific person. And while she may not clearly understand her actions herself, she's certainly the best source of information.

* * * * * * * * * * * * *

Other Woman

Dear Peggy,

Is there a perspective for the other party? We fell in love, deeply. The parting was and continues to be horrible. He wants to remain friends who see each other regularly as only friends. I refuse such a situation; it is too painful. He says it makes him feel warm to see me, watch me, be in my presence; it makes me sad and angry. He feels hurt and rejected. He is married; I am not. How do these relationships change? What do you think?

Dear Reader,

This letter describes a common plight of the third party—waiting in limbo without a commitment (or even the prospects of one in the above case), but where the married partner still wants to continue to have some kind of relationship. It's an extremely self-centered attitude on the part of the married partner who says it "makes him feel warm to see me, watch me, be in my presence."

While the married person may be kidding themselves that this comment is somehow flattering, it's actually insulting. It's expecting another human being to be a backdrop to their lives, to "stand by"—much like a professional photographer has an assistant just standing by to be available if/when they're wanted or needed. While this stand-by position is appropriate in some work situations, it's clearly demeaning in personal life. (It's not too different from the way people express their enjoyment of having a dog who "makes them feel warm to see, watch, and be in their presence.") People deserve to be treated with more respect and consideration.

It's also interesting to see how the perception of a situation can be so different according to where you stand. The married partner "feels hurt and rejected," and tries to make it appear that it is the third party's fault—and therefore their responsibility to take care of those feelings). But at the same time, there doesn't seem to be much consideration for the feelings of the third party.

As to "how these relationships change," they usually change only when the third party (or the spouse) changes it. The married partner seldom initiates change and may be willing to continue this kind of arrangement indefinitely— because they don't want to give up the benefits of either relationship. Since the common pattern is for the third party to eventually be left to pick up the pieces and get on with their own lives, it's probably better to start that process sooner rather than later.

* * * * * * * * * * * *

In love with a married man
(Here are 2 letters before my response.)

Dear Peggy, (letter #1)

I am a 21-year-old female. I have an 18-month-old daughter and my life was going really bad until I met, what I believe, might be the love of my life. There is only one problem...he is married. He said that he wants to be with me and that he will leave his wife, and I truly believe that. He does not love her and she doesn't love him. All she loves is his money and I love him for him. I am so sad because she will not leave him and he will not totally leave her for the reasons of court. He spends most of his time with me if he is not working, and even if he is, he still comes over all of the time... I cannot explain how much I love him. We make wonderful love all of the time. I have never felt so sexual around anyone else but him! He makes me feel like the only person on the earth. He is 42. I love him so much.... Please help me and give me some advice, anything would help. I have been told to leave him, but I can't. I love him way too much and so does my daughter. Please Help Me!!!!

Dear Peggy, (letter #2)

My man is married to a women he claims is sick with cancer and their marriage has been over for years due to her alcoholism.

I have had the best relationship with this man I have ever had. For once in my life I am truly happy. He satisfies me sexually as well as mentally. We only get to spend morning together on the weekdays. On the weekends I do get brief sessions with him but he is mainly with her. My friends call me a slut, bitch, and whatever comes to their mind. They don't understand how important this relationship is to me. I want to believe everything that he says. He tells me he loves me and he makes me laugh. Should I give up everything I ever looked for.!!! I've been looking for this man all my life. Should I believe him when he tells me it is me that he has been looking for all his life, but has yet to tell me that he is willing to leave that sick, drunk bitch that keeps me from my life's dream. What should I do? Listen to my friends or my crotch? Thanks. Helplessly confused.

Dear Reader,

These letters illustrate a common situation—where people ask for *help* or *advice* when it seems unlikely that they would actually accept it. It is sad that they have put themselves in a "no-win" situation. On some level, they *know* it—but somehow feel they have no power to do anything about it. Of course, they are the only ones who *can* do anything about it—and only when they decide they really want to.

Let me review some of the comments that cry out for clarity:

—"I met...what might be the love of my life."

There's no such thing as "the love of my life (especially when that person is already married to someone else)—except in romance novels and other unrealistic depictions of love.

—"only one problem...he is married."

This is not "only one problem;" it's a *huge* obstacle to any realistic hope of things working out. (Remember, only about 10 percent of people who divorce due to an affair wind up marrying the person with whom they had the affair.)

—"He said...he will leave his wife, and I truly believe that."

Unfortunately, when a 42-year-old man tells a 21-year-old woman that he will leave his wife—she should only believe it when she sees it happen. (And she shouldn't hold her breath.)

—"Give me some advice... I have been told to leave him, but I can't."

There's little reason to give advice to someone who goes right on to say that they reject the advice they're given.

—"My man is married to a woman..."

How can he be "*my* man" when he's married to someone else?

—"that sick, drunk bitch...keeps me from my life's dream."

Of course, it's *not* really this woman who is thwarting the life's dream; it's the man who is *not* choosing to leave her - despite whatever he says.

—"I want to believe everything that he says."

This shows some awareness of how someone could actually believe this typical statement: "I love you —but can't leave my wife....": because she *wants* to believe everything he says. Otherwise, it would be very difficult to believe that he really is "mainly with her [his wife]"—even though she is "sick with cancer and their marriage has been over for years due to her alcoholism."

Both of the above letters illustrate the problems when people let their emotions overwhelm their rational thinking. Everyone around them can see what they are unable/unwilling to see about the true nature of the situations. They will see it too whenever they are ready (which may or may not happen before they are terribly hurt). In the meantime, it is positive that they are at least writing out the confusion they are experiencing. Perhaps that process alone will help them think more clearly and take control of their lives instead of being blinded by too much denial and wishful thinking.

* * * * * * * * * * * * *

211

Lies to the other woman

Dear Peggy,

It's amazing that no one even considers the other woman in extramarital affairs; except to say she is the evil person. This is all so taboo that almost all the focus is on the married couple. That's not fair. I met a man online that convinced me he was divorced and had custody of his 3 minor teenage children. We finally met 3 months after we started talking online. He admitted before we met that his divorce was not final; however, he did convince me he had custody of the children and because of property settlement, custody, her extramarital affair, the divorce would take another year. We do not live in the same geographic location. Finally, after many more months he admitted that he was living under the same roof as his wife, separate but not apart, due to financial straits. He assures me that the divorce will be final in a few months and we will spend the rest of our lives together.

He will not tell the children or anyone in his life about me, he's waiting for the divorce to be final; yet it does not need to be kept a secret on my end. How does one fall in love with a man that has told so many lies, or better yet stay in contact with him? It's the same old story...you fall, you fall hard for a man who lied, and yet you want to believe that he is telling the truth now.

My question: If the wife committed adultery and the divorce is almost final, and this man professes his undying love and says he wants to spend the rest of his life with you—should he tell his three teenage children anything about this person? Should he keep that a secret too until the divorce is final? The children know about the pending divorce. Does the other woman have a right to expect that she not be hidden when the divorce is amicable, or at least as amicable as it can be? I know if more women respected other women by not having an affair unless the man "s__ts" or gets off the pot; the man would either stay in the marriage or obtain a divorce. However, when men lie, even if they have filed and intend to get the divorce, where does that leave the woman?

It's all so confusing and I see no area for women to commiserate...only the respective spouses. Do you know of any books on the subject that might be helpful?

Dear Reader,

This is a long, painful letter—like so many stories I have heard over the years. In this case, she obviously knows she's dealing with a man who lies, as evidenced by the long list of people to whom he's lied about all kinds of things. So the questions about what he *should* tell or not tell are really irrelevant— because it appears that his criteria for what he tells, when he tells, and who he tells is based on what best serves his own needs. And this pattern of lying is not one that is likely to stop. So it may be that if she "wins," she "loses." A lifetime of dealing with a person like this is likely to be a lifetime of continuing to be confused by his behavior.

I respect the fact that she obviously realizes the folly of what she's doing; she clearly states, "How does one fall in love with a man that has told so many lies, or better yet stay in contact with him?" So I suspect this letter is an invitation to have someone validate her own knowledge. She knows rationally that this is not a promising situation, but she's trying to apply her understanding to her emotional feelings.

Since I'm a big believer in the power of information (and books as a source of information) in helping overcome being controlled by feelings and emotions, I'm especially encouraged by the request for "any books on the subject that might be helpful." One of the best resources is a very old book (now out of print, but perhaps available in libraries) by Melissa Sands titled *"The Mistress' Survival Manual."* A more recent book that addresses this issue is Laurel Richardson's book, *"The New Other Woman."* It could also be helpful to expand the focus to thinking about life in a larger framework (not limited just to relationship issues) by doing some life-planning as presented in a number of good life-planning books, including our own "Life-Design Workbook."

It's sometimes hard to step back, take a deep breath, and change course. But simply writing this letter indicates a willingness to consider it before continuing to beat her head against this wall of confusion and frustration. The letter represents an initial effort to get more control over this situation—which is a positive first step toward taking back her life.

* * * * * * * * * * * *

Affair with boss

Dear Peggy,

I have been having an affair with my boss for over two years. He tells me how much he loves me and can't live without me. He tells me that he doesn't love his wife anymore; however, he and his wife are going on a cruise this winter together. I try to tell him that I don't understand how somebody can go on vacation with someone they don't love, but he just tells me I don't understand. When I talk about marriage, he tells me he wants to marry me but he doesn't know when. When I tell him I am going to leave the job and work elsewhere, he said he will hunt me down and drag me back. He can't work in that job without me. However, I have to sit at work while he is on a cruise with his wife. I don't know what to do. Please help!

Dear Reader,

While the specific problem presented above *seems* to relate to an issue of love, it sounds much more like a problem of *control*. Frankly, genuine love and a self-serving effort to control another person are simply not compatible. And a situation like the one described above sounds more like possessiveness than love.

It's also possible that a man like the one described above may not want to have to choose. Sometimes people don't want to give up either the stable home life or the affair. They're satisfied to keep juggling both for as long as

213

possible—and will use whatever pressure, intimidation, or promises that will prolong their not having to make a decision. Often, nothing changes until one of the other two people (in a case like this, either the wife or the other woman) makes their own decision. We can, after all, only take responsibility for our own actions—not for the actions of others. And waiting/hoping for someone else to take a certain action can sometimes go on for years and years.

Now to get back to the initial question of love, it appears that someone like the man described above may have his own (convenient) definition of love. Many people have an image of love as *only* the initial feelings of romantic love. By that narrow, simplistic definition, he may say he doesn't "love his wife anymore."

While I can't tell a specific person what to do—frankly, in most instances people already *know* what's best to do. It's just a matter of whether or not they're willing to do it. So I offer the above comments only as validation of what the writer of this letter already senses, but perhaps doesn't want to accept.

* * * * * * * * * * * *

"Other Woman" talking to wife?
(Here are 2 letters prior to my response.)

Dear Peggy, (letter #1)

I have been seeing this married man for 8 months. I have tried to be strong and stay away from him and we have for up to 6 weeks at a time, but he always ends up calling and we go back to the old routine. When I ask him if he is going to get a divorce he just says "yes, but I don't know when; I am waiting for a better time." I tell him it will only get worse the longer he waits. We have a wonderful time together, but I always feel awful when he has to leave. Last week, I finally decided "if he is not going to tell his wife, then I am," so I called and told her everything. She was very nice to me, said she suspected he was having an affair, but was not sure. I told her I would not see him anymore and was sorry. She said she did not blame me, but did not know what she was going to do. She loves him and wants it to work.

After I spoke with her, I called him to inform him that I told her everything. He was not as upset as I thought he would be. He said he understood, and he wished it would have just been a one-night stand; it would have made things much easier, but he really does care for me and does not know what to do. I told him I was not going to ever see him again and not to call me. He tried to call me 3 days later; I did not answer the phone, though he called 6 times. What should I do now? Should I call his wife and let her know he is still trying to contact me? Or leave it alone? I truly love him very much, more than I have anyone. But I am trying to do the right and moral thing now. It is so hard for me, because I want to be with him so bad. She asked me to call her if he tried to call me again. Any advice would be appreciated.

Dear Peggy, (letter #2)

    I was the other woman. My affair lasted for three months, and things tended to get really "sticky." I befriended his wife at his request. I ended things by telling his wife about the affair because I was hurt by him, and I really liked her as a person. I have avoided her since telling her. She wants to meet with me, and I do not think it is wise. I know she is hurt and insecure but I have told her I do not want her husband even though I still have a lot of feelings for him. I feel very remorseful for what I have done, but how should I deal with this woman who has sooo much hurt in her? How do I deal with myself for what I have done to her life? I am dealing with so many emotions I feel like I am on a roller coaster. Your suggestions would be much appreciated.

Dear Reader,

    These letters illustrate the fact that there's plenty of pain to go around when this sort of triangle exists. And it's also indicative of how often the wife and other woman are able to empathize with each other once they see each other as real people instead of just the role they are playing. However, in any such situation, it's the person in the pivotal role (in these cases, the husband having an affair) who needs to be responsible for dealing with the situation. Regardless of how much empathy or concern the other woman has for the wife, the sooner the other woman severs *all* contact with *both* the husband and the wife, the sooner everyone can get about the business of dealing with the situation.

    It is not the other woman's responsibility to *help* the wife or to "make up to the wife" for the harm that has been done. While it's admirable to have concern (and even regret), the best way to honor that feeling is to set about dealing with your own life in as caring and responsible a way as possible. As we go through our lives, there are invariably times when we're disappointed in ourselves when we do things that hurt others and damage our self-esteem. But no amount of trying to go back and *fix* things can change the past. So it's probably wise to use our energy in going forward, taking with us whatever lessons we learn from our experiences.

    Both letters above refer to wanting to do the "right and moral thing" and wondering how to "forgive myself." Those feelings tend to make a person feel they should *do* something, but avoiding any kind of involvement may be the best thing she can do. Even if the husband or wife *thinks* they want the other woman's involvement, it's probably a case of the less, the better. Avoiding all contact with the husband and the wife is probably preferable; but if it somehow can't be avoided, then perhaps it's best to simply explain that you're bowing out in order to leave the two of them to work together to resolve their situation— that they need to talk to each other, not to you. In the meantime, you have your own issues to deal with and your own decisions to make and your own life to get in order. The best thing you can do for *them* is to take care of your own future without them in it in any way.

* * * * * * * * * * * *

Other woman won—and lost

Dear Peggy,

I am the other woman in this story and after 3 years of crying and questioning the status of divorce, I finally gave up. Now my love has moved, followed me 1500 miles, and left his wife. Everything should be roses and sunshine now, right? It's not! We fight all the time and can't get back on track. Why?

Dear Reader,

It's really quite sad when someone believes they've found a special love—only to finally *win* the person of their dreams and find that it's more like a nightmare than the dream they envisioned. The wonderful feelings of love that existed during the affair somehow seem to have disappeared. As to why this happens, it's not too hard to explain. While in the midst of an affair, there's often a fantasy make-believe quality to the relationship—whereas when it becomes a committed relationship, it frequently takes on the same qualities the original marriage had. That's because the whole issue has more to do with the difference between affairs and a long-term committed relationship than with the particular people involved.

The other woman often pays a heavy price, regardless of whether the man stays with his wife (which is usually the case) or leaves his wife so they can be together. While, of course, there are exceptions, in most cases it's a lose-lose proposition for the other woman. While it doesn't always turn out to be as negative as the description above, it's quite common for there to be a significant shift when the roles change from being the other woman to being the wife or primary partner. In fact, it may be even more difficult because the new relationship bears the burden of being seen as *responsible* for whatever fallout (or regrets) result from the divorce. (Of course, this is even more likely if there are children involved).

Bottom line: it's unlikely that a couple can "get back on track"—because that track is no longer relevant to the new relationship. The challenge lies in trying to forge a new relationship that looks toward building a future together, not trying to recapture the past—which is likely to be a losing proposition.

* * * * * * * * * * * * *

Do I give him another chance?

Dear Peggy,

My current boyfriend (fiancée) is separated from his wife. He has been for one and a half years, on and off. That is the problem. He left her, we started dating. He left me 6 months later to go back to her, he said for the children. He left her 3 weeks later to go back to me, he said because he couldn't live without me. I was 3 months pregnant. He left me 3 months later to go back to his estranged wife. This time admitting that he had slept with her a few times while we were together. He did that when he went over to see his kids. She is now pregnant too and he has left her again, saying he can not live where he is not happy—even for the kids. He wants me to give him another chance. He says he has only been happy when we were together and he will wait as long as it takes for me to commit to him again.

I do love him, but am afraid. He wants to get married when his divorce is final. Do I give him this chance?

Dear Reader,

If I count correctly, the above letter describes a man who has left this woman twice and left his wife three times. The obvious question is, what evidence is there that it wouldn't happen again? (Obviously, there's no reason to believe that a person like this who says they want another chance actually deserves it—or would value an additional chance by acting any more responsibly in the future than in the past.)

Since he always seems to have some explanation for the repeated changes in what he wants, the next most likely part of the pattern would be to decide to go back to his wife because *she's* pregnant. This, of course, is only one of many uncertainties in this situation. Another obvious question is whether he will, in fact, ever get divorced.

It's quite understandable that this reader would be afraid; in this instance, the fear is a very rational fear. In fact, it's questionable as to whether to even say, "he wants to get married *when* his divorce is final"—since the first question is *whether* his divorce will ever happen. So any decision as to whether or not to "give him this chance" really doesn't need to be answered unless and until he actually gets a divorce.

* * * * * * * * * * * * *

Conflicting Wants

Dear Peggy,

I have been working with a man for 2-1/2 years. We are really close friends and tell each other everything. The problem is he is married, I am not. He has 2 children, I have 1 child. We want so badly to spend time together, yet we can't seem to get away from the office or our homes. We are both in unhappy relationships. I know now that I love him and that he loves me too. I can't stop thinking about him and spend most of my time at home wishing I were with him. He says that he feels the same. I need advice.

This is not a fling, we have never even slept together. We just really love to be around each other and can't help falling in love. What do I do? I don't want his children or my child to get hurt from this and I know he feels the same. We don't want to hurt them, yet we want so badly to give our relationship a fair chance. Do you have any suggestions?

Dear Reader,

There is probably no answer that will accomplish both of the things wanted:

—"I don't want his children or my child to get hurt..."

—"We want so badly to give our relationship a fair chance..."

217

This is a classic example of the truism: "You can have *anything* you want, but you can't have *everything* you want." In this situation, as with many life circumstances, there are tradeoffs. You can't have both. There is no magic solution and no way to avoid the realities of the potential problems involved in this kind of situation.

One possible way of getting more clarity is to deal with one matter at a time—instead of trying to deal with several issues at once. For instance, a woman in a position like the one described is unlikely to be able to rationally assess the situation unless she's out of the immediate work environment she shares with the other man. On the other hand, she's also unlikely to be able to rationally assess the relationship with the other man unless she's out of the "unhappy relationship" she now shares with someone else.

Another alternative for trying to accurately assess what she really wants is to do *both*: get out of the immediate work environment *and* get out of the "unhappy relationship." Only when independently assessing the situation "from the outside" is she likely to be able to think clearly and make the best decision. Otherwise, she may either remain in limbo or make a decision and then second-guess herself forever. In order to find satisfaction in whichever decision is made, such a life-altering decision deserves long, thoughtful consideration.

* * * * * * * * * * * *

Woes of the Other Woman
(Here are 2 letters before my response.)

Dear Peggy, (letter #1)
I am having an affair with a married man. We have known each other for 3 years, and I have also worked for him. We were friends first, best friends, and our love for each other grew. He said he fell in love with me the first time he saw me. He doesn't love his wife at all; he was supposed to leave her a few times in their marriage, but she said she would kill herself if he left. This was years before he met me. He says he loves me like his children, and has never felt this way before about another woman. We are so close and need each other so much. I was married for 16 years also, and he is married for 19 years. He hasn't made love to her since we have been together. He said he is going to leave her, but because of financial obligations he can't right now... Is there any hope for us, or am I dreaming? We love each other more and more each day. We are so...much alike, and every time we are together we have so much fun. It is really not about sex, although we both feel it's the best we have ever had.... Should I hang in there and wait, or should we back off until he makes up his mind? We can not go a day without talking and seeing each other... Does this kind of love really exist???? Please give me some advice...I'm lost without him.

Dear Peggy, (letter #2)
For the past 1-1/2 years I've accepted the role of being the other woman...the secret...this is with a man who is not married but has been in a live-

in relationship for the last 4-1/2 years. Without going into pages of past histories...will try to sum up briefly... This live-in relationship started out for purposes of financial and physical conveniences...to quote "it is not good nor bad...not what I want...nor the quality of life I want for myself"...which is why the man I am involved with continued to look elsewhere.

We have an intense physical and emotional relationship...We both recognize the importance of having found "the love of our life"... I might add we are not kids...we are both 51... It is becoming increasingly difficult to continue being the invisible woman with the man I love. His difficulty leaving his situation seems to be his sense of responsibility (financial) and guilt (this lady has a history of mental unstableness). I have asked him to tell me where his commitments and choices are (no time frame)...and he is having great difficulty expressing himself. What to do? Give an ultimatum...give him time away from me? At this point I feel like he's got the best of both worlds...and he does! It is time for me to know if I will ever be a visible person in his life. How? Well...would appreciate your input...

Dear Reader,

These letters represent the common "lines" heard by the other woman—and they are right to feel frustrated and confused. It's clear that there's a pattern of lines that are regularly used to keep the other woman "waiting in the wings" while the marriage (or other relationship) continues.

—"[his wife] would kill herself if he left."

—"because of financial obligations he can't [leave her] right now."

—"His difficulty leaving his situation seems to be his sense of responsibility (financial) and guilt (this lady has a history of mental unstableness)"

There's a clear pattern here: all the *excuses* sound so thoughtful and considerate, almost *noble*. Of course, they also happen to be extremely self-serving. Why bother to make the hard choices if you can continue to have *both*: a primary relationship and a lover on the side.

It's likely that each of the women who wrote these letters (as well as any woman in the role of other woman) recognizes the reality I've just described. It's just so hard to allow the rational understanding of the situation to overpower the strong emotional involvement. Hopefully, the process of writing these letters indicates a willingness to reevaluate their situations and act on what they probably already know. And it might help to remember that even if the man finally leaves his wife or other partner, only about 10 percent of men who actually divorce their wives (or leave a primary relationship like the one above) wind up marrying the other woman.

* * * * * * * * * * * *

Burning anger...

Dear Peggy,

I am so angry right now. Two years ago, I met a man. Of course, he was married and it isn't to me. He is a minister and marriage counselor, I had much respect for that...and felt comfortable talking to him about things I felt, the everyday things going on, things I looked forward to. He would share with me just the same. And then he would make flirting comments...and I was flattered by it... Since I didn't say no...to stop, that was a fatal mistake. He would became "friendlier" and not long after that he was pursuing me...and I loved it. I felt so cherished and I really believed his sincerity...after all, he's a minister. He wouldn't lead me astray with his feelings if they weren't genuine. He told me he married too young, and if he had to do it again, he wouldn't. He said he wished he would have met me instead. So, I am totally fallen for this guy. We would spend hours...up to 5 hours a day on the phone...just talking about everything. Of course, the bill was mine... Should I have been concerned that he never offered to pay any of it?? I would send him 5-hour phone cards to call me. I didn't just go through wonderful times with him, financially things were difficult for him...and I sent money a couple times to pay his health insurance, car insurance, money for Christmas...

And he was lying to his wife the whole time. She had found out about me... several months after we started talking on the phone...he had neglected to erase one of my messages. He told her it was over; she had him call me, with her on the phone, and tell me it was over. She accused me of pursuing a married man who was going through a rebellious time.

After that, he called and begged me to stay. He cried and begged me to stay...and felt really bad about how humiliated I felt. And I stayed. He begged me to see him in person (we live in different states) and I did. (I pawned all the jewelry I had ($5,000.00) for $1,500.00 to pay bills and have enough to travel and see him. But I didn't regret it, because he was wonderful. We found we were very attracted to one another and talked about me moving to be closer to him. This went on for another 7 months and he insisted that I come see him again. So I did, and at that point something in the relationship changed. It was never the same. I believe one of the reasons is that I asked him, why are we having an affair if he wasn't really going to leave his wife. She didn't deserve to have that kind of life, with him cheating on her. Every so often she would call me, to see what was going on...and she was so miserable...and I would lie and tell her that we were just friends. I told him I didn't want just phone sex every week for the rest of my life. That's when he started to withdraw; he would tell me he was busy trying to put his business back together, he would seem to avoid me online...and when I asked him about it, he would deny it and tell me not to take it personally. He stopped sharing with me...probably just the way he was with his wife when he started withdrawing from her.

When all this "withdrawing" started, I would ask what was wrong and he would just tell me that he was preoccupied. I would beg for him to tell me if he really wanted me out of his life just to say so...by this time I wasn't hearing from him for a couple of weeks at a time...and I was doing all the calling. He told me that all of his friends had to take the load of the friendship, he hadn't been calling anyone because of all the pressure he was under. But we were still having phone sex whenever I called...and he would initiate it. And then the last final call, he said everything was over, that the phone sex we'd had hadn't meant anything, that we were "never" going to be together. That we would just be friends, and would I still consider moving to where he lived and we could work together in the ministry.

I felt so betrayed...and so humiliated...my just reward. The last time we talked, I was telling him I would try to work at being "friends," but I couldn't have phone sex anymore. He said that if it confused me then we should quit...and then he said he had to leave because his boss was coming. We hung up...and I quickly dialed him back to ask one last question. Well, it wasn't his boss, it was his wife bringing him lunch. He was talking to his son...and all I could say was "that's your son?.." and he hung up on me. Then I called back and a woman answered, and I asked for his boss (to see if his boss was really there)...and she said no. I didn't leave a message. Then I realized it was his wife that I'd talked to...and I was so MAD that he'd lied to me...after all the times I'd struggled to make it right...or bend to whatever direction he wanted me to go...and he didn't want me to know it was his wife visiting him.

So I called back, and she answered again; she asked if I was calling about a job...might I move to the state where he lives. By this time, she thinks that her husband is having nothing to do with an affair with me...so I told her I wasn't going to lie anymore...that he had been enticing me with one hand and punching me with the other. I told her about the phone sex, the money, and finally that I had even slept with her husband. I know by doing that, that I have burned all the bridges. I should have walked away many, many months ago, that I didn't have to be malicious. And there are moments when I still get angry...I want to call the people in the church he works with and tell them what a liar he's been to them. How dirty I feel and how I hate being taken advantage of.

This anger, I know, is what I need to get rid of. Do I really want to continue to destroy this man's life? And his wife, she doesn't deserve any of this. She was so heartbroken. She could hardly speak. Some days, the anger builds so strong, I am on the verge of telling his coworkers. But I don't, hoping that it will go away.

How do you rid yourself of the anger? How can you love someone and be so mean to them? How do you let go?

Dear Reader,

This story is so painful to read because there is so much hurt here. While the letter-writer expresses "burning anger," it's probably strongly connected to the intense pain she feels about all this. And she also feels pain on behalf of the wife. This awareness can be used to defuse the power of her desire to "destroy this man's life." Clearly, any additional effort to do that would cause as much (or more) destruction to the wife than to the minister. And, as she has already indicated, the wife "doesn't deserve any of this."

Having the impulse to do something to get back at someone who has hurt you is normal—but *acting* on that impulse in the face of knowing the harm to the innocent people involved is quite a different matter. Getting revenge at their expense is in some ways even worse than the initial behavior that led to such anger. For instance, the man may have rationalized that "no one would get hurt," which is a common rationalization. He could therefore (in his own mind) proceed with his actions—which, of course, did eventually create lots of hurt for everyone.

But to deliberately set out to "destroy his life" at this point would be much more harsh—and lead her to be indulging in the very behavior (or worse) that had made her so angry in the first place. Inevitably, people who act out their revenge fantasies (thinking they will feel better after evening the score) find that they actually feel worse. They lose their self-respect, which is too high a price to pay.

Any crisis in life, however difficult, is also an opportunity to grow and learn for the future. Few people who develop in a significant way are able to do it without having faced (and overcome) some great life difficulty. So one way to let go of the anger is to use its energy as a motivator to move on in life, taking with you what you've learned from this experience.

In this instance, there is likely to be a significant learning related to "looking down the road" toward where any particular situation is leading rather than getting caught up in the moment and failing to think clearly and act responsibly. Another potential lesson is to decide to be less willing to be used by others—especially when any objective observer could clearly see the abuse going on in this relationship, for instance. We can learn to see this for ourselves while still in the middle of situations instead of only learning from hindsight.

So, all in all, there are good possibilities for using the energy of the anger to direct it toward improving life from here on out. Clearly understanding that prospect can make it much easier to let go of the anger.

* * * * * * * * * * * * *

How Do I Go On?

Dear Peggy,

I have just ended a year long affair with a man who I know that I love with all my heart. The original plan was that we were supposed to go off into the sunset together; but as you know, dreams like that (when a man is married) do not usually come true. Do you have some general suggestions for the other woman as to how they go on after the affair?

Dear Reader,

Of course, there's no formula or prescription for recovering from the loss of a dream. It might help, however, to more fully recognize just how much it was truly a dream as opposed to reality. Fortunately, the woman who wrote this letter shows some understanding of the situation by saying that "dreams like that when a man is married do not usually come true." However, it might be helpful to go further and recognize other aspects of the dream that may not have been true either.

For instance, thinking of the other man (and referring to him) as "wonderful" and a "gentleman" may make the loss seem even more painful. Realistically, her view of him probably wasn't very accurate because people do not usually present their full selves in a fantasy/affair situation that lasts a year or so. It takes years of jointly dealing with real life to know the full nature of another person. In other words, the qualities that are experienced during an affair are usually not as representative of the person as they are of the behavior inherent in playing that romantic role.

This woman sounds prepared to look realistically at her life and make decisions based on a clearer assessment of reality. And she is likely to better succeed at that by re-evaluating the true value (or lack thereof) of what she has lost by losing her dream. The dream may have been more a wake-up call than anything else—and she may be fortunate that it did not come true. Because she may have waked from the dream at some future time to find it wasn't what she had thought/expected/wanted it to be, leading to an even greater sense of loss.

* * * * * * * * * * * * *

Was "wife," now "other woman"

Dear Peggy,

I have a comment, somewhat of a question. I had been married for 14 years, very unhappily. I had been cheated on. I lived with it as best I could. Now I am the other woman. I hate it immensely, yet love this guy. I didn't think I was capable of love again. The whole thing is very painful. You need to give more advice for the "other woman" and how to end these relationships.

Dear Reader,

The above letter raises an issue many people can't quite comprehend: how could a person who had "been cheated on" turn around and become the other woman? This is a perfect example of how the behavior has more to do with the circumstances around the particular role a person is playing than who is playing the role. When a person has only been on one side of this situation, they can't imagine how this is possible, but it's much more common than people realize.

As for my giving advice for the other woman, I don't have specific advice to offer, only perspective. But it's true that the dilemmas and difficulties of the third party are often overlooked or diminished when compared with the dilemmas and difficulties of the spouse who is being deceived. It's clear that affairs have a way of eventually hurting everyone involved. Sometimes it takes longer than others, but that is the way it usually turns out.

Naturally, it's hard to think clearly about the long-term impact of an affair when caught up in feeling you're "in love"—but eventually the bubble bursts. So the sooner someone can start focusing on "how to end the relationship," the better. The longer it lasts, the more the chance for problems and complications that will make it even more painful when it ends. While any feelings of guilt or

223

of it being wrong may not be strong enough to fight the positive feelings of an affair, it might help to focus more on the fact that being the other woman is not a *smart* position to be in. The short-term pleasure is seldom worth the long-term pain.

* * * * * * * * * * * * *

Wants to Leave

Dear Peggy,

I have been in a relationship as the other woman for 7 years; I am 30 he is 37. The affair started when I became friends with his wife; (everyone in our circle of friends consider us to be "best friends"). So how can I be sleeping with my best friend's husband? Anyway, he does want to leave her, but I told him that if he does that, I will not have any more to do with him. How will I ever be able to trust him? At least while he stays married and with her, I know where he is every night. Yes, there are a lot of nights when I wish he could be with me, but I can't understand why I do not want him all the time if he is willing to give me that... Have you any answers for this?

Dear Reader,

This kind of "arms-length" relationship (without investment in a future together) is not uncommon among women today. Actually, this is not a new phenomenon. More than a decade ago, Laurel Richardson wrote a book called "The New Other Woman: Contemporary Single Women in Affairs with Married Men." She points to some of the factors that may be involved: the shortage of "good" men, a desire for independence in order to more easily pursue careers, easier and less-demanding, etc.

However, this best-of-both-worlds scenario grows stale over time and usually leaves women wanting *more*; so in many ways it's actually "settling for less." On the hopeful side, a woman who sees herself as being able to function independently and be responsible for her own security, is also capable of moving away from this role and forming an equal (non-deceitful) relationship with an unmarried man. So the very qualities that may lead a woman to currently prefer a situation as described above may also be the qualities that can allow her to have a more successful egalitarian relationship if/when she is ready to form a lasting bond.

* * * * * * * * * * * * *

The "love of my life"

Dear Peggy,

What do I do if the love of my life is married?? He says he's getting out; do I wait??

Dear Reader,

I'm always concerned when someone feels an unattainable person is the "love of their life." This dramatic view of the relationship gives it an unrealistic strength and specialness—and makes the pain all the greater at not attaining it.

The desperate feelings that can be evoked by this attitude make it all but impossible to think clearly about the prospects. Again, here are a few facts:

—Fewer than 10 percent of people who get divorced actually marry their lover.

—About 60 percent of all second marriages end in divorce.

—Over 75 percent of marriages that begin from an affair end in divorce.

So, in most cases, it's unreasonable to *wait* because he's unlikely to "get out." And even if he does get out, chances are it won't lead to marriage. And if it does lead to marriage, chances are great that the marriage will end in divorce. Since these are terrible odds, no sensible person would want to pursue this path. So, as the old saying goes, "be careful what you wish for; you might get it." And in a situation like this, getting what you want could be disastrous in the long term.

* * * * * * * * * * * * *

The View from Both Sides
(Here are 2 letters before my response.)

Dear Peggy, (letter #1, hoping things will eventually work out)

I met my soul-mate. The problem, of course, is that he is married. When I met him he had been separated for 4 years and avoiding the issue of ever doing anything about his marriage. Then we met! It was storybook from the beginning. One of those "and their eyes met across a crowded room" things. He was always honest with me about his life. He said that he always thought that he would meet the perfect person and then the questions would be answered. But when he met the perfect person (me), it wasn't that easy. I encouraged him to find out for himself what he wanted. I could not be the one to decide for him concerning his life. I encouraged him to go back to her. To discover if it is really over. He has two small children. I told him that if he could be happy with his wife, forgive her of her unfaithfulness, and love her again—then that is what is best.

We agreed to be just friends. We remained friends for 3 months. I never had sex with him, and we communicated regularly. I helped him learn to forgive his wife and to understand how she felt. I encouraged him and rebuilt his self-esteem. I poured a lot into helping him realize that he was not responsible for her choices, but that he was responsible for how he handled the situation. I let him know that it was not good for his daughters that they not have the benefit of a happy household...that they deserved to see their parents happy, not just cohabiting together. Well, I did such a good job that he is back with her. He says that he is happy and really loves her.

I wonder though. I know him almost better then he knows himself. He travels a lot in his business, so he is not home a lot. When he is home, he does things that don't include his wife, but his friends or his girls. When he is home, she isn't. They never do anything together. It seems to me that if you love someone then you want to be with them. He even asked me if, while he was out flying his plane, he could come and visit me. He is an engineer. If you know enough about

225

the personality type...they have a high achievement level. He once told me that he had never failed at anything that he had put his mind to. I think that maybe he has talked himself into this because he doesn't want to feel that he has failed at his marriage. I think that this is the honeymoon syndrome coming into effect again. He is not home enough to have to deal with a day-to-day relationship. So while he is home he can be the happy husband. Their sex life sucks. She is very rigid and timid in bed and uses it as a tool to reward him. He says that she jumps at every sound and he feels that she is just doing her duty. He says that he really has to work at helping her achieve orgasm and intercourse has to be fast so that she doesn't lose interest before he achieves orgasm.

He told me that he has never met anyone like me and doesn't feel that he will ever attain the level of devotion and admiration in his marriage that we have achieved together. But that he has this sense of duty to his daughters. That he couldn't live if his wife moved back to her home state with his daughters. When he told me that he had decided to stay with her, he finally told me that he loved me. That he knew he had always loved me, and that there would always be a place in his heart for me, but that he had to stay with her as long as he thought that he could make it work. I have no reason to doubt his word because he has never lied to me, and at that moment in time he did not have to say that. He had refrained from telling me that throughout everything else.

He still gives me his itinerary...lets me know all that is happening in his life...all the little things...the good and the bad. He calls himself one of my "buds." He knows how I feel about him. My decision is that I am going to play wait and see. I am not going to put my life on hold. If something else better comes by, then I will snatch it up. It will be hard to top this. I am going to be his "bud"...develop the friendship and see what happens in his marriage. One can only pretend so long. Eventually if his heart is not truly in his marriage, then he will become unhappy and unfulfilled again.

Dear Peggy, (letter #2), the likely reality even if things seem to have worked out)

I have been dating a married man for four years. We have been living together on and off for the last three years. His divorce will be final this month. He has gone back and forth from her to me for most of this time, trying to deal with his guilt on both ends. He has been with me exclusively for the past year, but last fall, when his wife filed for divorce, he spent four months living in my apartment (not contributing to expenses) while writing these long letters to her in his journal about how he couldn't live without her and the kids, listing the things about her that he loved, begging her to let him come back. I was devastated, but I felt that he was bordering on suicidal behavior, and I was his only friend, so I couldn't throw him out. His family lives two hours away, so I couldn't tell them to take care of him.

This was an excruciating period for me. He would tell me how he wanted to get over her and spend his life with me, but I would find evidence that he was still begging her for a chance. He would send notes back with the children in their coat pockets, things like that. Now he has turned things around, taking charge of his life, and pushing the divorce through, letting me know where he is at all times, but I still feel no trust. I'm afraid to be happy even for a minute because I might be tricked again. I have panic attacks at work where I think about things that happened years ago.

Paradoxically, he is my best friend. There is no one I would rather spend time with. But I'm constantly terrified that he is thinking about her. I am obsessed with her, trying to find things about her to put down, reasons to despise her. At the same time I find myself wanting to be like her sometimes. He says we can't go on unless I put the past behind us. He is tired of talking about things that happened three years ago. The thought of counseling is exhausting to me. How can I explain everything that has happened, everything I have felt? How do I move forward?

Dear Reader,

In both these letters—even when there's a desire and/or intention to get on with life, there's a great deal of difficulty in doing so. In the first letter, saying, "I am not going to put my life on hold..." is very hard to do when the other person is actively doing things that prevent that from happening—like giving his itinerary and sharing all that is happening in his life. In the second letter, there's a feeling of being trapped in the past (without having completely worked through the fallout from all that happened), thus life still being somewhat on hold.

Another similarity is that in the first letter, he wants to still be "buds"—while the second letter expresses the strong feeling of being best friends. (It sounds, however, as if the friendship in both instances is very one-sided.)

The first letter's final question is: "Am I doing the right thing?" But a better question might be, "Am I doing the *smart* thing?" The second letter provides some insight into the legacy of so much indecision, uncertainty and waffling. Also, any situation (whether like the one described in the first letter or the second one) is basically unequal and unfair—thus probably not a good position in which to be. Both these two women (and the countless others in their position) need/deserve to focus less on their partners and more on taking care of *themselves* and their own needs/joys/satisfactions in life. (This isn't being *selfish*; it's just taking charge of your own life instead of only reacting to the thoughts/actions of someone else.)

* * * * * * * * * * *

Lady-in-waiting

Dear Peggy,

I have been seeing a married man for 4 years now. He has a 4-year-old daughter and at first he would say, if it weren't for my daughter, I would not be married any more. Obviously as our relationship progressed, I want more. We have spoken about him getting a divorce, and to make a long story short, I gave him a deadline—because I have become very bitter, angry, jealous, etc., that I can't have more from this relationship. So of course he didn't think about my deadline until it was almost that time. And now he has told me he can't meet my deadline because of the Holidays. (I know he can't tell his wife he wants a divorce over Christmas—but he could give me an answer)

Anyway, I am at a complete loss—and a complete mess. I am so bitter all the time, it is ruining our relationship. I love this man so much. Please help. I need all the advice I can get. He is my best (and only) friend and I am so afraid of losing him, yet I don't want to be one of those women who never got married— and had an affair for 20 years.

Dear Reader,

This is such a sad, static situation—and so unbelievably common. At least this letter shows an awareness of what can happen if a situation like this is allowed to go on indefinitely. And awareness can be the first step toward taking action. In the meantime, this letter clearly shows the toll it takes when waiting/hoping for a married lover to decide to divorce. (Unfortunately, the excuses can go on forever.)

One of the first steps toward dealing with this kind of limbo situation is *not* relying on the lover as the *best* or *only* friend. (By the way, it's questionable as to how good a friend they really are—since a real friend doesn't put others through this kind of torment.)

Since the sense of helpless and hopelessness blocks out everything else in life, it's important to step back in order to see beyond this one aspect of life. Getting some distance from the situation and becoming involved with other people and other activities may allow for clearer thinking about the whole situation than is possible when totally focused on this one person.

Nothing is really lost by virtue of moving away unless/until a final decision is made—because in the final analysis, actions speak more than words. A person *saying* they want a divorce (and then offering reason/excuse after reason/excuse as to why now is not a good time) doesn't really mean much. It's what they *do* that counts. Not only is it not possible to *force* someone to take action, it's also not smart to try to force something like this anyway; it will only create resentment in the future (a little like winning the battle and losing the war.) While it's impossible to control another person's actions, it *is* possible to control our own.

So waiting for others to do something is useless at best and self-defeating at worst. No matter how much it hurts in the short-run, the long-term hurt may be even greater. So the awareness of the consequences of continuing to wait and hope (as expressed in the above letter) needs to be turned into action. "Knowing what to do" and "doing it" are not the same thing—but it's a first step in the right direction.

* * * * * * * * * * * * *

Waiting for Her to Leave

Dear Peggy,

I am a recently divorced 39-year-old male. Several months ago I began seeing a woman I have known for the past decade. She is married with three children and currently baby-sits my two children. We had talked to each other at our children's sporting events and I considered her my friend. One night she asked me to go out for a drink, and she told me she has had feelings for me for a long time. I never thought about her in that way because I thought she was happily married. We started seeing each other and quickly fell in love. After several months of sneaking around we both agreed that this was not right and stopped seeing each other intimately.

We still see and talk to each other every day and she wants to remain "best friends." For the time being she is staying in the marriage for the children. She told me it may take a year or two before she gets a job and leaves her husband. I truly love her and want to wait but have a tough time being only friends with her. Should I tell her that I can't be "just friends" and stop talking to her, hoping that someday we will be together? Or should I try to stay friends and hope that everything will fall into place?

Dear Reader,

Most of us have heard the saying, "Don't play with fire—because you might get burned." Well, a situation like the one described above (talking to each other every day and remaining best friends) is definitely playing with fire. And the person *most* likely to get burned is the one in the position of the letter-writer.

All the reasons (excuses) as to why they can't be together until later (for the sake of the children, etc.) are so common as to be somewhat meaningless. Whenever an unattached person is waiting/hoping for a potential future with someone who is married, there's little likelihood that they'll actually have a future together.

It's understandably flattering when someone declares their feelings for you. But getting caught up in the emotional reaction to this can cloud the ability to think clearly. And when the other person is thinking (or behaving) in an unclear, ambiguous way (like declaring love, then staying married), it's all the more important that there be some clear thinking on the part of someone in the position described above.

Unfortunately, having unrealistic hopes (like "hoping that someday we will be together" or "hoping that everything will fall into place") are not examples of clear thinking. It's much more like "wishful thinking." However, writing a letter like the one above and seeking input about the situation is a very a positive sign. It's the first step toward breaking out of the fantasy-thinking and gaining better perspective, possibly leading to better actions.

* * * * * * * * * * * * *

Man in turmoil over affair

Dear Peggy:

I recently made the decision to have another affair, and hoped that my second experience would be an improvement over the first. So, instead of choosing a man who had had numerous affairs in his life, I chose someone who never had one before. This experience turned out to be just as ungratifying as the first. It's funny how we always say there is something missing in our marriages causing us to have an affair, when there could be much more missing in an affair!

This man was tremendously guilty immediately afterwards. He did not speak to me or call me for a week. He has three children under the age of 10, and had told me that he had thought about having an affair for over a year, but had not found the right woman until I came along. He was tremendously attracted to me, and still is. He recently talked to me several times, saying he was dealing with his guilt and that he found it difficult since he never knew how he was going to react. But now that some time has passed, he said he wants to see me again to talk about what happened. I don't see the point in another meeting, and I don't want to cause this man more pain than he is already in. I suggested that there was no need to turn a one-night stand into an affair. We could just leave it at that. But he said he does not want to think of it in those terms. I think he is just trying to make sense out of this, and wants to give it some meaning. Or perhaps he is just stunned by what he was ultimately capable of doing. What do you think? Should I avoid meeting with him again at this time?

Dear Reader,

I think the above letter shows amazingly good insight into what might be in the head of the man who is in turmoil over his affair with her. Based on her understandings, it appears that she already recognizes that even though he *wants* to see her again, that is unlikely to actually help—and may even make things worse.

She also shows a degree of insight into her own situation by virtue of recognizing that "there could be much more missing in an affair!" This is a good indication of the confusion often felt by people involved in affairs. While there's that kind of understanding, there's also the interesting way of phrasing her experience with this second affair by saying she "recently made the *decision* to have another affair." This is not what people usually say. Having an affair is often not a conscious decision—because if affairs depended on consciously *choosing*, there would be far fewer affairs. Most people who wind up in affairs say just the opposite; they say, "I never intended to have an affair" or "It just happened."

The best thing about an experience like the one described above is that it seems to lead to reflecting on what happened instead of blindly going from one affair to the next without learning anything in the process. While in this particular instance, it seems that the man was the one who got hurt; in general, *everyone* usually winds up being negatively affected by affairs.

15: Dealing with a Friend's Affair

Doing The Right Thing

Dear Peggy,

I desperately need some help in "doing the right thing." I know for a fact that my friend's husband is having an affair. I'm not the only one who has seen him slipping around with this other woman when my friend is at work. I don't think she suspects. If she does, she hasn't let on to me. But I don't know whether I should tell her. What if I tell her and she doesn't believe me? Or what if I don't tell her, and then she blames me if she finds out some other way? It's killing me to stand by without doing anything. But I just don't know what to do.

Dear Reader,

Obviously, this is a tough decision that needs to be made as responsibly as possible for the sake of everyone concerned.

Here are some general guidelines for determining whether/when to tell:

When friends have a prior agreement that they want to be told if either of them ever learns about the other's partner having an affair, then it's responsible to honor that agreement.

When friends *don't* have such an understanding with each other, then it's important to consider whether someone *wants* to know. (I know from my own experience that sometimes a person doesn't want to be forced to face something like this if they're not ready to deal with it.)

Bottom Line: "Don't lie if asked, but don't volunteer if *not* asked." If they ask about their partner's affair, they're showing a readiness (or at least a willingness) to face it. If they *don't* ask, it's usually better to wait for some indication that they want to know and are prepared to handle it.

In the meantime, its reasonable to talk to the person having the affair to let them know that you know. This does not mean threatening or demanding, but simply telling them that you're aware of what's going on and that you won't lie to cover for them. This gives them the opportunity to tell their partner—or at least to end the affair.

*   *   *   *   *   *   *   *   *   *   *   *   *

Friends didn't tell me

Dear Peggy,

I feel like such a fool. I've suspected his many affairs for years... My friends all knew. They saw my pain (as did he) they offered everything but the answers I needed to know. My husband bragged about having sex with one of my friends, in our bed, right under my nose. No one said anything. They felt sorry for me. My husband said that I was insane and needed to be committed. My friends just watched my soul die...over and over again. No one said anything. Now I'm alone. My husband still denies everything.

My friends look at me with sad eyes. I feel so stupid. I have no one to turn to. I don't trust anyone anymore. If they would have just told me. I knew what was going on. There were so many women he was screwing around with that it really did sound like I was crazy. Yet it was true, they all new, and they let me suffer for four years. I was desperate for answers. Proof that I wasn't insane. It came too late. How could my dearest friends do that to me? How could they watch me fall apart over and over? How could he?? He loves me, right? Now I'm all alone. He's still here, they're still here, but I'm all alone. What do I do now? Who do I trust?

Dear Reader,

This is a perfect description of the crazy-making process of believing/knowing your partner is having an affair—but not having confirmation, not knowing for *sure*. (Trying to make you feel like you're crazy is a typical defensive tactic by the person having an affair.)

Now for some general observations about the two main points of this letter.

First, "My husband still denies everything." This is absolutely common. As I've mentioned before, there's a sort of unwritten rule among people having affairs to deny, deny, deny.

Second, "No one said anything." Friends are in a very difficult position in this situation. No matter what they do, it's likely to be wrong—which is why they often do nothing. In situations like the above, the responsibility lies with the person who is suspicious to specifically *ask* the friends (in a very direct way) if they know about a partner's affair. It is *not* responsible for a friend to arbitrarily decide to *offer* this information without being asked.

The writer of the above letter doesn't clearly indicate whether or not she ever asked—only that the friends didn't *offer* the information. If she asked and they lied, then her feelings toward the friends are warranted. However, if she didn't ask, then the friends' actions are quite reasonable. In any case, everyone loses in these kinds of secretive, deceptive situations. And the responsibility for the pain created by the secrecy lies with the person who had an affair rather than with the friends who are caught in the middle.

* * * * * * * * * * * *

Should I snitch?
(Here are 2 letters before my response.)

Dear Peggy, (letter #1)

I believe my minister is having an affair. I'm not sure yet, but the whole church has noticed except his wife. I feel really bad with her not knowing, but I don't know if I should tell her or have her figure out what's going on for herself????

Dealing with a Friend's Affair

Dear Peggy, (letter #2)

I rent out a basement apartment. My landlady's 45-year-old son (who is married) is allowed to come over (usually when no one is home) by my landlady and use the upstairs bedroom to have sex with his newfound honey. He will have an attitude if I'm home during the day and hint that he'd like to be alone with his girlfriend. I feel offended because I pay rent and I think he should get a motel room if he wants to be a dog. My landlady only allows it because she's pressured.... Should I snitch to his wife (with or without him knowing) or not?

Dear Reader,

As illustrated above, there are many reasons a person might wonder about whether to tell the spouse of a person who is having an affair. Sometimes it's for the benefit of the spouse (as with the minister's wife) and sometimes it's for the benefit of the person who is considering telling. No matter what the reasons, the most important (and only *responsible* reason) is to tell because there's an indication that the person whose spouse is having an affair actually *wants* to know. If they are in denial or unprepared to face the truth, they should not be forced to do so—either out of someone's genuine desire to be helpful or out of someone's personal need to see the situation end.

This is a clear indication of the fallout for *many* people when someone is having a secret affair. Both the personal distress and the inconvenience (as illustrated by the two letters above) are indicative of the degree to which supposedly personal behavior has an impact far beyond the individuals involved.

16: Dealing with a Parent's Affair

My mom's having an affair!

Dear Peggy,

I recently got solid proof that my mom has been having an affair, although I have suspected it for almost a year. I am sure my father has no idea this is going on. I would like my mom to stop and see how much it hurts me and will hurt my dad. I know my dad loves my mother to pieces. What should I do? Should I confront her? Or maybe the man she's sleeping with?

Dear Reader,

This letter appears to be from a young person, perhaps a teenager. Often, when people are engaged in affairs, there's some concern about the impact on the kids, but it's often kept in the background (usually with the belief that they'll never find out and therefore never be hurt by it). But typically, children are far more aware than their parents think. In fact, children (of all ages) are usually quite perceptive of their surroundings and are not as likely as adults to try to rationalize away whatever they notice.

When a young person (such as the writer of this letter) gets "solid proof" of an affair, it puts them in an unbelievably difficult situation. The general guidelines for an adult friend who finds out about an affair may not be as appropriate in this situation—because there's so much more at stake. But, in general, it's better not to talk directly to the third party. It's better to talk to the person (in this case, the mom) who is having the affair, letting them know that you know. Especially when dealing with a parent, this is not to be done in a *threatening* way, but just pointing out the difficult position you're in and explaining that while you wouldn't voluntarily tell the other parent about the affair, you also couldn't lie if they asked you about it.

There are two primary reasons for talking to the parent having the affair instead of the other parent. First, the parent who doesn't know about the affair may already know (or at least suspect), but not be ready to deal with it. Second, this kind of approach may lead the parent who is having an affair to tell their partner themselves—or at least stop to the affair.

One final consideration when a young person is in the position of deciding who to talk to, it may be helpful to talk to one other safe, trusted adult—(probably not a family member) before talking to the parent who is having the affair. This is just to know that there's someone else who knows what you're going to do and is there for support. In the final analysis, each person (whether adult or child) needs to decide for themselves exactly how to proceed with something this sensitive. But this situation illustrates the need for more focus on the special predicament of the children of those who engage in affairs.

* * * * * * * * * * * * *

Can't "get over" our father's affair

Dear Peggy,

About a year ago my siblings and I discovered that my father was having an affair. We are in our 20's and 30's, my parents are in their 50's. After a horrible 3 months of lawyer visits with my mother, she decided she could work things out with my father and a therapist. They seem to have things back on track. The only problem is, we do not. My brothers and sisters still are enraged with my father about this never-discussed issue. Some of my family feel we will never get over this, if my mother does or not. I have seen elements of distrust of relationships in my siblings and myself. Is this a natural occurrence? Will we ever "get over" this?

Dear Reader,

I want to take this opportunity to appeal to everyone (whether dealing with parents, other family members or friends) to respect that it's *their* life and *their* decision—and no matter how it may affect anyone else, it has nowhere near the impact on others that it has on the individuals themselves. So if the couple themselves (who are personally struggling with it) can get over it, anyone who loves them can do so as well.

It will help to remember that "getting over it" does not imply *approving* of any actions or decisions. It simply means trying to *understand* why someone may choose to stay.

Here are some common reasons a person may choose to stay and work to get over it:

— They may still love their spouse. Yes, despite the hurt and anger, love can still survive. This was an important point for me personally.

— They may value their shared history. My husband and I had grown up together, been childhood sweethearts, and been married eighteen years when I learned of his affairs.

— They may recognize that affairs are not just a reflection of a specific marriage but are also a reflection on broader forces in their environment that undermine monogamy. Having affairs has more to do with other factors than with who is a good or bad person.

— They may consider the prospects for the future of the marriage if they stay. If I had left when my husband told me about his affairs 25 years ago, I would have missed all those years of having an honest, monogamous marriage—one that has now lasted 44 years.

— They may look realistically at their spouse's other qualities and find that on balance they prefers their spouse to other potential partners. Although being alone is a perfectly legitimate choice, many people prefer to have a mate.

While these are a few of the reasons people choose to stay with spouses who have affairs (and manage to get over it), I want to be very clear that I'm *not* saying anyone *should* stay. What I *am* saying is that we should respect and support each person's individual choices about significant issues in their lives— even when we disagree or fail to understand.

Finally, as for the question as to whether it's a "natural occurrence to find elements of distrust of relationships in my siblings and myself"—people can take from an experience like this whatever they choose to focus on. Instead of focusing on the potential damage, a more positive possibility is that it can allow a recognition of the reality of such risks in marriage, leading people to take the steps necessary to establish deep trusting relationships built on a commitment to honesty. There is no specific cause and effect as to the impact this can have. As with any life crisis, each person can use this experience as a learning experience to improve their own lives.

* * * * * * * * * * * * *

Father with 25 year mistress/dual life

Dear Peggy,

My father has Alzheimer's. Recently he lost his drivers license, so we hired a caretaker to drive him around. Through this caretaker we discovered that my father has been sharing an apartment with a mistress for 25 years. That would make me 5 years old when they met. We have wondered for years exactly what he does during the day, but for all those years he's been coming home between 6:30 and 7 p.m. for dinner. He has provided well for our family financially, but has always been secretive and aloof. As a single adult female (who was unaware of this until quite recently), what do you think the implications are for my patterning and imprinting with regards to my own potential relationships?

Dear Reader,

There are several key points to this letter that can provide learning for all of us. First, we often think we *know* our family in a way that frequently turns out to be an illusion. Especially in times of illness or death, facts often come to light that would otherwise never have been known. And those facts frequently create two feelings at the same time. The first reaction is usually "how could I not have known about something like this?" And the second is an awareness that somehow this "makes sense" of something that had been unclear for many years.

As for the question about whether there are "implications regarding the potential relationships" for the daughter of a man like the one described above, there's no reason that should be the case. To clarify, the patterning to be concerned about would be one of being secretive and aloof, not of the specific behavior. While some people do maintain secret relationships for years (as described above), the relevance for the woman who wrote this letter would be in the secretive nature of the parent's life rather than the way in which the secretiveness was acted out. Also, any tendencies toward secretiveness are not indelibly imprinted; they are subject to deliberately changing that pattern, based on making a conscious decision about how to relate to others. In fact, this kind of experience could provide a timely wake-up call to be deliberate about living life in a more open and honest way.

* * * * * * * * * * * *

My Dad's Secrets

Dear Peggy,

I'm a teenager. I recently found a window on AOL that lists all the sites explored in the last month. I was stunned to find pages of x-rated sites (including teen and gay sites, accessed by my dad. (I have solid proof that he spends about half an hour every day looking at pornography on the Internet and having cyber sex with online prostitutes.)

I can't look my dad in the face, and I feel dirty around him. I can't stand for him to touch me, even when he just puts his hand on my shoulder and asks how I'm doing. He doesn't know why I'm so touchy and gets hurt. I feel like I'm dying inside.

Should I tell my mom? Or should I just pretend I don't know? If I tell her, our formerly cozy family will be destroyed—if it doesn't kill her. But there's a part of me that feels like she has a right to know. If I don't say anything, I'll be covering for him, and I don't want to do THAT. But I don't want her to be hurt.

I don't think I can live here with him, knowing what he does, and keeping it from my mom. But if I move out, she'll know something's wrong. Oh, I'm so confused! I've cried myself to sleep every night since I found out. The secret is killing me, and I don't know what to do. If I don't settle this soon, I think I'm going to collapse. Please help me.

Dear Reader,

It's so sad that people don't stop to think about all the people affected by their actions, especially when it creates this kind of stressful situation for their children. Since it's especially difficult to handle this *alone* (with its serious ramifications for the mom, the dad, and the teenager), it's extremely important to find some personal support in dealing with this kind of issue. There are many factors to be considered.

While there's no really good alternative, it's important to realize that there's risk both in whatever *is* done and in whatever is *not* done. Too often, we only see the risk in taking action, failing to see that there are also risks involved in *not* taking action. Then turning to the question of what action might be appropriate: in general, it's better to tell the father exactly what you know—just so he knows you know. It's usually better not to tell the mother unless or until you think she suspects or wants to know. However, not *volunteering* the information to mom is different from *covering* for dad.

So the first step *may* be first telling someone else who is totally trusted (for advance support in this effort), then telling dad everything expressed in this letter—in order to put the responsibility for how to handle this squarely on dad's shoulders (where it belongs), instead of silently struggling alone.

* * * * * * * * * * * * *

Angry at my father

Dear Peggy,

My parents almost got a divorce because my daddy had an affair. I still feel so much anger inside, and I'm not yet able to overcome this anger. How do I deal with this?

Dear Reader,

It's obvious that this person is having great difficulty dealing with this situation. While the anger is not surprising, it might help to get clear about whether the anger is primarily for the mother's sake (because of the pain to her) or whether it's mostly personal.

Obviously, there's personal disappointment when a parent turns out not to be the person we thought/hoped they were. But holding onto the anger on behalf of the mother is another matter. If she has decided to stay and try to work things out, a loving child needs to respect that decision and do everything possible to support her in that process. So it may help in dealing with the anger if there's an appreciation of the fact that a child's anger may also be making it more difficult for the mother (who already has enough to deal with).

So if the mother (who is personally struggling with the situation) can deal with her hurt and anger, anyone who loves her can surely do as much. It won't be easy, but if there's a genuine desire to get over it (and a thoughtful effort to do so), it can be done.

* * * * * * * * * * * * *

My Parents

Dear Peggy,

I have a really big problem. See, my dad did have a brief relationship, although I don't quite know how serious it was. But my mother has always been a faithful wife and this week is their 21st anniversary. Mom is the kind of person who is strong and likes to get back at people. Dad is calm and sensitive. About an hour ago, my brother who is 16 and I (13) talked with my dad while my mom was out. My dad understands that he did something very wrong. Very, very, very, wrong. But he can't turn back the hands of time and undo it. He has apologized, but my mom is merciless.

While talking to me, she said that she was sorry for him, but there was nothing that she could do to forgive him. Yesterday, all she had was a Slim Fast with vodka and orange juice with vodka. My mom hasn't had a drink other than an occasional strawberry daiquiri every July on vacation. She ate today, but is still drinking to calm herself down.

I've never seen my dad cry before. I've seen my mom cry, but never my dad. He did tonight. I can't stand to see this happen to my family. My mom went to a local club tonight and said that she would be home by 3 a.m. She doesn't want

241

to meet a guy, but she wants to drink and watch people dance. I know I'm going into details, but I can't help it. My brother has been really great to me, and is being unbelievably grown-up about this. But, I'm scared.

What can my dad do? How can he at least make amends? I know my parents won't split up. They always say that my brother and I are the most important things to them in the world. But I want things to go back to the way they were. Even if my mom can't forgive him, I know my dad will never do it again. I just want everything to be normal.

Please help me. I can't eat and I can't sleep. I need your help and so does the rest of my family.

Dear Reader,

Once an affair is discovered (which is far more often than people expect), it creates a crisis (both emotional and practical) for everyone who is touched by the situation—including the children. Teenagers can have an especially difficult time in that they often assume a far more mature/adult posture than would otherwise be warranted at their age. Of course, some teens primarily react with their own outrage at the situation, but many are like the brother and sister described in the above letter who try to assume responsibility for figuring out how to solve this dilemma.

However, no matter how much the children of parents involved in this situation might want to make things right, it's completely up to the parents to do the work that is called for. In the meantime, the child is left hoping for the best by making such statement as those above, including:

— "I know my parents won't split up."

Unfortunately, there's no way to absolutely know this, but it's helpful to believe it's possible.

— "I want things to go back to the way they were."

This is an understandable desire, but actually it wouldn't be good for things to simply "go back to the way they were"—because whatever situation existed before led to the current crisis.

— "I know my dad will never do it again."

This, too, is an understandable belief, but there is no guarantee that one or the other of the parents won't ever do anything like this again, despite the current pain and guilt.

— "I just want everything to be normal."

Again, this is perfectly understandable, but unrealistic. This will take a very long time to deal with, even if everyone makes their best effort. And by the time things become somewhat normal again, these two young people are likely to be grown and moving out on their own.

The bottom line is that there's not much the kids can do except try to take care of *themselves* and hope that the parents will do the necessary work to recover from this crisis.

17: Affairs at Work

I can't stop fantasizing about my boss

Dear Peggy,
I have worked with the same man for 6 years and I am finding myself thinking about him all the time. I dream and day-dream about being with him. I love my husband and would never hurt him, but he is the only sexual partner I have ever had. Why am I so infatuated?

Dear Reader,

This is a much more common situation than many people realize. Being infatuated with a boss usually relates to their powerful position in our lives. Women often have a great deal of admiration for a boss's ability and success and come to value him not only as a boss, but also as a friend and mentor. In addition, the boss often has a lot of control over a woman's future in terms of her economic well-being and her opportunities for advancement. This is not to say that women are trying to "sleep their way to the top." Most ambitious women today recognize that this is clearly not a good path to success. But the boss may play such an important part in a woman's life that she has difficulty separating their professional relationship from her personal feelings.

This situation is one that I understand firsthand. Many years ago when I was 25 years old, working for a 50-year-old boss, I became so impressed with his power, sophistication, success, etc., that I couldn't clearly see the person behind the position. This was all the more appealing by virtue of the fact that he made *me* feel better about myself. (After all, here was this highly successful person who thought I was so *special*—smart, attractive, competent...) I finally came to my senses before it was too late, but I saw how this kind of attention can lead to seeing the boss through rose-colored glasses.

Fortunately, this woman is recognizing that she has a problem. Many people who never intend to have an affair fail to take steps necessary to prevent it from happening. They let their private fantasies blind them to the reality of the consequences of their thinking. The very process of keeping the feelings secret tends to make them stronger. It allows for focusing *only* on the positive aspects of being with the boss and avoids focusing on the potential consequences. So talking about it (in whatever way can bring it into reality without creating additional problems) is probably a good way to cut through the fantasy. This talking can be with a professional or a friend or family member who can be totally trusted. There's something about discussing your thinking out loud (and seeing it through the eyes of someone else) that allows you to view it more realistically.

243

If what this reader says is true: "I love my husband and would never hurt him," the current path is almost guaranteed to do just that. So it's foolish to pretend there's some way to continue the current situation without that risk.

* * * * * * * * * * * *

Affair with my boss
(Here are two letters before my response.)

Dear Peggy, (letter #1, from a woman who has not yet had an affair)
I'm attracted to my boss. I think he knows it and I'm afraid something might come out of this. We haven't said anything to each other yet...but I can tell that he likes me, as I'm sure he feels it too. I love my husband very much. We've been married for 10 years now and have 2 children. My boss is married too and has a child. I'm afraid that if I have an opportunity I might take it. Please help and tell me how not to go through with it... Do you believe in trying it and letting go at the same time?

Dear Peggy, (letter #2, from a woman already involved with her boss)
I'm 41 years old and just went back to work last year, after 15 years of a very rocky marriage. I have started having an affair with my 61-year-old married boss. I love him very much and he loves me. My husband caught us a few months ago and I told him that it has been over since then. But it hasn't. We are just more careful. My marriage is in terrible shape (worse now then before the affair obviously).

I can't seem to stop seeing this man no matter how hard I try. I am totally consumed with thoughts of him and he is with me. I don't know what my attraction to this man is, but I love him and I don't know what to do. My husband told me if I leave him, he will KILL this man, and if he finds out I am still seeing him he told me he will kill him. I really believe he will do it; I shouldn't have to be a prisoner to his threats, but I'm afraid of what he will do to this man. I also don't want to give him up. Please advise me.

Dear Reader,
In understanding the appeal of a boss (or some other man met at work), it's important to realize that while they may appear to have special qualities (like being more thoughtful or communicative than husbands), it's not that they are particularly special in their ability to relate to women in a satisfying way; it's the circumstances that make the difference. For instance, a man who seems so thoughtful and communicative at work may behave very differently at home. His wife sees a different side of him and may complain about him in much the same way as the woman he's having an affair with complains about her own husband.

At work, people present a side of themselves that is not representative of the whole person. They're usually committed to looking their best and being on their best behavior. Also, when people work together on projects involving large budgets or high stakes, the work environment becomes filled with a sense of vitality and importance, making the office setting a very sexy place. Given this potent atmosphere, it's no wonder that the office has become one of the most popular sources of contact for extramarital affairs.

Even though there are tremendous risks involved in having an affair with a boss, women often lose sight of the risks. So here are some "blinding glimpses of the obvious" about this kind of situation. Most affairs (whether in the office or not) eventually become some kind of problem, either because it becomes known to others or because it ends. When this happens, women in the workforce are generally the ones who are penalized—and this is especially true when the man is her boss. When the affair with her boss ends, her job is also likely to end.

However, the risk at work pales in comparison to the risk at home. Much more critical than the risk of losing the job is the risk of losing the marriage. And, as illustrated by the second letter, there's the even greater risk of physical danger—which is very real and can not be ignored without risking dire consequences. Affairs are an emotional issue both for the person engaging in an affair as well as for the spouse who discovers an affair—and the irrational actions involved in engaging in an affair may very well lead to irrational actions by the spouse who discovers it. So the time to focus on more rational behavior is in the beginning, before anything takes place.

* * * * * * * * * * * *

My Boss and I

Dear Peggy,

I am a 28-year-old female who is currently in a relationship with a 34-year-old man and have been for 4 years now. I also have a boss that is 39 and married for 12 years now with 2 children. My boss has made it clear to me that he wants a relationship with me and I am rather interested in this man. He told me that he is leaving his wife and it has been long coming for 2 years now, and he plans to do it. (I have nothing whatsoever to do with his departure from his wife.) I respect this man and believe in him; I have worked for him for 6 years now and it was always strictly business. We just got caught up with getting to know each other online here for about a month now...

My problem is my current boyfriend; I do love this man very much and we have been through a lot together in the last 4 years. I do not live with him. I have finally convinced him to trust me, though I can tell it isn't complete yet. I get along with him very good at times, but there are others that we just fight it seems like forever. When we get along, we get along awesome; when we fight the walls come down (so to speak).

I have talked to my boss about a future with him; I also have discussed a future with my boyfriend in great lengths throughout the years. I just don't know what to do, I don't want anyone to get hurt. And if I do have to let one of them go (which I know I do), I just don't know how to find the words. I think with my boss, the attraction has a lot to do with the power he holds—and the boyfriend is time put into the relationship and lots of caring. These men are a lot alike in many ways; they are also a lot like me. My boyfriend and I share the same birthday, and my boss and I share the same thoughts, meaning we know what the other is thinking a lot... I just don't know what to do.

Dear Reader,

As is often the case when someone is trying to choose between A and B, the real answer (which is not on their scorecard) is likely to be "none of the above." With this degree of confusion and mixed feelings and trying to "make things fit," it's clear that whichever decision is made would probably lead to all kinds of second-guessing. No matter which man is chosen, there will likely always be doubts as to whether it was the right choice.

In situations like this, especially when someone is still in their 20s, it's far more likely that there's a real need to *first* establish a clear sense of personal identity, not figuring out what parts of the person *match* with someone else. This means having a clear sense that you can make it on your own—emotionally, psychologically, and financially. While there are exceptions, in most instances, for a woman in our culture, this takes until about the age or 30—*if* there's been a conscious effort to establish a clear personal identity in the world during that time. If the process is only begun at age 28, then 30 will still be too soon to have a clear sense of yourself as an independent person.

Unfortunately, many relationships end (or marriages end in divorce) because of this effort to choose or fit with someone else. However, waiting until you've established a clear sense of yourself as a separate person (rather than part of a couple) can permit a recognition of a potential partner that is very clear. Whenever the choice is as unclear as described above, neither choice is likely to be a good one—at least not at this point.

* * * * * * * * * * * * *

Affair at Work

Dear Peggy,

How can I possibly get over the shocking experience of being part of an affair? We worked for the same company, he quit. He moved and I couldn't get to talk to him. Not even say good-bye. I loved him very much. I lost so much. Was it only an illusion? Was it really just an illusion? Please tell me.

We were very compatible. But I was very lonely at that time and he had many things I had always looked for in a man: he is good looking and suave; romantic and with good manners; smart, sexy, adorable. Simply adorable. And he said he loved me. And I believed him. How, How can I possibly get over him?

Everyone at work knew about it; that made the shock even greater. I considered myself a decent person and having to deal with the fact that my reputation is so damaged (and with the fact that I was exposed) is a thing that I haven't quite learned. The new company that I started to work for called for my references and they mentioned the episode. That was devastating, as I relived the same situation and felt crushed. How can I learn to live with it when it seems that it follows me everywhere I go?

I still feel betrayed. Only when I got to work for the second job (that I have already quit because I couldn't handle the gossip) did I learn that he had said I was obsessed with him. I can't believe he said that. I am sure he had never felt so close to anyone in his life before, and that holds true for me too.

Just last week a guy threw the whole thing in my face (indirectly) and I felt just as the first day of the scandal: devastated. How can I get over it? I have done counseling, do I still need to do more? Are there any books on the "other woman?" Does anybody ever take a look at us? We lose, and we lose a lot too.

Dear Reader,

This is a sad (but typical) commentary on the plight of a woman who has an affair with a man at work. This letter illustrates two of the most common fallacies: 1) that the man is somehow *special* and 2) that the affair can take place without dire consequences as far as the job itself is concerned.

Fallacy #1. The man is *special*.

According to the description above: "He had many things I had always looked for in a man: he is good looking and suave; romantic and with good manners; smart, sexy, adorable. Simply adorable."

Fact: It's not that a man at work is particularly special; it's the circumstances.

For instance, a man who seems so wonderful at work may behave very differently at home. At work, people present a side of themselves that is not representative of the whole person. They're usually committed to looking their best and being on their best behavior.

Fallacy #2. The affair can take place without consequences to the job.

Office affairs (where at least one of the partners is married) carry extremely high risks to the job—and these risks are much greater for women than for men.

Fact: The double standard in society as a whole exists in the office as well.

Both men and women are likely to be more harsh in their judgment of the woman than the man when it comes to an office affair. Even if coworkers bring no moral judgment to her actions, they're likely to make a professional judgment that she's not really serious about her career. And when an affair ends, or if it becomes a problem in the office, it's the woman whose job is likely to be jeopardized. And even if she is able to get or keep a job, her peers' assessment of her as a worker will probably be lowered. This is a very high price to pay for an affair.

As for books or other resources, it's true that there is very little help for the other woman. The very best book is one that is no longer in print, called *"The Mistress' Survival Manual"* by Melissa Sands. I've mentioned it before, but it's worth trying to find it in a used bookstore or a library—because it perfectly describes the above situation. Also, Laurel Richardson's *"The New Other Woman"* can be helpful in thinking through this issue. Unfortunately, the fate of the other woman is usually doomed from the beginning. Hopefully, more women will educate themselves about their potential plight before they reach the point described in the above letter.

* * * * * * * * * * * * *

At Work Affair???

Dear Peggy,

I'm a working mother and wife. My husband and I both work nights. I feel he always has his free time to golf or do whatever, whereas I don't. This has been an ongoing problem for all the 4 years we have been married. Therefore, it has caused many disagreements. I have a friend at work that I don't feel I have cheated with. But I will let you be the judge of it. We have only gotten as far as a few kisses here and there. That is all I ever wanted from this guy, nothing more. After this has happened, I come home and feel very loving towards my husband. I have to put myself in his place that I wouldn't want this to happen to me, but the aftereffects towards my husband are great!!!!! Got any advice????

Dear Reader,

This letter describes a very real struggle that many people face. On one hand, they acknowledge that they wouldn't want their spouse to do what they're doing. On the other hand, it feels so good that it's hard to see the problem.

An added feature (that is also quite common) is to find things about life circumstances that somehow *justify* the behavior that a person wants to pursue. It's more common with women than men that they point to a husband's shortcomings or unfairness in the marriage as evidence that they *deserve* this break. When someone *wants* to do something, there are many ways to convince themselves that it's OK.

Another question raised by the above description, however, is a classic question in our culture today: "How much is enough?" Whether it's money or success or love—we usually want *more*. So the idea that "all I ever wanted...nothing more..." is "a few kisses here and there" may be true *for now*, but will almost certainly change if things continue.

It's common to feel this kind of euphoria when connecting with someone new in this way, but it's usually a huge rationalization to make the case that it also benefits the spouse. Any potential benefit is likely to be temporary, just the calm before the storm. Things seldom remain the same; they change—for everyone—and the changes can be more than anyone bargained for.

* * * * * * * * * * * * *

Still in love with my boss

Dear Peggy,

I have been with my husband for 9 years and I just fell out of love with him. I met my boss when he came to be my manager 4 years ago. One night, I stayed late and (feeling very stressed out) we decided to go out to have a drink. Then it happened, we hit it off. He has been tied up with another coworker in an affair which caused our relationship to lose trust. He is a married man with 3 children. His wife knows about the affair with the other coworker and never

248

would expect us together, nor does my husband know. I still have strong feelings for him and he is still my boss. I have dreams about him. He won't leave his wife and I'm ready to leave mine. What should I do?

Dear Reader,

This letter is extremely typical of the kind of complicated situation that can develop when people get caught up in such an unrealistic romantic view of life/love. It's easy to see that everything about this letter is filtered through a lens that distorts reality and focuses through a dramatic/romantic view of the world. So the problem is not really "What should I do?" It's "How should I *think*."

There doesn't appear to be much clear thinking at this point, as illustrated by several statements:

— "I...fell out of love (with my husband)" and "...it happened, we hit it off."

Love is not something you fall into or fall out of. Love has many stages, and the above description seems to be referring either to lust or to a very unrealistic fascination with love.

— His "affair with the other coworker"..."caused our relationship to lose trust."

It's hard to see how/why there was ever any meaningful trust in this relationship. Trust does not appear to be the strong suit of people who have multiple affairs. And it's hard to see how trust can be lost when there was no basis for being trusting in the first place.

— "I have dreams about him. He won't leave his wife and I'm ready to leave mine."

This whole situation sounds like a dream (or a soap opera or romance novel)—but not real life. As for "what to do," leaving a marriage for such a dream is not a good reason. As I said earlier, it's not so much a matter of what to *do*, but how to go about *thinking* more clearly about the entire situation—and basing actions on that thinking instead of on a romantic fantasy. Also, a part of the actions one might choose (if basing them on thinking instead of dreaming) would be to separate from the source of the dream—to see whether this improves the ability to think more clearly about the whole situation.

18: Homosexual Affairs

Distraught

Dear Peggy,

I've been in a lesbian relationship with my partner for 2 years and counting...we committed to each other last year after we moved into our first home together. Our neighbors befriended her, and I became suspicious of her activity after she began coming home less and less. She admitted to sleeping with the neighbor's wife.

It was not really a shock; it was what I felt all along. That was last year. Since then she feels I should warm up to her, what is past is past, but I still don't think she knows the magnitude of what she has done. I have tried to get over it. I tried acting like it never happened, that did not work; that attitude gave her leverage to believe she could hurt me and not be the love I once knew her to be... She has become lazy, inconsiderate, and unaware she is losing the only woman that has ever loved her... She blames her activities on her mother's dying. Well that's just displacement if you ask me. What do you think?

Dear Reader,

This letter clearly illustrates how the emotional impact of a partner's affair is universal, regardless of the gender of the people involved—including the sensing that something is happening before knowing for sure, the pain of being deceived, the effort to move on without dealing with it, and blaming something or someone else for what happened.

In any relationship, deception is extremely hurtful, as is a partner's unwillingness to put in the time and effort to deal with the impact of their actions. It's typical in situations like this for both people to wish they could pretend it never happened and to try to get over it and just go on. But that's virtually impossible. With something as important as this, "acting like it never happened" simply doesn't work in the long run. People may temporarily get a little relief, but it is likely to continue to stand between them and prevent them from having a close and trusting relationship.

As for "blaming her activities on her mother's dying," there's virtually never one single reason why someone does something like this—(unless it's a willingness to be deceptive). Of course, it's common to look for some particular reason to try to legitimize something we want to do anyway. Since most of us want to feel good about ourselves, it's typical that people in this situation will not only rationalize the reasons behind their actions but also fail to acknowledge "the magnitude of what she has done."

As with any situation where this has happened, it's a long, slow process to rebuild the trust that has been broken. And the first step is for both people to be willing to invest the time and energy it takes to deal with what happened and commit to ongoing honest communication in the future.

* * * * * * * * * * * *

Honesty in Homosexual Affairs

(Here are 4 letters before my response.)

Dear Peggy, (letter #1)

I don't know if you will help me with this but I really need some advice bad. Anyway, the situation is this: I have been with my girlfriend for over a year and it has all been great except one thing, the sex. I mean I don't have a real problem with it, but she does. She says that she just doesn't have the drive for sex anymore. I have asked her repeatedly if it was me or something that I was doing or even if she thought that it was getting boring, all of that stuff. She has told me no to all of them, it is just her. She will want to have sex, but once we get to bed she doesn't have the drive for it. I guess that I just don't understand it. We didn't have a problem about sex at all until we moved here to be closer to her family, then things started to change with it. I am really confused about this whole thing. I don't know what to do. I am scared of rejection that if I try to pursue sex with her then she will get upset with me. I don't know what else to do about it. I mean she says that it isn't me, but I don't know how to get our sex life back to the way it was. I feel like it is me and she just doesn't want to hurt my feelings by saying so. I have asked her that and she still tells me no. What should I do?????? Very Confused.

Dear Peggy, (letter #2)

I have been married 15 years and have children. My husband and I are high school sweethearts and have really grown up together. We have a really great physical and emotional relationship, plus a lot of humor. Recently, my husband disclosed to me that for about the past 5 years he'd been having "feelings" towards other men. I am devastated and at times feeling hopeless. I have set up an appointment with a therapist, but I feel like I need answers now. He says that he can no longer ignore how he feels and as much as he loves us, he can't handle the conflict. We're going to work through this together for all of our sakes, but I know the overall feeling is that we're over. He is attracted to me in all ways, but then there's these other feelings that he doesn't understand, but feels as if he wants a relationship with a man. Could there possibly be any hope for a situation like this? Shocked and Depressed.

Dear Peggy, (letter #3)

My spouse and I have had a relationship with a friend for approximately 3 years. During that time, I have noticed that the 'other' male seems to relish the threesome more than I do at this point. He feels more relaxed with the threesome than just a one-on-one. He feels like he's cheating when it's just the

252

two of us. I find it sometimes difficult to express my emotional feelings while my spouse is present. Now this extra has been seeing someone and she has no clue at all of his behavior. He knows how I feel, but he still wants to get together. I don't think it's fair for him to try to build a life with someone (he's still legally married) and to continue to see me/us. I know if I let this continue the way it is, that it would be fine with him. How can I still maintain the friendship, even though I can't seem to get through to him? I guess I really know the answer, but just asking someone else helps.

Dear Peggy, (letter #4, edited for length)
    Where to start. Male, 50, married 30 years, two married children, one fantastic grandchild. Upper middle class. Nice home and lifelong collection of furnishings. Before puberty was always interested in the guys. After puberty was really interested in the guys. Dated some in high school; never had sex with a girl. Had a few adolescent experiences with male friends that I fully enjoyed. First year of college, met a girl who was three years older and a graduate. Had my first through third heterosexual experience when she comes up pregnant. Being Mr. Responsible, we hastily married. We were both totally ignorant with regards to sexuality. It was something that she could/would not talk about. Very early on, discovered tremendous sexual 'limits.' She would not touch me below the shoulders. Sex was cordial, but not much reciprocation.
    Now, after 30 years of marriage, I literally had to kill my emotions and sexuality. I went into a spiral of depression. I sought counseling, asked her to join me, but she was (and remains) of the opinion that she was not the one with a problem. So, I'm still not interested in chasing a woman, but my repressed orientation has taken on a new meaning. There is a lot of baggage I carry, and I still do not want to intentionally hurt anyone. But I am so weary of denying myself for others. When is it going to be my turn? I am very close to meeting the gay community to explore my feeling. I will try to be discrete. I am not considering divorce, but who knows...

Dear Reader,
    While homosexuality in this society has created unwarranted strains on individuals and on their relationships, the *primary* problems for anyone in a significant relationship are *not* related to whether they are heterosexual or homosexual—but the degree to which there can be *honesty* between the two people. Relationships can be difficult even *with* complete responsible honesty, but *without* it, it's almost impossible to have a really satisfying long-term relationship. For instance, when you look behind the presenting problems in each of the above letters, there's the honesty factor lurking just beneath the surface.
    In the first letter, it *appears* that they "didn't have a problem about [the disinterest in sex]...at all until we moved here to be closer to her family." This immediately leads to the suspicion that the family is either not totally aware of

253

(or not completely approving of) the relationship. While keeping a major secret like this doesn't necessarily stifle sexual feelings, it's quite common to have problems due to the close proximity to other family members—whether in a situation like the one above or one where a heterosexual couple has problems due to the close proximity of their children in the house. So working *directly* on the lack of sex drive may be missing the primary problem—which *may* be a lack of honesty with the family as well as a lack of honesty in acknowledging to the partner that this is the basic problem. Any dishonesty (with anyone) about the nature of a relationship is likely to create problems of all kinds, including sexual ones.

In the second letter, we see a somewhat different way that secrecy (or the lack thereof) can impact a situation. The fact that the wife is looking for "hope for a situation like this" is probably greatly influenced by the fact that her husband honestly volunteered the information about his feelings toward other men. The more honesty there is between people, the more likely they are to be able to resolve even the most difficult issues—like this one. The connection that results from this kind of honesty is what makes it possible for them to "work through this together for all of our sakes."

In the third letter, there's a lot of hair-splitting about the value of honesty. For instance the other man feels less comfortable with a one-on-one situation—probably in large part because it *feels* like cheating/secrecy/deception (even if there's a general awareness by the wife that this is happening.) Then the writer of the letter is making another kind of judgment when *seeming* to be concerned about the unfairness of the other man in trying to build a life with his wife—while personally seeing the writer and *his* wife. Again, the concern is *probably* related more to the writer's personal displeasure with the situation than with genuine concern for the fairness to the other man's wife. Honesty really begins with being honest with *ourselves*—and it's clear from the conclusion of the letter that this man does *know* this on some level.

Finally, the last letter (which was considerably longer but edited for length) *appears* to be describing a relationship that has had an overtone of dishonesty during the entire 30 years—which can be a tremendous burden to bear (as indicated by saying "there is a lot of baggage I carry"). While there's no way to know for sure just from this letter, it's *possible* that his wife has suspected his repressed orientation all these years—which *may* be a factor in her lack of responsiveness. This, of course, is not to *blame* him for her reaction, only to possibly help explain what seems so sad and unfair. Of course, it *is* a sad situation—for two people to spend so many years together without sexual fulfillment. But genuine satisfaction is probably only possible when there's total *responsible* honesty.

* * * * * * * * * * * * *

Best Friend vs. Boy Friend

Dear Peggy;

I hope it is OK to ask a gay-related extramarital affairs question. Several years ago I realized that I may have an interest in other guys. I was almost ready to give up on this interest and pursue a future with a woman (and hopefully family) when I came across this one guy... We met via AOL and I find myself very much in love with him. He has said the same to me, but is also still in love with his significant other of 6 years. They have had troubles before and again recently, but I don't want to fuel a breakup. Yet I am in love with him. I have never said I loved anyone in my life before this, nor have I ever felt this strongly about anything. What can I do? The one I love reciprocates my affections of love but doesn't want to leave the other nor does he want me to talk to other people (guy or girl). I'd wait forever for him (or at least I keep saying I will), but I am going crazy not knowing what I should do... Please Help me!

Dear Reader,

The experience described in this letter illustrates the universality of some of the issues related to affairs, including:

—prevalence of initial meeting online
—the strength of the feelings of new love
—the other person being torn between primary partner and new relationship
—feeling crazy or confused or in limbo while waiting for resolution

This letter is an articulate description of the typical battle between what a person feels emotionally and what they *know* based on a more rational assessment of the situation. It illustrates the key elements that are so common:

— online meetings are often begun as more fantasy-based than reality-based
— the flush of the initial phase of love invariably feels like true love, whether or not it is
— the other person's indecisiveness is typical of a desire to avoid giving up either person—unless or until forced to choose
— feelings of desperation (craziness) are understandable when waiting in limbo (especially when told, "don't talk to other people")—which also raises issues of fairness

Naturally, it's very difficult to think clearly in the midst of such strong emotions, but it's the best hope for getting a grasp on the situation and making a rational decision.

* * * * * * * * * * * *

Husband's affair with another man

Dear Peggy,

I am struggling with a confession my husband made to me this past summer. He had an affair with another man. I am still reeling from this. He swears to me this was just a result of the extreme pressure he was under (our business was failing), and says it will never happen again. He had a whole past filled with

255

sexual abuse when he was a child. We have been married over 15 years and I never knew this. I know the person he was with very well, although I don't have to face him anymore. I think I can forgive, but I can't seem to forget. I feel so betrayed and wonder how he really feels. He says he loves me and wants our marriage, but he doesn't seem to be able to show it. I am so worried he's just putting up a front because he doesn't want anyone to know about what he did. I am so sad and confused, I just don't know what to do. I don't think he is gay, but maybe bisexual because he does enjoy sex. He swears this is the only time in all of our years together, but I wonder. I am angry he betrayed me.

Dear Reader,

It's pretty obvious that there have been *many* secrets, not just about sexual orientation—for instance, not knowing about the husband's childhood sexual abuse. This is a very big secret that may or may not relate to the question of whether he's gay or bisexual. There's probably a great deal of confusion, not just on the part of the writer of this letter, but on the part of her husband as well. Perhaps they could use this as an opportunity to forge a much closer connection based on talking more honestly and in more detail (about all important life issues) than they have done in the past. It's only through that process that they may be able to get more understanding of what has happened and why. And in the meantime, they can find strength in simply facing issues that have been kept hidden—and working together to deal with them.

We're much more likely to be angry and confused when we try to figure things out by ourselves than when we're talking about them, especially talking about them with the other person involved in the whole situation. So I hope that the process of coming to grips with the current situation can bring about a willingness to talk through it in order for both people to be better able to deal with the emotional impact of all of these serious and complicated issues.

* * * * * * * * * * * *

Bisexual Desires

Dear Peggy,

I know this might sound bizarre, but although I am deeply in love with my husband and I find him very attractive, as well as other men, I also find women very attractive on a sexual level. I am not interested in developing a relationship with another man besides my husband, even though I find other men attractive, but I feel very strongly about wanting to have sex with other women. I have had sex with a woman in the past, so it isn't just about curiosity (although probably all extramarital affairs have some roots in that), but sometimes it seems like an even painful desire. I don't want to hurt my husband for anything, nor do I plan on destroying my family (we have two small children), but I feel like a freak because it seems like a struggle inside about what to do. Anyway, I hope I have made some sense.

Dear Reader,

This letter articulates what many people feel but simply don't say. Since it's so seldom voiced, it leaves a person in this situation feeling (as stated above) "like a freak." However, there's nothing bizarre about this. Some studies of human nature have concluded that bisexuality is, in fact, quite *natural*—that the way we make heterosexual/homosexual delineations actually misses the point. So as far as having bisexual desires, they're quite understandable.

However, as is alluded to in the letter, the *real* issue is not whether the desires are bisexual but rather the problems related to acting on *any* sexual desires (with the risk of "destroying the family...with two small children"). Most people have various desires and fantasies at different times, but that doesn't mean they decide to act on them. It's probably more effective to focus on the issue of honesty than on the desires themselves—or on whether they're bizarre.

In fact, simply writing this letter show there's a degree of thoughtfulness and openness to thinking more clearly about this whole situation. Private fantasies (never expressed) sometimes take on a life of their own, growing stronger by virtue of their secrecy. Even the extra taboo nature of feeling they're bizarre can add to their power. So talking about the desires (especially talking about the potential consequences of acting on the desires) is, in an of itself, a positive step toward feeling more in control of the situation.

19: Sexually Open Marriage

Open Marriage
(Here are excerpts from 5 letters prior to my response.)

Dear Peggy, (excerpt #1)

My husband and I have recently decided to have an open marriage. Everything is going wonderful, it looks as if we have found the best of both worlds. Any suggestions or tips on how to keep our relationship healthy and happy in this new environment? Should we talk about our experiences with others?

Dear Peggy, (excerpt #2)

Should I marry a very fair, intelligent, good-looking, hard-working, nice, caring, with great sense of humor single man who wants our relation to be open? We trust each other and we are very transparent. I am in love with him, but he is not—and says he will never be (with me or anybody else). We have talked about marriage but I am not sure if I can manage an open relationship. We both are open-minded but I can't help feeling a little bit jealous about his "relations" with other women. What would be your advice?

Dear Peggy, (excerpt #3)

What should do? My husband is allowing us to have an open marriage for now. I have told him I can't give this other man up because I love him very much, and I also love my husband, but not as much. This other man and I are spiritually together, our spirits are together and he wants to marry me. My heart wants to marry him badly, but my mind is holding me back. I just don't know what to do.

Dear Peggy, (excerpt #4)

Do you consider swinging a form of extramarital affairs when both partners are willing participants? Why do you think people get into swinging? What is your overall opinion on swinging?

Dear Peggy, (excerpt #5)

How do I bring about the subject of couples in our relationship (read swing)? I have a solid marriage. We both have a good sex drive and enjoy our time together (really enjoy). I think my spouse would be agreeable but...

Dear Reader

The first thing I noticed about these letters related to "open marriage" is that what they are actually asking about is "*sexually* open marriage." The term "Open Marriage" originated with the book of that title written by Nena and

George O'Neill. For those who want solid information about the whole subject of open marriage, I suggest reading this classic (written in the early 70s) that is still the best resource on the subject. (Nena O'Neill is a close personal friend— and I have learned much about this issue from her through the years.)

Unfortunately, most people completely missed the O'Neill's point in their book. They were only saying that sexually open marriage might be possible for some couples who had already evolved an open relationship *in all other ways*. The sexual aspect was a very small part of the overall kind of open marriage they were suggesting *might* be possible for a *few* couples who have developed a relationship based on honesty and a commitment to fairness and equality.

Unfortunately, most people jump to trying to have a *sexually* open marriage when they haven't developed an "open marriage" in all other aspects of their relationship. There's often an idealistic view of an "open marriage," thinking somehow you can "have the best of both worlds"—a solid, satisfying marriage *and* the excitement of affairs. But realistically, that's not likely to happen. Because talking through the issues involved in a sexually open marriage (and processing all the feelings involved) requires an enormous amount of time and energy—which has a dramatic impact on the quality of the primary relationship. In the final analysis, most people determine that the tradeoffs are just not worth it.

I've known couples involved in sexually open marriages, but I've known only a few who were able to sustain them over a long period of time. Ironically, neither long-term monogamy nor long-term sexually open marriages are either easy or prevalent. Most people *profess* monogamy, but deceptively have affairs in secret.

20: Loves/Affairs from the Past

Ex-Boyfriend

Dear Peggy,

After 28 years I still have strong feelings for this person. I am happily married but cannot forget this guy... He was my first love and we had a son together but didn't marry... He also has a family... We met last year for a weekend, and we both cried and wished we didn't have to leave the other... See when I became pregnant in high school, our parents separated us... We both were devastated, for at the time we both loved each other... As time went on we both married and have our own lives and family...but for some reason we both still care for each other. It's been 28 years... I have a strong feeling we may end up together one of these days... Can I ever get over him ?? Will I ever get over him? Please help me!

Dear Reader,

This is a poignant letter, illustrating the power of first love—especially when it produces a child! It's fairly predictable that "for some reason we both still care for each other." Young love makes an indelible imprint on us, especially if it was a good experience. Obviously, in this case, there was a huge negative aspect to it as well—due to the high-school pregnancy and family intervention. So while wishing to turn back the clock is understandable, the strong feelings probably are tied to the memory of the person as they were many years ago rather than to the real person who exists today. All of us change dramatically over time, and in many respects we're not the same people we were when we were young.

For instance, I wound up marrying my first love—and after 44 years, we're still married. But we're extremely different now from the way we were when we were teenagers. Each of us has changed in countless ways. (In some ways it's hard to look back and recognize that we're even the same people.)

To some degree, it's common to never quite get over our feelings for our first love. And there's no problem with that; it's a very special experience. The problem comes when we allow the memory of the past (and the fantasy of a possible future) to intrude on the present in such a way as to jeopardize the lives we have now. Being "happily married" is a great blessing, not to be taken lightly or put at risk because of such feelings. It can be pleasant to hold a thought of "what might be some day" as long as we don't get carried away and try to make it happen. Life has many twists and turns, and the older we get, the more we realize that it's very hard to predict what the future may hold. It's more important to protect and preserve what's good about the present.

DEAR PEGGY

* * * * * * * * * * * * *
Old Feelings

Dear Peggy,

Sixteen years ago I was a seventeen-year-old who had been dating the same boy since I was 13 years old. We were making plans to get married after I finished high school. Then my father was transferred to a new job several hours away. After a very ugly incident, my family very much discouraged this relationship. We grew apart and I married a man when I was 19. We have been married for 12 years and have four children. Through all this I have never forgotten my first love. I think of him often and see his family also, as we have stayed friends. I believe my husband knows these feelings have never died. My parents have since voiced regret over the situation. I can not talk about this man and have had opportunities to see him, but I don't trust myself. I'm afraid the feelings would overwhelm me.

My husband believes I should talk with him to get some type of closure which we never had. I don't know what to do. Can you give me some advice. Thank you.

Dear Reader,

There is absolutely nothing to compare with first love. (My husband and I refer to our years as teenagers, learning about love and sex with each other, as our period of "young, hot love.") It's special precisely *because* it's "first." But many people maintain a fantasy image of that special first love and elevate it to some mystical place of perfection.

My first love also became my lasting love partner, and the couple we were as teenagers remains a special memory—but it is *not* the same couple that made a life together, through pain and pleasure and kids and affairs.... While it may be tempting to pine for the fantasy of young love, it's important to know that the reality of being married, raising kids, and facing all of life's challenges together is the basis for lasting love. Unfortunately, we have this notion that love is that first flush of romantic love, but as I've explained before, this is only the first stage of love. It either changes or it withers and dies.

So it's not reasonable to compare a kind of fairy-tale image based on teenage love with real-life married love over a period of years. As for whether seeing a young love again would bring any kind of closure, there's no way to know. It certainly isn't necessary. What's important is to value it for what it represents (the first experience of young love), but not to assume that it was the particular person who made it special. The specialness was in the experience itself, not the person with whom it was shared. So it's not necessary to try to *forget* a first love; but it *is* important to put it in its proper place—as just a stepping-stone to growing up and engaging in a real love based on making a life together.

* * * * * * * * * * * * *

Old flame...

Dear Peggy,

I am very confused. I am a 36-year-old mom of three lovely children. I have been married for 12 years to a very wonderful man. I met my husband two weeks after breaking up with a boyfriend I had since I was 13 (he was 15) whom I dated off and on for 8 years. This guy was my first lover. We had very deep, intense feelings for each other. We broke up because we were so young and were unable to stay faithful to each other. We both had other people we dated and slept with. We both got married to different people and went our separate ways. We didn't talk to each other for 10 years.

Recently I found out he was very unhappy in his marriage and one day I decided to pick up the phone and called him. I was just calling to talk and offer my friendship. We talked on the phone for two hours and it felt like old times. We met two months later for lunch and ended up in a motel. I found out my feelings for him never died. We have met twice since that day. We talk on the phone a lot. He says I am very special to him and that he will never find anyone like me again. He wants to separate from his wife because he doesn't love her anymore; (she slept with her old boyfriend and he can't forgive her). He is not making any promises to me about getting married if we both leave our spouses. He says he does not want to be responsible for breaking up my family.

My husband and I have never had passionate feelings for each other. I love him but not as intensely as I love my first love, the love of my life. After we broke up and all these years, I often dream of him and always wake up feeling sad thinking about what could have been. We have so much in common, we enjoy spending time together, we communicate so well. My husband and I don't have any of that. I feel the only thing we have in common is our children. I am not happy with my husband. I don't want to leave him but I can't stop loving this other man. He is my soul-mate.

Dear Reader,

Yes, there *is* a special magic about our first love—whether we stay together or part. If couples stay together, they find that that those feelings of new love can't be sustained through the years. But if people do *not* stay together—yet come back together later (as in the above letter), they may kind of pick up where they left off in feeling how special this love is.

This specialness, of course, is reinforced when there's the feeling that one "doesn't love [his wife] anymore" and the other is "not happy with [her] husband." This sounds nice and neat. But it fails to appreciate that it's the timing and the situation that have recreated this first flush of love. If people reconnect (and stay reconnected for many years), the relationship does *not* sustain this specialness that is inherent in it's (revised) "newness." It feels glorious when someone feels they've found their soul-mate, but in reality there's no such thing as *one special person* who is meant for any certain person.

Naturally, any relationship (whether continuing from youth or being rejoined later as the one described above) can be satisfying and can develop into the deep, rich kind of love connection that forges over time in living together and dealing with real life together. But it's important to go beyond focusing *only* on the positive memories of the early days without also taking note of the negative aspects of the relationship that might still continue. For instance, note the statement that "We broke up because we were so young and were unable to stay faithful to each other." While the "too young" part may no longer be relevant, it sounds as if the "staying faithful" part might still be a problem. While it may *sound* like thoughtfulness to say "he does not want to be responsible for breaking up my family," it's also a way of protecting against expectations and responsibilities that he may not be prepared to assume.

* * * * * * * * * * * *

What to do?
(Here are 2 letters before my response.)

Dear Peggy, (letter #1)

My wife of 22 years recently confessed to me about a "sort of" affair which happened about 20 years ago with her boss. She says she met with the man 6 or 8 times but that they never actually had intercourse, so she didn't actually cheat. The problem is that when I question her about what did or did not take place, now she says she doesn't remember. Should I confront the man (who still lives in the area) about his account of what happened 20 years ago or just forget it???

Dear Peggy, (letter #2)

I've been married for over 25 years. Five years ago my husband told me he tried to have an affair with my sister-in-law, but she turned him down. He told me he tried this 20 years ago and was just telling me now because there was some trouble going on in the family and he was afraid it would come out. So he told me. Then he told me he was having an affair at work. Then after 2 weeks of really hurting, he said he lied and he just wanted to hurt me because I was playing the lottery. After all these years all this comes out, and he says he is sorry and he wants me to just forget it because it was so long ago. But he has changed so much; he doesn't even buy me a birthday gift. Is this proving his love or just trying to see how long I'll hold on. I feel the whole 25 years have been a lie. Am I wrong in being so confused or should I just grow up and get over it as he says.

Dear Reader,

Many people falsely assume that if they have an affair, there's no harm as long as their spouse never finds out. But they underestimate the difficulty of keeping something like this a secret for 20 years or more. It is a terrible strain—not only wondering if the spouse will someday find out, but simply the strain of carrying a secret like this for so long.

The most disturbing part of the above descriptions is not in the details of the affairs from so many years ago, but in the current attitude of insensitivity to the spouse's feelings. In the first letter there's still a justification/rationalization that it was just "sort of" an affair and that she "doesn't remember" things. And in the second letter, there's an attempt to shift the guilt to make the wife feel she should just "grow up and get over it."

It's much easier to deal with actions from 20 years ago when the *current* actions are thoughtful and caring. So the current difficulties in coping with this kind of information may have much more to do with the lack of sensitivity to its impact than to the events themselves. The past can't be changed, but the present and future warrant much more of an effort to deal with this issue than is described in these letters. And it's not so much getting the specific details that is likely to make a difference; it's the willingness of the spouse to be responsible in trying to provide whatever information is requested—and to demonstrate their consideration for the impact of that information on their spouse.

* * * * * * * * * * * *

Past lovers

Dear Peggy,

I am a 27-year-old-female and have been with my current husband since 10th grade in high school. When he was young, he lied a lot and slept with many people—and then we got married. Then he was still too young, I guess, and he continued to lie and sleep with people, some of which I knew; he also had a major drinking problem. I now find that since we have gotten remarried, after divorcing for 2 years, that I have become steadily more insecure—and this time it's for no reason. I feel fat and inferior, ugly and paranoid; we can't even watch a TV program that has a pretty woman in it without me feeling anger or inferior to her because of what I think his thoughts are. I don't even want to go to the beach and I feel like it is ruining our relationship and my self esteem, but is this caused by my past experience with him, or could it very well be my very own problem that has always been there? Please give me advice. I feel like the only thing I have to offer is my mind, which I respect, as does he. I am 5' 4" and weigh 118 pounds and try to take care of myself as best I can, feeling this way. Please Help Me!

Dear Reader,

This letter verbalizes the feelings of *many* women—being dissatisfied with their looks and thinking they're not attractive enough. Unfortunately, our society is saturated with images of women that are not realistic; but these images tend to be used as points of comparison—which inevitably leaves a normal woman feeling somehow less. Obviously, a woman who is 5' 4" weighing 118 pounds is in no way "fat." But as long as we hold these unrealistic images in our heads, we're likely to be dissatisfied—no matter *how* we look.

So while part of the cause of these feelings is unclear thinking, it's not *paranoid*—because women have a real uphill struggle to *avoid* thinking this way in a culture like the one in the U.S. (Other parts of the world are not necessarily quite so distorted in their view of beauty.) So while we need to try to be more realistic in our thinking, it's a constant battle to overcome the unrealistic standards we see all around us.

This battle can be all the more difficult when there has been an affair—because this almost always affects a person's self-esteem and sense of themselves. There's a tendency to constantly wonder if our spouse is viewing someone else in a more favorable light. So, again, it's important to think clearly—which means recognizing that it's unreasonable to feel in competition with every other person in the world and that it's normal for people to be attracted to others.

Also, it's important to recognize that any perceived lack on the part of the spouse (whether physical or something else) does not *cause* a spouse to have an affair—just as beauty does not *prevent* a spouse from having an affair. These are just convenient, simplistic excuses for affairs. Affairs are much more about deception than about looks.

What we need is to constantly remind ourselves of the *facts* (as I mentioned above) that can offset the unrealistic judgments we make about our looks. One extremely positive thing about the above letter is the writer's acknowledgment that she has a good mind. Now the task is to continue to *use* that good mind to fight back the emotion-based thoughts that lead to being unreasonably judgmental about her looks.

* * * * * * * * * * * * *

Lost Love Found Again

Dear Peggy,

Forty years ago I married a very lovely girl and loved her very much. Losing our baby upset her so that she went home to Mama. I tried to phone her every day, but was told she didn't want to talk to me. (Later I found out that her parents wouldn't let her talk to me.) I am married now to another lovely girl and have been for 30 years, but she now requires 24-hour-a-day care, with lots of medication. To make a long story short, I have located my ex-wife, and our love for each other hasn't died after the 40 years we've been apart. The doctor is treating me for stress. I'm going to spend a week with my other love, and I feel like a teenager in love. I don't really feel like I am cheating on my wife. I know I should, but I've loved the other girl all these years too. In 30 years I've never cheated on my wife. Should I feel guilty? Or am I justified in trying to show the other lady how much she means to me. She is as excited as I am about spending a week together. We're not kids. She's 66 and I'm 70. I really do love both of these ladies.

Dear Reader,

This is obviously a thoughtful person dealing with a complicated situation. He is understandably struggling with his intense feelings of stress and guilt and his intense feelings of joy and excitement. I feel compassion for all three people involved, but feel that he is in a better position to determine his own course than anything I could say about his particular situation.

Nevertheless, I think this letter touches on some important issues for discussion. First of all, it illustrates the power of first love or young love (especially if it had a Romeo and Juliet quality like the one described above). I know the power of that first, young love. I'm fortunate that my husband was also my first love. And I've often felt that if we had not somehow managed to end up together, I would have carried that special connection for the rest of my life. We were childhood sweethearts and (due to outside influences) had a very brief break in our relationship in our teens. I discovered during that short time apart that he would always be in my heart—no matter what! I'm thankful that I never had to test my belief in the enduring quality of our connection, but the above story reminded me of the power of that early love.

The other issue that comes to mind in reading the above letter is the powerful feelings of love that can and do exist when people are *older*. We have the mistaken idea in this culture that exciting love is only for the young. Wrong! As the above expressions of joy clearly indicate, love has nothing to do with age. I have a dear friend who describes his loving relationship with the woman he married when he was 71 years old—as "bliss." Never underestimate the power of real love.

21: Second Time Around

Falling in Love, Staying There

Dear Peggy,

My lover and I met on AOL nearly 2 years ago. We both were unhappily married. We met and fell in love. We are both now in the middle of divorces, I left my husband a year ago, he left his wife 1 year ago. His wife learned of the affair several months ago. Our relationship is magical, but very complex. He lives part of the week in Los Angeles, and part of the week in the Bay Area, where I reside. His kids are in the Bay Area. I have a four-year-old son. The goal is to have him be here permanently, career situation permitting. We wish to share our lives.

My question is two-fold:

1. What is the likelihood of a successful, happy relationship with the person with whom you had an affair?

2. What is the ideal time to introduce our children into our relationship?

I would love a response. There is so much literature on affairs, but none that I've found regarding the persons really finding happiness past the deception to the spouses. We never thought we would have affairs. But we were lucky to find each other. Help!

Dear Reader,

There is very little information available about situations like this—because this is not what usually happens. In most instances, an affair doesn't lead to divorce. And when there *is* a divorce, in most cases, it does not lead to marrying the person who was involved in the affair. However, anyone who studies statistics knows that the only relevant statistic is the one that fits you personally. Since the relationship described above has already beaten the odds, there's no reason to assume it *can't* succeed.

Having said that, it's important, of course, to recognize that other hurdles lie ahead in situations like this. Even when divorce actions are undertaken before an affair comes to light, the affair often affects the willingness of former spouses to cooperate in helping the children adjust to the new relationship. So when it comes to the "ideal time to introduce the children into the relationship," how it's done is probably more important than when. It's probably essential to first appeal to the former spouses to cooperate (or at least not undermine) this effort.

Finally, as with all marriages, there are standard marital issues to deal with; and statistically, there are more divorces in second marriages than in first. But none of this in and of itself can *predict* the prospects for a particular union.

While it's not appropriate to identify them at this time, there are a number of high-profile, long-term, successful marriages (greatly admired by the public) where the relationship began as an extramarital affair. So it's wise to take heed of the statistics and the odds for success—but in the final analysis, it's up to each couple (and each individual within the couple) to do what it takes to beat the odds and develop a solid, long-term relationship.

* * * * * * * * * * * * *

Going nowhere fast

Dear Peggy,

I've been married for two years now to my second husband, who is the complete opposite of my first husband. With a lot of therapy, I've realized that the first man I married was someone who was incapable of loving me the way I felt I should be loved (he could care less about me). The problem is with my second husband. He has been supportive, caring, feeling, open and honest— however, I'm feeling completely smothered. This is a grown man who pouts if I tell him I want to do something with my friends until I can no longer stand it, so I end up not going out. Of course I get resentful, but he Never goes Anywhere without me—not even to a family function if I'm sick or not feeling well. (I've tried these tactics before, just to get some free time, but to no avail). I have two children from my first marriage and a child with my second, and I almost feel as if I can't run fast enough or far enough away from all of them. I love my kids, but lately I've been feeling as if my "children" have multiplied; either that, or my husband is too stern, and I end up feeling like a child. Please help!

Dear Reader,

This is a situation that would be amusing if it weren't so serious. It reminds me of the saying, "Be careful what you ask for; you might get it!" When a spouse cares too little, we want more. But if they care too much, we want less. Of course, the kind of smothering described above is not really a reflection of caring. It's more a reflection of an effort to control. I don't know whether the effort to control is based on concern for her well-being or on a desire to exert power over her. Any person in this situation can sense for themselves what the likely motive is for the behavior. But whatever the motive, it doesn't feel good.

One common reason for men behaving in this protective (possessive) way is that they're afraid of losing their wife to another man. Most men fail to understand that for many women, their desire is not for another man but for freedom for themselves. A favorite passage of mine that reflects this understanding about women's lives is from the book "Playing After Dark" by Barbara Lazear Ascher:

"I have a friend, happily married, who says that she can't imagine leaving her husband for another man. What she can imagine is leaving him for solitude. It's harder to win than a lover, but it may better nourish the soul. If my friend left, her husband might find it hard to believe that it was a quest for solitude rather than sexual adventure that called her away."

While there's no resolution in knowing that personal feelings and desires to "run away" are common among women, it can nevertheless allow for a certain recognition of both the good and the bad aspects of our role as "caretakers of the family." We may value our contribution to the well-being of those we love, but we need to balance this with also finding ways to increase our own well-being. Sometimes if a spouse understands that being "boxed in" can lead to desperate thoughts (and potentially desperate actions), they can appreciate that there may be more risk in trying to restrain their wives than in accepting more mutual independence within the relationship. The word that accurately describes that balance point worth seeking between stifling dependence and fearful independence is *interdependence*—where each person appreciates that they are two whole people who come together, rather than two halves trying to make a whole.

22: Complicating Circumstances

Affair (Abuse)

Dear Peggy,

I wish I didn't need to write to you about this. I have been married since 1991 to a husband who can be the sweetest man alive and the most abusive one as well. For the past 2 years his abuse has me hiding in the bedroom. (I rarely go out in the rest of house unless it's to cook his dinner, which I then serve to him while he lies in front of the TV.) This has been happening at least for the past 2 years. Three months ago, he was asked to take a job out of town for his company; we expected it to last a couple of weeks, not 3 months. Since our communication was not so good (in fact nil) when he left, I felt he didn't want me anymore and he felt I didn't want him anymore. Well, to make a long story short, he had an affair while working out of town.

Now he's back with me, we are talking more than we have ever done since day one of our marriage—and it's not all fighting; our sex life is better too. But I am not sure I know how to begin trusting him again. We have an appointment to see a counselor; he will have been back for a week by then. I'm doing my best to be amateur counselor to both of us, talking calmly; I even took out some of my old self-help books to read sections and discuss. He says it was because he was lonely. But I was lonely too. He says she was a substitute for me—because I wasn't there and he needed "it."

It's only been a couple of days since he's been home and things look like they might be on the upswing in the marriage. I know it's going to take a long time. I knew this was going to happen; I'm not sure I really wanted it to but now that it has, I'm trying to deal with it sensibly. I love my husband and he says he loves me. Do you see any hope for us or should we just part?

Dear Reader,

While the subject that was sent with the above letter was "Affair," I couldn't resist adding "Abuse"—because that's an absolute trump card (overriding any other consideration). I can't really address the issue of affairs in the context of a description of "a husband [who] can be the sweetest man alive and the most abusive one as well."

According to this letter, "we have an appointment to see a counselor." It's absolutely critical to get counseling and/or some kind of professional help whenever abuse is involved.

Of course, it's reasonable to wonder "how to begin trusting him again." In fact, as I've often said, trust is the by-product of ongoing actions that demonstrate trustworthiness. And a few months is too short a time to determine

273

the degree to which the behavior will warrant earning trust. This is even more important because of the issue of abuse.

* * * * * * * * * * * *

What are some warning signs?

Dear Peggy,

I'm now divorcing my third husband after learning that he molested my teenage daughter. I've since discovered many other lies and infidelities with many others since the very beginning of our relationship—(and I was convinced my husband was the most faithful and great guy in the world). It was a total shock. Both of my other marriages ended because of abuse and infidelity. I've always made it clear I won't stand for either, yet the degree of "how crummy can he be" got progressively worse. What am I doing that is attracting guys like this to me?

I've always placed honesty and fidelity at the top of my priorities, and thought my husband(s) did the same. I don't want this to happen again. My marriages were happy with good sexual relations between us. There were no reasons for wanting another woman. I could've done nothing different or better that would have made a difference. So, in case I ever want to get involved again, what signs should I look for in a guy? Before, if there was ever a question, I gave the benefit of the doubt. This has proven to be disastrous, yet I don't want to become a pessimist; I want to be able to trust that the person I give my heart and soul to will be honorable.

Where do you draw that line? How do you know when to and when not to trust the person you love and who proclaims to have your best interests in mind? Finding trust again will be difficult at best, and I don't know that I could take anything like this again.

Dear Reader,

This is a startling example of how people can *appear* to be one way and actually be completely different. It's understandable that the writer of this letter feels she is "attracting guys like this," and wants to know "what signs to look for..." However, she's already answered her own questions by saying: "I gave the benefit of the doubt" and "I don't want to become a pessimist." It's as if she believes that *wishing* will make it so. However, "failing to always give the benefit of the doubt" is not being a pessimist. It's being a realist.

Unfortunately, the world today is a place where we need to be especially vigilant when it comes to protecting children. And, frankly, while this got the least amount of attention in the above letter, it is the far more serious issue. Extramarital affairs are extremely prevalent and there can be many reasons why an otherwise reasonable person might have an affair. But this is not true of "molesting" a teenage stepdaughter; *no* reasonable person would do this. (An obvious way of seeing this distinction is the fact that child sexual abuse is *illegal*, whereas an extramarital affair, while painful, is not against the law.)

Of course, far beyond the legal aspects are the *human* aspects of the damage of sexual abuse to a teenager. So as for the question of "knowing when to and when not to trust the person you love:" when it comes to protecting children, there should never be blind trust. This is a lesson (whether related to child sexual abuse or to extramarital affairs) that is often only learned the hard way, but it's critical to understand that trust should come only with trustworthy behavior.

* * * * * * * * * * * *

Abusing me and cheating

Dear Peggy,

After 6-1/2 years of marriage my husband began an affair with a coworker and voluntarily told me about it. For the following eight months I lived in what I would call nothing other than hell. He refused to stop the affair, he refused to leave our home, he threatened me and my life if I were to leave with our child. He became physically abusive towards me and the emotional abuse was also extremely painful. His girlfriend (mother of 4 who left her husband for mine) became pregnant with my husband's child; he forced her to have an abortion. After he attacked me for the third time (had to go to hospital), I filed charges against him and he was removed from our home.

I filed for divorce and it will probably be finalized around the holidays. My questions are these: Why would a man (while he was abusing me and cheating) claim he still loved me? Why would a man risk everything (as though nothing would ever really be lost) for someone that he also claimed to love but would never marry, live with or even commit to? (probably mostly due the fact that he really doesn't at all like other people's children). Can you possibly explain this man to me, because I've been married to him now for a total of eight years, and just maybe before the divorce is final I can gain some kind of understanding as to what kind of person I said "I do" to.

Dear Reader,

While the question relates to trying to *understand* this person, my initial reaction is to be far more concerned about being *protected* from this person. I certainly can't analyze the psyche of the abuser, but I very much hope this woman (and any others in this situation) will seek out any and all sources of support and help in avoiding physical abuse. While the woman who wrote this letter has taken the important step of getting a divorce, there still needs to be great caution in dealing with such a person.

I do understand her need to have someone explain his behavior (because there's a normal desire to make sense of all this); but there's no good "explanation" for a physically abusive person. I will, however, try to address the general issue of how a person can "claim he still loved me...and risk everything." It's part of an elaborate rationalization process that allows someone to justify in their own mind that they have a "right" to have whatever they want—and that there's no risk (meaning there will be no consequences). Trying

275

to make sense of something like this is a fruitless endeavor—because it simply makes no sense. However, it's quite common among people having affairs. They simply ignore or deny the potential consequences of what they're doing and have a strange sense of what it means to "love" someone.

*   *   *   *   *   *   *   *   *   *   *   *

Cheating Dead Husband

Dear Peggy:

I am a thirty-something woman who was married for 20 years until my husband passed away suddenly a few months ago. My husband was the "love of my life." He was an excellent father and good husband (or so I thought).

While going through some of his personal belongings, I discovered that he was having an affair. I am not sure when this affair occurred or if it had ever ended. The woman he was having the affair with worked with him. She is also married. When he passed away, she was very helpful during the wake and the funeral regarding work issues and personal matters. She was actually trying to be my friend.

I cannot begin to explain how devastated I am about this affair. I really had no clue that this was going on. There was never any indication that we had a problem in our marriage. Our sex life was still very active. I just don't understand what could have happened and have no way of finding out how it could have happened with him being gone and not being able to talk to me.

I have so much anger and hurt about this affair that I feel that because I cannot confront my husband, I must confront this other woman. I also believe her husband should know. I feel very vindictive (which is not like me). I know that if I told her boss about this affair that she would be demoted (at the very least). The company that she and my husband worked for does not condone this behavior and it is prohibited. I know that wanting to "blow her in" is because of my anger, but I seem to be losing control of what is considered practical thinking. My grief support counselors have told me not to confront her, but I cannot get myself together because I feel that I should. They have also asked me if I think the husband deserves to be hurt. I think he should know what type of woman he is living with.

What do you think? Can you help me shed some light on this? Is there anyone out there with the same problem? I am really at a loss on how this could have happened? Any insight is welcome.

Dear Reader,

It's a very normal human desire to bring some kind of closure to significant events in our lives. And certainly, grieving the death of a spouse is compounded by the unfinished business expressed by the statement: "I...have no way of finding out how it could have happened with him being gone and not being able to talk to me." This desire to find out why an affair happened is almost universal, and unfortunately, many people never fully come to an understanding of "why"—even if their spouse is alive and willing to try to talk about it. (Often, however, there is not a willingness to try to explain *why*, so this feeling of being unfinished is not exclusive to the situation described above.)

While this particular situation is too complicated and too serious to be responsibly addressed in a brief response, everyone can learn something by noting some of the key elements in this situation. For instance, it sounds like there's good support/help in that there's mention of grief support counselors. And, based on my own experience through the years, their advice about not telling the husband of the other woman is wise counsel. Most people who struggle with this particular issue convince themselves that they're telling "for the good of the other spouse," but there's an underlying awareness that it's mostly vindictive. And it almost never provides any relief to the person doing the exposing; in fact, it often makes them feel worse about themselves and about the situation.

The same is true for exposing the other woman in order to bring punishment to her. While it's understandable to feel it's not fair for her to go unpunished, it's also unwise to think that her punishment will change anything for the better. Of course, privately confronting the other woman is a reasonable action to take, especially if there will be any further contact. If, on the other hand, there's never any reason to have contact with her in the future, that might make a difference. I've known many people who have confronted the third party; sometimes it works out well—while other times it makes things even worse. This is a decision each person must make for themselves, knowing that they cannot predict the outcome.

One other common problem is allowing a significant negative fact like this to wipe out all the good things about their spouse. Most people have both some good and some bad qualities/behaviors—and even having an affair doesn't erase the fact that they *also* may have been "an excellent father and good husband." As for the confusion based on the feeling that "there was never any indication that we had a problem in our marriage"—as strange as it may seem, an affair does not necessarily have anything to do with whether or not the marriage has any serious problems. Most of us have assumed that our husband wouldn't have an affair if we had a *good* marriage, but many men (like my own husband) simply valued *both*—the good marriage and having affairs.

So as difficult and devastating as it is to learn that your marriage was not the way you believed it to be, it's helpful to remind yourself (over and over) that the new *bad* information does not negate all the *good* that was also part of your life together. It's when we re-write the script of our lives in light of the new information, completely deleting all the good parts, that life becomes more difficult to bear. We can make it even worse—or we can save whatever parts may give us comfort. We can only hope that time and perspective will ease some of the pain for those who face such a difficult time.

P.S. While I don't know whether or not it was based on a true story, there was a movie some years ago that described a situation almost precisely like the one above. The title had to do with "Friends" (perhaps "Between Friends"). Anyway, I think it starred Mary Tyler Moore, Christine Lahti, and Ted Danson. I recall that it depicted a remarkable coming together of these two women following the death of the husband/lover. It was probably far too much of a Hollywood treatment to be realistic, but it might provide some different ways of thinking about this kind of situation.

* * * * * * * * * * * *

Death adds to confusion
(Here are 2 letters before my response.)

Dear Peggy, (letter #1)
My husband has been visiting, late at night, a woman whom I thought was a friend of mine, although she knew him before I met her. Anyway, I have believed in this man for 14 years, but when I found his car at her home at 1:30 a.m., it devastated me.

I still question him about this and all we end up doing is fighting. Another problem is that we have recently lost our only daughter to Leukemia. She was only 6 years old when she died. This has been such a strain on all of us and I know my husband blames me for it. He thought she should go have more chemo and I said no, it wouldn't do any good; so we all went to Disneyland instead of chasing after more treatments.

Dear Peggy, (letter #2)
I have been involved with my best friend's husband, not sexually though!! I recently lost my only sibling to a tragic death. He has been the only person who has been there for me and I/we have fallen in love. We are both going through a divorce as we speak.

My obvious issue pertains to my girlfriend!! We have been friends for 15 years. I never thought I would ever do something like this. He and I have discussed moving in together after both of our divorces are final. But I hate to imagine the pain that will cause her!! I am so confused—I am prepared to lose her friendship. Is it right, though?

He has been my salvation through my grieving and I need that so much right now!! I have always liked him even before the death of my sibling. Therefore, I know it is not just because of that!! Can you help such a lost person???

Dear Reader,
These letters both describe a situation where an affair seems to be related to the difficulty of dealing with the death of a significant person. While the reason for an affair is never as simple as being caused by one single event, there is, nevertheless, almost certainly an impact on the situation by virtue of the emotions involved in grieving the death of a loved one.

While the circumstances are different in the two situations described above, the common thread is that in both instances someone went outside the marriage to find comfort in dealing with their grief. It's important to understand that

278

sharing strong emotions with *anyone* creates a special bond—so whatever feelings existed toward the other person were no doubt strengthened by sharing this vulnerable feeling of pain and grief with them.

We might ask why this sharing wasn't done within the primary relationship. But sometimes it's easier to share our pain with someone other than the person with whom we have other issues, based on years of sharing the daily problems of marriage and family. Sharing with a new person doesn't involve integrating the feelings into whatever other residual feelings exist due to dealing with previous difficulties.

So while the new connection may not be based *only* on the comfort and support offered during the grieving process, this certainly plays a large part in the attraction and the connection to this other person. And once that grieving process (and its impact) have subsided somewhat, the same connection is unlikely to continue—because the connection is forged through an unusual situation, not based on normal daily functioning.

Unless and until a relationship is based on a *normalized* situation, there's no accurate way to judge just what it means. The only fairly certain thing about an affair under these circumstances is that it is more connected to trying to escape the pain and grief from the death than to choosing one person over another.

Recognizing the nature of the new connection, however, does not diminish its power to disrupt (and potentially to break) the primary relationship. This understanding may make it easier to handle the feelings related to the situation and make it possible to be more effective in dealing with it.

* * * * * * * * * * * * *

Lover's wife just died

Dear Peggy,

Have been having an affair for the last 8 years The gentleman I've been having this affair with just lost his wife unexpectedly from an auto accident. He lost her and I feel like I lost him; we both have such an overwhelming feel of guilt but still have a sense of needing to stay in contact with one another. How can I get past this horrible pain I keep feeling inside? It is always in the back of my mind; it's hard to eat, sleep, even enjoy everyday activities. Do you have any advice? I feel like I'm the widow...

Dear Reader,

This situation is typical of the totally unpredictable twists and turns that can happen in the course of having an affair. The feelings described above are obviously very deep, very painful—and very unexpected, which makes them all the more difficult to deal with.

No matter what issues we are dealing with in our lives, most of them get trumped by a *death*, especially an unexpected death. So there's sure to be some confusion in trying to deal with the new feelings related to the death—while continuing to experience the strong feelings of attachment to the man with whom she's having the affair. (Frankly, it would be much more disturbing if there were a *failure* to feel this kind of conflict.)

Many of the issues that arise when we deal with a person's death are related to feelings of guilt—regardless of whether it has anything to do with affairs. We usually feel regret about things undone or things unsaid, feeling unfinished and in limbo. It's as if all the balls are thrown up in the air and we're waiting to see how they'll land. In most such instances, this process (however uncomfortable it may be) simply takes time. This means there's unlikely to be a quick resolution to the poignant question: "How can I get past this horrible pain I keep feeling inside?"

There's probably no specific action that can remove this kind of pain. It's a matter of surviving it, not eliminating it. It also can't be ignored, can't be gone around, and can't be buried; it has a life of it's own and simply needs to be gotten through. It will be difficult for everyone involved, but honestly acknowledging the conflicting feelings (as in the above letter) is a good beginning. Then it might help just to accept the situation and try to be as patient as possible while recovering from the shock of these difficult circumstances.

* * * * * * * * * * * * *

Long-term Affairs

Dear Peggy,

What would make two "happily married" people (in this case both parties are in committed relationships) remain in a long term affair, i.e. seven years or more, with each other? These two people actually support each other's marriage. They speak often by telephone but only get together for passionate times occasionally, perhaps once a month or sometimes less depending on their busy schedules. They are both professionals. Apparently, they are both aware that this is a fantasy relationship, referring to each other as a breath of fresh air. Neither party wants to end their marriage; they both love their spouses and families. They keep each other abreast of their work schedules (both in and out of town), family events, vacations, etc., and there seems to be no end to the relationship.

Is this love, albeit a different kind of love? If not, what keeps this affair intact? I look forward to your response.

Dear Reader,

I hesitated to respond to this letter since the writer didn't indicate whether they are one of the parties involved in the affair, whether their spouse is one of the parties, or whether it's someone else. However, it raises the question of close emotional attachments with someone of the opposite sex outside the marital relationship—which is an issue for many people. The fact that this couple "get together for passionate times occasionally" certainly takes it beyond just an emotional connection and makes it a sexual connection as well. But I'll try to address the emotional attachment aspect of this relationship, a subject I've addressed before.

When someone has a "good marriage," yet still develops this kind of strong attachment outside the marriage, it usually indicates an effort to "have the best of both worlds"—in that they value the marriage and the sense of belonging but also value the freedom to relate closely to someone else with whom they don't share the burdens and responsibilities of daily life: kids, finances, etc. It's often easy to candidly share details with someone whose life will not be affected by the decisions you make in the way that your spouse is affected. (Since the friend will suffer no direct ramifications of choices or decisions, they are free to simply support the person in whatever they want to do.) Whether or not this connection can be called love, it is clearly valued because of its supportive nature.

However, this is basically a self-centered way of dealing with life: making it easier on yourself at someone else's (the spouse's) expense—and ultimately at your own expense, in that this kind of "having it all" attitude can't usually be sustained over time without serious repercussions. So while they may say they "support each other's marriage," that's just a convenient rationalization. Their actions speak louder than their words, indicating that they're actually supporting each other personally, not "the marriage."

* * * * * * * * * * *

Confusion about Feelings for Ex

Dear Peggy,

I am in a state of utter confusion and maybe you can help me out. I am married 30 years, and have been separated 2-1/2 years because my husband had an affair—which has resulted in his girlfriend having his baby 8 months ago. They do live together but it doesn't look like it will be for much longer. I thought we had a good marriage and he had a mid-life crisis and the affair happened. When I found out about it and confronted him, I got the usual story, "It's not you, it's me, I love you, I don't know why, I need my space."

Somehow we have managed to remain close friends, and I still love him, although I'm not in love with him anymore. It's taken 2-1/2 years to get myself "healthy" again. I enjoy his company and friendship but I'm now feeling like I have the best of both worlds. I see him when I want to (no sex involved) and then I get to go to my own home and do my own thing without having to consider anyone else. Is this wrong?

What confuses me is that I feel so sorry for him; he has made a mess of every aspect of his life and has no happiness anymore. After all that he has done and all the pain that I've gone through, how can I care about his happiness? It hurts me to see him so depressed and unhappy. Am I nuts to worry about Him?

Dear Reader,

There is noting *nuts* about being a thoughtful, responsible, loving person who can still feel empathy for the pain of others, even under circumstances such as this. This kind of attitude only becomes a problem if someone lets it somehow interfere with their willingness to take care of themselves. There is certainly nothing wrong with enjoying life and being healthy again. (An important part of staying healthy is the "no sex involved" part of this situation.)

I've seen this kind of empathy before, often when the ex-spouse has faced some serious consequence such as having a pregnancy result from the affair. It's somehow easier to feel empathy for someone who is suffering due to the consequences of their own actions—rather than through anything you did to make them suffer. It's when people seem to have avoided paying any price for their actions that there's more likely to be feelings of vengeance. And, of course, it's far preferable to have feelings of empathy rather than revenge. At the same time, it's also important to go on with life and not be unduly controlled by any intense feelings about the ex-spouse, even positive ones.

* * * * * * * * * * * * *

Very bizarre

Dear Peggy,

A man is in love with me...he just got a divorce...he is very emotionally involved, but since the divorce (past 4 months) he feels very alone, and I can never spend enough time with him because I have a life that needs to be lived. His wife lived life through him the whole marriage. He knows that she is stupid and lacks a lot of common sense.

Here's what happened...we became very close. He tells me he doesn't love her anymore, but that he could never hate her...and he still has feelings for her. He then feels so lonely one night when I couldn't be there that he had his ex-wife spend the night. They had sex and began to get along a little better. I judged him. He says that I have a very powerful effect on him. He says I am his soul-mate and that I make him feel the way nobody ever has before and wants to spend the rest of his life with me... We are perfect for each other...we know it, and his wife doesn't even have a problem with it! She just says whatever makes him happy. After he had sex the first time after they separated, she stayed until they fought non-stop, then she'd go back to her apartment. Then his loneliness would overcome him and they'd have sex again. He still loves her, but isn't in love with her and still wants to only be with me. He says the voice inside his soul tells him and he's soooo emotionally attracted to me that he can't do anything about it. I'm not ready for a sexual relationship either yet; so we did a lot of fooling around, but no sex.

He always knew what he wanted up until a few weeks ago. I came back from a trip...I had planned on spending a lot of time with him. But he was so hurt that I didn't right away, that within five days of my arrival he had sex with his ex again, and she has been living there for the last two weeks and will be until he's decided what he wants. He now says he's in love with her, but still in love with me. I have no one to go to when I feel lonely and I am very hurt and betrayed by all of this. He said his counselor told him not to get so emotionally involved. He's trying, but then he has his ex staying with him and she is still living her life through him. As far as I know, we both feel that I am his soul-mate, but I've received enough heartache and want to know what I should do. Should I tell him to go to hell? Should I wait longer? What I don't think is fair is that his ex, whom he is now "in love" with, is spending all the time with him and I'm just sitting here. He doesn't talk to me anymore, I never really know what is going on. He has what he wants all figured out except for the relationship he wants. He's thinking that maybe the feelings he has for both of us will never go away, but then how on earth can a person live like that. He doesn't even trust his ex. He trusts me!!!! What is up with him?

He says that he and his ex still have a relationship... He says it's weird, but I (along with many others) think that it is purely sexual, and it has to come to a stop because sex won't solve any of his problems... What should happen? What will happen? What can be done? What should I do in the mean time? Very hurt.

Dear Reader,

This very long letter is printed in its entirety to demonstrate how much confusion can develop in these kinds of situations. If this person could step back and take an objective look at what is being described, there would be no need to write a letter asking "What can be done?" I dare say anyone reading this letter would *hope* that she would decide to extricate herself from this situation—and the sooner the better.

A smarter, safer attitude toward this situation would probably involve *not* trying to figure out who he loves or who he trusts or what he'll do. It could take quite a long time for him to figure out what he wants, so sitting around waiting for him to decide "what he wants" is probably a losing proposition.

I would also question the opening statement, "a man is in love with me." This is not the way someone behaves toward someone they love. So this might be a starting point for finding the strength to walk away unless and until his words and actions are more coherent. Finally, anyone who has been divorced for only 4 months (as described here) is seldom in any condition to make a responsible choice about future love relationships.

So there's really little use in trying to figure out someone who is in no condition to think straight. When they don't even understand themselves, there's little chance that someone else will understand them. The very question about "what to do in the meantime" implies a belief that there will soon be a definitive clarity to this situation—which is unlikely. The more reasonable question is "how can I get on with my life?"

* * * * * * * * * * * * *

Alcoholism and/or affair

Dear Peggy,

My husband of 18 years has always been a "partier"—he plays softball and goes out drinking afterward. Five years ago, he began his own company and has in the past year achieved a lot of success. He has a lot of money to burn now, and in addition to softball nights, has begun going out after work frequently. He often comes home as late at 2:30-3:30 a.m., and not come home at all twice. Two of these late evenings occurred immediately after recent out-of-town trips with me (during which he did not drink excessively.) A recent life insurance health screen showed elevated liver enzymes. Since then, I have been asking him to go to a doctor and/or consider treatment. He refuses to do either.

He moved out last Friday, saying that we were both unhappy. He refuses to get marriage counseling. In retrospect, there are signs of an affair. He went to extreme lengths to make sure I did not ever go out with him in the town where he has his business and does much of his drinking. On one occasion when I showed up at a bar where he was drinking with his ball team, a friend of his rushed ahead of me to tell him I was coming in. He seemed very startled but then treated me nicely. I saw no women with the ball team, but the bar is a "meat market," and later other members of the team who are single were dancing.

He has trouble maintaining an erection when we make love, a situation which has grown progressively worse for over a year now. He claims that he still loves me, that he is not having an affair, but needs his space and wants to just work and play ball this summer, and not have me on his case. He has made some statements that are classic midlife crises kinds of statements: "his life is passing him by..."

I believe that he is an alcoholic and that if there is an affair, it's with someone who is willing and available to drink with him. I am hurt and confused; my children are too. I believe the primary issue we have to deal with is alcoholism, but in your experience do men who are "protecting" their drinking display behavior similar to a man hiding an affair? Do you think it's likely that he is having an affair? Should I take measures to find out, or concentrate on the alcohol situation and assume that if that's resolved, he will discontinue such a relationship?

Thank you for your response. We are in touch with Al-Anon and other professional organizations as well, but this aspect is something that keeps eating at me.

Dear Reader,

There is often a correlation between drinking and having affairs—although it is not necessarily a "cause-and-effect" situation. For instance, my husband was *not* an alcoholic, but there *was* a relationship between his drinking and having affairs. Both were part of a pattern of rationalization that it "wouldn't do any harm." So the drinking was simply part of the lifestyle that included having affairs—since he was more comfortable "chasing" (as he called it) when he'd had some drinks. As a consequence, once he told me about his affairs, he also decided to stop drinking. (This was a way of breaking the whole lifestyle behavior that he had been engaging in.) While he didn't drink anything at all for several years, he did eventually resume very moderate drinking—but did not resume having affairs. So while the two issues coexisted, there was never a direct cause and effect between the two.

As for other direct relationships between drinking and affairs (like whether or not hiding the drinking and hiding affairs are related), certainly the deceptive behavior is similar. In both instances, there's an effort to "put on a front" of behaving one way while in fact behaving in a different way. Again, this does not necessarily represent a cause and effect; it may simply represent similar ways of rationalizing behavior.

Of course, until there's clear evidence or admission, there's no way to know whether an affair is actually taking place. But regardless of whether or not there is an affair, whenever there is a situation as described above, there are surely some serious issues that need to be addressed. On one hand, it might be helpful to try to get some sense of priority as to which are the *greater* concerns amidst all the possibilities: the health issues, the mid-life crisis, the possibility of an affair, or the alcoholism.

On the other hand, there may be no clear 1, 2, 3 priority; it may be a general breakdown of the connection that allows a couple to know what's really going on in each other's lives. Addressing that overarching issue may be a good first step—since there's little likelihood of having an impact on any of the various issues without improving the ability to relate in a more honest way. Couples often get to the point of engaging in "satellite" conversation (where they're not talking *directly* about what's going on; they just send out *signals*). The more clear and direct the communication, the more likelihood of finding a way to improve the situation.

* * * * * * * * * * * *

More attractive after marriage

Dear Peggy,

I am a 37-year-old male who just felt he was getting old; I recovered from a heart attack that I felt was the end. Then I met my young and beautiful wife and was quite startled when she told me she was in love with me. She is a wonderful woman and we were friends for 2 years, but I don't know where I was at the time. A lot of things were happening so fast, and people were giving me fair warning that I had finally reached the plateau where I could have anything I wanted. Being lonely, I chose her. It was not a god-awful choice, but since then I have had more women than ever walk up to me and be blatant about sleeping with me and all the things they could do for me. I am not terribly handsome, but all these women are on me like never in my life. I haven't even done anything and I'm feeling guilty. Am I a dog for finding other women attractive—or better yet, how do I control those come-ons, especially when they're handing me their phone number and addresses.

I went to a 50th anniversary celebration, and I promised my wife that I would make our marriage that strong to survive a 50th—but the truth is, I care about my wife but I don't love her like I should. I feel she's the one in love and I'm trapped in this marriage where I feel disgust at even taking her to bed. She's beautiful, any man would be proud, but she was a friend and I crossed the line.

And there were circumstances that pushed her towards me so fast that it didn't give me enough time to date her: her Mother (need I say more). Sorry for the novella... Thanks.

Dear Reader,

Many of the dilemmas discussed in this letter are ones that people wake up to later, after they're married. First of all, too often people enter marriage for all the wrong reasons. Far more prevalent is the situation where someone falls head-over-heels and gets married on that basis. But occasionally (as above) someone *doesn't* feel sexual chemistry with the other person, but *decides* to marry anyway. Either of these is likely to lead to problems. The best chance of actually making it to a 50th anniversary is to enter marriage with *both*: feeling the sexual chemistry *and* feeling your partner is a friend. (Personally, I think that's what has seen us through 44 years of marriage so far; we were friends and we were truly attracted to each other.)

Having said that, it's not to say that either aspect without the other is doomed to failure. For many years, "arranged" marriages (where the partners didn't even *meet* until the wedding) worked out quite well. Similarly, some marriages, that begin only because of sexual attraction, develop into a deeper connection so that they become true friends.

No matter how someone initially enters marriage, the best path to finding how/whether to continue it (successfully) is to develop as much honesty as possible. This does *not* mean frank, brutal, hurtful honesty; it means carefully, thoughtfully sharing more and more about their deepest hopes, fears, desires, etc. In the final analysis, this is the primary way a couple either draws closer together or moves further apart. The degree to which they share their *real* selves primarily determines the kind of relationship that is possible. Any relationship based on wearing masks and hiding your true feelings has very little chance of success.

As for having other women find a man more attractive when he's married, that may have very little to do with the man per se. It usually has more to do with the fact that being unattainable or being safe (in that less will be expected from a woman if the man is already married) is appealing to some women who really don't want more. It says nothing about whether these other women would be available for marriage (or even a long-term relationship) if the man *were* available.

On the other hand, finding other women attractive does not make someone a "dog;" it just makes them normal. However, *acting* on the attractions is a totally different matter. If a couple develop the kind of honest communication that every marriage deserves, they will avoid the deception inherent in secretly acting on attractions. If someone truly wants to avoid "hurting their partner, they will recognize the hurt involved in secrecy as much as the hurt involved in sharing more of their true feelings with each other.

It's especially common to second-guess a decision that doesn't feel like it was our own decision, that someone else pushed it on us. But that doesn't mean we can't still re-think the entire situation and determine that (perhaps) we would have made the same decision even if we hadn't been pushed. So everyone needs to take responsibility for whatever actions they take in their lives—both in the past and especially in the future. Overcoming the tendency to feel like a "victim of circumstances" makes it much more likely that this will be possible.

* * * * * * * * * * * *

Separation, one year

Dear Peggy,

I am a single parent of two teenagers...a few months ago I met a very nice man my age...we have a wonderful relationship, however the distance of the two hours seems not to be the problem... Rather, he has been separated from his wife for over one year...he lives in an apartment while she kept the house, they also share joint full care of their young child of 8 years old...

We are both in love, have a nice relationship; however, he has not yet filed for divorce... When I ask him why this has not happened, he tells me that it is a money issue, revolving around finances for the future, as in retirement, and that his wife would come out in a better position... When I ask him what he would like to see happen, he wants definitely to file for divorce, divide up the property, seek what is best for his son, and have a life in the future with me.

My main question is: I am not worried that he will return to her at any point, but I really don't want to wait for 2-3 years until he decides to get his legal work resolved... I don't want to tell him that I will not see him, but I do want to assert myself and tell him that he needs to do what is best in his and his child's best interest.

He is a very caring and decent man. I really worry that if I say something, I may upset the potential in the relationship...yet this procrastination is upsetting me in the last few weeks. Also we have a distance of two hours between us...which is also a concern. Thanks for listening...I don't know what to do.

Dear Reader,

This is a very thoughtful letter, providing a clear description of a difficult situation. As with many letters, I find that people often already know what is best; they just need reinforcement or encouragement to trust themselves to do it.

For instance, it sounds reasonable "to assert myself and tell him" based on the description of him as "...a very caring and decent man." If someone really is caring, they want to know when they're behavior is distressing to someone they care about. And if sharing that distress triggers a negative response, that's information that needs to be known—because it brings into question the degree of caring in the first place.

Also, an essential aspect of a close, meaningful relationship is being able to share real feelings. Feeling afraid to "say something that may upset the potential in the relationship" is a sign of a bigger problem than the one being addressed.

Actually, even if they initially succeed in realizing the potential in the relationship, that's just the first step; then come the many years of *sustaining* the relationship. And sustaining a good relationship over time requires being able to talk about deep feelings.

So it's important to be able to talk about deeply-held feelings and to honestly share your concerns. Just waiting (and hoping) that things work out allows all kinds of delays, procrastinations, rationalizations, etc., to be acted out. It's important to bring more clarity to whether delays are based on an *inability* to act or an *unwillingness* to act. For instance, the "2-3 years" mentioned above does not reveal whether it's due to waiting for everything to be optimum (just to minimize tradeoffs or inconveniences) or whether it's really essential. While some reasons for delays may be necessary, some probably are not. And the bottom line is that a person's actions usually reflect their real priorities.

23: Learnings from Affairs

Affair was expensive lesson

Dear Peggy,

My affair ended one year ago...the biggest mistake in my life. I've hurt so many people, I live with this every day. And my husband reminds me of it every morning, when I look down at the resetable odometer and it is on 0. I feel like a prisoner in my own home... I can't go anywhere without him. My kids...they don't know about what I did....and I'm too ashamed to tell them...

We are in counseling...but it's been interrupted by "little league season." That's where it all started...at the little league field, and now the rumors continue to fly at the field about what happened. My husband hears them and then the nightmare begins all over for me...the endless questioning. My life is a disaster...some days are just so hard to get through...I want everything to get better...just forget it all, but I know it is impossible for my husband to forget. I've done everything he has asked of me, even giving up my dreams of going to school to be a teacher. This is the most expensive lesson in life I will ever learn.

Dear Reader,

This letter clearly illustrates some of the consequences that can come from an affair. It's a gripping description of the life-altering nature of this experience—for everyone involved. We're more aware of the impact on the spouse because there's seldom much attention paid to the potential impact on the person who had the affair. All too often people tend to think that if the marriage survives, then that's a good outcome. However, it's much more complicated than that.

Whether or not a person (regardless of which role they play) fully recovers from the impact of this experience does not depend on whether they stay married or get a divorce. It has more to do with whether they devote the time and effort involved in overcoming the emotional impact.

Recovery involves:
1. Accepting the fact that it happened.
   This doesn't mean "liking" it; it just means giving up the "if only..." and facing the reality.
2. Understanding that affairs are not due *only* to "personal failure."
   It's a mistake to think that "bad" people have affairs and "good" people don't. In fact, anyone is vulnerable and no one is immune.
3. Allowing time to heal.
   Time alone won't do it, but healing doesn't happen quickly.
4. Deliberately focusing on dealing with it.

It can't be avoided, so face it head-on.
5. Believing it's *possible* to recover.
   This is critical—for both partners.

* * * * * * * * * * * * *

The Impact of Secrecy

Dear Peggy,

Since extramarital affairs are taboo, they are not talked about; and the secrecy, I think, fuels the fire. I was on the verge of an affair...via the Internet...but have decided the price is too high...way, way too high. Unfortunately, so many people think they can get away with it, but the marriage suffers regardless, I would assume.

I don't know why I feel personally like having an affair. I feel I can handle two loves in my life, but if my husband would, I would feel betrayed and hurt. That's why I won't. Keep the lines of communication open!!

Dear Reader,

These thoughts and awarenesses usually come only after an affair has happened, when a person learns firsthand about the true impact of the secrecy of having an affair. It's refreshing to hear someone being able to think this clearly prior to learning it the hard way.

Another point in this letter that is well-taken is that many people might rationalize that it's all right for them to have an affair, but not for their partner to have one. Since very few people are prepared to have a sexually open marriage, few affairs would happen if there were no secrecy. This is where secrecy has the most impact of all.

Here's a partial list of some of the effects of Secrecy:

—It adds to the excitement of having affairs.

—It leads those having affairs to assume they won't get caught.

—It leads those who suspect an affair to be alone with their anxiety.

—It leads those who learn of a partner's affair to be alone with their pain.

—It contributes to feelings of shame by the partner who did *not* have an affair.

—The *secret* creates emotional distance even if the affair is never discovered.

—It perpetuates the hypocrisy in society as a whole in that the secrecy allows us to pretend we're a monogamous society, leaving each couple to think they are unusual in failing to be monogamous—which makes recovery more difficult, whether or not they stay together.

* * * * * * * * * * * * *

My Affair/Myself

Dear Peggy,

About 3 months ago I had a very passionate affair. I could not stand everyone knowing but my wife, so I told her. We have spoken in detail about it. I have not seen or communicated with the person since telling my wife. My wife says that she understands why I did it: her job, our kids, I was the last one on the list of love... She has also assured me that she forgives me and loves me very much. *This statement is proven everyday by both of us. My problem is I can hardly look her in the eye, let alone look at my own face in the mirror. She whom I have hurt so much forgives me. But it seems I am the real loser as I can't forgive myself. If you have any ideas or directions for me, I would be very grateful. Thank you for your time.*

Dear Reader,

Many people who have had affairs and whose spouse has not reacted in the way described in this letter would feel this man was very fortunate. However, it's clear that he doesn't *feel* fortunate. Actually, in some ways it creates a challenge, albeit a different kind of challenge, in dealing with a situation like this. (It's sometimes easier to feel justified in defending yourself when your spouse tells you what a terrible person you are.) But when you get love in the face of the hurt that has been caused, you may feel unworthy. In the above letter, both the feelings of unworthiness and the initial desire to tell his wife because he "couldn't stand everyone knowing but her" indicate a commitment to fairness and equality—which is a rare and valuable quality in a marital relationship.

One factor that might help offset some of the negative feelings is to deliberately focus on these qualities of fairness and equality, which are certainly admirable. Another factor that might soften the internal criticism is recognizing the gift of honesty indicated by the statement, "we have spoken in detail about it." A willingness to talk and to answer questions the spouse might have about the affair is one of the most critical factors in a person's ability to recover. Not withholding this kind of information also indicates a commitment to fairness and equality in the relationship.

So while no couple would rationally *choose* to go through this kind of pain in order to achieve a closer, more honest and more committed relationship, that can, in fact, be the result. Nothing can be done at this point to change the past, but the opportunity to use this crisis to forge a stronger relationship for the future can mean that something good can be built from this bad experience. Focusing on the ways in which this experience can be used to create that better future together is a good way to begin putting things in perspective and once again looking in the mirror with some pride.

* * * * * * * * * * * * *

Want to be Forgiven

Dear Peggy,

I need some guidance. I had an affair about 4 years ago. I was very mean and hateful towards my husband, and my family stuck by my side and angered him even more. We had 3 children at the time, and although they were young, they were involved also. I finally got my head on straight and came back to my husband and family. It has been a long battle, and I understand that he is angry and has every right to be, but I want to know what I have to do to get him through the depression, hurt, pain etc.

Even though it has been 4 years, he is still very depressed and angry. He says he has no hope for the future and lives day to day. I have tried to find information to help guide us through the stages of forgiveness, but there isn't that much help out there for this type of thing. (It surprises me too, as prominent as it appears to be in society.) Any info that you can give me would be of great help. Like I said, I realize that I have made a grave error in judgment and only want to be forgiven and to get on with our lives.

Dear Reader,

Most people involved in this kind of situation want closure—and feel that *forgiveness* can bring the kind of closure that allows them to "get on with our lives." Usually when this much time has passed and there's still depression and anger that stands in the way of forgiveness, it's because the couple has tried to put the affair behind them and go on without fully dealing with it. Any time this issue is set aside without thoroughly discussing it and getting as much understanding as possible, the emotions do not get thoroughly dealt with—and the depression and anger can continue indefinitely.

It's not enough for someone to say they're sorry for their actions or to make promises about the future. It takes concrete answers that can only come when all aspects of this situation are fully explored and dealt with. Any effort at forgiveness without having fully addressed the whole situation is usually an empty forgiveness. Only when people gain information, understanding, and perspective (about the issue of affairs in general and about their own experience in particular) are they prepared to overcome the depression and anger and truly forgive.

* * * * * * * * * * * *

Long-term relationship
(Here are two letters before my response.)

Dear Peggy, (letter #1)

I am in desperate need of direction. I have been involved with a married man for over 10 years; I was divorced at the time we met. I used to think it was enough to just be able to love someone and have that loved returned. Over the years I have developed the sense of coping with the situation by working endlessly and isolating myself from family and not letting friends in. Now that I am getting older, I realize that I want more for myself. I want to be able to share things with someone. I want to grow old with someone. I love the man I have been seeing. He won't leave his wife and I haven't made him make any decisions. I don't want to hurt him and I can't imagine my life without him. How can I be strong?

Dear Peggy, (letter #2)

How can you manage to get over things like a female that has been in my life for years and she is not my wife? I can't get over her, but I can't leave my wife... I love my wife, but that woman is so much in my life that I can't get her out of my life even if I want to. I feel that she has a magic or something; all I know is this is killing me, and I know that the end is not good. I have a 3-year-old and I love him, but I feel that she has a strong hold on me. I wish I could let go, but too much memory and pain. I feel that I destroyed everybody's life: son, wife, and that woman; and that's killing me...

Dear Reader,

These two letters were *not* describing two sides of the same relationship. (There was no evidence that this man and this woman were involved with each other.) But they clearly illustrate the pain for everyone involved in this kind of long-term, secret affair. What's especially sad is that both people clearly state the sense of pain and loss involved in this kind of situation. But while they are able to intellectually understand that it is doomed, they can't seem to use their intellectual understanding to break the emotional control of their feelings.

While there's no magical way to stop the feelings, it is possible to gradually shift the power from the emotions to the intellect by repeatedly (and consistently) stopping the *involuntary* thoughts about the other person every time you begin fantasizing about or obsessively thinking about them—and *voluntarily*, deliberately begin focusing on *other* important people and aspects of life that are meaningful.

Focusing on the futility of staying in this *stuck* position (continuing to dwell on "what might have been") may help to shorten the period of time of staying in limbo. It also may help to realize that a quick, clean break is likely to be *less* painful than a long, drawn-out one. There's no way to avoid some pain, but there are smarter choices that can lessen the time that the pain continues. Once there's a final acceptance of the fact that there's no future for *anyone* in this situation, the sooner the pain can be alleviated for everyone concerned.

24: Preventing Affairs

Will he have an affair?

Dear Peggy,

I am 25 years old and married to a wonderful man 12 years older than me. I love him very much, but sometimes he worries me. Especially when it comes to other women. When we first started seeing each other, he was still friends with his last lover, which didn't bother me until they wanted to go places together without me. I put my foot down because I felt that she was still interested in him. A couple of years ago, before we were married, my neighbor's friend came over one day and I could tell she was attracted to my husband. Soon I was finding out that he was going over to her house and just "visiting" her. I'm pretty sure that nothing happened, but when asked why he was there he couldn't (or wouldn't) say.

One more thing I want to mention is that my husband had told me one time that he's been attracted to 3 or 4 other women (physically and mentally) since we've been together. I tried not to let this hurt my feelings and to just be happy knowing that he was trying to confide in me, but it did. My question is: does my husband sound like he's able to cheat, or am I being a big neurotic baby about this? And should I stop asking questions about other women when he starts talking about them because I can see sometimes that it hurts his feelings when I don't believe that he loves me? I'm almost totally sure that he's been faithful to me because that's what he tells me, but I'm scared of losing him.

Dear Reader,

This kind of thinking is common, and there's no clear answer as to whether the suspicions are justified. While no one is immune from affairs (and anyone is vulnerable or "able to cheat"), that doesn't mean they will. So blind trust is not warranted, but neither is rampant suspicion.

On one hand, when people can openly communicate about natural attractions to others, it makes it less likely that they will act on those attractions. It's when attractions are hidden away as secret fantasies that they're more likely to grow and take on a life of their own, blocking out the reality of any consequences.

On the other hand, casual comments about attractions can also be used to deliberately "throw a partner off guard" by creating a false sense of security that they're being *totally* honest, thereby providing more opportunity to pursue attractions without arousing suspicion.

Regardless of how much we might wish otherwise, monogamy is an issue that's never settled "once and for all." It requires ongoing, honest communication. This is important perspective for anyone who seriously wants to prevent an affair.

* * * * * * * * * * * * *

Insecure about his feelings

Dear Peggy,

I am a 22-year-old who has been married for 5 years. In the beginning, before we were married, things were really great. He was always happy, thoughtful, and caring. But now, its completely changed, and the past 5 years have been a slow ride in this direction. I don't understand him sometimes; I can't tell what he thinks or feels. I want to know if he still loves and cares for me the way he used to. We've talked about our relationship, as well as relationships in general. He feels that kissing another girl is not cheating, and as long as the other person does not find out, its not a problem at all. This worries me.

He occasionally goes out for a drink or two after work with the guy he carpools with; they always go to the same pool hall. I never had a problem with it until last weekend when a group of us went out to play pool at this particular pool hall, and he could not keep his eyes off of one of the waitresses. He wasn't flirting, or even talking to her, just staring at her. I mean, every time she walked through the room, he was completely enthralled in staring at her. It made me feel stupid. There I was sitting next to him, and he's paying total attention to her!

I don't think that he has ever cheated on me, but I am beginning to wonder if he has thought about it, or is thinking about it. Are there any signs that I could maybe look out for? I don't know what to do. I do love him very much. I hope that things can work for us, but the way that we've been slipping farther and farther away from each other scares me. I need to know how to turn us back in the right direction. I hope you can help.

Dear Reader,

This letter is relevant for everyone in that no one is ever absolutely positive that their partner would *never* have an affair. So the final thoughts in this letter are somewhat universal: "I don't think that he has ever cheated on me." "I am beginning to wonder if he has thought about it, or is thinking about it." "Are there any signs that I could maybe look out for?"

First of all, it's extremely important to communicate about this issue. Most people are like the person who wrote this letter in that they have all kinds of private fears that they're afraid to confront. They look for "signals" or try to find meaning in various actions (or inactions). For instance, the fact that your partner "looks" at others (or even is attracted to others) is not, in and or itself, a problem; in fact, it's natural to be attracted to others. The problem comes if the attraction is acted on. And the best way to decrease the likelihood of that happening is to honestly discuss this issue and your feelings about it on an ongoing basis. That's because attractions become a much greater threat to the relationship if it's taboo to acknowledge them. If you can't talk about these feelings, they become your own private secret and are likely to grow in intensity and desire. But openly discussing your feelings brings a degree of reality to the issue that leads to a more sensible and responsible way of thinking, which in turn reduces the desire to act on the attractions.

The bottom line is that when most couples start getting "serious," they start to feel jealous and competitive with others and they make it clear by words or actions that they don't like it when their partner looks at anyone else or admires anyone else in any way. This, of course, does not stop the interest in others; it just means the interest goes "underground" in that the person simply stops letting their partner know of their interest in others. This begins a cycle of secrecy: if you can't tell your partner when you find someone attractive, you won't tell them when you're tempted to act on that attraction, and you certainly won't tell them if and when you *do* take any action. While this should not be taken as a license to be gross or crude or embarrassing, couples do need to be able to talk candidly (and realistically) about this whole issue in order to prevent the very thing they fear.

* * * * * * * * * * * *

Is fidelity possible?

Dear Peggy,

I have been living with my boyfriend for a little over two years. I thought we had a good relationship. I very much wanted to marry him. However, I recently found out that he cheated on me with his ex-fiancée...twice. Once about five months ago, and the first time was almost a year ago. He didn't tell me about it—I overheard him telling one of his guy friends. He says that he didn't tell me because I had told him in the past that if he ever cheated on me I would leave him and that "living with the guilt was easier than living without me." He also says that he doesn't want to be with anyone other than me, that he is not in love with her, and the reason for the infidelity was "because there are aspects of the relationship that he had with her that are missing in our relationship...and that those qualities made her attractive to him, and it manifested itself in a physical way." Now, I want to know if it is possible for someone to be faithful, if they have been unfaithful in the past. And, of course, the question everyone asks...how do I trust again??

Dear Reader,

This letter reflects a very common dilemma: the idea of saying in advance that an affair would not be tolerated, then feeling trapped by that statement if there is a different feeling if/when it actually happens. In fact, no one *knows* what they will do if they discover their partner has had an affair. Almost everyone *feels* or *says* that they wouldn't stand for it—which is understandable in the abstract. But when faced with the reality, there are many other factors involved, and people don't necessarily feel the same way.

The next important issue in this letter is the idea that the *reason* for the affairs was because of "aspects in the other relationship that were missing in the marriage." If that were a legitimate reason for an affair, literally *everyone* would have an affair—because there's no such thing as a marriage where *nothing* is "missing." No one person (with their own individual personal characteristics) is going to meet *all* of the desires someone might have for their relationship.

Finally, as to whether it's "possible for someone to be faithful if they have been unfaithful in the past:" Of course, it's possible. Everything depends on whether they learned from their experience. This kind of crisis provides an opportunity to develop a marriage that is stronger than it ever was before (or than it would have been without working through such a crisis). The key to whether or not this happens depends upon committing to honesty in the future. By that I mean *responsible honesty*—which involves not withholding relevant information from each other. If people are truly honest, they're unlikely to have a secret affair, regardless of whatever temptations or desires there may be. It's the willingness to be deceptive and dishonest that leads to affairs.

(I use the term "responsible honesty" to differentiate this kind of honesty from the kind that might be blunt or brutal or hurtful. Responsible honesty is undertaken for the clear purpose of *improving* the relationship—*not* to cause hurt to anyone. The motives for honesty make a tremendous difference in the way the honesty can be received and the information can be dealt with—regardless of the specific nature of the information.)

* * * * * * * * * * * * *

Dreaming about another guy

Dear Peggy,

I met someone that I find extremely attractive but I am only married for two years. I would NEVER have an affair, but I do dream about what it would be like to have a relationship with this guy. Am I a terrible spouse?

Dear Reader,

It's normal to feel attractions to other people—no matter how much we love our spouse. It's helpful to remember that it's also natural for your partner to find others attractive. It's probably something you don't want to think about. You'd like to believe it won't happen, so you may convince yourself that somehow your relationship will be different. But understanding that attractions to others are normal and inevitable (no matter how much you love each other), can be the first step toward being able to keep them in perspective. If you see attractions as a direct threat to your love (thinking that if you and your partner love each other, neither of you would ever be attracted to anyone else), you're granting power to attractions that they would not otherwise possess.

While it seems scary at first, talking honestly about your attractions and how to deal with them actually reduces their power and effect. Talking also reduces the danger that you will actually act on your attractions. But if you try to deny the possibility of attractions, you send a subtle (or not so subtle) signal to your partner that you don't want to know about any of their feelings of attraction toward others. Since attractions are both normal and inevitable, you're in essence sending a message that says, "Lie to me; pretend you're never attracted to anyone else." This, of course, causes other problems related to honesty that can have serious consequences for your relationship.

* * * * * * * * * * * * *

Would he do it again?

Dear Peggy,

My husband had an affair. I stayed with him after this. We have an 8-week old baby girl. He was there through the whole birth. But would he do it again? I couldn't go through that again!! Should I stay? He says he wants to, but for me or for the baby? Married 6 years. Not all great !! Help.

Dear Reader,

There's no "one-time" promise or event that can guarantee monogamy; it's an ongoing process of honest communication that allows you to really "know" each other, thus not deceive each other. You can significantly increase the chances that your marriage can be monogamous by recognizing "what doesn't work" and "what is more likely to work" in preventing future affairs.

What doesn't work:

—Repeating the marriage vows doesn't prevent affairs.

—Love doesn't prevent affairs.

—Being the "perfect" partner doesn't prevent them.

—Threats don't prevent them.

—Simple promises don't prevent them.

—Getting caught doesn't prevent them.

What is most likely to work:

—Awareness that no one is immune to having an affair.

—Discussion and agreement about your commitment to monogamy.

—Regular renewal of your commitment.

—Ongoing, honest communication.

* * * * * * * * * * * * *

Husband's Online Affair

(Here are 2 letters before response.)

Dear Peggy, (letter #1)

My husband, whom I love very much, has recently had a relationship with a woman he met online. He began talking to her online just after I had a baby and was going through postpartum depression. Because the depression made me seem distant, he reached out to this woman and has continued contact with her even after I had asked him not to talk with her. Now I find he has met her in person and has had phone sex with her. I am very distraught. As more of this is uncovered, it seems there is more to the affair. At first, it was just friends. Then it was he was her shoulder, and now who knows??? Can I trust him again?

What do I need to do to change the situation? I feel as if the whole world has vanished beneath my feet. Please help!

Dear Peggy, (letter #2)
My husband just recently had an affair with an online friend. We are trying to put our marriage back together. I am working really hard on changing issues that brought him to the point of going to someone else, but I am having a very difficult time emotionally. I keep getting very angry about the whole situation to the point I feel I am losing control. It is so unfair and he won't be honest about who the affair was with. I feel I am fighting a ghost. I feel that without complete honesty, how can I ever feel secure and trust him again. The more I try to read up on information to try to help myself and my husband, the more angry I get about the whole thing—yet I don't want to just shove my emotions under the carpet and forget about them, only to have them keep resurfacing over and over again in the future. I really need help. I really love my husband and want to keep our marriage of 17 years together—not only for myself, but we have two children. I think he loves me too still, but this is so hard. What can I do to get over the anger and deep hurt of this situation?

Dear Reader,
One factor that makes it even harder to deal with the affairs (which is tough enough in and of itself) is the fact that in both cases these women are attributing the *reason* for the affairs as specific problems in their particular marriages, somehow blaming themselves for the affairs. One reader says, "Because the depression made me seem distant, he reached out to this woman." And the other says: "I am working really hard on changing issues that brought him to the point of going to someone else..."

These explanations make it appear that somehow the affairs could have been prevented if these women had done something different. Naturally, once an affair is discovered, it's easy to go back and identify whatever problems existed in the marriage and say that's why the affair happened. But if it hadn't been these particular problems, it would have been some other problems—and *those* would have been given as the "reasons" for the affairs.

It's important to recognize that you can't understand why your partner has an affair by looking *only* at the problems in your marriage—or *only* at whatever shortcomings your partner may have had that made them vulnerable to an affair. Affairs happen to all kinds of people in all kinds of marriages.

However, the best advice on how to best *prevent* affairs as well as *recover* from an affair is contained in one of the above letters: "I feel that without complete honesty, how can I ever feel secure and trust him again." A commitment to honesty, backed up by *testing* it with ongoing honest communication (about attractions, temptations, and everything relevant to the relationship) is the best way to recover or to prevent an affair in the first place.

And getting a better general understanding of affairs can help in dealing with your own personal situation.

* * * * * * * * * * * * *

I am considering an affair

Dear Peggy,

I'm very unhappy in my marriage. My husband does not show me the affection I feel I deserve. I know a man that is in love with me. He makes me happy to know he is in love with me. But I don't think I love him. I am strongly considering an affair. I feel love and affection is missing in my life. I really need help.

Dear Reader,

The statement in this letter about considering an affair just because it "makes me happy to know he is in love with me" (even though "I don't think I love him")—is a classic description of what is all too often the case with women: "wanting to be wanted." While everyone needs and deserves feeling loved and having affection in their lives, this particular way of seeking it is likely to be very disappointing. It's also likely to add some new problems to whatever problems already exist.

We frequently look for validation from others when what we really need is to value ourselves and seek ways to feel good about ourselves and about life in general. So the dissatisfaction described above can best be viewed as a wake-up call to make some life changes aimed at finding ways to "feel *loving*" rather than "feeling *loved*." It's much more satisfying to have a reciprocal loving relationship than one that is one-way. And it's also more satisfying to have a relationship based on honesty than on deception. So a satisfying resolution of the dilemma described above almost certainly won't happen through having an affair.

* * * * * * * * * * * * *

Morality

Dear Peggy,

We work together. This is his third separation from her, and he says final. The desire has been building up in both of us, and this weekend we had sex. It was great, and I do not expect anything from him. I know he has not had sex with other people. I don't believe that he is getting divorced soon, nor do I believe that we will end up together somewhere dreamy... I am trying to be realistic.

My question to you is, how wrong is this in God's eyes? I know what the Ten Commandments say about affairs; is this one? And what do you think I should be cautious of? All my friends say this is silly/dumb, but I want to live so that at the end of my life I don't have regrets. What specifically is wrong with this? I know if anyone gets hurt it will probably be me, but I would like to see him again. And if he and his wife decide to start living in the same home again, it will all be totally over on my part. Also I fully intend to keep dating other single

301

and available men so that I can find my true soul-mate, to whom I will be true. I used to think that these sort of things happened only on the soaps, but I now know that they can happen to anyone at all, even me. I would very much appreciate your comments or insights...

Dear Reader,

The struggle is clear in this letter: trying to think clearly—and questioning whether there is, in fact, clear thinking. My reaction is that the answer is both yes and no.

There are indications of clear thinking:

— While he says the "separation is final," she "doesn't believe he is getting divorced soon." At least she's not kidding herself; she is *trying* to be realistic.

— She realizes this "can happen to anyone," not just on the soaps. This is true.

But there are other indications of a *lack* of clear thinking:

— "I know he has not had sex with other people."

That is not something she can *know*.

— "What is wrong with this? ...if anyone gets hurt it will probably be me."

It's strange to think there's "nothing wrong" with doing something that will probably hurt yourself.

— "I will date to find my true soul-mate..."

There is no *one* soul-mate; this is fantasy-thinking.

— "If he and his wife live together, it will be totally over."

People usually don't intend to get as deeply attached as they wind up getting, especially the *other woman*. Whether or not there's an intention to get hooked, the classic, sad stories indicate that's usually what happens.

As for the "morality" questions, I think each person is capable of answering those for themselves. The key is to be honest with yourself; you'll know what you really think—without looking to friends (or to me) for answers.

* * * * * * * * * * * * *

Affair after 42 years

Dear Peggy,

How do you respond to a 60-year-old wife's affair after 42 years of marriage?

Dear Reader,

As for the question as to "how to respond" to this situation, the initial response is almost always shock, anger/hurt, and emotional upheaval. But regardless of what has happened in the past (either during all the years of monogamy or during the time of the affair), the critical factor is what happens now that it's out in the open. Is there a willingness to talk about what happened and to try to learn from it? Is there a willingness to commit to honesty and to honestly discussing everything that is important to the relationship? And is there evidence of a willingness to engage in ongoing honest sharing of thoughts and feelings about subjects other than affairs?

In other words, can this crisis be used to develop a stronger bond and connection or is it a sign that the connection is severely damaged. Each person needs to honestly assess the overall desires for the future and do whatever best serves moving in that direction. It won't be easy (and it may not be possible) to recover the relationship, but it's difficult at *any* age—whether after 2 years of marriage or 42 years as above. As this letter illustrates, this issue is the same, regardless of age or anything else; so it's necessary to develop a better ability to talk about it, understand it, and resolve it in whatever way best fits for the individuals involved.

* * * * * * * * * * * * *

Strong attraction

Dear Peggy,

I am a very sensible woman. I have been truly in love with my husband for years. Although we are just shy of our 2-year anniversary—we have been together for 5 years before that. Well, recently upon meeting a friend, by introduction of my brother, I am awestruck. He is so attractive to me—not just physically but emotionally (even though we haven't reached a deep emotional level in our friendship).

I think about him a lot—but I still feel as strongly about my husband as ever. I just "think" of little things I'd like to see played out......mostly flirting, but I wonder if this type of thought is "healthy" or if I should separate myself from this situation before temptation actually rears it's head. It's actually all innocent fun—and I do hear that he enjoys our time together too. He's always looking for an excuse to come over to my brother's when I'm visiting, and my sister-in-law has confirmed he talks about me a lot. He is single, but has a girlfriend. Tell me this is normal and will pass. The feelings are always strongest after I see him.

Dear Reader,

This letter is timely in that it offers the possibility of stopping a situation before it "gets out of hand." Over and over through the years I've heard people say (after their marriages have been devastated): "I didn't *mean* to have an affair." But the above scenario seems to be headed in that direction.

To address some of the specifics: It's easy to be attracted to some new, interesting person of the opposite sex. In fact, it's "normal." There's no real problem in *feeling* attraction; it's what you do with the feelings that makes all the difference. And the *doing* involves what you *think*. Also, the "thinking of little things, mostly flirting" is not the problem; it's the *secrecy* about those thoughts that leads to problems.

People naturally fear the idea of sharing their attractions with their partner. And hopefully, you don't wait until you feel a strong attraction to begin the process of acknowledging as a couple that attractions are normal and that you need to discuss this issue on an ongoing basis in order to keep them under

303

control. On the other hand, a failure to have this kind of ongoing conversation about attractions allows them to take on a life of their own—and in the process puts the primary relationship in jeopardy. So the fact that the feelings are "normal" doesn't mean they aren't also "dangerous," especially if they're kept secret. The key to avoiding problems is to avoid the secrecy.

* * * * * * * * * * * *

Not an issue of sex

Dear Peggy,

I have been married 3 years. I have had 3 extramarital relationships during that time. I have spent much time trying to figure out why I do this—why I take this awful risk despite my love for my husband and my family. I think I have figured out the reasons, but I don't know how to stop.

Sex is not the goal or the issue with my affairs. I have a need to make men fall in love with me. This is a pattern that I developed in high school. I must make every man I get to know love me, to the extent of being obsessed with me. Then once that goal is achieved, I move on, often hurting my latest "victim" very much. Please don't think I am trying to be conceited—I am really not that attractive, but I have always been able to make men fall for me. It is a game of manipulation that I have mastered over the years. I have taken perfectly wonderful men and manipulated them this way—some that were devoted to their wives. Just to give an example of this, I can tell you that I have had a relationship with every boss I have ever had, and with many of the professors I had in college, despite the fact that they all originally had strong ethical beliefs about not crossing that line.

When I met my husband, I knew I was in love with him when I realized that I did not feel the need to manipulate him. We have a great marriage, good communication, wonderful sex life, etc. I really thought that my "problem" would go away after we got married. However, within 6 months after saying my vows, I was at the old game again.

These relationships always start out innocent and platonic, and I (somewhat subconsciously) become whatever I think is that man's desires in a woman. I never make the first move towards progression of the relationship, but it eventually happens. Sometimes this happens very quickly—sometimes it takes many months. Sex is not an issue until it becomes the next logical step in the relationship, and when it finally happens, I never enjoy it. I have never enjoyed sex with anyone other than my husband.

I am riddled with guilt over this. I often consider leaving my loving husband because I know it would be best for him. But there are two children involved, and I lead this life in secret to keep my family together. I feel guilty towards him for betraying him, I feel guilty towards these other men for hurting them, I feel guilty towards my children for not deserving their respect, and I feel guilty towards God for this horrible sin. I have dreams of losing everything, of going to hell, of getting beaten or killed by one of my ex-lovers, of one of my children finding out, etc.

Despite all of this guilt, and despite telling myself over and over that I won't do it anymore, it continues. I always have a conquest in the works. I don't think I do this out of some lack of self-esteem. If anything, I can be quite arrogant about my ability to do this, but only to myself. I have talked to my husband about my need to have other people love me, but I have always denied a progression to actual sex. He is able to cope with this need as long as he believes that I do not love another man in return, or make love to him. However, he worries that someone will eventually get angry with me and hurt me. I worry about this too.

I need to know how I can stop this behavior. The guilt is killing me, and I don't want to get hurt. I spend hours at night while I lie in bed praying to God for the strength to stop, and apologizing for the pain I have caused and the pain I could cause for my family.

Dear Reader,

The kind of "secret" life expressed in the above letter (that sometimes even the person themselves doesn't fully understand) is almost surely related to the *isolation* with which it is dealt. The very fact of writing the letter is a positive step. And even the minimal sharing with a spouse about temptations can be extremely helpful. But many, many people can't make changes *alone*—without some kind of *accountability*. In other words, someone else needs to know (what is being thought, what actions are being taken, what actions are being considered, etc.)

Anything done (and kept) in secret leaves the person completely alone with no resources to turn to for help/strength/support in changing. This same principle applies when trying to stop other habitual behaviors—like smoking, drinking, overeating. This is why groups such an alcoholics anonymous have been so helpful; they provide an automatic (and ongoing) source of accountability. While it doesn't need to be a formal group, there is almost always the need to have at least one other person with whom everything is shared *before* the actions are taken. Simply talking to another person ("reporting" to them) can act as a deterrent in doing something they would otherwise feel fairly "comfortable" because it's done in secret.

Guilt is not necessarily a motivator; in fact, often it just becomes part of a cycle of "doing something, feeling guilty, doing it again, feeling guilty again." (The whole process gets to be a habit, repeated over and over.) It's not how a person *feels* (guilty); it's what they *do* that counts. And they can certainly do more to break the old habits by finding someone in whom to confide on an ongoing basis (who can serve as an "external conscience") instead of relying solely on personal conscience or individual strength.

Getting back to the specifics of the above letter, the process described above is fairly common inasmuch as women often get caught up in situations that go beyond what they "intended." As I frequently point out, it's quite common for women to "want to be wanted." But then if they do all the little tricks to actually succeed in being wanted, they find they've gone so far that they don't know how to easily turn back—so they go ahead and have an affair. Preventing the affairs requires stopping the whole process at the *beginning*, not waiting until it escalates to the point of including sex.

* * * * * * * * * * * * *

Never been faithful...

Dear Peggy,

This is my second marriage. I have had lots of negative feelings in the past about marriage, so this was a BIG step for me. I've been married for 8 months My husband shared with me that he had never been faithful with his "other" wives (2) da!! Now, am I so stupid or do you believe that he can be faithful Now??? What are the odds??

Dear Reader,

Naturally, I can't know about any particular individual's likelihood of being faithful in the future after having had affairs in the past. I do know it's *possible*. My own husband had over a dozen affairs in a 7-year period, but hasn't had any affairs since 1973.

Many people hold on to the belief that people "can't change;" that a person who has had affairs will inevitably do it again. However, everything depends on whether or not they "learn" from their experience—specifically learn how to be more *honest*. The description above indicates the possibility that something has been learned. However, there's no way to interpret the learning from the scarce amount of information. For instance, it all depends on the *intent* behind his sharing that he "had never been faithful with his other wives." If it was said casually, or uncaringly, or in a sort of bragging way, then obviously it would not bode well for being monogamous in the future. However, if it was said as an effort to establish honesty (and perhaps even to help *prevent* future affairs by virtue of exposing past failures to be monogamous), then it would obviously mean something entirely different.

As far as I know, there are no "odds"—and it wouldn't really tell anything about a particular situation anyway. The chances of maintaining monogamy in any specific marriage probably have more to do with what happens *next* than in whatever happened in the past. For instance, honest disclosure about the past can be used as the basis for ongoing honest communication about how, as a couple, attractions to others will be handled in the future. There's nothing like honesty to defuse the fascination of private fantasies about possible other partners. So it's not a matter of just "waiting to see" whether someone remains monogamous. It's much more a matter of actively talking honestly about all issues important to the relationship, aimed at diminishing the secrecy within the marriage.

* * * * * * * * * * * * *

Fear of being cheated on

Dear Peggy,

I've been going out with my girlfriend for a year and a half, we are engaged and we are planning to get married a year from now. I am worried and in fear of having to go through something like this, so I want to find a way to prevent an affair from happening. I'm really scared, because I love my girlfriend and I would be so hurt if this would happen to our relationship. The funny thing is that I know for myself, I would never cheat on her (because I don't want her to be hurt and because I love her and I trust her), but you said that nobody is free of an extramarital affair and you can't prevent this from happening. How can I reassure myself? Or how can I just be happy? In a way I feel like I can't be happy anymore because of this fear of being cheated on!!!!! What should I do???

Dear Reader,

This letter represents a misunderstanding of what I've said, as demonstrated by the statement: "you said...you can't prevent this from happening." I'm *not* saying you *can't* prevent it. What I'm saying is that "anybody is *vulnerable*" a nd "no one is *immune*." This is simply a basic awareness from which to *motivate* people to do the necessary thinking and talking (on an ongoing basis throughout the life of the relationship) that *can*, in fact, prevent affairs.

The time to begin this "prevention" is in the very beginning of a relationship. Unfortunately, one of the first things that happens when a relationship gets serious is that one or both people start to feel jealous or possessive—*and* they let their partner know that they don't like the idea that they're ever attracted to anyone else. But this disapproval of attractions doesn't *stop* them; it just means your partner will keep them secret and not discuss them. Also, it starts a pattern of dishonesty that causes the relationship to be filled with jealousy and suspicion, as well as making it less likely that it will be monogamous.

But if both partners realize that attractions to others are likely, indeed inevitable (no matter how much they love each other), they can engage in ongoing honest communication about the reality of the temptations and how to avoid the consequences of acting on them. The effect on the relationship is to create a sense of closeness and a knowledge of each other that replaces suspicion with trust, making it *more* likely that it will be monogamous.

So it's *not* that affairs can't be prevented. It's that by not understanding the realistic risks involved, couples fall into the normal pattern of ignoring the issue, making them more vulnerable. But by committing to honesty and discussing this issue on an ongoing basis, they *can* prevent it from happening.

* * * * * * * * * * * *

Why aren't I enough?

Dear Peggy,

My husband of five months just confided in me that he has always had fantasies about our female friends. He has not had an affair but states if the

307

opportunity with these women presented itself he probably would not be able to be faithful to me. I feel as if he has already cheated on me mentally since he admits he would if he had the chance with them. This has left me feeling hurt, humiliated, and angry with both him and our female friends.

He claims he cannot control this and it has nothing to do with his love for me or his desire to be with me. However, he admits it is because he does not find me attractive enough. He loves me but just isn't attracted to me. How can this be when these other five women are the same size/build as me? He feels no matter what I do I will be unable to turn him on as much as they do. I was overweight when we met but now have lost the weight. At no time during our relationship has he been attracted to me so I don't see anything that will help. This has seriously affected our sex life and now I am afraid that will make him seek out the opportunity with our friends.

What should we do? How do I deal with this information? How do I trust him? Please help me. I feel this has shattered our chances of a happy marriage.

Dear Reader,

Having "fantasies" about other women (even female friends) is extremely common. In fact, *in general*, having fantasies is a normal aspect of human sexuality. And even discussing fantasies with your spouse is not *necessarily* a negative thing. In fact, it *can* be positive if used to maintain honest communication and a deeper "knowing" of each other. However, it's quite different when someone shares this kind of information in a way that feels "threatening" (like saying they "probably would not be able to be faithful").

Although I can't know the reasoning behind any particular person's comment of this type, it *could* be a "test" to gauge the reaction or a way of giving themselves permission to do something—having already announced it. But whatever the possible intention behind the statement, saying they "probably wouldn't be able to be faithful" is a cop-out—as if we don't have free will to make decisions, regardless of whatever "desires" we might have. And more important, this kind of statement of unwillingness to take responsibility for their actions (with the resulting hurt to their partner) shows a lack of caring for their partner that is far more critical than the fantasies themselves.

As for "being able to turn him on as much as the others," *no* long-term, established relationship is likely to carry the same turn-on potential as a new one—and this is an incredibly shallow basis for comparison. Also, the idea that a spouse "at no time has been attracted" to me—simply doesn't make sense. (It's unlikely there would have been a marriage in the first place had there been no attraction.)

As for what can be done regarding dealing with the information or about trusting or about the chance for a happy marriage, there's not *one* thing to be done—and certainly not something to be done by only *one* of the partners. When one person is thinking primarily of themselves (without regard for the fallout on their partner), the other person generally needs to insist on fairness and equality. And in the meantime, they need to take care of themselves as much or more than they take care of the relationship. It's only when *both* people try to resolve these issues that they can effectively be addressed.

* * * * * * * * * * * * *

Male-Female Friends???
(Here are 3 letters before my response.)

Dear Peggy, (letter #1)
   My husband and I have had a mutual male friend for the past year and a half. Recently this male friend and I have become very close. My husband knows of some of the conversations but not all. Recently we admitted to each other that we are both very attracted to one another and care very much for each other. He even said he's scared because he feels he can tell me anything, which he reiterated several times. We decided to cool our friendship off a bit, we don't want to hurt anyone. We've never had physical contact except for hugging every time we saw each other; we've both decided not to even do that.
   Of course all this makes us feel very confused and pained—because we want to be close. We've seen each other a couple times since our talk and it's very difficult, there's a lot of tension. We still plan on hanging out together with my husband. We don't say a whole lot to each other, but I have found him gazing at me a few times, but I just glance at him and avert my gaze because I'm afraid. My dilemma is can this man and I be just friends after admitting the sexual attraction and after coming to care so much for one another, or are we just fooling ourselves? I'm very confused and distraught.

Dear Peggy, (letter #2)
   My husband is a contractor and was hired by this woman. After he started working at her house, they became "friends." She would call my home and tell him shows he liked were on TV. She would constantly call his beeper, just to tell him of her personal problems. This has been going on for a year now. She is married and has 2 children. I found Email my husband sent to her, then I started to check cellular phone bills. There were over 50 phone calls to her home or her cellular number. I feel my husband is liking the attention from her, but I also see her wanting more from my husband.
   After I confronted my husband about the calls and Email, he was upset that he hurt me. I feel I can no longer trust him. (He does work for her because of the contract.) I had also confronted her about all this, she told me they were only "friends." I feel I can't believe her either. I've asked him many times why don't we all get together; he always says I know how you feel about her. I don't like her and he has never given me a reason to like her.
   I'm still very angry at him and her. I don't know if anything has happened between them; and if it did, I'm not sure if I will ever know the truth. I just don't think a man or woman should have friends of the opposite sex without the other being included. Am I wrong to feel this way?

Dear Peggy, (letter #3)

One night, when I was hanging out with our next door neighbor and friend, he suddenly kissed me. I was shocked, but I didn't stop him and it went on for a half hour or so. The next day, I told him that it couldn't happen again. I felt convinced of that at the time, but there was electricity in the air every time we saw each other after that. I was stunned to discover my intense attraction to this man whom I had known for almost two years. I thought we just had the kind of attraction that exists between friends of the opposite sex or persuasion and I never, ever, though it would turn into a reality. But it was a passion I've never felt before and, despite my better instincts, I couldn't stop longing for him, even as I knew I loved my husband and hated what was happening.

I started seeing this neighbor sporadically after we met one night to talk things over and I had tried to put it all to rest. That night, though, we ended up kissing and more than just kissing. We became lovers when my husband was out of town. Shortly thereafter, my husband found us talking intimately and a terrible fight ensued. I eventually moved out to a friend's house and I thought I would soon be divorced since I had done such an awful thing and had fallen in love on top of it. I am still, a few months later, separated from my husband.

The neighbor, as I'll call him, and I had an affair until he stopped it because he wants us to have a future together and will not see me until I'm divorced. I am in a state of utter confusion and torment. I know I still love my husband, but I am absolutely attracted to this other guy and love him, too. I don't feel this passion for my husband and I do not know if that is because we are actually through and I am denying it or if it's a kind of love that is more akin to friendship. My uncertainty goes even further, though. I long for the neighbor but am very angry that he would give up on what we started. I feel abandoned in mid-stream and I do not trust him because of it. Suffice it to say that I am really torn and do not know what to do. I hope you have a couple of words of wisdom.

Dear Reader,

This is a question that arises in almost every relationship: "Is it possible for men and women to *just* be Friends?" It was the subject of much debate several years ago with the release of the movie "When Harry Met Sally." But it's an ongoing debate—both internally (as illustrated in the above letters) and among people who are willing to talk openly about this issue.

Actually, precisely what is needed is more open discussion—*especially* with the primary partner. When any aspect of an opposite-sex "friendship" is kept hidden or secret from the primary partner, it becomes *much* more dangerous. Any new attraction carries with it lots of emotional (even physical, biochemical) aspects that tend to block a person's ability to think or behave *rationally*.

There's a very old song with a line that reflects this dynamic:

"There's a line between love and fascination
that's hard to see in a moment such as this.
'Cause they both give the very same sensation

310

when you're lost in the magic of a kiss..."

So the feelings are not *really* love—but they *feel* like love. However, even before reaching the "feeling like love" stage, there's usually a growing degree of secrecy—and that's when opposite-sex friendships initially become a threat to the primary relationship. For instance, if your partner knows everything about your friendship, it's probably OK. If they don't, it's probably not. Even if there's nothing "inappropriate" going on, any conversations or activities with the opposite-sex friend that are kept hidden from the primary partner are likely to create a problem. So the issue boils down to being honest—meaning not withholding information from your primary partner about anything related to your relationship with the friend.

Many people think the same "rules" should apply to opposite-sex friends that exist for same-sex friends. But that's just rationalization and not very realistic—because the nature of the relationship with an opposite-sex friend often involves a sexual overtone that doesn't exist with same-sex friends—except, of course, in the relationships of gay and lesbian couples.

If it's really just a friendship, your partner should be able to see/know about all your interactions. If something needs to be kept secret, then it becomes a potential threat. So you can have your primary relationship and an opposite-sex friend without jeopardizing your relationship *only* if you keep *no* secrets from your primary partner. And whenever either you or your partner are sharing secrets with others that you are *not* sharing with each other, the outside relationship is likely to escalate to some degree, whether or not it finally leads to "sex." And an outside emotional attachment (while not initially seen as being as threatening as a sexual relationship) can still create significant problems in a primary relationship.

As we can see from the above letters (representing different stages of dealing with this whole issue), there are likely to be serious consequences for secretly pursuing opposite-sex friendships. Since the secrecy allows people to ignore or deny the potential consequences, stopping the secrecy can help break the fantasy-attraction and help bring a sense of reality and accountability to the whole issue of male-female friendships. Remember, it's not the friendships per se that create the problem; it's the *secrecy* that allows them to go beyond just *friendship*.

* * * * * * * * * * * * *

How to improve marriage?

Dear Peggy,

I was looking for ways to improve our marriage. Neither of us has cheated on the other. Instead, we are at a spot in our relationship that may end us. The communication has become difficult and the relationship is not the same as previously. We are planning on seeking marriage counseling, but I do like to do my part and would like to be able to be a part of a list or community that encourages ways to improve current marriages. Do you know of any such places?

Dear Reader,

What a refreshing question—and how smart: to take action to improve the marriage before an out-and-out crisis.

There are many wonderful marriage enrichment programs throughout the country. A listing of the best marital education programs in the country can be found in the Directory of CMFCE (Coalition for Marriage, Family and Couples Education). A list of professionals and courses in the area of "marriage education" can be found at www.smartmarriages.com/directory_browse.html.

CMFCE is a coalition of the best, most responsible people in this field—and I am proud to be listed with this group. In addition to reviewing the programs in the CMFCE Directory, it is also a good way to identify a group of professionals who have authored some excellent books for self-study. For instance, while I'm best known for "The Monogamy Myth," my book on dealing with affairs, my husband and I also have a book aimed at helping improve marriages (not related to affairs) called "Making Love Stay." I encourage couples who want to prevent problems, work on problems, or recover from problems in their relationships to seek out the many good books and courses that can help them in this process.

For ongoing information about all aspects of affairs, as well as other books and resources, we invite you to visit our Website: www.dearpeggy.com.

* * * * * * * * * * * * *

About the Author

Peggy Vaughan has been married to James, her childhood sweetheart, for 55 years. They have two grown children and three grandchildren. She and James have been life-long partners, both at work and at home.

In 1970 they began working as an independent husband-wife consulting team, helping individuals, organizations, and corporations deal with a wide range of personal and professional issues.

In 1974 they faced the challenge of dealing with the extramarital affairs James had secretly engaged in for the previous seven years of their marriage. After spending several years privately working through this experience and developing a stronger, more honest marriage, they decided to use their experience to help others. They're willingness to share their personal lives sets them apart from most professionals.

In 1980, they "went public" with their own story, writing a book, *Beyond Affairs* describing their personal experience. They also appeared on Donahue as the first couple to deal with extramarital affairs, stay together and appear on national TV together to discuss their experience. Since that time, they have done hundreds of media appearances.

Peggy has written many other books aimed at helping people deal with affairs, including her classic, *The Monogamy Myth*, and her most recent book on preventing affairs: *To Have and To Hold*.

Since 1996 Peggy has reached thousands of people through her Website, DearPeggy.com, which serves as an Extramarital Affairs Resource Center. It has several hundred pages of free information, including Articles about Affairs, a list of therapists who have been recommended as being effective in dealing with affairs, Links to other sites, book reviews of other books as well as a Bookstore where she sells her own books.

Peggy is committed to fostering more public discussion of issues some consider "personal," but which she believes to be issues in society as a whole.

CPSIA information can be obtained at www.ICGtesting.com
Printed in the USA
LVOW061742220512

282826LV00002B/63/P